## The Editors

PETER HULME is Professor in Literature at the University of Essex. His recent books include *Remnants of Conquest: The Island Caribs and Their Visitors, 1877–1998* and the co-edited *Cambridge Companion to Travel Writing*.

WILLIAM H. SHERMAN is Professor of Early Modern Studies in the Department of English and Related Literature at the University of York. He is the author of *John Dee: The Politics of Reading and Writing in the English Renaissance* and of articles on Renaissance literature and the history of the book. He has also edited *"The Tempest" and Its Travels* with Peter Hulme and the new Cambridge edition of Ben Jonson's *The Alchemist* with Peter Holland.

# W. W. NORTON & COMPANY, INC.
## *Also Publishes*

ENGLISH RENAISSANCE DRAMA: A NORTON ANTHOLOGY
*edited by David Bevington et al.*

THE NORTON ANTHOLOGY OF AFRICAN AMERICAN LITERATURE
*edited by Henry Louis Gates Jr. and Nellie Y. McKay et al.*

THE NORTON ANTHOLOGY OF AMERICAN LITERATURE
*edited by Nina Baym et al.*

THE NORTON ANTHOLOGY OF CHILDREN'S LITERATURE
*edited by Jack Zipes et al.*

THE NORTON ANTHOLOGY OF DRAMA
*edited by J. Ellen Gainor, Stanton B. Garner Jr., and Martin Puchner*

THE NORTON ANTHOLOGY OF ENGLISH LITERATURE
*edited by M. H. Abrams and Stephen Greenblatt et al.*

THE NORTON ANTHOLOGY OF LITERATURE BY WOMEN
*edited by Sandra M. Gilbert and Susan Gubar*

THE NORTON ANTHOLOGY OF MODERN AND CONTEMPORARY POETRY
*edited by Jahan Ramazani, Richard Ellmann, and Robert O'Clair*

THE NORTON ANTHOLOGY OF POETRY
*edited by Margaret Ferguson, Mary Jo Salter, and Jon Stallworthy*

THE NORTON ANTHOLOGY OF SHORT FICTION
*edited by R. V. Cassill and Richard Bausch*

THE NORTON ANTHOLOGY OF THEORY AND CRITICISM
*edited by Vincent B. Leitch et al.*

THE NORTON ANTHOLOGY OF WORLD LITERATURE
*edited by Sarah Lawall et al.*

THE NORTON FACSIMILE OF THE FIRST FOLIO OF SHAKESPEARE
*prepared by Charlton Hinman*

THE NORTON INTRODUCTION TO LITERATURE
*edited by Alison Booth and Kelly J. Mays*

THE NORTON READER
*edited by Linda H. Peterson and John C. Brereton*

THE NORTON SAMPLER
*edited by Thomas Cooley*

THE NORTON SHAKESPEARE, BASED ON THE OXFORD EDITION
*edited by Stephen Greenblatt et al.*

For a complete list of Norton Critical Editions, visit
www.wwnorton.com/college/English/nce_home.htm

A NORTON CRITICAL EDITION

# William Shakespeare
# THE TEMPEST

AN AUTHORITATIVE TEXT
SOURCES AND CONTEXTS
CRITICISM
REWRITINGS AND APPROPRIATIONS

*Edited by*

## PETER HULME

UNIVERSITY OF ESSEX

AND

## WILLIAM H. SHERMAN

UNIVERSITY OF YORK

**W. W. NORTON & COMPANY**

*New York • London*

W. W. Norton & Company has been independent since its founding in 1923, when William Warder and Mary D. Herter Norton first published lectures delivered at the People's Institute, the adult education division of New York City's Cooper Union. The Nortons soon expanded their program beyond the Institute, publishing books by celebrated academics from America and abroad. By mid-century, the two major pillars of Norton's publishing program—trade books and college texts—were firmly established. In the 1950s, the Norton family transferred control of the company to its employees, and today—with a staff of four hundred and a comparable number of trade, college, and professional titles published each year—W. W. Norton & Company stands as the largest and oldest publishing house owned wholly by its employees.

The text of this book is composed in Fairfield Medium
with the display set in Bernhard Modern.
Composition by PennSet, Inc.
Manufacturing by the Maple-Vail Book Group.
Book design by Antonina Krass.
Production Manager: Ben Reynolds.

Library of Congress Cataloging-in-Publication Data
Shakespeare, William, 1564–1616.
The Tempest : sources and contexts, critcism, rewritings and appropriations / William Shakespeare; edited by Peter Hulme and William H. Sherman.
    p. cm. — (A Norton critical edition)
Includes bibliographical references.

**ISBN 0-393-97819-2**

1. Survival after airplane accidents, shipwrecks, etc—Drama.
2. Shakespeare, William, 1564–1616. Tempest. 3 Fathers and daughters—Drama. 4. Castaways—Drama. 5. Magicians—Drama.
6. Islands—Drama. I. Hulme, Peter. II. Sherman, William H. (William Howard) III. Title. IV. Series.

PR2833.A2H85 2003
822.3'3—dc22

2003060936

W. W. Norton & Company, Inc., 500 Fifth Avenue, New York, N.Y. 10110
www.wwnorton.com

W. W. Norton & Company Ltd., Castle House,
75/76 Wells Street, London W1T 3QT

*5  6  7  8  9  0*

# Contents

Preface      vii

## The Text of *The Tempest*
The Tempest      3
A Note on the Text      78

## Sources and Contexts
MAGIC AND WITCHCRAFT      85
   Ovid • [Medea]      85
   Giovanni Pico della Mirandola • Oration on the
      Dignity of Man      86
   Anonymous • [Friar Bacon's Magical Exploits]      88
   William Biddulph • [An English Conjuror on the
      High Seas]      89
   Reginald Scott • [How to Enclose a Spirit]      89
POLITICS AND RELIGION      91
   Isaiah XXIX      91
   Samuel Purchas • Virginia's Verger      93
   Gabriel Naudé • [Master Strokes of State]      95
GEOGRAPHY AND TRAVEL      97
   Anonymous • Primaleon of Greece      97
   Gaspar Gil Polo • [A Mediterranean Storm]      99
   Walter Ralegh • A Map of Tunis and Carthage      101
   Richard Eden • [A Voyage to the Patagonians]      102
   Capt. Wyatt • [An Atlantic Storm]      105
   Michel de Montaigne • [The Cannibals of Brazil]      107
   William Strachey • [Storms and Strife in Bermuda]      110
   Sir Henry Mainwaring • The Seaman's Dictionary      115

## Criticism
   John Dryden • [The Character of Caliban]      119
   Nicholas Rowe • [The Magic of *The Tempest*]      119
   Samuel Taylor Coleridge • Notes on *The Tempest*      121
   Ludwig Tieck • Shakespeare's Treatment of the
      Marvellous      125
   Fanny Kemble • [Some Notes on *The Tempest*]      127

Henry James • [Surrendering to *The Tempest*]   131
Lytton Strachey • Shakespeare's Final Period   134
G. Wilson Knight • [Prospero's Lonely Magic]   137
   • A Chart of Shakespeare's Dramatic Universe   141
Frank Kermode • [Art vs. Nature]   142
George Lamming • A Monster, a Child, a Slave   148
Barbara A. Mowat • Prospero, Agrippa, and Hocus
   Pocus   168
David Lindley • Music, Masque, and Meaning in
   *The Tempest*   187
Stephen Orgel • Prospero's Wife   201
John Gillies • Shakespeare's Virginian Masque   215
Peter Hulme • Prospero and Caliban   233
Andrew Gurr • *The Tempest*'s Tempest at Blackfriars   250
Barbara Fuchs • Conquering Islands: Contextualizing
   *The Tempest*   265
Leah Marcus • The Blue-Eyed Witch   286

# Rewritings and Appropriations

DRAMA AND FILM   301
John Fletcher and Philip Massinger • The Sea Voyage   301
Thomas Heywood • The English Traveller   305
John Dryden and William Davenant • The Enchanted
   Island   308
Thomas Duffett • The Mock-Tempest   312
Robert and William Brough • [Raising the Wind]   315
Aimé Césaire • A Tempest   321
Peter Greenaway • Prospero's Books   325
POEMS   332
Percy Bysshe Shelley • With a Guitar. To Jane.   332
Robert Browning • Caliban upon Setebos; or, Natural
   Theology in the Island   335
Joaquim Maria Machado de Assis • At the Top   337
Rainer Maria Rilke • The Spirit Ariel   338
H.D. • By Avon River   339
Suniti Namjoshi • Snapshots of Caliban   342
Lemuel Johnson • Calypso for Caliban   343
Heiner Müller • [Go Ariel]   347
Edwin Morgan • Ariel Freed   348
Ted Hughes • Setebos   349

Selected Bibliography   351

# Preface

The earliest recorded performance of *The Tempest* was at court, before King James, on "Hallomas nyght" (November 1), 1611. A year and a half later, on May 20, 1613, the play was performed again for the King, during the festivities leading up to the marriage of his daughter. The play was probably also performed for a wider public by the company formed under the patronage of King James, the King's Men—either indoors at the Blackfriars Theatre or outdoors at The Globe. But the text's first appearance in print (as with roughly half of Shakespeare's plays) was seven years after Shakespeare's death, when it was published as the opening title in the First Folio of 1623.

This privileged position has given weight to *The Tempest*'s status as Shakespeare's swan song. Although Shakespeare had a major hand in at least two plays after this one (*Henry VIII* and *The Two Noble Kinsmen*), and although scholars now tend to be suspicious of simplistic identifications between Prospero and Shakespeare (making the former's renunciation of illusions and charms the latter's farewell to the stage), the play's position as both a crowning and an inaugural work is entirely appropriate. *The Tempest* offers some of Shakespeare's most profound meditations on the cycles of life, shuttling between a sense of an ending and a sense of a beginning, and culminating in a potent (and potentially unstable) mixture of death and regeneration, bondage and release.

The editors of the First Folio divided Shakespeare's plays into three generic groupings—comedies, histories, and tragedies. They placed *The Tempest* in the first of these categories, but few modern readers have been entirely content to leave it there. The play shares some of the otherworldly setting and romantic playfulness of *A Midsummer Night's Dream*, and it moves, like other Shakespearean comedies, toward reconciliation and marriage; but the seriousness of its tone, the suffering experienced by all of the play's characters, and the presence of themes such as exile, enslavement, and mortality have led many modern critics to label it a tragicomedy or to group it with Shakespeare's other late plays in a special category called the "romance."

In most of Shakespeare's plays the plot is adapted from readily identifiable historical or literary texts. No such source has been identified for the story of *The Tempest*, but the search has turned up echoes of a wide range of texts, including Virgil's *Aeneid*, Ovid's *Metamorphoses*, Montaigne's essay "Of the Cannibals," and one or more of the contemporary accounts of the shipwreck of the *Sea Venture* on the coast of

Bermuda in July 1609. The only accepted source for a name in the play
is for Caliban's "dam's god, Setebos" (1.2.372), who is borrowed from
Antonio Pigafetta's account of Magellan's circumnavigation of the
world, in which Setebos is named among the gods of the Patagonians.
But echoes have been heard from the Bible (particularly Isaiah XXIX),
earlier plays featuring magicians (especially Friar Bacon and Doctor
Faustus), histories of Renaissance Italy, and prose romances from Italy,
France, and Spain (which often featured shipwrecks, sorcerers, monsters, and long-deferred marriages between knights and maidens).

Similarly, alongside the clear responses to and rewritings of *The
Tempest*, a number of texts written by Shakespeare's contemporaries
seem to contain echoes of the play, as when Samuel Purchas writes in
the 1620s about the native conspiracies against the English colonists
in Virginia, or Gabriel Naudé writes in the 1630s about the theatrical
exercise of political power. A selection of these materials—few of which
can count as indisputable sources, but all of which cast light on the
play—is featured in "Sources and Contexts," providing some sense of
the contemporary discourses that *The Tempest* was informed by (and
that it, in turn, helped to shape). These texts are here divided into
three overlapping subsections, "Magic and Witchcraft," "Religion and
Politics," and "Geography and Travel."

It is the last of these that is immediately invoked by the play's title
and opening scene, and that accounts for some of its exploratory
themes and nautical language: the plot of *The Tempest* begins with a
dramatic storm that wrecks a ship off the coast of an "uninhabited island." We find out in 1.2 that the island is, in fact, inhabited by as
strange a cast of characters as can be found in any Renaissance play.
Some twelve years before the play begins, the Italian magician Prospero had been the legitimate Duke of Milan; but by withdrawing into
his studies and turning over the ducal duties to his ambitious brother
Antonio, he lost power in a coup d'etat—the reversal of which provides
the central plot for the play. Prospero was put to sea with his young
daughter Miranda, some basic provisions, and at least some of the
books from his precious library ("volumes that / I prize above my dukedom"). Their little boat took them to the island where the play is set,
and which the geographical references in the text seem to place in both
the Mediterranean and the Atlantic: the course being followed by the
entourage of Alonso after the celebration of his daughter Claribel's
wedding to the King of Tunis is back across the Mediterranean toward
his kingdom of Naples, but Ariel refers to the Bermudas and the word
Setebos comes from Patagonia.

Prospero and Miranda are attended by two characters who were already on the island when they arrived—their servant Caliban and the
spirit Ariel. We are told by Prospero and Ariel that Caliban had been
brought to the island by his now-dead mother, the Algerian witch Sycorax (who had herself been exiled to the island, spared from execution
because of her pregnancy), and, after an attempted rape of Miranda,
he had been confined to a rock and forced to gather fuel for Prospero's
fire. Caliban's appearance is one of the most enigmatic aspects of the

play: in this and the following scenes he is described by various characters as "earth," "tortoise," "hag-seed," "fish," "monster," "moon-calf,"
"puppy-headed," "misshapen," and a "thing of darkness," but he also
speaks some of the most beautiful lines in the play and in several
places is acknowledged as having human features, feelings, and aspirations. Ariel is also in the service of Prospero, who freed him from the
tree in which he was imprisoned by Sycorax. Prospero has promised
him (or her, as Ariel is often played) that if he performs all of his magical commands for the duration of the play, he will earn his freedom
and return to the elements.

If Prospero's books are the cause of his banishment, they are also the
source of the power he uses to overcome it: he raises the storm in order to bring to the island the Italian noblemen who had deposed him
and forced him from Milan. The first member of the wedding party encountered by Prospero and Miranda is Alonso's son Ferdinand, the
young prince of Naples, who believes himself to be the sole survivor of
the shipwreck. According to Prospero's plan, he falls in love with Miranda at first sight. One plotline follows their brief courtship (in the
play's central scene, 3.1); the action of the play is brought to a climax
with their betrothal in 4.1 and presentation to Alonso and the other
courtiers in 5.1.

In 2.1 we are introduced to the rest of the wedding party—notably
Gonzalo (the old and noble councillor), Antonio (Prospero's usurping brother), and Sebastian (Alonso's younger brother). While the exhausted King and courtiers sleep, Antonio tries to persuade Sebastian
to murder the King and, like himself, take over his brother's role—but
Prospero, through Ariel, prevents this first of two conspiracies in the
play. The other conspiracy is hatched by Caliban, who (in 2.2 and 3.2)
encourages the jester Trinculo and the butler Stephano to seize control
of the island from Prospero by killing the magical tyrant, burning his
books, and taking his daughter as their queen. For their part, Stephano
and Trinculo are more interested in the alcohol they have managed to
rescue from the ship, and their mock-conspiracy (along with Caliban's
dreams of freedom) degenerates into drunken banter. In 3.2 they are
led off by an invisible Ariel and his music.

In 3.3 the busy Ariel arranges for an edifying (and mystifying) dumb
show, which presents the hungry courtiers with the image of a feast before snatching it away and chastising them for their wrongs. While they
are wandering in despair, Prospero (in 4.1) takes the opportunity to
unite Miranda and Ferdinand and celebrates their engagement with a
masque featuring the goddesses Iris, Juno, and Ceres. Suddenly remembering the threat of Caliban and his co-conspirators, Prospero
breaks off the show and delivers the play's most famous speech ("Our
revels now are ended").

Having foiled Caliban's conspiracy by tempting Trinculo and
Stephano with gaudy clothing, Ariel and his spirits chase them through
a filthy swamp. In the play's final act, Prospero resolves to give up his
magic and, once the King's ship is safely on its way back to Italy, to
grant Ariel his freedom and turn his own thoughts to preparing for

death. The King and his courtiers are reunited with Ferdinand and his future princess—and queen—Miranda. Ariel returns the ship and the mariners, miraculously restored, and after general statements of apology and forgiveness, the Italians prepare for their departure while Prospero (in a brief epilogue) asks for the audience's applause.

The Tempest is, after The Comedy of Errors, Shakespeare's shortest play, and it is full of loose ends and open questions. Where (indeed, what) is the island on which the play is set? How are we supposed to feel toward Caliban? What are we to make of the play's absent women? What happens to the balance of power at the end of the play, as the ship prepares to return to Milan? And what is the source of Prospero's power? Does it derive from his study of the "liberal arts" and the books from his library that he took into exile? From his magical book, robe, and staff, and the assistance of Ariel and other supernatural spirits? From his ability (like Shakespeare's) to enchant an audience with words and images? Or from his tyrannical control over those he has placed in a position of weakness?

The range and openness of these questions has guaranteed a long and lively critical history, reflected in the section called "Criticism," which contains material from four centuries and includes such notable literary figures as Dryden, Coleridge, and Henry James. Over the last fifty years The Tempest has been at the heart of critical debates about matters as diverse as postcolonialism, textual editing, and Renaissance magic, all of which are discussed in the latter part of the "Criticism" section.[1]

The universality of The Tempest's relationships (father and daughter, husband and wife, older brother and younger brother, king and subject, master and servant, colonizer and colonized) have helped make it one of the most adaptable texts of the entire literary canon, and it has been reread and rewritten more radically than any other of Shakespeare's works. The play has in fact been adapted from the outset, and the text as we now know it has only been used on stage for just over half of its existence. The section "Rewritings and Appropriations" offers extracts from some of the earliest theatrical responses by Shakespeare's contemporaries or near-contemporaries that imitate or parody aspects of The Tempest, as well as from Dryden and Davenant's 1667 adaptation for the Restoration theater, The Enchanted Island, which displaced the version printed in Shakespeare's First Folio (and itself became the subject of imitation and parody). In addition, we offer representative examples of the astonishing array of altered forms—including burlesque, comic opera, and postcolonial appropriation—in which the play has continued to appear.

The play's interest in magical illusions and musical charms and its physical and psychological struggles in remote locations are some of the factors that have made it attractive to filmmakers. It provided the plot for the pioneering science-fiction film Forbidden Planet (1956),

---

1. A thorough overview of critical approaches to The Tempest is Patrick M. Murphy, "Interpreting The Tempest: A History of Its Readings," in The Tempest: Critical Essays, ed. Patrick M. Murphy (New York: Routledge, 2001), pp. 3–72.

which featured the first completely electronic score in cinematic history, and it was filmed as *Prospero's Books* by Peter Greenaway in 1991. This section concludes with Greenaway's fantastic list of the twenty-four books that Prospero might have taken to his island—and that served, literally or metaphorically, as the source of his power.

As a play that foregrounds the power of books, *The Tempest* has been an enduring source of inspiration and provocation to contemporary writers working in a wide range of genres and styles. Novels and longer narrative poems are difficult to excerpt, so here we merely gesture toward them with the opening and closing sections of Robert Browning's "Caliban upon Setebos"; but within the lyric tradition, Shelley, Rilke, and many others have given new voice to the play's characters in their meditations on the music of the theatrical island, the power of language, and the ends of art. Contemporary authors have been drawn less to Prospero than to Ariel and Caliban; some—like contemporary critics—have also been fascinated by the shadowy presence of Sycorax, Claribel, and Setebos, who never appear on stage. Ted Hughes's coruscating use of the whole range of the play's characters to relate the story of his marriage provides a dramatic and powerful conclusion to this section.

The editors would like to thank the authors of several of the pieces included in this volume for either suggesting ways of editing their material or allowing the editors a free hand in doing so. Particular thanks go to George Lamming, Barbara Mowat, Stephen Orgel, John Gillies, and Leah Marcus. We would also like to thank Susan Forsyth for her assistance with securing permissions for reprinted materials. Finally, we regret that the fees requested by some publishers put a few crucial essays and rewritings out of our (and your) reach.

# The Text of
# THE TEMPEST

# The Tempest

## List of Characters

ALONSO, King of Naples
SEBASTIAN, his brother
PROSPERO, the right Duke of Milan
ANTONIO, his brother, the usurping Duke of Milan          5
FERDINAND, son to the King of Naples
GONZALO, an honest old councillor
ADRIAN and FRANCISCO, lords
CALIBAN, a savage and deformed slave
TRINCULO, a jester                                         10
STEPHANO, a drunken butler
MASTER of a ship
BOATSWAIN
MARINERS
MIRANDA, daughter to Prospero                             15
ARIEL, an airy spirit
IRIS
CERES
JUNO    } [presented by] spirits
NYMPHS                                                    20
REAPERS

THE SCENE: An uninhabited island

2. **Alonso:** As King of Naples he controls the large area of southern Italy that in Shakespeare's time was controlled by Spain.
3. **Sebastian:** second in line to the throne of Naples after Ferdinand.
4. **Prospero:** an Italian word meaning favorable or propitious. He is the "right," that is legitimate, Duke of Milan (pronounced throughout the play with the accent on the first syllable). Milan was one of the most powerful states in Renaissance Italy, but it was taken over first by France and then by Spain.
5. **Antonio:** As Prospero explains in 1.2, he had usurped Prospero's dukedom twelve years earlier.
6. **Ferdinand:** heir to the throne of Naples.
7. **Gonzalo:** gives advice (counsel) to his king.
9. **Caliban:** often considered an anagram of "canibal."
10. **Trinculo:** a name probably derived from the Italian *trincare*, to drink. He is a jester, a fool employed by the royal house for entertainment.
12. **The Master:** the ship's captain.
13. **The Boatswain:** pronounced "bosun"; he is in charge of the ship's rigging and anchors and acts as intermediary between the Master and the sailors.
15. **Miranda:** a word derived from the Latin verb *miror*, meaning "she who is to be wondered at or admired." She is next in line to Prospero's dukedom.
16. **Ariel:** a word glossed in the Geneva Bible as "lion of God," but which probably just denotes "airiness."

3

## Act 1, Scene 1

[*On a ship at sea.*] *A tempestuous noise of thunder and lightning heard. Enter a* SHIPMASTER *and a* BOATSWAIN.

MASTER    Boatswain!

BOATSWAIN    Here Master. What cheer?

MASTER    Good, speak to th' mariners. Fall to't yarely, or we run ourselves aground. Bestir, bestir!                    *Exit.*

*Enter* MARINERS.

BOATSWAIN    Heigh, my hearts! Cheerly, cheerly, my hearts!    5
Yare, yare! Take in the topsail. Tend to th' Master's whistle. [*To the storm*] Blow till thou burst thy wind, if room enough!

*Enter* ALONSO, SEBASTIAN, ANTONIO, FERDINAND, GON-
ZALO, *and others.*

ALONSO    Good Boatswain, have care. Where's the Master?
Play the men!                                                                         10

BOATSWAIN    I pray now, keep below.

ANTONIO    Where is the Master, Boatswain?

BOATSWAIN    Do you not hear him? You mar our labor. Keep your cabins: you do assist the storm!

GONZALO    Nay, good, be patient.                                        15

BOATSWAIN    When the sea is. Hence! What cares these roarers for the name of king? To cabin! Silence! Trouble us not.

GONZALO    Good, yet remember whom thou hast aboard.

BOATSWAIN    None that I more love than myself. You are a councillor: if you can command these elements to silence,    20
and work the peace of the present, we will not hand a rope more—use your authority. If you cannot, give thanks you have lived so long, and make yourself ready in your cabin for the mischance of the hour, if it so hap. [*To the mariners*]

3. **Good:** good fellow; **yarely:** quickly.
5. **hearts:** hearties.
6. **Take . . . topsail:** the first stage in reducing the ship's speed; **Tend:** attend. Both Master and Boatswain would convey orders by means of a whistle.
7–8. **Blow . . . enough:** Blow as hard as you like, as long as we have room between the ship and the rocks. Winds were often pictured as faces with puffed cheeks.
10. **Play the men!:** either (to the mariners) "Act like men!" or (to the Boatswain) "Ply the men!" that is, put them to work.
15. **good:** my good man; **patient:** composed.
16. **cares:** a plural subject with a singular form of the verb was a common formulation in the period; **roarers:** roaring winds and waves, with a metaphoric link to social disorder ("roaring boys" were riotous young men).
21. **work . . . present:** bring peace to the present turmoil; **hand:** handle.
24. **hap:** happen.

Cheerly, good hearts! [*To the courtiers*] Out of our way, I say! 25
Exit [*Boatswain with mariners*].

GONZALO  I have great comfort from this fellow. Methinks he
hath no drowning mark upon him; his complexion is perfect
gallows. Stand fast, good Fate, to his hanging; make the rope
of his destiny our cable, for our own doth little advantage. If
he be not born to be hanged, our case is miserable. 30
Exit [*with courtiers*].

Enter BOATSWAIN.

BOATSWAIN  Down with the topmast! Yare! Lower, lower! Bring
her to try with main-course. (*A cry within.*) A plague
upon this howling! They are louder than the weather or our
office.

Enter SEBASTIAN, ANTONIO, *and* GONZALO.

Yet again? What do you here? Shall we give o'er and drown? 35
Have you a mind to sink?

SEBASTIAN  A pox o' your throat, you bawling, blasphemous,
incharitable dog!

BOATSWAIN  Work you, then.

ANTONIO  Hang, cur, hang, you whoreson insolent noise- 40
maker! We are less afraid to be drowned than thou art.

GONZALO  I'll warrant him from drowning, though the ship
were no stronger than a nutshell and as leaky as an un-
stanched wench.

BOATSWAIN  Lay her a-hold, a-hold! Set her two courses. Off 45
to sea again! Lay her off!

Enter MARINERS *wet*.

MARINERS  All lost! To prayers, to prayers! All lost!
[*Exit mariners in confusion.*]

BOATSWAIN  What, must our mouths be cold?

26. **Methinks:** it seems to me.
26–28. **he . . . gallows:** The proverb was "He that is born to be hanged will never be drowned."
27. **complexion:** appearance; temperament.
29. **doth little advantage:** is of little use.
31–32. **Bring . . . try:** move forward tentatively under minimum sail; **main-course:** mainsail.
34. **office:** (the noise we make at) our work.
35. **give o'er:** stop working.
37. **blasphemous:** Unless some original blasphemy was cut from the Boatswain's speech, this simply implies "abusive" or "disrespectful."
42. **warrant . . . drowning:** guarantee he'll never drown.
43–44. **leaky . . . wench:** The phrase may refer to a menstruating woman, with the flow of blood unstopped; but *leaky* could also mean sexually insatiable.
45–46. **Lay . . . off:** bring the ship close toward the wind by setting foresail and mainsail (the two *courses*), then take her out to sea.
48. **must . . . cold?** must we die?

GONZALO   The King and Prince at prayers! Let's assist them,
  For our case is as theirs.
SEBASTIAN                    I'm out of patience.                    50
ANTONIO   We are merely cheated of our lives by drunkards.
  This wide-chopped rascal—would thou mightst lie drowning
  the washing of ten tides!
GONZALO   He'll be hanged yet, though every drop of water
  swear against it and gape at widest to glut him.                  55
[MARINERS]   (A confused noise within:) "Mercy on us!"—
  "We split, we split!"—"Farewell, my wife and children!"—
  "Farewell, brother!"—"We split, we split, we split!"
                                            [Exit Boatswain.]
ANTONIO   Let's all sink with th' King.
SEBASTIAN   Let's take leave of him.          Exit [with Antonio].   60
GONZALO   Now would I give a thousand furlongs of sea for an
  acre of barren ground: long heath, brown furze, anything.
  The wills above be done, but I would fain die a dry death.
                                                        Exit


### Act 1, Scene 2

[On the island.] Enter PROSPERO [in his magic cloak] and
MIRANDA.

MIRANDA
  If by your art, my dearest father, you have
  Put the wild waters in this roar, allay them.
  The sky, it seems, would pour down stinking pitch
  But that the sea, mounting to th' welkin's cheek,
  Dashes the fire out. O, I have suffered                            5
  With those that I saw suffer: a brave vessel
  (Who had no doubt some noble creature in her)
  Dashed all to pieces! O, the cry did knock
  Against my very heart! Poor souls, they perished.
  Had I been any god of power, I would                              10

---

51. **merely:** completely, utterly.;
52. **wide-chopped:** big-mouthed.
53. **the . . . tides:** an exaggerated form of the sentence passed on pirates, who were hanged
on the shore at low-water mark and left there until three tides had flowed.
55. **glut:** swallow.
61. **furlongs:** equal to 220 yards.
62 **heath:** heather; **furze:** gorse.
63. **fain:** gladly.
1. **art:** learning; magic powers.
2. **allay:** set to rest.
3. **pitch:** tar.
4. **welkin's cheek:** face of the sky.
6. **brave:** fine, noble.

Have sunk the sea within the earth, or ere
It should the good ship so have swallowed, and
The fraughting souls within her.
PROSPERO                                Be collected.
No more amazement. Tell your piteous heart
There's no harm done.
MIRANDA                        O, woe the day!
PROSPERO              ·                No harm.                      15
I have done nothing but in care of thee—
Of thee my dear one, thee my daughter—who
Art ignorant of what thou art, naught knowing
Of whence I am, nor that I am more better
Than Prospero, master of a full poor cell,                      20
And thy no greater father.
MIRANDA                        More to know
Did never meddle with my thoughts.
PROSPERO                                'Tis time
I should inform thee farther. Lend thy hand
And pluck my magic garment from me.

    [*She helps him remove the cloak, and he puts it aside.*]

                      So,
Lie there my art. Wipe thou thine eyes; have comfort.          25
The direful spectacle of the wrack, which touched
The very virtue of compassion in thee,
I have with such provision in mine art
So safely ordered that there is no soul—
No, not so much perdition as an hair                            30
Betid to any creature in the vessel
Which thou heard'st cry, which thou saw'st sink. Sit down,
For thou must now know farther.
MIRANDA    [*sitting*]              You have often
Begun to tell me what I am, but stopped
And left me to a bootless inquisition,                          35
Concluding, "Stay: not yet."

11. **or ere:** before.
13. **fraughting souls:** people who were the cargo; **Be collected:** compose yourself.
14. **amazement:** bewilderment; anguish; **piteous:** pitying.
19. **whence I am:** where I came from; **more better:** higher in rank.
20. **full poor cell:** small, humble dwelling (with a monastic overtone).
21. **no greater:** of no higher status than the dwelling suggests.
22. **meddle with:** intrude upon.
25. **my art:** that is, the cloak.
26. **direful:** having dire consequences; **wrack:** shipwreck; loss.
27. **virtue:** essence.
28. **provision:** foresight.
30. **perdition:** loss.
31. **Betid:** happened.
35. **bootless inquisition:** fruitless inquiry.

PROSPERO                          The hour's now come;
   The very minute bids thee ope thine ear.
   Obey, and be attentive. Canst thou remember
   A time before we came unto this cell?
   I do not think thou canst, for then thou wast not          40
   Out three years old.
MIRANDA                           Certainly, sir, I can.
PROSPERO
   By what? By any other house or person?
   Of anything the image tell me that
   Hath kept with thy remembrance.
MIRANDA                                          'Tis far off,
   And rather like a dream than an assurance                   45
   That my remembrance warrants. Had I not
   Four or five women once that tended me?
PROSPERO
   Thou hadst, and more, Miranda. But how is it
   That this lives in thy mind? What seest thou else
   In the dark-backward and abysm of time?                     50
   If thou rememb'rest aught ere thou cam'st here,
   How thou cam'st here thou mayst.
MIRANDA                                     But that I do not.
PROSPERO
   Twelve year since, Miranda, twelve year since,
   Thy father was the Duke of Milan and
   A prince of power.
MIRANDA                          Sir, are not you my father?        55
PROSPERO
   Thy mother was a piece of virtue, and
   She said thou wast my daughter, and thy father
   Was Duke of Milan, and his only heir,
   And princess, no worse issued.
MIRANDA                                     O the heavens!
   What foul play had we that we came from thence?             60
   Or blessèd was't we did?
PROSPERO                          Both, both, my girl.
   By foul play (as thou say'st) were we heaved thence,
   But blessedly holp hither.

---

41. **Out**: fully, that is, not yet three years old.
44. **with thy remembrance**: within thy memory.
46. **warrants**: guarantees as true.
50. **abysm**: abyss; chasm.
51. **aught**: anything.
56. **piece**: model.
59. **no worse issued**: of no less noble birth (than her father).
63. **holp**: helped.

MIRANDA                    O, my heart bleeds
  To think o' th' teen that I have turned you to,
  Which is from my remembrance! Please you, farther.                    65
PROSPERO
  My brother and thy uncle, called Antonio—
  I pray thee mark me, that a brother should
  Be so perfidious!—he whom next thyself
  Of all the world I loved, and to him put
  The manage of my state, as at that time                    70
  Through all the signories it was the first
  And Prospero the prime duke, being so reputed
  In dignity, and for the liberal arts
  Without a parallel; those being all my study,
  The government I cast upon my brother                    75
  And to my state grew stranger, being transported
  And rapt in secret studies. Thy false uncle—
  Dost thou attend me?
MIRANDA                    Sir, most heedfully.
PROSPERO
  Being once perfected how to grant suits,
  How to deny them, who t' advance, and who                    80
  To trash for overtopping, new-created
  The creatures that were mine, I say, or changed 'em,
  Or else new-formed 'em; having both the key
  Of officer and office, set all hearts i' th' state
  To what tune pleased his ear, that now he was                    85
  The ivy which had hid my princely trunk
  And sucked my verdure out on't.—Thou attend'st not?
MIRANDA
  O, good sir, I do.
PROSPERO                    I pray thee, mark me.
  I, thus neglecting worldly ends, all dedicated
  To closeness and the bettering of my mind                    90
  With that which, but by being so retired,

64. **teen . . . to:** trouble I've been to you.
65. **from:** not present in.
70. **manage:** administration.
71. **signories:** lordships; territories.
72. **prime:** senior.
73. **liberal arts:** the arts and sciences studied at universities, specifically grammar, logic, and rhetoric (the trivium), and arithmetic, geometry, music, and astronomy (the quadrivium).
76. **transported:** carried away.
79. **perfected:** completely versed in; **suits:** petitions.
81. **trash for overtopping:** check (as in the training of hounds) for undue ambition.
82. **or:** either.
83–84. **key . . . office:** control over positions and those who held them.
85. **that:** so that.
87. **verdure:** vitality, therefore power; **on't** of it.
90. **closeness:** privacy.

O'erprized all popular rate, in my false brother
Awaked an evil nature; and my trust,
Like a good parent, did beget of him
A falsehood in its contrary as great                              95
As my trust was, which had indeed no limit,
A confidence sans bound. He being thus lorded,
Not only with what my revenue yielded,
But what my power might else exact, like one
Who, having into truth by telling of it,                         100
Made such a sinner of his memory
To credit his own lie, he did believe
He was indeed the duke, out o' th' substitution
And executing th' outward face of royalty
With all prerogative. Hence his ambition growing—               105
Dost thou hear?
MIRANDA                 Your tale, sir, would cure deafness.
PROSPERO
To have no screen between this part he played
And him he played it for, he needs will be
Absolute Milan. Me, poor man, my library
Was dukedom large enough. Of temporal royalties                 110
He thinks me now incapable; confederates
(So dry he was for sway) with th' King of Naples
To give him annual tribute, do him homage,
Subject his coronet to his crown, and bend
The dukedom yet unbowed (alas, poor Milan!)                     115
To most ignoble stooping.
MIRANDA                         O, the heavens!
PROSPERO
Mark his condition, and th' event; then tell me
If this might be a brother.
MIRANDA                         I should sin
To think but nobly of my grandmother.
Good wombs have borne bad sons.

91–92. With . . . rate: with studies that were more valuable than public appreciation,
except that they withdrew me from the people.
97. sans bound: without limit; lorded: made a lord.
100. into: unto or against; it: that is, his own lie.
103. out o' th' substitution: by virtue of having taken my place.
105. prerogative: privileges of office.
107–9. part . . . Milan: The distinction is between Antonio playing the part of duke on behalf of Prospero (him he played it for) and becoming the real duke (Absolute Milan).
110. temporal royalties: secular power.
111. confederates: allies; conspires.
112. dry: thirsty, hence eager; sway: power.
114. Subject . . . crown: Antonio conspires to make the dukedom of Milan, symbolized by
the coronet, subject to the control of the crown of Naples.
115. yet: hitherto.
117. his condition . . . event: the terms of his agreement with Naples and its outcome.
119. but: other than.

PROSPERO                              Now the condition.     120
  This King of Naples, being an enemy
  To me inveterate, hearkens my brother's suit;
  Which was that he, in lieu o' th' premises
  Of homage, and I know not how much tribute,
  Should presently extirpate me and mine          125
  Out of the dukedom and confer fair Milan,
  With all the honors, on my brother. Whereon,
  A treacherous army levied, one midnight
  Fated to th' purpose did Antonio open
  The gates of Milan, and i' th' dead of darkness,     130
  The ministers for th' purpose hurried thence
  Me and thy crying self.
MIRANDA                       Alack, for pity!
  I, not remembering how I cried out then,
  Will cry it o'er again; it is a hint
  That wrings mine eyes to't.
PROSPERO                           Hear a little further,     135
  And then I'll bring thee to the present business
  Which now's upon's, without the which this story
  Were most impertinent.
MIRANDA                        Wherefore did they not
  That hour destroy us?
PROSPERO                       Well demanded, wench:
  My tale provokes that question. Dear, they durst not,     140
  So dear the love my people bore me; nor set
  A mark so bloody on the business; but
  With colors fairer painted their foul ends.
  In few, they hurried us aboard a bark,
  Bore us some leagues to sea, where they prepared     145
  A rotten carcass of a butt, not rigged,
  Nor tackle, sail, nor mast—the very rats
  Instinctively have quit it. There they hoist us
  To cry to th' sea that roared to us; to sigh
  To th' winds, whose pity, sighing back again,        150
  Did us but loving wrong.

122. **hearkens:** listens attentively to.
123. **in . . . premises:** in return for the conditions.
125. **presently:** immediately; **extirpate:** literally, to pull up by the roots, therefore to drive out.
129. **Fated:** appointed by fate.
131. **ministers:** agents.
134. **hint:** occasion.
137. **the which:** that is, the present business.
138. **impertinent:** irrelevant; **Wherefore:** why.
139. **demanded:** asked; **wench:** young girl.
144. **In few:** in short; **bark:** small boat.
145. **leagues:** A league is three miles.
146. **butt:** literally, a barrel or tub.

MIRANDA                    Alack, what trouble
  Was I then to you!
PROSPERO          O, a cherubin
  Thou wast that did preserve me. Thou didst smile,
  Infusèd with a fortitude from heaven,
  When I have decked the sea with drops full salt,                 155
  Under my burden groaned; which raised in me
  An undergoing stomach, to bear up
  Against what should ensue.
MIRANDA                    How came we ashore?
PROSPERO
  By providence divine.
  Some food we had, and some fresh water, that             160
  A noble Neapolitan, Gonzalo,
  Out of his charity (who being then appointed
  Master of this design) did give us, with
  Rich garments, linens, stuffs, and necessaries
  Which since have steaded much. So, of his gentleness,    165
  Knowing I loved my books, he furnished me
  From mine own library with volumes that
  I prize above my dukedom.
MIRANDA                    Would I might
  But ever see that man.
PROSPERO                    Now I arise.
  Sit still, and hear the last of our sea-sorrow.          170
  Here in this island we arrived, and here
  Have I, thy schoolmaster, made thee more profit
  Than other princes can, that have more time
  For vainer hours, and tutors not so careful.
MIRANDA
  Heavens thank you for't. And now I pray you, sir,        175
  For still 'tis beating in my mind, your reason
  For raising this sea-storm?
PROSPERO                    Know thus far forth:
  By accident most strange, bountiful Fortune
  (Now my dear Lady) hath mine enemies

152. **cherubin:** The plural of cherub (angel) could be used as a singular form.
155. **decked:** adorned.
156. **which:** that is, your smile.
157. **undergoing stomach:** determination to persevere.
164. **stuffs:** utensils or fabrics.
165. **steaded:** been useful; **gentleness:** kindness; nobility.
168–69. **Would . . . ever:** I wish that some day I might.
169. **Now I arise:** either an implicit stage direction or an allusion to Prospero's rising fortunes.
172. **made . . . profit:** provided a better education.
173. **princes:** a generic term for royal children of either sex. **can:** that is, can gain.
174. **careful:** caring; attentive.

Brought to this shore; and by my prescience                    180
I find my zenith doth depend upon
A most auspicious star, whose influence
If now I court not, but omit, my fortunes
Will ever after droop. Here cease more questions.
Thou art inclined to sleep. 'Tis a good dullness,                    185
And give it way. I know thou canst not choose.

    [MIRANDA *sleeps.*]

Come away, servant, come! I am ready now.
Approach, my Ariel. Come!

    *Enter* ARIEL.

ARIEL
All hail, great master, grave sir, hail! I come
To answer thy best pleasure; be't to fly,                    190
To swim, to dive into the fire, to ride
On the curled clouds. To thy strong bidding task
Ariel and all his quality.
PROSPERO                  Hast thou, spirit,
Performed to point the tempest that I bade thee?
ARIEL    To every article.                    195
I boarded the King's ship. Now on the beak,
Now in the waist, the deck, in every cabin,
I flamed amazement. Sometimes I'd divide
And burn in many places; on the topmast,
The yards, and bowsprit would I flame distinctly,                    200
Then meet and join. Jove's lightnings, the precursors
O' th' dreadful thunderclaps, more momentary
And sight-outrunning were not. The fire and cracks
Of sulfurous roaring the most mighty Neptune

181. **my zenith:** the highest point (in my fortunes).
182. **influence:** astrological power.
183. **omit:** disregard.
185. **dullness:** drowsiness.
186. **give it way:** give in to it.
192. **task:** set tasks for; test.
193. **quality:** skills; fellow spirits.
194. **to point:** exactly.
196. **beak:** bow.
197. **in the waist:** amidships.
198. **flamed amazement:** appeared as terrifying fire, as in the marine phenomenon of St. Elmo's fire.
200. **yards:** crossbars on masts; **bowsprit:** pole to which the lower part of the sail is fastened; **distinctly:** separately.
201. **Jove:** the most powerful of the Roman gods, traditionally armed with lightning bolts.
202. **momentary:** transitory.
203. **sight-outrunning:** faster than the eye could follow.
204. **Neptune:** Roman god of the sea, usually pictured with his trident.

Seem to besiege and make his bold waves tremble,          205
Yea, his dread trident shake.

PROSPERO                    My brave spirit!
Who was so firm, so constant, that this coil
Would not infect his reason?

ARIEL                    Not a soul
But felt a fever of the mad and played
Some tricks of desperation. All but mariners          210
Plunged in the foaming brine and quit the vessel,
Then all afire with me; the King's son Ferdinand,
With hair upstaring (then like reeds, not hair),
Was the first man that leapt, cried "Hell is empty,
And all the devils are here!"

PROSPERO                    Why, that's my spirit.          215
But was not this nigh shore?

ARIEL                    Close by, my master.

PROSPERO    But are they, Ariel, safe?

ARIEL                    Not a hair perished.
On their sustaining garments not a blemish,
But fresher than before; and, as thou bad'st me,
In troops I have dispersed them 'bout the isle.          220
The King's son have I landed by himself,
Whom I left cooling of the air with sighs
In an odd angle of the isle, and sitting,
His arms in this sad knot.

PROSPERO                    Of the King's ship,
The mariners, say how thou hast disposed,          225
And all the rest o' th' fleet.

ARIEL                    Safely in harbor
Is the King's ship; in the deep nook where once
Thou call'dst me up at midnight to fetch dew
From the still-vexed Bermudas, there she's hid;
The mariners all under hatches stowed,          230
Who, with a charm joined to their suffered labor,
I have left asleep; and for the rest o' th' fleet
(Which I dispersed) they all have met again,
And are upon the Mediterranean float

207. **coil**: tumult.
209. **of the mad**: of the kind suffered by lunatics.
213. **upstaring**: standing on end.
220. **troops**: groups (actually one group and three separate individuals).
223. **angle**: corner.
224. **in . . . knot**: folded, a conventional sign of melancholy.
229. **Bermudas**: in Shakespeare's time, a group of uninhabited Atlantic islands feared for their dangerous reefs and ferocious storms.
230. **under hatches**: below deck.
231. **suffered labor**: exertions during the storm.
234. **float**: sea.

Bound sadly home for Naples,                                    235
Supposing that they saw the King's ship wrecked
And his great person perish.
PROSPERO                            Ariel, thy charge
Exactly is performed; but there's more work.
What is the time o' th' day?
ARIEL                               Past the mid-season.
PROSPERO
At least two glasses. The time 'twixt six and now              240
Must by us both be spent most preciously.
ARIEL
Is there more toil? Since thou dost give me pains,
Let me remember thee what thou hast promised,
Which is not yet performed me.
PROSPERO                            How now? Moody?
What is't thou canst demand?
ARIEL                               My liberty.                   245
PROSPERO
Before the time be out? No more.
ARIEL                               I prithee,
Remember I have done thee worthy service,
Told thee no lies, made no mistakings, served
Without or grudge or grumblings. Thou did promise
To bate me a full year.
PROSPERO                Dost thou forget                          250
From what a torment I did free thee?
ARIEL                                No.
PROSPERO
Thou dost, and think'st it much to tread the ooze
Of the salt deep,
To run upon the sharp wind of the north,
To do me business in the veins o' th' earth                     255
When it is baked with frost.
ARIEL                          I do not, sir.
PROSPERO
Thou liest, malignant thing! Hast thou forgot

239. **mid-season:** noon.
240. **two glasses:** two hours.
241. **preciously:** valuably, carefully.
242. **pains:** tasks; troubles.
243. **remember:** remind.
244. **Moody:** stubborn; sullen.
249. **or . . . or:** either . . . or.
250. **bate me:** deduct from the period of my servitude.
252. **ooze:** muddy bottom.
254. **salt deep:** sea.
255. **veins:** channels; seams of metal.
256. **baked:** hardened.

The foul witch Sycorax, who with age and envy
Was grown into a hoop? Hast thou forgot her?

ARIEL
No, sir.

PROSPERO          Thou hast. Where was she born? Speak. Tell me.          260

ARIEL
Sir, in Algiers.

PROSPERO          O, was she so? I must
Once in a month recount what thou hast been,
Which thou forget'st. This damned witch Sycorax,
For mischiefs manifold, and sorceries terrible
To enter human hearing, from Algiers,          265
Thou know'st, was banished. For one thing she did
They would not take her life. Is not this true?

ARIEL
Ay, sir.

PROSPERO
This blue-eyed hag was hither brought with child
And here was left by th' sailors. Thou, my slave,          270
As thou report'st thyself, was then her servant;
And for thou wast a spirit too delicate
To act her earthy and abhorred commands,
Refusing her grand hests, she did confine thee,
By help of her more potent ministers,          275
And in her most unmitigable rage,
Into a cloven pine; within which rift
Imprisoned thou didst painfully remain
A dozen years, within which space she died,
And left thee there, where thou didst vent thy groans          280
As fast as mill-wheels strike. Then was this island
(Save for the son that she did litter here,
A freckled whelp, hag-born) not honored with
A human shape.

ARIEL          Yes, Caliban her son.

PROSPERO
Dull thing, I say so: he, that Caliban          285

258. **envy:** malice.
259. **grown . . . hoop:** bent, or doubled, over.
266. **one thing:** generally assumed to be her pregnancy.
269. **blue-eyed:** blue eyelids were associated with pregnancy, but also with malevolent women; the epithet also suggests that Sycorax would be an unusual figure in Algiers, where dark eyes would be the norm; **hag:** witch.
272. **for:** because.
274. **hests:** commands.
275. **ministers:** agents.
280. **vent:** emit.
281. **as . . . strike:** as the blades of waterwheels strike the water.
282–83. **litter . . . whelp:** terms usually associated with animal births.

Whom now I keep in service. Thou best know'st
What torment I did find thee in: thy groans
Did make wolves howl, and penetrate the breasts
Of ever-angry bears. It was a torment
To lay upon the damned, which Sycorax                    290
Could not again undo. It was mine art,
When I arrived and heard thee, that made gape
The pine, and let thee out.
ARIEL                            I thank thee, master.
PROSPERO
If thou more murmur'st, I will rend an oak
And peg thee in his knotty entrails till                    295
Thou hast howled away twelve winters.
ARIEL                                Pardon, master.
I will be correspondent to command
And do my spriting gently.
PROSPERO                    Do so; and after two days
I will discharge thee.
ARIEL                    That's my noble master!
What shall I do? Say what! What shall I do?                    300
PROSPERO
Go make thyself like a nymph o' th' sea. Be subject
To no sight but thine and mine, invisible
To every eyeball else. Go, take this shape
And hither come in't. Go! Hence with diligence. *Exit* [ARIEL].
[*To* MIRANDA] Awake, dear heart, awake! Thou hast slept well.    305
Awake!
MIRANDA    The strangeness of your story put
Heaviness in me.
PROSPERO            Shake it off. Come on,
We'll visit Caliban, my slave, who never
Yields us kind answer.
MIRANDA                    'Tis a villain, sir,
I do not love to look on.
PROSPERO                    But, as 'tis,                    310
We cannot miss him. He does make our fire,
Fetch in our wood, and serves in offices
That profit us. What ho! Slave! Caliban!
Thou earth, thou! Speak!

292. **made gape:** opened up.
294. **murmur'st:** complain.
297. **correspondent:** answerable.
307. **Heaviness:** drowsiness.
309. **villain:** evil or low-born person.
311. **miss:** do without.
312. **offices:** tasks.

CALIBAN   (*within*)          There's wood enough within.
PROSPERO
Come forth, I say! There's other business for thee.          315
Come, thou tortoise! When?

    *Enter* ARIEL *like a water-nymph.*

Fine apparition! My quaint Ariel,
Hark in thine ear. [*He whispers to* ARIEL.]
ARIEL          My lord, it shall be done.          *Exit.*
PROSPERO
Thou poisonous slave, got by the devil himself
Upon thy wicked dam, come forth!          320

    *Enter* CALIBAN.

CALIBAN
As wicked dew as e'er my mother brushed
With raven's feather from unwholesome fen
Drop on you both! A southwest blow on ye
And blister you all o'er!
PROSPERO
For this, be sure, tonight thou shalt have cramps,          325
Side-stitches that shall pen thy breath up; urchins
Shall, for that vast of night that they may work,
All exercise on thee; thou shalt be pinched
As thick as honeycomb, each pinch more stinging
Than bees that made 'em.
CALIBAN          I must eat my dinner.          330
This island's mine by Sycorax my mother,
Which thou tak'st from me. When thou cam'st first
Thou strok'st me and made much of me; wouldst give me
Water with berries in't; and teach me how
To name the bigger light, and how the less,          335
That burn by day and night. And then I loved thee
And showed thee all the qualities o' th' isle,
The fresh springs, brine-pits, barren place and fertile.
Cursèd be I that did so! All the charms
Of Sycorax—toads, beetles, bats—light on you!          340
For I am all the subjects that you have,
Which first was mine own king; and here you sty me

317. **Fine:** exquisitely fashioned; **quaint:** skillfull.
323. **southwest:** Winds from the southwest brought warm and damp air and were therefore considered unwholesome.
326. **pen . . . up:** stop you breathing; **urchins:** goblins in the form of hedgehogs.
328–29. **pinched . . . honeycomb:** pinched with as many holes as a honeycomb has cells.
337. **qualities:** characteristics.
339. **charms:** spells.
342. **sty:** confine (as with swine).

In this hard rock, whiles you do keep from me
The rest o' th' island.

PROSPERO                Thou most lying slave,
Whom stripes may move, not kindness. I have used thee          345
(Filth as thou art) with humane care, and lodged thee
In mine own cell till thou didst seek to violate
The honor of my child.

CALIBAN                O ho, O ho! Would't had been done!
Thou didst prevent me; I had peopled else
This isle with Calibans.

MIRANDA                Abhorrèd slave,          350
Which any print of goodness wilt not take,
Being capable of all ill. I pitied thee,
Took pains to make thee speak, taught thee each hour
One thing or other. When thou didst not (savage)
Know thine own meaning, but wouldst gabble like          355
A thing most brutish, I endowed thy purposes
With words that made them known. But thy vile race,
Though thou didst learn, had that in't which good natures
Could not abide to be with; therefore wast thou
Deservedly confined into this rock,          360
Who hadst deserved more than a prison.

CALIBAN
You taught me language, and my profit on't
Is, I know how to curse. The red plague rid you
For learning me your language!

PROSPERO                Hag-seed, hence!
Fetch us in fuel; and be quick, thou'rt best,          365
To answer other business. Shrugg'st thou, malice?
If thou neglect'st or dost unwillingly
What I command, I'll rack thee with old cramps,
Fill all thy bones with aches, make thee roar,
That beasts shall tremble at thy din.

CALIBAN                No, pray thee.          370
[Aside] I must obey. His art is of such power,
It would control my dam's god, Setebos,
And make a vassal of him.

---

345. **stripes:** strokes of the whip.
349. **Thou . . . else:** had you not prevented me, I would have populated.
351. **print:** imprint.
357. **race:** natural or inherited disposition.
364. **learning:** teaching; **Hag-seed:** offspring of a witch.
366. **answer other business:** perform other tasks.
368. **old cramps:** the pains of old age.
372. **Setebos:** a devil of the Patagonian natives, according to Richard Eden's 1555 translation of Antonio Pigafetta's account of Magellan's circumnavigatory expedition.

PROSPERO                    So, slave, hence.      *Exit* CALIBAN.

*Enter* FERDINAND; *and* ARIEL, *invisible, playing and*
*singing.*

ARIEL   [*Sings*]
                Come unto these yellow sands,
                And then take hands.          .                            375
                Curtsied when you have, and kissed,
                The wild waves whist.
                Foot it featly here and there,
                And sweet sprites the burden bear.
                        Hark, hark                                        380
                        The watch-dogs bark
                        Bow-wow, bow-wow.
                [*Spirits echo the burden "bow-wow" within.*]
                        Hark, hark! I hear
                        The strain of strutting Chanticleer,
                        Cry cock-a-diddle-dow.                           385

        [*Spirits echo the burden "cock-a-diddle-dow" within.*]

FERDINAND
        Where should this music be? I' th' air or th' earth?
        It sounds no more; and sure it waits upon
        Some god o' th' island. Sitting on a bank,
        Weeping again the King my father's wrack,
        This music crept by me upon the waters,                          390
        Allaying both their fury and my passion
        With its sweet air. Thence I have followed it,
        Or it hath drawn me rather; but 'tis gone.
        No, it begins again.
ARIEL      [*Sings*]
                Full fathom five thy father lies,                        395
                Of his bones are coral made;
                Those are pearls that were his eyes;
                Nothing of him that doth fade,

---

373 **SD. playing:** probably a lute.
377. **whist:** becoming silent.
378. **featly:** nimbly.
379. **burden:** refrain.
382. **SD.** Here, as in the stage directions following lines 385 and 402, the Folio adds the direction *dispersedly*, that is, not in unison.
384. **strain:** song; **Chanticleer:** rooster.
387. **waits upon:** attends.
391. **passion:** literally, suffering.
395. **Full fathom five:** A fathom—the nautical measure of the depth of the sea—is about
six feet, so five full fathoms is about thirty feet.
398. **fade:** decay.

But doth suffer a sea-change
Into something rich and strange.                    400
Sea-nymphs hourly ring his knell.
Hark, now I hear them: ding dong bell.

[*Spirits echo the burden "ding dong bell" within.*]

FERDINAND
The ditty does remember my drowned father.
This is no mortal business, nor no sound
That the earth owes. I hear it now above me.                    405
PROSPERO    [*To Miranda*]
The fringèd curtains of thine eye advance
And say what thou seest yond.
MIRANDA                                    What is't? A spirit?
Lord, how it looks about. Believe me, sir,
It carries a brave form. But 'tis a spirit.
PROSPERO
No, wench, it eats, and sleeps, and hath such senses                    410
As we have, such. This gallant which thou seest
Was in the wrack; and, but he's something stained
With grief (that's beauty's canker), thou mightst call him
A goodly person. He hath lost his fellows
And strays about to find 'em.
MIRANDA                                    I might call him                    415
A thing divine, for nothing natural
I ever saw so noble.
PROSPERO    [*Aside*]    It goes on, I see,
As my soul prompts it. Spirit, fine spirit, I'll free thee
Within two days for this.
FERDINAND                                    Most sure, the goddess
On whom these airs attend! Vouchsafe my prayer                    420
May know if you remain upon this island,
And that you will some good instruction give

399. **suffer:** undergo.
403. **ditty does remember:** song commemorates.
404. **mortal:** earthly.
405. **owes:** owns.
406. **advance:** raise.
407. **yond:** yonder.
409. **brave:** handsome.
411. **gallant:** fine gentleman (perhaps spoken ironically).
412. **but:** except for the fact that; **something:** somewhat.
413. **canker:** something that corrodes or consumes.
417. **It:** that is, my plan.
418. **As . . . it:** according to the direction of Prospero's intellectual power.
419–20. **Most . . . attend:** This sentence recalls Aeneas's phrase in the *Aeneid* when he meets his mother, Venus, disguised as a huntress: "O dea certe" [Oh, surely the goddess].
420. **airs:** Ariel's songs; **Vouchsafe:** grant.
421. **May know:** that I may know; **remain:** live.

How I may bear me here. My prime request,
Which I do last pronounce, is (O you wonder!)
If you be maid or no?

MIRANDA                    No wonder, sir,                    425
But certainly a maid.

FERDINAND                 My language? Heavens!
I am the best of them that speak this speech,
Were I but where 'tis spoken.

PROSPERO                        How? The best?
What wert thou if the King of Naples heard thee?

FERDINAND
A single thing, as I am now, that wonders                    430
To hear thee speak of Naples. He does hear me,
And that he does I weep. Myself am Naples,
Who with mine eyes, never since at ebb, beheld
The King my father wracked.

MIRANDA                         Alack, for mercy!

FERDINAND
Yes, faith, and all his lords, the Duke of Milan            435
And his brave son being twain.

PROSPERO   [Aside]             The Duke of Milan
And his more braver daughter could control thee
If now 'twere fit to do't. At the first sight
They have changed eyes. Delicate Ariel,
I'll set thee free for this! [To Ferdinand] A word, good sir.   440
I fear you have done yourself some wrong. A word!

MIRANDA
Why speaks my father so ungently? This
Is the third man that e'er I saw; the first
That e'er I sighed for. Pity move my father
To be inclined my way.

FERDINAND                     O, if a virgin,                  445
And your affection not gone forth, I'll make you
The Queen of Naples.

PROSPERO                     Soft, sir! One word more.
[Aside] They are both in either's powers. But this swift
     business

423. bear me: conduct myself; prime: most important.
425. maid: a girl, as opposed to either a goddess or a married woman.
430. A single thing: without family; unmarried; weak.
431–32: Because Ferdinand believes his father to have drowned, he thinks of himself as
(King of) Naples; so *he* (the King) and *me* are for Ferdinand the same person.
433. at ebb: at low tide, that is, the tears have never since stopped.
436. his brave son: the only reference in the play to Antonio's son; twain: two of them.
437. more braver: worthier; control: contradict.
439. changed eyes: exchanged glances, with the implication of falling in love; Delicate: artful.
441. *You* (Ferdinand) *have done yourself* (the King of Naples) *some wrong.*
444. Pity: let pity.

I must uneasy make, lest too light winning
Make the prize light. [*To* FERDINAND] One word more! I                450
    charge thee
That thou attend me. Thou dost here usurp
The name thou ow'st not, and hast put thyself
Upon this island as a spy, to win it
From me, the lord on't.

FERDINAND                          No, as I am a man!

MIRANDA
There's nothing ill can dwell in such a temple.                         455
If the ill spirit have so fair a house,
Good things will strive to dwell with't.

PROSPERO      [*To* FERDINAND]                Follow me.
    [*To* MIRANDA] Speak not you for him: he's a traitor. [*To* FER-
    DINAND] Come!
I'll manacle thy neck and feet together.
Sea water shalt thou drink; thy food shall be                           460
The fresh-brook mussels, withered roots, and husks
Wherein the acorn cradled. Follow!

FERDINAND                          No!
I will resist such entertainment till
Mine enemy has more power.

        *He draws [his sword], and is charmed from moving.*

MIRANDA                          O dear father,
Make not too rash a trial of him, for                                   465
He's gentle, and not fearful.

PROSPERO                          What, I say,
My foot my tutor? [*To* FERDINAND] Put thy sword up, traitor,
Who mak'st a show but dar'st not strike, thy conscience
Is so possessed with guilt. Come from thy ward,
For I can here disarm thee with this stick,                             470
And make thy weapon drop.

MIRANDA                          Beseech you, father—

PROSPERO
Hence! Hang not on my garments.

MIRANDA                          Sir, have pity.
I'll be his surety.

449. **uneasy:** difficult.
449–50. **light . . . light:** easy . . . cheap.
450. **charge:** command.
452. **ow'st:** owns.
461. **fresh-brook mussels:** These are inedible.
463. **entertainment:** treatment.
465. **rash:** hasty.
466. **not fearful:** not a cause of fear; not afraid.
469. **Come . . . ward:** give up your defensive stance.

PROSPERO            Silence! One word more
Shall make me chide thee, if not hate thee. What,
An advocate for an imposter? Hush!                               475
Thou think'st there is no more such shapes as he,
Having seen but him and Caliban. Foolish wench,
To th' most of men this is a Caliban,
And they to him are angels.
MIRANDA                        My affections
Are then most humble. I have no ambition                         480
To see a goodlier man.
PROSPERO    [*To* FERDINAND] Come on, obey.
Thy nerves are in their infancy again,
And have no vigor in them.
FERDINAND                     So they are.
My spirits, as in a dream, are all bound up.
My father's loss, the weakness which I feel,                     485
The wrack of all my friends, nor this man's threats
To whom I am subdued, are but light to me,
Might I but through my prison once a day
Behold this maid. All corners else o' th' earth
Let liberty make use of. Space enough                            490
Have I in such a prison.
PROSPERO    [*Aside*]        It works. [*To* FERDINAND] Come on!
[*To* ARIEL] Thou hast done well, fine Ariel. [*To* FERDINAND]
    Follow me.
[*To* ARIEL] Hark what thou else shalt do me.
MIRANDA    [*To* FERDINAND]                 Be of comfort,
My father's of a better nature, sir,
Than he appears by speech. This is unwonted                      495
Which now came from him.
PROSPERO    [*To* ARIEL]         Thou shalt be as free
As mountain winds; but then exactly do
All points of my command.
ARIEL                        To th' syllable.
PROSPERO    [*To* FERDINAND] Come, follow. [*To* MIRANDA] Speak
not for him.                                   *Exeunt.*


478. **To:** compared to.
482. **nerves:** sinews.
487. **light:** minor burdens.
489. **All corners else:** all other corners.
493. **do me:** do for me.
495. **unwonted:** unusual.
497. **then:** that is, in order to be free.

### Act 2, Scene 1

[*Another part of the island.*] *Enter* ALONSO, SEBASTIAN, ANTONIO, GONZALO, ADRIAN, *and* FRANCISCO.

GONZALO
    Beseech you, sir, be merry. You have cause
    (So have we all) of joy; for our escape
    Is much beyond our loss. Our hint of woe
    Is common: every day some sailor's wife,
    The master of some merchant, and the merchant          5
    Have just our theme of woe. But for the miracle—
    I mean our preservation—few in millions
    Can speak like us. Then wisely, good sir, weigh
    Our sorrow with our comfort.
ALONSO                          Prithee, peace.
SEBASTIAN    [*To* ANTONIO] He receives comfort like cold porridge.
ANTONIO    [*To* SEBASTIAN] The visitor will not give him o'er so.    10
SEBASTIAN
    Look, he's winding up the watch of his wit;
    by and by it will strike.
GONZALO    [*To* ALONSO] Sir—
SEBASTIAN    One. Tell.                                              15
GONZALO    When every grief is entertained
    That's offered, comes to th'entertainer—
SEBASTIAN    A dollar.
GONZALO    Dolor comes to him, indeed. You have spoken truer
    than you purposed.                                              20
SEBASTIAN    You have taken it wiselier than I meant you
    should.
GONZALO    [*To* ALONSO] Therefore, my lord—
ANTONIO    Fie, what a spendthrift is he of his tongue!
ALONSO    I prithee, spare.                                         25
GONZALO    Well, I have done. But yet—
SEBASTIAN    He will be talking.

---

3. **hint:** occasion.
5. **merchant . . . merchant:** trading ship . . . shipowner.
9. **with:** against.
10. **porridge:** pottage, sometimes made of peas, therefore a pun on "peace."
11. **visitor:** one taking comfort to the sick, as Gonzalo is doing; **give him o'er:** abandon him.
15. **Tell:** keep count.
16. **entertained:** accepted.
17. **th'entertainer:** the recipient.
18. **dollar:** at this time, a German or Spanish coin in wide circulation.
19. **dolor:** grief.
20. **purposed:** intended.
25. **spare:** stop.

ANTONIO   Which, of he or Adrian, for a good wager, first begins to crow?

SEBASTIAN   The old cock.                                      30

ANTONIO   The cockerel.

SEBASTIAN   Done. The wager?

ANTONIO   A laughter.

SEBASTIAN   A match.

ADRIAN   Though this island seem to be desert—                 35

ANTONIO   Ha, ha, ha!

SEBASTIAN   So, you're paid.

ADRIAN   Uninhabitable and almost inaccessible—

SEBASTIAN   Yet—

ADRIAN   Yet—                                                  40

ANTONIO   He could not miss't.

ADRIAN   It must needs be of subtle, tender, and delicate
temperance.

ANTONIO   Temperance was a delicate wench.

SEBASTIAN   Ay, and a subtle, as he most learnedly delivered.   45

ADRIAN   The air breathes upon us here most sweetly.

SEBASTIAN   As if it had lungs, and rotten ones.

ANTONIO   Or as 'twere perfumed by a fen.

GONZALO   Here is everything advantageous to life.

ANTONIO   True, save means to live.                            50

SEBASTIAN   Of that there's none, or little.

GONZALO   How lush and lusty the grass looks! How green!

ANTONIO   The ground indeed is tawny.

SEBASTIAN   With an eye of green in't.

ANTONIO   He misses not much.                                  55

SEBASTIAN   No, he doth but mistake the truth totally.

GONZALO   But the rarity of it is, which is indeed almost beyond credit—

SEBASTIAN   As many vouched rarities are.

GONZALO   That our garments, being, as they were, drenched    60

---

29. crow: speak.
30. old cock: that is, Gonzalo.
31. cockerel: that is, Adrian.
34. A match: agreed.
35. desert: uninhabited.
41. miss't: avoid saying "yet"; miss the island.
42. must needs be: has to be; subtle: delicate; delicate: pleasant.
43. temperance: mildness of climate.
44. Temperance: a woman's name; delicate: voluptuous.
45. subtle: crafty; delivered: uttered.
50. save: except.
52. lush: tender; lusty: vigorous.
53. tawny: yellowish brown.
54. eye: tinge.
56. but: merely.
59. vouched rarities: strange phenomena accepted as true.

in the sea, hold notwithstanding their freshness and gloss,
being rather new-dyed than stained with salt water.

ANTONIO    If but one of his pockets could speak, would it not
say he lies?

SEBASTIAN    Ay, or very falsely pocket up his report.                    65

GONZALO    Methinks our garments are now as fresh as when
we put them on first in Afric, at the marriage of the King's
fair daughter Claribel to the King of Tunis.

SEBASTIAN    'Twas a sweet marriage, and we prosper well in our
return.                                                                    70

ADRIAN    Tunis was never graced before with such a paragon to
their queen.

GONZALO    Not since widow Dido's time.

ANTONIO    Widow? A pox o' that! How came that "widow" in?
Widow Dido!                                                                75

SEBASTIAN    What if he had said "widower Aeneas" too? Good
Lord, how you take it!

ADRIAN    "Widow Dido," said you? You make me study of that.
She was of Carthage, not of Tunis.

GONZALO    This Tunis, sir, was Carthage.                                  80

ADRIAN    Carthage?

GONZALO    I assure you, Carthage.

ANTONIO    His word is more than the miraculous harp.

SEBASTIAN    He hath raised the wall and houses too.

ANTONIO    What impossible matter will he make easy next?                 85

SEBASTIAN    I think he will carry this island home in his pocket,
and give it his son for an apple.

ANTONIO    And sowing the kernels of it in the sea, bring forth
more islands.

GONZALO    Ay.                                                            90

ANTONIO    Why, in good time.

GONZALO    [To ALONSO] Sir, we were talking, that our garments
seem now as fresh as when we were at Tunis at the marriage
of your daughter, who is now queen.

ANTONIO    And the rarest that e'er came there.                           95

SEBASTIAN    Bate, I beseech you, widow Dido.

ANTONIO    O widow Dido? Ay, widow Dido.

---

63–64. would . . . lies: that is, because it would still be holding water.
65. pocket up: conceal.
71. to: for.
75. Widow Dido!: In Virgil's version of the story in the *Aeneid*, Dido, founder of Carthage,
was already a widow when Aeneas met her; however, Antonio takes Gonzalo's use of the
term as an overdelicate way to describe a woman deserted by her lover.
77. take: interpret.
78. study of: think about.
83. miraculous harp: the mythical harp of Amphion, which raised the walls of Thebes.
96. Bate: Except.

GONZALO   Is not, sir, my doublet as fresh as the first day I
wore it? I mean, in a sort.

ANTONIO   That "sort" was well fished for.                              100

GONZALO   When I wore it at your daughter's marriage.

ALONSO
You cram these words into mine ears, against
The stomach of my sense. Would I had never
Married my daughter there; for coming thence
My son is lost, and (in my rate) she too,                               105
Who is so far from Italy removed
I ne'er again shall see her. O thou mine heir
Of Naples and of Milan, what strange fish
Hath made his meal on thee?

FRANCISCO                        Sir, he may live.
I saw him beat the surges under him,                                    110
And ride upon their backs. He trod the water
Whose enmity he flung aside, and breasted
The surge most swol'n that met him. His bold head
'Bove the contentious waves he kept, and oared
Himself with his good arms in lusty stroke                              115
To th' shore, that o'er his wave-worn basis bowed,
As stooping to relieve him. I not doubt
He came alive to land.

ALONSO                     No, no, he's gone.

SEBASTIAN
Sir, you may thank yourself for this great loss,
That would not bless our Europe with your daughter,                     120
But rather lose her to an African,
Where she, at least, is banished from your eye,
Who hath cause to set the grief on't.

ALONSO                             Prithee, peace.

SEBASTIAN
You were kneeled to and importuned otherwise
By all of us; and the fair soul herself                                 125
Weighed, between loathness and obedience, at
Which end o' th' beam should bow. We have lost your son,

98. **doublet:** close-fitting jacket.
99. **in a sort:** in a way.
103. **stomach of my sense:** appetite for listening to them.
105. **rate:** opinion.
110. **surges:** waves.
116. **o'er . . . bowed:** the cliff, eroded by waves, projected outward.
117. **As:** as if.
120. **That:** you who.
123. **Who:** that is, Claribel.
124. **importuned:** begged.
127. **Which . . . bow:** which end of the scales should lower.

I fear, forever. Milan and Naples have
More widows in them of this business' making
Than we bring men to comfort them. The fault's                    130
Your own.
ALONSO          So is the dearest o' th' loss.
GONZALO   My lord Sebastian,
   The truth you speak doth lack some gentleness,
   And time to speak it in: you rub the sore
   When you should bring the plaster.
SEBASTIAN                         Very well.                    135
ANTONIO   And most chirurgeonly.
GONZALO   [To ALONSO]
   It is foul weather in us all, good sir,
   When you are cloudy.
SEBASTIAN               Foul weather?
ANTONIO                            Very foul.
GONZALO
   Had I plantation of this isle, my lord—
ANTONIO   He'd sow't with nettle-seed.
SEBASTIAN                         Or docks, or mallows.   140
GONZALO   And were the king on't, what would I do?
SEBASTIAN   Scape being drunk for want of wine.
GONZALO
   I' th' commonwealth I would by contraries
   Execute all things. For no kind of traffic
   Would I admit; no name of magistrate;                    145
   Letters should not be known; riches, poverty,
   And use of service, none; contract, succession,
   Bourn, bound of land, tilth, vineyard, none;
   No use of metal, corn, or wine, or oil;
   No occupation, all men idle, all;                    150
   And women too, but innocent and pure;
   No sovereignty—
SEBASTIAN          Yet he would be king on't.
ANTONIO   The latter end of his commonwealth forgets the
   beginning.

---

**131. dearest:** heaviest.
**136. chirurgeonly:** like a surgeon.
**139. plantation:** colonization.
**140. docks, or mallows:** weeds used to rub on nettle stings.
**141. on't:** of it.
**142. want:** lack.
**143. by contraries:** opposite to customary practice.
**144. traffic:** trade.
**146. Letters:** literature.
**148. Bourn . . . tilth:** Boundaries, property limits, tillage.
**149. corn:** grain.

GONZALO
  All things in common nature should produce                    155
  Without sweat or endeavor. Treason, felony,
  Sword, pike, knife, gun, or need of any engine
  Would I not have; but nature should bring forth
  Of its own kind, all foison, all abundance,
  To feed my innocent people.                                       160
SEBASTIAN    No marrying 'mong his subjects?
ANTONIO    None, man, all idle: whores and knaves.
GONZALO
  I would with such perfection govern, sir,
  T' excel the golden age.
SEBASTIAN           'Save his majesty!
ANTONIO    Long live Gonzalo!                              165
GONZALO    And do you mark me, sir?
ALONSO
  Prithee, no more. Thou dost talk nothing to me.
GONZALO    I do well believe your highness, and did it to
minister occasion to these gentlemen, who are of such
sensible and nimble lungs that they always use to laugh at    170
nothing.
ANTONIO    'Twas you we laughed at.
GONZALO    Who, in this kind of merry fooling, am nothing to
you. So you may continue, and laugh at nothing still.
ANTONIO    What a blow was there given!                    175
SEBASTIAN    An it had not fall'n flatlong.
GONZALO    You are gentlemen of brave mettle; you would lift
the moon out of her sphere if she would continue in it five
weeks without changing.

*Enter* ARIEL [*invisible,*] *playing solemn music.*

SEBASTIAN    We would so, and then go a-batfowling.          180
ANTONIO    Nay, good my lord, be not angry.
GONZALO    No, I warrant you, I will not adventure my discretion so weakly. Will you laugh me asleep, for I am very
heavy.

157. **engine:** machine used in warfare.
159. **foison:** plenty.
164. **'Save:** God save.
169. **minister occasion:** provide the opportunity.
170. **sensible:** sensitive; **use:** are accustomed.
176. **An:** if; **flatlong:** with the flat of the blade.
177. **mettle:** spirit.
178. **sphere:** orbit.
180. **a-batfowling:** hunting birds with a stick.
182. **warrant:** promise.
182–83. **adventure . . . weakly:** risk my reputation for discretion for so weak a cause.
184. **heavy:** sleepy.

ANTONIO   Go sleep, and hear us.                                    185

    [*All sleep except* ALONSO, SEBASTIAN, *and* ANTONIO.]

ALONSO   What, all so soon asleep? I wish mine eyes
  Would, with themselves, shut up my thoughts. I find
  They are inclined to do so.
SEBASTIAN                         Please you, sir,
  Do not omit the heavy offer of it.
  It seldom visits sorrow; when it doth,                         190
  It is a comforter.
ANTONIO             We two, my lord,
  Will guard your person while you take your rest,
  And watch your safety.
ALONSO                    Thank you. Wondrous heavy.
             [ALONSO *sleeps. Exit* ARIEL.]

SEBASTIAN
  What a strange drowsiness possesses them!
ANTONIO
  It is the quality o' th' climate.
SEBASTIAN                         Why                                195
  Doth it not then our eyelids sink? I find
  Not myself disposed to sleep.
ANTONIO
  Nor I: my spirits are nimble.
  They fell together all, as by consent
  They dropped, as by a thunder-stroke. What might,             200
  Worthy Sebastian, O, what might?—No more.
  And yet, methinks I see it in thy face,
  What thou shouldst be. Th' occasion speaks thee, and
  My strong imagination sees a crown
  Dropping upon thy head.
SEBASTIAN                    What? Art thou waking?                 205
ANTONIO
  Do you not hear me speak?
SEBASTIAN                    I do; and surely
  It is a sleepy language, and thou speak'st
  Out of thy sleep. What is it thou didst say?
  This is a strange repose, to be asleep
  With eyes wide open; standing, speaking, moving,             210
  And yet so fast asleep.
ANTONIO                    Noble Sebastian,
  Thou let'st thy fortune sleep—die rather; wink'st

189. omit: refuse; heavy offer: chance to sleep.
199. consent: agreement.
203. Th' occasion speaks thee: The opportunity calls upon you.
212. wink'st: (you) shut your eyes.

Whiles thou art waking.

SEBASTIAN                              Thou dost snore distinctly;
There's meaning in thy snores.

ANTONIO
I am more serious than my custom. You                          215
Must be so too, if heed me; which to do,
Trebles thee o'er.

SEBASTIAN                    Well, I am standing water.

ANTONIO
I'll teach you how to flow.

SEBASTIAN                              Do so. To ebb
Hereditary sloth instructs me.

ANTONIO                                        O!
If you but knew how you the purpose cherish                     220
Whiles thus you mock it; how in stripping it
You more invest it. Ebbing men, indeed,
Most often do so near the bottom run
By their own fear or sloth.

SEBASTIAN                              Prithee say on.
The setting of thine eye and cheek proclaim                     225
A matter from thee; and a birth, indeed,
Which throes thee much to yield.

ANTONIO                                        Thus, sir:
[*Pointing to Gonzalo*] Although this lord of weak remem-
    brance, this,
Who shall be of as little memory
When he is earthed, hath here almost persuaded                  230
(For he's a spirit of persuasion, only
Professes to persuade) the King his son's alive.
'Tis as impossible that he's undrowned
As he that sleeps here swims.

SEBASTIAN                              I have no hope
That he's undrowned.

---

216. **if heed me**: if you are to heed me.
217. **Trebles thee o'er**: makes you three times as important; **standing water**: that is, at a standstill.
218. **ebb**: decline.
219. **Hereditary sloth**: that is, idleness imposed on Sebastian by his position as younger brother.
220–21. **If . . . mock it**: if only you realized how in mocking your indolence you in fact show how you desire to embrace my plan.
221–22. **how in stripping . . . invest it**: how in attacking it you show its value.
223. **bottom**: that is, where they might miss the turning tide of fortune.
225. **setting**: fixed expression.
226. **matter**: matter of importance.
227. **throes . . . yield**: causes you pain to say it.
228. **this lord**: Gonzalo; **weak remembrance**: poor memory.
230. **earthed**: buried.
231. **spirit**: embodiment (as a councillor).

ANTONIO                     O, out of that no hope                235
  What great hope have you! No hope that way is
  Another way so high a hope that even
  Ambition cannot pierce a wink beyond,
  But doubt discovery there. Will you grant with me
  That Ferdinand is drowned?
SEBASTIAN                     He's gone.
ANTONIO                               Then tell me,            240
  Who's the next heir of Naples?
SEBASTIAN                          Claribel.
ANTONIO
  She that is Queen of Tunis; she that dwells
  Ten leagues beyond man's life; she that from Naples
  Can have no note, unless the sun were post—
  The man i' th' moon's too slow—till new-born chins      245
  Be rough and razorable; she that from whom
  We all were sea-swallowed, though some cast again,
  And, by that destiny, to perform an act
  Whereof what's past is prologue, what to come
  In yours and my discharge.
SEBASTIAN                     What stuff is this? How say you?   250
  'Tis true my brother's daughter's Queen of Tunis,
  So is she heir of Naples, 'twixt which regions
  There is some space.
ANTONIO                     A space whose ev'ry cubit
  Seems to cry out, "How shall that Claribel
  Measure us back to Naples? Keep in Tunis,              255
  And let Sebastian wake." Say this were death
  That now hath seized them: why, they were no worse
  Than now they are. There be that can rule Naples
  As well as he that sleeps; lords that can prate
  As amply and unnecessarily                            260
  As this Gonzalo; I myself could make
  A chough of as deep chat. O, that you bore
  The mind that I do! What a sleep were this
  For your advancement! Do you understand me?

---

**238. wink:** glimpse.
**243. Ten leagues . . . life:** that is, beyond the journey of a lifetime.
**244. note:** news; **post:** messenger.
**246. from:** coming from.
**247. cast:** disgorged.
**250. discharge:** responsibility.
**253. cubit:** old unit of measurement, about twenty inches.
**255. Measure:** retrace; **Keep:** stay.
**258. There be:** There are those.
**259. prate:** speak foolishly.
**261–62. make . . . chat:** teach a jackdaw to speak as profoundly.

SEBASTIAN
  Methinks I do.
ANTONIO                And how does your content                265
  Tender your own good fortune?
SEBASTIAN                          I remember
  You did supplant your brother Prospero.
ANTONIO                                      True:
  And look how well my garments sit upon me,
  Much feater than before. My brother's servants
  Were then my fellows; now they are my men.                   270
SEBASTIAN    But, for your conscience?
ANTONIO
  Ay, sir, where lies that? If 'twere a kibe,
  'Twould put me to my slipper; but I feel not
  This deity in my bosom. Twenty consciences
  That stand 'twixt me and Milan, candied be they,            275
  And melt ere they molest. Here lies your brother,
  No better than the earth he lies upon,
  If he were that which now he's like—that's dead;
  Whom I with this obedient steel (three inches of it)
  Can lay to bed forever. Whiles you doing thus,              280
  To the perpetual wink for aye might put
  This ancient morsel, this Sir Prudence, who
  Should not upbraid our course. For all the rest,
  They'll take suggestion as a cat laps milk;
  They'll tell the clock to any business that                 285
  We say befits the hour.
SEBASTIAN                    Thy case, dear friend,
  Shall be my precedent. As thou got'st Milan,
  I'll come by Naples. Draw thy sword; one stroke
  Shall free thee from the tribute which thou payest,
  And I the King shall love thee.
ANTONIO                            Draw together;          290
  And when I rear my hand, do you the like
  To fall it on Gonzalo.

265. **content:** inclination.
266. **tender:** regard.
269. **feater:** more fittingly.
272. **kibe:** chilblain.
273. **put me to:** make me wear.
274. **This deity:** that is, conscience.
275. **candied:** frozen into ice; **be they:** may they be.
276. **molest:** interfere.
281. **perpetual wink:** everlasting sleep; **for aye:** forever.
283. **Should not:** could not then; **upbraid:** criticize.
284. **suggestion:** prompting.
285. **tell the clock to:** agree with.
292. **fall it:** let it fall.

SEBASTIAN                   O, but one word. [*They talk apart.*]

*Enter* ARIEL [*invisible*] *with music and song.*

ARIEL
  My master through his art foresees the danger
  That you, his friend, are in, and sends me forth
  (For else his project dies) to keep them living.                    295

    *Sings in Gonzalo's ear.*

  While you here do snoring lie,
  Open-eyed conspiracy
    His time doth take.
  If of life you keep a care,
  Shake off slumber and beware.                                       300
    Awake, awake!
ANTONIO
  Then let us both be sudden.

    [ANTONIO *and* SEBASTIAN *draw their swords.*]

GONZALO   [*Waking*] Now, good angels preserve the King.

    [*He wakes* ALONSO.]

ALONSO
  Why, how now? Ho! Awake? Why are you drawn?
  Wherefore this ghastly looking?
GONZALO                          What's the matter?                   305
SEBASTIAN
  Whiles we stood here securing your repose,
  Even now, we heard a hollow burst of bellowing,
  Like bulls, or rather lions; did't not wake you?
  It struck mine ear most terribly.
ALONSO                          I heard nothing.
ANTONIO
  O, 'twas a din to fright a monster's ear,                           310
  To make an earthquake: sure it was the roar
  Of a whole herd of lions.
ALONSO                    Heard you this, Gonzalo?
GONZALO
  Upon mine honor, sir, I heard a humming,
  (And that a strange one too) which did awake me.
  I shaked you, sir, and cried. As mine eyes opened,                  315

**298. time:** chance.
**302. sudden:** quick.
**315. cried:** called out.

I saw their weapons drawn. There was a noise,
That's verily. 'Tis best we stand upon our guard,
Or that we quit this place. Let's draw our weapons.

ALONSO
Lead off this ground, and let's make further search
For my poor son.

GONZALO                    Heavens keep him from these beasts:          320
For he is sure i' th' island.

ALONSO                              Lead away.

ARIEL
Prospero my lord shall know what I have done.
So, King, go safely on to seek thy son.          *Exeunt.*


### Act 2, Scene 2

*Enter* CALIBAN, *with a burden of wood.*

CALIBAN
All the infections that the sun sucks up
From bogs, fens, flats, on Prosper fall, and make him
By inchmeal a disease!

*A noise of thunder heard.*

                              His spirits hear me,
And yet I needs must curse. But they'll nor pinch,
Fright me with urchin-shows, pitch me i' th' mire,          5
Nor lead me, like a fire-brand, in the dark
Out of my way, unless he bid 'em. But
For every trifle are they set upon me;
Sometimes like apes that mow and chatter at me,
And after bite me; then like hedgehogs, which          10
Lie tumbling in my barefoot way and mount
Their pricks at my footfall; sometime am I
All wound with adders, who with cloven tongues
Do hiss me into madness.

*Enter* TRINCULO.

---

317. **verily:** true.
2. **flats:** swamps.
3. **inchmeal:** inch by inch.
4. **needs must:** have to; **nor:** neither.
5. **urchin-shows:** goblin-shows.
6. **fire-brand:** burning piece of wood.
9. **mow:** grimace.
13. **wound with:** entwined by.

Lo, now lo!
Here comes a spirit of his, and to torment me                    15
For bringing wood in slowly. I'll fall flat.
Perchance he will not mind me.

[*He falls to the ground and covers himself with his cloak.*]

TRINCULO   Here's neither bush nor scrub to bear off any
weather at all, and another storm brewing: I hear it sing i' th'
wind. Yond same black cloud, yond huge one, looks like a      20
foul bombard that would shed his liquor. If it should thunder
as it did before, I know not where to hide my head. Yond
same cloud cannot choose but fall by pailfuls. [*He sees* CAL-
IBAN.] What have we here? A man or a fish? Dead or alive? A
fish: he smells like a fish; a very ancient and fishlike smell; a     25
kind of not-of-the-newest poor-John. A strange fish. Were
I in England now (as once I was) and had but this fish
painted, not a holiday fool there but would give a piece of
silver. There would this monster make a man; any strange
beast there makes a man. When they will not give a doit       30
to relieve a lame beggar, they will lay out ten to see a dead
Indian. Legged like a man, and his fins like arms. Warm, o'
my troth! I do now let loose my opinion, hold it no longer:
this is no fish, but an islander, that hath lately suffered by
a thunderbolt. [*Thunder.*] Alas, the storm is come again.    35
My best way is to creep under his gaberdine; there is no
other shelter hereabout. Misery acquaints a man with
strange bedfellows. I will here shroud till the dregs of the
storm be past. [*He crawls under* CALIBAN'S *cloak.*]

*Enter* STEPHANO [*with a bottle*], *singing.*

STEPHANO
I shall no more to sea, to sea,                                  40
Here shall I die ashore.
This is a very scurvy tune to sing at a man's funeral. Well,
here's my comfort. (*Drinks.*)

(*Sings.*)

17. **mind:** notice.
18. **bear off:** keep off.
21. **bombard:** leather jug.
26. **poor-John:** salted fish.
28. **painted:** that is, on a sign outside a booth.
29. **make a man:** make a man rich.
30. **doit:** small coin.
32–33. **o' my troth:** upon my faith.
36. **gaberdine:** cloak.
38. **shroud:** take shelter.
42. **scurvy:** worthless.

The master, the swabber, the boatswain and I,
　　The gunner and his mate,　　　　　　　　　45
Loved Moll, Meg, and Marian, and Margery,
　　But none of us cared for Kate.
　　For she had a tongue with a tang,
　　Would cry to a sailor, "Go hang!"
She loved not the savor of tar nor of pitch,　　50
Yet a tailor might scratch her where'er she did itch.
　　Then to sea, boys, and let her go hang!
This is a scurvy tune too; but here's my comfort. (*Drinks.*)

CALIBAN　Do not torment me! O!

STEPHANO　What's the matter? Have we devils here? Do you　55
put tricks upon's with savages and men of Ind? Ha? I have
not scaped drowning to be afeared now of your four legs; for
it hath been said, "As proper a man as ever went on four
legs, cannot make him give ground"; and it shall be said so
again, while Stephano breathes at' nostrils.　　60

CALIBAN　The spirit torments me! O!

STEPHANO　This is some monster of the isle with four legs,
who hath got, as I take it, an ague. Where the devil should
he learn our language? I will give him some relief if it be but
for that. If I can recover him, and keep him tame, and get to　65
Naples with him, he's a present for any emperor that ever
trod on neat's leather.

CALIBAN　Do not torments me, prithee! I'll bring my wood
home faster.

STEPHANO　He's in his fit now, and does not talk after the　70
wisest. He shall taste of my bottle. If he have never drunk
wine afore, it will go near to remove his fit. If I can recover him, and keep him tame, I will not take too much
for him; he shall pay for him that hath him, and that
soundly.　　75

CALIBAN　Thou dost me yet but little hurt; thou wilt anon, I
know it by thy trembling. Now Prosper works upon thee.

STEPHANO　Come on your ways. Open your mouth: here is

---

44. **swabber:** seaman who washes down the decks.
48. **tang:** sting.
50. **savor:** smell.
56. **Ind:** the Indies.
63. **ague:** fever.
63–64. **should he learn:** could he have learned.
65. **for that:** that is, for speaking our language.
67. **neat's leather:** cowhide.
70–71. **after the wisest:** in the wisest manner.
72. **afore:** before.
74. **hath:** that is, buys.
76. **anon:** soon.
78. **on your ways:** that is, come here.

that which will give language to you, cat. Open your mouth:
this will shake your shaking, I can tell you, and that soundly.    80
[*Caliban drinks.*] You cannot tell who's your friend. Open
your chaps again. [CALIBAN *drinks again.*]

TRINCULO    I should know that voice. It should be—but he is
drowned, and these are devils. O, defend me!

STEPHANO    Four legs and two voices: a most delicate monster!    85
His forward voice now is to speak well of his friend; his
backward voice is to utter foul speeches, and to detract. If all
the wine in my bottle will recover him, I will help his ague.
Come. [CALIBAN *drinks.*] Amen. I will pour some in thy other
mouth.                                                              90

TRINCULO    Stephano!

STEPHANO    Doth thy other mouth call me? Mercy, mercy! This
is a devil, and no monster. I will leave him; I have no long
spoon.

TRINCULO    Stephano! If thou beest Stephano, touch me, and      95
speak to me; for I am Trinculo—be not afeard—thy good
friend Trinculo.

STEPHANO    If thou beest Trinculo, come forth: I'll pull thee
by the lesser legs. If any be Trinculo's legs, these are they.
[*Pulls him out.*] Thou art very Trinculo indeed! How cam'st    100
thou to be the siege of this moon-calf? Can he vent Trincu-
los?

TRINCULO    I took him to be killed with a thunder-stroke. But
art thou not drowned, Stephano? I hope now thou art not
drowned. Is the storm over-blown? I hid me under the dead    105
moon-calf's gaberdine, for fear of the storm. And art thou
living, Stephano? [*Dancing with him*] O Stephano, two
Neapolitans scaped!

STEPHANO    Prithee, do not turn me about, my stomach is not
constant.                                                          110

CALIBAN    [*Aside*] These be fine things, an if they be not
sprites. That's a brave god, and bears celestial liquor. I will
kneel to him.

STEPHANO    How didst thou scape? How cam'st thou hither?
Swear by this bottle how thou cam'st hither. I escaped upon    115

82. chaps: jaws.
87. detract: make scornful remarks.
88. help: cure.
93–94. long spoon: playing on the proverb "He must have a long spoon that will eat with
the devil."
100. very: the real.
101. siege: excrement; moon-calf: misshapen creature; vent: expel, that is, defecate.
109–10. not constant: unsettled.
111. an if: if.
112. brave: fine; bears: he carries.

a butt of sack which the sailors heaved o'erboard, by this
bottle, which I made of the bark of a tree, with mine own
hands, since I was cast ashore.

CALIBAN     I'll swear upon that bottle to be thy true subject, for
the liquor is not earthly.                                                    120

STEPHANO     Here. Swear then how thou escapedst.

TRINCULO     Swum ashore, man, like a duck. I can swim like a
duck, I'll be sworn.

STEPHANO     [*Giving him the bottle*] Here, kiss the Book.
Though thou canst swim like a duck, thou art made like a      125
goose.

TRINCULO     O Stephano, hast any more of this?

STEPHANO     The whole butt, man. My cellar is in a rock by the
seaside, where my wine is hid. [*To* CALIBAN] How now, moon-
calf, how does thine ague?                                                   130

CALIBAN     Hast thou not dropped from heaven?

STEPHANO     Out o' th' moon I do assure thee. I was the man i'
th' moon, when time was.

CALIBAN     I have seen thee in her, and I do adore thee. My mistress showed me thee, and thy dog, and thy bush.                 135

STEPHANO     [*Giving the bottle to* CALIBAN] Come, swear to that:
kiss the Book. I will furnish it anon with new contents.
Swear.

TRINCULO     By this good light, this is a very shallow monster. I
afeared of him? A very weak monster. The man i' th' moon? A      140
most poor credulous monster. Well drawn, monster, in good
sooth.

CALIBAN     I'll show thee every fertile inch o' th' island, and I
will kiss thy foot. I prithee, be my god.

TRINCULO     By this light, a most perfidious and drunken mon-      145
ster! When god's asleep he'll rob his bottle.

CALIBAN     I'll kiss thy foot. I'll swear myself thy subject.

STEPHANO     Come on then: down and swear.

TRINCULO     I shall laugh myself to death at this puppy-headed
monster. A most scurvy monster. I could find in my heart to      150
beat him—

STEPHANO     [*To* CALIBAN] Come, kiss.

TRINCULO     —but that the poor monster's in drink. An abom-
inable monster.

116. **butt:** cask; **sack:** Canary wine.
118. **since:** after.
133. **when time was:** once upon a time.
135. **thy dog, and thy bush:** The Man in the Moon has with him a dog and a thornbush.
141. **drawn:** pulled (on the bottle).
141–42. **in good sooth:** indeed.
153. **in drink:** drunk.

CALIBAN

   I'll show thee the best springs; I'll pluck thee berries;     155
   I'll fish for thee, and get thee wood enough.
   A plague upon the tyrant that I serve!
   I'll bear him no more sticks, but follow thee,
   Thou wondrous man.

TRINCULO   A most ridiculous monster, to make a wonder of a   160
poor drunkard.

CALIBAN

   I prithee let me bring thee where crabs grow;
   And I with my long nails will dig thee pig-nuts,
   Show thee a jay's nest, and instruct thee how
   To snare the nimble marmoset. I'll bring thee     165
   To clust'ring filberts, and sometimes I'll get thee
   Young scamels from the rock. Wilt thou go with me?

STEPHANO   I prithee now, lead the way without any more
talking. Trinculo, the king and all our company else
being drowned, we will inherit here. [*To Caliban*] Here,   170
bear my bottle. Fellow Trinculo, we'll fill him by and by
again.

CALIBAN   (*Sings drunkenly*) Farewell, master, farewell, farewell.

TRINCULO   A howling monster; a drunken monster.   175

CALIBAN   [*Singing*]

      No more dams I'll make for fish,
      Nor fetch in firing
      At requiring,
      Nor scrape trencher, nor wash dish,
         Ban, ban, Ca-caliban   180
      Has a new master: get a new man.
  Freedom, high-day, high-day freedom, freedom high-day,
    freedom.

STEPHANO   O brave monster, lead the way!     *Exeunt.*

---

163. **pig-nuts:** edible wild tubers.
165. **marmoset:** small monkey.
166. **filberts:** hazelnuts.
167. **scamels:** possibly sea mews, a seabird; possibly a lost dialect word for a kind of mollusk.
169. **else:** apart from us.
177. **firing:** firewood.
178. **At requiring:** On demand.
179. **trencher:** wooden plate.
182. **high-day:** holiday.

## Act 3, Scene 1

[*Near* PROSPERO'S *cell.*]

*Enter* FERDINAND, *bearing a log.*

FERDINAND
There be some sports are painful, and their labor
Delight in them sets off. Some kinds of baseness
Are nobly undergone, and most poor matters
Point to rich ends. This my mean task
Would be as heavy to me as odious, but                         5
The mistress which I serve quickens what's dead
And makes my labors pleasures. O, she is
Ten times more gentle than her father's crabbed,
And he's composed of harshness. I must remove
Some thousands of these logs and pile them up,                10
Upon a sore injunction. My sweet mistress
Weeps when she sees me work and says such baseness
Had never like executor. I forget;
But these sweet thoughts do even refresh my labors,
Most busilest when I do it.

      *Enter* MIRANDA, *and* PROSPERO [*unseen*].

MIRANDA               Alas, now pray you,              15
Work not so hard. I would the lightning had
Burnt up those logs that you are enjoined to pile.
Pray set it down and rest you. When this burns
'Twill weep for having wearied you. My father
Is hard at study: pray now rest yourself.                     20
He's safe for these three hours.

FERDINAND               O most dear mistress,
The sun will set before I shall discharge
What I must strive to do.

MIRANDA            If you'll sit down
I'll bear your logs the while. Pray give me that:

---

1. **sports:** activities, physical exertions.
2. **sets off:** compensates; **baseness:** degradation.
3. **undergone:** undertaken.
5. **but:** except that.
6. **quickens:** gives life to.
8. **crabbed:** sour.
11. **sore injunction:** harsh order.
13. **Had . . . executor:** Was never undertaken by such a person; **I forget:** that is, to work.
15. **Most . . . it:** when I am busiest at my work.
18. **this:** that is, the log.
19. **weep:** exude resin as tears.
21. **safe:** withdrawn.
22. **discharge:** complete.

I'll carry it to the pile.
FERDINAND                         No, precious creature,                    25
    I had rather crack my sinews, break my back,
    Than you should such dishonor undergo
    While I sit lazy by.
MIRANDA                    It would become me
    As well as it does you; and I should do it
    With much more ease, for my good will is to it,                        30
    And yours it is against.
PROSPERO    [*Aside*]         Poor worm, thou art infected:
    This visitation shows it.
MIRANDA                         You look wearily.
FERDINAND
    No, noble mistress, 'tis fresh morning with me
    When you are by at night. I do beseech you
    Chiefly, that I may set it in my prayers,                              35
    What is your name?
MIRANDA                    Miranda.—O, my father,
    I have broke your hest to say so!
FERDINAND                              Admired Miranda!
    Indeed the top of admiration, worth
    What's dearest to the world! Full many a lady
    I have eyed with best regard, and many a time                         40
    Th' harmony of their tongues hath into bondage
    Brought my too diligent ear. For several virtues
    Have I liked several women, never any
    With so full soul but some defect in her
    Did quarrel with the noblest grace she owed                           45
    And put it to the foil. But you, O you,
    So perfect and so peerless, are created
    Of every creature's best!
MIRANDA                     I do not know
    One of my sex; no woman's face remember,
    Save, from my glass, mine own. Nor have I seen                        50
    More that I may call men than you, good friend,
    And my dear father. How features are abroad

34. **by**: nearby.
35. **Chiefly**: principally.
37. **hest**: command.
39. **dearest**: most valuable.
40. **eyed . . . regard**: held in highest esteem.
42. **diligent**: attentive.
45. **owed**: owned.
46. **put  . . . foil**: foiled it.
48. **Of**: out of.
50. **glass**: mirror.
52. **How . . . abroad**: what people elsewhere look like.

I am skilless of; but by my modesty
(The jewel in my dower) I would not wish
Any companion in the world but you,                          55
Nor can imagination form a shape,
Besides yourself, to like of. But I prattle
Something too wildly, and my father's precepts
I therein do forget.
FERDINAND                    I am in my condition
A prince, Miranda—I do think a king—                         60
I would not so!—and would no more endure
This wooden slavery than to suffer
The flesh-fly blow my mouth. Hear my soul speak:
The very instant that I saw you did
My heart fly to your service, and there reside              65
To make me slave to it, and for your sake
Am I this patient log-man.
MIRANDA                         Do you love me?
FERDINAND
O heaven, O earth, bear witness to this sound
And crown what I profess with kind event
If I speak true! If hollowly, invert                        70
What best is boded me to mischief! I,
Beyond all limit of what else i' th' world,
Do love, prize, honor you.
MIRANDA    [Weeping]          I am a fool
To weep at what I am glad of.
PROSPERO    [Aside]           Fair encounter
Of two most rare affections. Heavens rain grace            75
On that which breeds between 'em!
FERDINAND                        Wherefore weep you?
MIRANDA
At mine unworthiness, that dare not offer
What I desire to give, and much less take
What I shall die to want. But this is trifling,
And all the more it seeks to hide itself                    80
The bigger bulk it shows. Hence, bashful cunning,

---

53. **skilless:** ignorant; **modesty:** chastity.
54. **dower:** dowry.
57. **like of:** be fond of.
58. **Something:** somewhat.
59. **condition:** rank.
63. **flesh-fly:** insect that lays eggs in dead flesh; **blow my mouth:** lay its eggs in my mouth.
69. **kind event:** happy outcome.
70. **hollowly:** insincerely; **invert:** turn.
71. **boded:** in store for; **mischief:** harm.
72. **what:** whatever.
79. **to want:** if I lack it.

And prompt me, plain and holy innocence!
I am your wife if you'll marry me;
If not, I'll die your maid. To be your fellow
You may deny me, but I'll be your servant                       85
Whether you will or no.
FERDINAND                    My mistress, dearest,
  And I thus humble ever.
MIRANDA    My husband, then?
FERDINAND                       Ay, with a heart as willing
  As bondage e'er of freedom. Here's my hand.
MIRANDA    [*Taking his hand*]
  And mine, with my heart in't. And now farewell               90
  Till half an hour hence.
FERDINAND                    A thousand thousand!

            *Exeunt* [FERDINAND *and* MIRANDA, *separately*].

PROSPERO
  So glad of this as they I cannot be,
  Who are surprised with all; but my rejoicing
  At nothing can be more. I'll to my book,
  For yet ere suppertime must I perform                        95
  Much business appertaining.                      *Exit.*

                    Act 3, Scene 2

            [*Another part of the island.*]

        *Enter* CALIBAN, STEPHANO, *and* TRINCULO.

STEPHANO    [*To* TRINCULO] Tell not me. When the butt is out
  we will drink water, not a drop before. Therefore bear up and
  board 'em. [*To* CALIBAN] Servant monster, drink to me!
TRINCULO    "Servant monster"? The folly of this island! They
  say there's but five upon this isle. We are three of them; if th'   5
  other two be brained like us, the state totters.
STEPHANO    Drink, servant monster, when I bid thee. Thy eyes
  are almost set in thy head.

---

84. **maid**: servant and unmarried; **fellow**: bedfellow.
86. **will or no**: want it or not; **My mistress**: that is, the woman I serve.
88–89. **willing . . . freedom**: desirous as slaves always are to be free.
91. **thousand thousand**: that is, farewells.
93. **with all**: by everything that happens.
96. **appertaining**: related to this.
1. **out**: empty.
2–3. **bear . . . 'em**: approach and attack (the language of naval battles is used to refer to
their assault on the alcohol).
6. **be brained like us**: have brains in a condition like ours.
8. **set**: sunk.

TRINCULO   Where should they be set else? He were a brave
monster indeed if they were set in his tail.                              10

STEPHANO   My man-monster hath drowned his tongue in
sack. For my part, the sea cannot drown me. I swam ere I
could recover the shore, five and thirty leagues off and on.
By this light, thou shalt be my lieutenant, monster, or my
standard.                                                                 15

TRINCULO   Your lieutenant, if you list; he's no standard.

STEPHANO   We'll not run, Monsieur Monster.

TRINCULO   Nor go neither, but you'll lie like dogs and yet say
nothing neither.

STEPHANO   Moon-calf, speak once in thy life, if thou beest a     20
good moon-calf.

CALIBAN
How does thy honor? Let me lick thy shoe.
I'll not serve him; he is not valiant.

TRINCULO   Thou liest, most ignorant monster; I am in case to
jostle a constable. Why, thou debauched fish thou, was there      25
ever man a coward that hath drunk so much sack as I do today? Wilt thou tell a monstrous lie, being but half a fish and
half a monster?

CALIBAN
Lo, how he mocks me. Wilt thou let him, my lord?

TRINCULO   "Lord," quoth he? That a monster should be such a      30
natural!

CALIBAN
Lo, lo again! Bite him to death, I prithee.

STEPHANO   Trinculo, keep a good tongue in your head. If you
prove a mutineer—the next tree! The poor monster's my subject and he shall not suffer indignity.                           35

CALIBAN
I thank my noble lord. Wilt thou be pleased
To hearken once again to the suit I made to thee?

STEPHANO   Marry, will I. Kneel and repeat it. I will stand, and
so shall Trinculo.                                 [*Caliban kneels.*]

9. **set:** placed; **brave:** fine.
13. **recover:** reach; **leagues:** that is, about a hundred miles; **off and on:** in fits and
starts.
14. **By this light:** an oath.
15. **standard:** standard-bearer.
16. **list:** like; **no standard:** that is, not standing up.
18. **go:** walk; **lie:** lie down; tell lies.
24. **in case:** in a condition to.
25. **constable:** officer of the law; **debauched:** seduced away from proper allegiance.
27. **monstrous:** enormous; told by a monster.
31. **natural:** idiot.
34. **the next tree:** that is, you will hang from . . .
38. **Marry:** indeed; originally "by the Virgin Mary."

*Enter* ARIEL, *invisible.*

CALIBAN

As I told thee before, I am subject to a tyrant,                    40
A sorcerer, that by his cunning hath
Cheated me of the island.

ARIEL                                    Thou liest.

CALIBAN        [*To Trinculo*]

Thou liest, thou jesting monkey, thou!
I would my valiant master would destroy thee.
I do not lie.                    45

STEPHANO    Trinculo, if you trouble him any more in's tale, by
this hand, I will supplant some of your teeth.

TRINCULO    Why, I said nothing.

STEPHANO    Mum then, and no more.—Proceed.

CALIBAN

I say by sorcery he got this isle;                    50
From me he got it. If thy greatness will
Revenge it on him—for I know thou dar'st,
But this thing dare not—

STEPHANO    That's most certain.

CALIBAN

Thou shalt be lord of it, and I'll serve thee.                    55

STEPHANO    How now shall this be compassed? Canst thou
bring me to the party?

CALIBAN

Yea, yea, my lord. I'll yield him thee asleep,
Where thou mayst knock a nail into his head.

ARIEL    Thou liest; thou canst not.                    60

CALIBAN

What a pied ninny's this! Thou scurvy patch!
I do beseech thy greatness give him blows
And take his bottle from him. When that's gone,
He shall drink naught but brine, for I'll not show him
Where the quick freshes are.                    65

STEPHANO    Trinculo, run into no further danger. Interrupt the
monster one word further and, by this hand, I'll turn my
mercy out o' doors, and make a stockfish of thee.

44. **valiant master:** that is, Stephano.
47. **supplant:** displace.
49. **Mum:** keep quiet.
51. **thy greatness:** that is, Stephano.
53. **this thing:** that is, Trinculo.
56. **compassed:** accomplished.
57. **party:** person you're talking about, that is, Prospero.
61. **pied ninny:** jester in a motley costume; **patch:** fool.
65. **quick freshes:** running springs.
68. **stockfish:** saltfish, beaten before cooking.

TRINCULO   Why, what did I? I did nothing. I'll go farther off.

STEPHANO   Didst thou not say he lied?                                    70

ARIEL   Thou liest.

STEPHANO   Do I so?

> [*Beats* TRINCULO.]

Take thou that! As you like this, give me
the lie another time.

TRINCULO   I did not give the lie! Out o' your wits, and hearing too? A pox o' your bottle. This can sack and drinking          75
do. A murrain on your monster, and the devil take your fingers!

CALIBAN   Ha, ha, ha!

STEPHANO   Now forward with your tale. [*To* TRINCULO] Prithee
stand further off.                                                       80

CALIBAN   Beat him enough. After a little time I'll beat him too.

STEPHANO   Stand farther. [*To* CALIBAN] Come, proceed.

CALIBAN

Why, as I told thee, 'tis a custom with him
I' th' afternoon to sleep. There thou mayst brain him,
Having first seized his books; or with a log                            85
Batter his skull, or paunch him with a stake,
Or cut his weasand with thy knife. Remember
First to possess his books; for without them
He's but a sot, as I am, nor hath not
One spirit to command—they all do hate him                            90
As rootedly as I. Burn but his books.
He has brave utensils (for so he calls them)
Which, when he has a house, he'll deck withal.
And that most deeply to consider is
The beauty of his daughter. He himself                                95
Calls her a nonpareil. I never saw a woman
But only Sycorax my dam and she;
But she as far surpasseth Sycorax
As great'st does least.

STEPHANO   Is it so brave a lass?                                       100

---

69. **off:** away.
72–73. **give me the lie:** call me a liar.
76. **murrain:** plague.
86. **paunch:** stab in the belly.
87. **weasand:** windpipe.
89. **sot:** fool.
91. **but:** only.
92. **brave:** splendid.
93. **deck withal:** furnish it with.
96. **nonpareil:** that is, without equal.
100. **brave:** fine.

CALIBAN
    Ay, lord. She will become thy bed, I warrant,
    And bring thee forth brave brood.
STEPHANO   Monster, I will kill this man. His daughter and
    I will be king and queen, save our graces; and Trinculo
    and thyself shall be viceroys. Dost thou like the plot, Trin-   105
    culo?
TRINCULO   Excellent.
STEPHANO   Give me thy hand. I am sorry I beat thee. But
    while thou liv'st, keep a good tongue in thy head.
CALIBAN
    Within this half hour will he be asleep.                        110
    Wilt thou destroy him then?
STEPHANO   Ay, on mine honor.
ARIEL   [Aside] This will I tell my master.
CALIBAN
    Thou mak'st me merry. I am full of pleasure,
    Let us be jocund. Will you troll the catch                      115
    You taught me but whilere?
STEPHANO   At thy request, monster, I will do reason, any rea-
    son. Come on, Trinculo, let us sing.

        [They sing.]

        Flout 'em, and scout 'em
        And scout 'em, and flout 'em.                               120
            Thought is free.
CALIBAN    That's not the tune.

        ARIEL plays the tune on a tabor and pipe.

STEPHANO   What is this same?
TRINCULO   This is the tune of our catch, played by the picture
    of Nobody.                                                      125
STEPHANO   If thou beest a man, show thyself in thy likeness.
    If thou beest a devil, take't as thou list.
TRINCULO   O, forgive me my sins!
STEPHANO   He that dies pays all debts. I defy thee! Mercy
    upon us!                                                        130
CALIBAN    Art thou afeard?

101. become: suit
104. save: God save.
115. jocund: jolly; troll the catch: sing the round.
116. but whilere: just a short time ago.
117–18. reason, any reason: anything reasonable.
119. flout: mock; scout: deride.
122 SD. tabor: small drum.
124–25. picture of Nobody: allusion to a figure with limbs but no body.
127. as thou list: however you want to.

STEPHANO    No, monster, not I.

CALIBAN
  Be not afeard: the isle is full of noises,
  Sounds, and sweet airs that give delight and hurt not.
  Sometimes a thousand twangling instruments                    135
  Will hum about mine ears; and sometimes voices,
  That, if I then had waked after long sleep,
  Will make me sleep again; and then, in dreaming,
  The clouds methought would open and show riches
  Ready to drop upon me, that, when I waked,                    140
  I cried to dream again.

STEPHANO    This will prove a brave kingdom to me, where I
  shall have my music for nothing.

CALIBAN    When Prospero is destroyed.

STEPHANO    That shall be by and by: I remember the story.     145

                [Exit ARIEL, playing music.]

TRINCULO    The sound is going away; let's follow it, and after
  do our work.

STEPHANO    Lead, monster, we'll follow. I would I could see
  this taborer: he lays it on.

TRINCULO    [To CALIBAN] Wilt come? I'll follow Stephano.      150

                                            Exeunt.


### Act 3, Scene 3

*Enter* ALONSO, SEBASTIAN, ANTONIO, GONZALO, ADRIAN,
FRANCISCO, *etc.*

GONZALO
  By'r lakin, I can go no further, sir:
  My old bones ache. Here's a maze trod indeed
  Through forthrights and meanders. By your patience,
  I needs must rest me.

ALONSO                    Old lord, I cannot blame thee,
  Who am myself attached with weariness                          5
  To th' dulling of my spirits. Sit down and rest.
  Even here I will put off my hope, and keep it
  No longer for my flatterer: he is drowned

---

**145. by and by:** in good time.
**149. lays it on:** bangs it vigorously.
**1. By 'r lakin:** By our ladykin (Our Lady).
**3. forthrights and meanders:** straight and crooked paths; **By your patience:** With your
permission.
**4. needs must:** need to.
**5. attached:** seized.
**6. To . . . spirits:** To the point of being dispirited.
**8. for:** as.

Whom thus we stray to find, and the sea mocks
Our frustrate search on land. Well, let him go.          10
ANTONIO     [*Aside to Sebastian*]
I am right glad that he's so out of hope.
Do not, for one repulse, forgo the purpose
That you resolved t' effect.
SEBASTIAN     [*Aside to* ANTONIO] The next advantage
Will we take throughly.
ANTONIO     [*Aside to* SEBASTIAN] Let it be tonight;
For now they are oppressed with travel, they          15
Will not nor cannot use such vigilance
As when they are fresh.
SEBASTIAN     [*Aside to* ANTONIO] I say tonight: no more.

> *Solemn and strange music, and* [*enter*] PROSPERO *on the*
> *top (invisible).*

ALONSO
What harmony is this? My good friends, hark!
GONZALO
Marvellous sweet music.

> *Enter several strange shapes, bringing a banquet; and*
> *dance about it with gentle actions of salutations, and*
> *inviting the King etc. to eat, they depart.*

ALONSO
Give us kind keepers, heavens! What are these?          20
SEBASTIAN
A living drollery. Now I will believe
That there are unicorns; that in Arabia
There is one tree, the phoenix' throne, one phoenix
At this hour reigning there.
ANTONIO                                    I'll believe both;
And what does else want credit, come to me,          25
And I'll be sworn 'tis true. Travelers ne'er did lie,
Though fools at home condemn 'em.

---

10. **frustrate:** frustrated.
11. **right:** very.
12. **for:** on account of; **repulse:** setback.
13. **advantage:** opportunity.
14. **throughly:** thoroughly.
15. **now:** now that.
17 SD. **on the top:** on a third level above the gallery.
20. **kind keepers:** guardian angels.
21. **living drollery:** comic picture come to life.
23. **phoenix:** mythical Arabian bird, of which only one is alive at any time, said to reproduce itself every five hundred years by dying in flames and being reborn.
25. **want credit:** lacks credibility.

GONZALO                                    If in Naples
I should report this now, would they believe me?
If I should say I saw such islanders
(For certes these are people of the island)                              30
Who, though they are of monstrous shape, yet note,
Their manners are more gentle, kind, than of
Our human generation you shall find
Many—nay, almost any.
PROSPERO    [*Aside*]          Honest lord,
Thou hast said well; for some of you there present           35
Are worse than devils.
ALONSO                      I cannot too much muse
Such shapes, such gesture, and such sound, expressing
(Although they want the use of tongue) a kind
Of excellent dumb discourse.
PROSPERO    [*Aside*]          Praise in departing.
FRANCISCO
They vanished strangely.
SEBASTIAN                   No matter, since                    40
They have left their viands behind; for we have stomachs.
Wilt please you taste of what is here?
ALONSO                              Not I.
GONZALO
Faith, sir, you need not fear. When we were boys,
Who would believe that there were mountaineers,
Dewlapped like bulls, whose throats had hanging at 'em       45
Wallets of flesh? Or that there were such men
Whose heads stood in their breasts? Which now we find
Each putter-out of five for one will bring us
Good warrant of.
ALONSO                   I will stand to and feed;
Although my last, no matter, since I feel                     50
The best is past. Brother, my lord the duke,
Stand to and do as we.

---

30. **certes:** certainly.
36. **muse:** wonder at.
39. **Praise in departing:** Keep your praise till it finishes.
41. **viands:** food; **stomachs:** appetites.
44. **mountaineers:** mountain dwellers.
45. **Dewlapped:** with a fold of skin hanging from the neck, like cattle.
47. **heads . . . breasts:** one of the classical and medieval monstrous races, also referred to in *Othello*: "men whose heads / Do grow beneath their shoulders" (1.3.144–45).
48. **putter-out of five for one:** traveler who deposited a sum of money with an underwriter before a journey that, if successfully completed, would net him five times the deposit.
49. **warrant:** proof; **stand to:** set to work.
50. **Although my last:** even if it turns out to be my last meal.

*Thunder and lightning. Enter* ARIEL, *like a harpy; claps his wings upon the table, and with a quaint device the banquet vanishes.*

ARIEL
You are three men of sin, whom destiny—
That hath to instrument this lower world
And what is in't—the never-surfeited sea                            55
Hath caused to belch up you, and on this island,
Where man doth not inhabit, you 'mongst men
Being most unfit to live. I have made you mad;
And even with suchlike valor men hang and drown
Their proper selves.

[*The courtiers draw their swords.*]

                        You fools, I and my fellows                  60
Are ministers of Fate. The elements
Of whom your swords are tempered may as well
Wound the loud winds, or with bemocked-at stabs
Kill the still-closing waters, as diminish
One dowl that's in my plume. My fellow ministers       65
Are like invulnerable. If you could hurt,
Your swords are now too massy for your strengths
And will not be uplifted. But remember—
For that's my business to you—that you three
From Milan did supplant good Prospero;                         70
Exposed unto the sea, which hath requit it,
Him and his innocent child; for which foul deed
The powers, delaying, not forgetting, have
Incensed the seas and shores, yea, all the creatures
Against your peace. Thee of thy son, Alonso,            75
They have bereft; and do pronounce by me
Ling'ring perdition (worse than any death
Can be at once) shall step by step attend

**52 SD. harpy:** mythical creature with the face and breasts of a woman and the body
of a vulture, an instrument of divine vengeance; **quaint:** ingenious.
**54. instrument:** control.
**59. suchlike valor:** the bravado of the mad.
**60. proper:** own.
**61. ministers:** agents.
**62. whom:** which.
**63. bemocked-at:** scorned.
**64. still-closing:** always closing again when parted.
**65. dowl:** feather.
**66. like:** similarly; **If:** Even if.
**67. massy:** heavy.
**69. business:** message.
**71. requit it:** repaid the deed.
**76. bereft:** deprived.
**77. perdition:** ruin.

You and your ways; whose wraths to guard you from,
Which here, in this most desolate isle, else falls          80
Upon your heads, is nothing but heart's sorrow
And a clear life ensuing.

> *He vanishes in thunder; then, to soft music, enter the*
> *shapes again, and dance with mocks and mows, and [then*
> *depart], carrying out the table.*

PROSPERO [*Aside*]
Bravely the figure of this harpy hast thou
Performed, my Ariel; a grace it had, devouring.
Of my instruction hast thou nothing bated                   85
In what thou hadst to say. So, with good life
And observation strange, my meaner ministers
Their several kinds have done. My high charms work,
And these, mine enemies, are all knit up
In their distractions. They now are in my power;            90
And in these fits I leave them, while I visit
Young Ferdinand, whom they suppose is drowned,
And his and mine loved darling.              [*Exit.*]
GONZALO
I' th' name of something holy, sir, why stand you
In this strange stare?
ALONSO                    O, it is monstrous, monstrous!       95
Methought the billows spoke and told me of it,
The winds did sing it to me, and the thunder,
That deep and dreadful organ-pipe, pronounced
The name of Prosper. It did bass my trespass.
Therefore my son i' th' ooze is bedded; and                 100
I'll seek him deeper than e'er plummet sounded,
And with him there lie mudded.              [*Exit.*]
SEBASTIAN                           But one fiend at a time,
I'll fight their legions o'er!

---

79. **whose:** that is, the heavenly powers'.
80. **else:** otherwise.
81. **is nothing:** there is no option.
82. **clear:** unblemished.
82 SD. **mocks and maws:** mocking gestures and grimaces.
84. **a grace . . . devouring:** you gracefully made the food disappear.
85. **bated:** omitted.
86. **So:** similarly; **good life:** lifelike actions.
87. **observation strange:** exceptional care; **meaner:** lesser.
88. **several . . . done:** various parts have played.
90. **distractions:** confusions.
96. **billows:** waves; **it:** that is, my sin.
99. **bass my trespass:** proclaim my guilt in a bass voice.
100. **Therefore:** for that reason.
101. **plummet:** lead weight (to measure depth of water); **sounded:** tested.
102–3. **But . . . o'er:** If the fiends come one at a time, I'll fight all of them.

ANTONIO                    I'll be thy second.
                           *Exeunt* [SEBASTIAN *and* ANTONIO].

GONZALO

All three of them are desperate: their great guilt,
Like poison given to work a great time after,                    105
Now 'gins to bite the spirits. I do beseech you,
That are of suppler joints, follow them swiftly,
And hinder them from what this ecstasy
May now provoke them to.

ADRIAN                     Follow, I pray you. *Exeunt omnes.*

## Act 4, Scene 1

*Enter* PROSPERO, FERDINAND, *and* MIRANDA.

PROSPERO    [*To* FERDINAND]

If I have too austerely punished you,
Your compensation makes amends, for I
Have given you here a third of mine own life,
Or that for which I live; who once again
I tender to thy hand. All thy vexations                          5
Were but my trials of thy love, and thou
Hast strangely stood the test. Here, afore heaven,
I ratify this my rich gift. O Ferdinand,
Do not smile at me that I boast her of,
For thou shalt find she will outstrip all praise                10
And make it halt behind her.

FERDINAND

I do believe it against an oracle.

PROSPERO

Then, as my gift, and thine own acquisition
Worthily purchased, take my daughter. But
If thou dost break her virgin-knot before                       15
All sanctimonious ceremonies may

103. **second:** assistant.
104. **desperate:** in despair; reckless.
106. **'gins:** begins; **bite:** sap.
108. **ecstasy:** frenzy.
1. **austerely:** severely.
3. **a third . . . life:** that is, Miranda. It is not clear whether Prospero means she represents a large part of what he cares about, or whether he has devoted a third of his life to her upbringing.
5. **tender:** offer.
7. **strangely:** wonderfully.
8. **ratify:** confirm.
9. **boast her of:** that is, boast of her.
11. **halt:** limp.
12. **against an oracle:** even if an oracle should pronounce otherwise.
14. **purchased:** earned.
16. **sanctimonious:** sacred.

With full and holy rite be ministered,
No sweet aspersion shall the heavens let fall
To make this contract grow; but barren hate,
Sour-eyed disdain, and discord shall bestrew                    20
The union of your bed, with weeds so loathly
That you shall hate it both. Therefore take heed,
As Hymen's lamps shall light you.

FERDINAND                              As I hope
For quiet days, fair issue, and long life,
With such love as 'tis now, the murkiest den,                    25
The most oppòrtune place, the strong'st suggestion
Our worser genius can, shall never melt
Mine honor into lust, to take away
The edge of that day's celebration
When I shall think or Phoebus' steeds are foundered,              30
Or night kept chained below.

PROSPERO                              Fairly spoke.
Sit then and talk with her: she is thine own.
What, Ariel! My industrious servant, Ariel!

       *Enter* ARIEL.

ARIEL
What would my potent master? Here I am.

PROSPERO
Thou and thy meaner fellows your last service                    35
Did worthily perform; and I must use you
In such another trick. Go bring the rabble,
O'er whom I give thee pow'r, here to this place.
Incite them to quick motion, for I must
Bestow upon the eyes of this young couple                        40
Some vanity of mine art. It is my promise,
And they expect it from me.

ARIEL                              Presently?

---

**18. aspersion:** sprinkling of water.
**23. Hymen's lamps:** wedding torches (Hymen was the Roman god of marriage); **shall light you:** If the torches burned brightly, it was a good omen for a happy marriage: Prospero warns them not to behave in a way that will jeopardize their good fortune.
**24. fair issue:** beautiful children.
**26. suggestion:** temptation.
**27. worser genius:** evil attendant spirit; **can:** that is, can make.
**29. edge:** sharpness of appetite or pleasure.
**30. or:** either; **Phoebus' . . . foundered:** the sun-god's horses are made lame (that is, he will be kept waiting for the wedding night).
**35. meaner fellows:** lesser spirits.
**37. trick:** ingenious device; theatrical performance; **rabble:** that is, the spirits, not the courtiers.
**41. vanity:** trifle, minor display.
**42. Presently:** immediately.

PROSPERO
    Ay, with a twink.

ARIEL
    Before you can say "come" and "go,"
    And breathe twice and cry "so, so,"                    45
    Each one tripping on his toe,
    Will be here with mop and mow.
    Do you love me master? No?

PROSPERO
    Dearly, my delicate Ariel. Do not approach
    Till thou dost hear me call.

ARIEL                               Well; I conceive.          *Exit.*   50

PROSPERO    [*To* FERDINAND]
    Look thou be true; do not give dalliance
    Too much the rein. The strongest oaths are straw
    To th' fire i' th' blood. Be more abstemious,
    Or else good night your vow.

FERDINAND                       I warrant you, sir,
    The white cold virgin snow upon my heart                55
    Abates the ardor of my liver.

PROSPERO                             Well.
    Now come, my Ariel: bring a corollary
    Rather than want a spirit. Appear, and pertly.

     *Soft music.*

    No tongue! All eyes! Be silent!

     *Enter* IRIS.

IRIS
    Ceres, most bounteous lady, thy rich leas               60
    Of wheat, rye, barley, vetches, oats, and peas;
    Thy turfy mountains, where live nibbling sheep,
    And flat meads thatched with stover, them to keep;
    Thy banks with pionèd and twillèd brims,

43. **with a twink:** in the time it takes to wink.
47. **mop and mow:** grimaces.
50. **conceive:** understand.
51. **true:** steadfast, true to your word.
51–52. **do not . . . rein:** do not give flirtation too much freedom.
54. **Or . . . vow:** or else say "good night" to your promise; **warrant:** assure.
55–56. **The . . . liver:** that is, keeping his or Miranda's chastity (pure and cold as snow) in his heart will balance his hot passions (thought to have their seat in the liver).
57–58. **Bring . . . spirit:** bring one too many spirits rather than lack enough.
59. **No tongue:** that is, no speaking.
60. **Ceres:** goddess of the earth; **leas:** meadows.
61. **vetches:** tares, weedy plants grown for fodder.
63. **thatched . . . stover:** covered with winter forage.
64. **pionèd:** dug out; **twillèd:** braided (perhaps suggesting the use of woven foliage to prevent erosion from the current).

Which spongy April at thy hest betrims                          65
To make cold nymphs chaste crowns; and thy broom-groves,
Whose shadow the dismissed bachelor loves,
Being lass-lorn; thy poll-clipped vineyard,
And thy sea-marge, sterile and rocky-hard,
Where thou thyself dost air—the queen o' th' sky,              70
Whose wat'ry arch and messenger am I,
Bids thee leave these, and with her sovereign grace,
Here on this grass-plot, in this very place
To come and sport. Her peacocks fly amain.

    [JUNO's *chariot appears above the stage.*]

Approach, rich Ceres, her to entertain.                        75

    *Enter* CERES.

CERES
Hail; many-colored messenger, that ne'er
Dost disobey the wife of Jupiter;
Who, with thy saffron wings, upon my flow'rs
Diffusest honey drops, refreshing show'rs,
And with each end of thy blue bow dost crown                   80
My bosky acres and my unshrubbed down,
Rich scarf to my proud earth. Why hath thy queen
Summoned me hither to this short-grassed green?

IRIS
A contract of true love to celebrate
And some donation freely to estate                             85
On the blessed lovers.

CERES                              Tell me, heavenly bow,
If Venus or her son, as thou dost know,
Do now attend the Queen? Since they did plot
The means that dusky Dis my daughter got,
Her and her blind boy's scandaled company                      90
I have forsworn.

65. **spongy:** wet; **hest:** behest.
66. **cold:** chaste; **broom-groves:** clumps of broom or gorse (thorny shrubs with yellow flowers).
68. **poll-clipped:** pruned.
69. **sea-marge:** shore.
70. **queen o' the sky:** Juno.
71. **wat'ry arch:** rainbow.
74. **peacocks:** the sacred birds that pull Juno's chariot; **amain:** quickly.
75. **entertain:** greet.
81. **bosky:** covered with bushes; **unshrubbed down:** bare hills.
82. **rich scarf:** that is, the rainbow.
85. **estate:** bestow
87. **son:** that is, Cupid; **as:** as far as.
88–89. **they . . . got:** According to Ovid, Venus and Cupid arranged for Proserpina (daughter of Ceres) to be abducted by Pluto (*dusky Dis,* god of the underworld).
90. **blind:** Cupid was traditionally pictured wearing a blindfold (to suggest that "love is blind").

IRIS                    Of her society
Be not afraid. I met her deity
Cutting the clouds towards Paphos, and her son
Dove-drawn with her. Here thought they to have done
Some wanton charm upon this man and maid,                         95
Whose vows are, that no bed-right shall be paid
Till Hymen's torch be lighted; but in vain.
Mars's hot minion is returned again,
Her waspish-headed son has broke his arrows,
Swears he will shoot no more, but play with sparrows              100
And be a boy right out.

     JUNO *descends*.

CERES                         Highest queen of state,
Great Juno comes; I know her by her gait.
JUNO
How does my bounteous sister? Go with me
To bless this twain, that they may prosperous be
And honored in their issue.                                      105

    [*Singing*]

Honor, riches, marriage-blessing,
Long continuance, and increasing,
Hourly joys be still upon you,
Juno sings her blessings on you.
[CERES]    [*Singing*]
Earth's increase, and foison plenty,                             110
Barns and garners never empty,
Vines, with clust'ring bunches growing,
Plants, with goodly burden bowing;
Spring come to you at the farthest,
In the very end of harvest.                                      115
Scarcity and want shall shun you,
Ceres' blessing so is on you.
FERDINAND
This is a most majestic vision, and
Harmonious charmingly. May I be bold

91. **society:** company.
93. **Paphos:** a city in Cyprus, sacred to Venus and her followers.
94. **Dove-drawn:** Venus's chariot was pulled by doves.
95. **wanton:** lewd.
97. **Hymen's . . . lighted:** that is, until they have been married.
98. **Mars's . . . minion:** that is, Venus, lover of Mars.
99. **waspish-headed:** referring to the sting both of his arrows and of his personality.
101. **right out:** simply.
110. **foison:** abundance.
111. **garners:** granaries.
114–15 **Spring . . . harvest:** may spring follow the harvest (so that there will be no winter).

To think these spirits?
PROSPERO                          Spirits, which by mine art          120
I have from their confines called to enact
My present fancies.
FERDINAND              Let me live here ever;
So rare a wondered father and a wise
Makes this place paradise.

    JUNO *and* CERES *whisper, and send* IRIS *on employment.*

PROSPERO                    Sweet now, silence!
Juno and Ceres whisper seriously.                                    125
There's something else to do. Hush and be mute,
Or else our spell is marred.
IRIS
You nymphs called naiads of the windring brooks,
With your sedged crowns, and ever-harmless looks,
Leave your crisp channels, and on this green land             130
Answer your summons; Juno does command.
Come, temperate nymphs, and help to celebrate
A contract of true love. Be not too late.

    *Enter certain nymphs.*

You sunburned sicklemen of August weary,
Come hither from the furrow and be merry,                     135
Make holiday; your rye-straw hats put on,
And these fresh nymphs encounter every one
In country footing.

    *Enter certain reapers, properly habited. They join with
    the nymphs in a graceful dance, towards the end whereof
    *PROSPERO *starts suddenly and speaks, after which, to a
    strange, hollow, and confused noise, they heavily vanish.*

PROSPERO
I had forgot that foul conspiracy
Of the beast Caliban and his confederates                     140
Against my life. The minute of their plot
Is almost come. [*To the spirits*] Well done! Avoid! No more!

122. **fancies:** illusions; whims.
123. **wondered:** wondrous; full of wonders.
128. **nymphs:** the female spirits who peopled the countryside; **naiads:** spirits associated
with water; **windring:** This is the only known use of this word, which may combine the
senses of wandering and winding.
129. **sedged crowns:** garlands made from sedges (rushlike plants growing at the edges of
rivers).
137–38. **encounter . . . footing:** join in a rustic dance.
138 SD. **habited:** dressed.
142. **Avoid:** leave.

FERDINAND
    This is strange: your father's in some passion
    That works him strongly.
MIRANDA                              Never till this day
    Saw I him touched with anger so distempered.                    145
PROSPERO
    You do look, my son, in a movèd sort,
    As if you were dismayed. Be cheerful, sir.
    Our revels now are ended. These our actors,
    As I foretold you, were all spirits and
    Are melted into air, into thin air;                             150
    And, like the baseless fabric of this vision,
    The cloud-capped towers, the gorgeous palaces,
    The solemn temples, the great globe itself,
    Yea, all which it inherit, shall dissolve,
    And, like this insubstantial pageant faded,                    155
    Leave not a rack behind. We are such stuff
    As dreams are made on, and our little life
    Is rounded with a sleep. Sir, I am vexed.
    Bear with my weakness: my old brain is troubled.
    Be not disturbed with my infirmity.                            160
    If you be pleased, retire into my cell
    And there repose. A turn or two I'll walk
    To still my beating mind.
FERDINAND and MIRANDA    We wish your peace.        [*They*] *Exit.*
PROSPERO
    Come with a thought. I thank thee, Ariel. Come.

        *Enter* ARIEL.

ARIEL
    Thy thoughts I cleave to. What's thy pleasure?
PROSPERO                                    Spirit,          165
    We must prepare to meet with Caliban.
ARIEL
    Ay, my commander. When I presented Ceres

---

**144. works:** affects; afflicts.
**146. movèd sort:** perturbed state.
**148. revels:** entertainment: technically, the dances concluding court masques.
**151. baseless fabric:** structure without foundation (or, possibly, purpose).
**153. great globe:** the world, but also recalling the Globe Theater.
**154. all . . . inherit:** that is, succeeding generations.
**155. pageant:** a technical term referring to a symbolic scene performed on a stage or to the stage itself; also, a theatrical trick (like the "vanity" of line 40).
**156. rack:** cloud; mist.
**157. on:** that is, of.
**158. rounded:** surrounded; concluded.
**167. presented Ceres:** either "played the role of Ceres" or "produced the masque of Ceres."

I thought t' have told thee of it, but I feared
Lest I might anger thee.

PROSPERO

Say again, where didst thou leave these varlets?                 170

ARIEL

I told you, sir, they were red-hot with drinking;
So full of valor that they smote the air
For breathing in their faces, beat the ground
For kissing of their feet; yet always bending
Towards their project. Then I beat my tabor,                     175
At which like unbacked colts they pricked their ears,
Advanced their eyelids, lifted up their noses
As they smelt music. So I charmed their ears
That calf-like they my lowing followed through
Toothed briars, sharp furzes, pricking gorse, and thorns,        180
Which entered their frail shins. At last I left them
I' th' filthy-mantled pool beyond your cell,
There dancing up to th' chins, that the foul lake
O'erstunk their feet.

PROSPERO            This was well done, my bird.
Thy shape invisible retain thou still.                           185
The trumpery in my house, go bring it hither
For stale to catch these thieves.

ARIEL                       I go, I go.                  *Exit.*

PROSPERO

A devil, a born devil, on whose nature
Nurture can never stick; on whom my pains,
Humanely taken, all, all lost, quite lost;                       190
And, as with age his body uglier grows,
So his mind cankers. I will plague them all,
Even to roaring.

*Enter* ARIEL, *loaden with glistering apparel, etc.*

Come, hang them on this line.

[ARIEL *hangs up the clothing and they stand apart.*]

170. **varlets:** servants; probably also "rogues."
174. **bending:** that is, moving.
176. **unbacked:** unbroken.
177. **advanced:** raised.
178. **As:** as if.
179. **lowing:** mooing.
182. **filthy-mantled:** covered with scum.
184. **O'erstunk:** smelled worse than.
186. **trumpery:** gaudy clothing.
187. **stale:** bait.
192. **cankers:** festers or decays.
193. **line:** probably a linden or lime tree rather than a clothesline.
193 SD. **stand apart:** Alternatively, they may exit and re-enter with the spirits at line 253.

*Enter* CALIBAN, STEPHANO, *and* TRINCULO, *all wet.*

CALIBAN
Pray you tread softly, that the blind mole may not
Hear a foot fall. We now are near his cell.                                    195
STEPHANO   Monster, your fairy, which you say is a harmless
fairy, has done little better than played the jack with us.
TRINCULO   Monster, I do smell all horse-piss, at which my
nose is in great indignation.
STEPHANO   So is mine. Do you hear, monster? If I should take   200
a displeasure against you, look you—
TRINCULO   Thou wert but a lost monster.
CALIBAN
Good my lord, give me thy favor still.
Be patient, for the prize I'll bring thee to
Shall hoodwink this mischance. Therefore speak softly;          205
All's hushed as midnight yet.
TRINCULO   Ay, but to lose our bottles in the pool!
STEPHANO   There is not only disgrace and dishonor in that,
monster, but an infinite loss.
TRINCULO   That's more to me than my wetting. Yet this is your   210
harmless fairy, monster.
STEPHANO   I will fetch off my bottle, though I be o'er ears for
my labor.
CALIBAN
Prithee, my King, be quiet. Seest thou here:
This is the mouth o' th' cell. No noise, and enter.                  215
Do that good mischief which may make this island
Thine own forever, and I, thy Caliban,
For aye thy foot-licker.
STEPHANO   Give me thy hand. I do begin to have bloody
thoughts.                                                                       220
TRINCULO   [*Seeing the apparel*] O King Stephano, O peer! O
worthy Stephano, look what a wardrobe here is for thee.
CALIBAN
Let it alone, thou fool. It is but trash.
TRINCULO   O ho, monster! We know what belongs to a frip-
pery. [*He puts on a gown.*] O King Stephano!                      225
STEPHANO   Put off that gown, Trinculo: by this hand, I'll have
that gown.

197. jack: knave.
202. lost: ruined; banished (as in Stephano's threat at lines 249–50).
205. hoodwink . . . mischance: drive our current misfortune from sight and memory.
218. For aye: forever.
221. O . . . peer: An allusion to the old ballad beginning "King Stephen was a worthy peer."
224. frippery: secondhand-clothing shop (that is, this is *not* "trash").

TRINCULO    Thy grace shall have it.

CALIBAN

The dropsy drown this fool! What, do you mean
To dote thus on such luggage? Let't alone                    230
And do the murder first. If he awake,
From toe to crown he'll fill our skins with pinches,
Make us strange stuff.

STEPHANO    Be you quiet, monster. Mistress line, is not this
my jerkin? [*He takes it.*] Now is the jerkin under the line.    235
Now, jerkin, you are like to lose your hair and prove a bald
jerkin.

TRINCULO    Do, do! We steal by line and level, an't like your
grace.

STEPHANO    I thank thee for that jest. Here's a garment for't.    240
Wit shall not go unrewarded while I am king of this country.
"Steal by line and level" is an excellent pass of pate. There's
another garment for't.

TRINCULO    Monster, come put some lime upon your fingers,
and away with the rest.                                      245

CALIBAN

I will have none on't. We shall lose our time
And all be turned to barnacles, or to apes
With foreheads villainous low.

STEPHANO    Monster, lay to your fingers. Help to bear this
away, where my hogshead of wine is, or I'll turn you out of    250
my kingdom. [*Loading* CALIBAN *with clothing.*] Go to, carry
this.

TRINCULO    And this.

STEPHANO    Ay, and this.

---

229. **dropsy:** a disease characterized by excess fluid in the body; an insatiable thirst.
230. **luggage:** cumbersome baggage.
234. **Mistress line:** addressed to the tree.
235. **jerkin:** leather jacket; **Now . . . line:** under the tree, but punning on the sense of having journeyed below the equinoctial or equatorial line.
236. **like:** likely.
236–37. **lose . . . jerkin:** Sailors on long voyages were said to lose their hair (from scurvy, fever, or other diseases), but Stephano is also playing crudely on the loss of hair from syphilis.
238. **by line and level:** with plumb line and carpenter's level, that is, properly; **an't like:** if it please.
242. **pass of pate:** witty stroke (a fencing metaphor: a *pass* was a thrust and the *pate* was the head, the seat of wit).
244. **lime:** birdlime, to make Caliban's fingers sticky.
245. **away:** make off.
247. **barnacles:** a type of goose, thought to be hatched from barnacles growing on trees (though the word was derived from the term for "torturing with pinches," so there may be a connection to Prospero's threatened punishments).
248. **villainous:** churlishly; wretchedly.
249. **lay to:** set to work.

*A noise of hunters heard. Enter divers spirits in shape of dogs and hounds, hunting them about,* PROSPERO *and* ARIEL *setting them on.*

PROSPERO    Hey, Mountain, hey!                   255
ARIEL    Silver! There it goes, Silver!
PROSPERO
   Fury, Fury! There, Tyrant, there! Hark, hark!

         [CALIBAN, STEPHANO, *and* TRINCULO *are chased off by spirits.*]

   [*To* ARIEL] Go, charge my goblins that they grind their joints
   With dry convulsions, shorten up their sinews
   With agèd cramps, and more pinch-spotted make them     260
   Than pard or cat o' mountain.
ARIEL                        Hark, they roar!
PROSPERO
   Let them be hunted soundly. At this hour
   Lies at my mercy all mine enemies.
   Shortly shall all my labors end, and thou
   Shalt have the air at freedom. For a little,            265
   Follow, and do me service.              *Exeunt.*

## Act 5, Scene 1

*Enter* PROSPERO *in his magic robes, and* ARIEL.

PROSPERO
   Now does my project gather to a head.
   My charms crack not, my spirits obey, and time
   Goes upright with his carriage. How's the day?
ARIEL
   On the sixth hour, at which time, my lord,
   You said our work should cease.
PROSPERO                I did say so       5
   When first I raised the tempest. Say, my spirit,
   How fares the King and's followers?
ARIEL                 Confined together
   In the same fashion as you gave in charge,
   Just as you left them; all prisoners, sir,

260. **agèd:** like those of old age.
261. **pard or cat o' mountain:** both refer to the leopard or panther.
1–2. **project . . . crack:** Prospero is using the language of alchemy to describe the climax of his plan. The materials, when heated, would *gather to a head*; if the experiment failed, the container would *crack*, and if it succeeded the alchemist would achieve the philosopher's stone (and with it the means of *projection*, or transmutation of base metals into gold or silver).
3. **carriage:** burden.
7. **and's:** and his.

In the line-grove which weather-fends your cell.                    10
They cannot budge till your release. The King,
His brother, and yours abide all three distracted,
And the remainder mourning over them,
Brimful of sorrow and dismay; but chiefly
Him that you termed, sir, the good old lord Gonzalo.          15
His tears runs down his beard like winter's drops
From eaves of reeds. Your charm so strongly works 'em
That if you now beheld them, your affections
Would become tender.
PROSPERO                    Dost thou think so, spirit?
ARIEL
Mine would, sir, were I human.
PROSPERO                          And mine shall.          20
Hast thou, which art but air, a touch, a feeling
Of their afflictions, and shall not myself,
One of their kind, that relish all as sharply
Passion as they, be kindlier moved than thou art?
Though with their high wrongs I am struck to th' quick,          25
Yet with my nobler reason 'gainst my fury
Do I take part. The rarer action is
In virtue than in vengeance. They being penitent,
The sole drift of my purpose doth extend
Not a frown further. Go, release them, Ariel.                    30
My charms I'll break, their senses I'll restore,
And they shall be themselves.
ARIEL                          I'll fetch them, sir.

                                        *Exit.*

        [PROSPERO *makes a circle on the stage.*]

PROSPERO
Ye elves of hills, brooks, standing lakes, and groves,
And ye that on the sands with printless foot
Do chase the ebbing Neptune, and do fly him          35
When he comes back; you demi-puppets that

10. **line-grove:** grove of lime or linden trees; **weather-fends:** defends from the weather.
11. **till your release:** until you release them.
17. **eaves of reeds:** thatched roofs; **works:** acts upon; agitates.
21. **touch:** sense.
23–24. **relish . . . they:** feel suffering just as acutely as they do.
24. **kindlier:** more humanely.
25. **quick:** center; most sensitive part.
27. **rarer:** less common; more noble.
33–50. Prospero's speech paraphrases Medea's invocation in Book 7 of Ovid's *Metamorphoses.*
35. **ebbing Neptune:** that is, the waves or tide.
36. **demi-puppets:** small puppets (that is, fairies).

By moonshine do the green sour ringlets make,
Whereof the ewe not bites; and you, whose pastime
Is to make midnight-mushrooms, that rejoice
To hear the solemn curfew; by whose aid                    40
(Weak masters though ye be) I have bedimmed
The noontide sun, called forth the mutinous winds,
And twixt the green sea and the azured vault
Set roaring war; to the dread rattling thunder
Have I given fire, and rifted Jove's stout oak             45
With his own bolt; the strong-based promontory
Have I made shake, and by the spurs plucked up
The pine and cedar. Graves at my command
Have waked their sleepers, oped, and let 'em forth
By my so potent art. But this rough magic                  50
I here abjure; and when I have required
Some heavenly music (which even now I do)
To work mine end upon their senses that
This airy charm is for, I'll break my staff,
Bury it certain fathoms in the earth,                      55
And deeper than did ever plummet sound
I'll drown my book.

> *Solemn music. Here enters* ARIEL *before; then* ALONSO
> *with a frantic gesture, attended by* GONZALO; SEBASTIAN
> *and* ANTONIO *in like manner attended by* ADRIAN *and*
> FRANCISCO. *They all enter the circle which* PROSPERO *had*
> *made, and there stand charmed; which* PROSPERO *observ-*
> *ing, speaks.*

A solemn air, and the best comforter
To an unsettled fancy, cure thy brains,
Now useless, boiled within thy skull. There stand,         60
For you are spell-stopped.
Holy Gonzalo, honorable man,
Mine eyes e'en sociable to the show of thine,
Fall fellowly drops. [*Aside*] The charm dissolves apace,

37. **green sour ringlets:** circles made by fairies in the grass.
40. **curfew:** evening bell.
41. **Weak masters:** agents of limited power.
43. **azured vault:** that is, the sky.
45. **fire:** lightning; **rifted:** split.
46. **promontory:** land jutting into the sea.
47. **spurs:** roots.
51. **required:** requested.
57 SD. **frantic:** excited; insane.
58. **air:** musical tune; **and:** which is.
59. **fancy:** imagination.
63. **sociable:** sympathetic.
64. **Fall:** let fall.

And as the morning steals upon the night,                        65
Melting the darkness, so their rising senses
Begin to chase the ignorant fumes that mantle
Their clearer reason.—O good Gonzalo,
My true preserver, and a loyal sir
To him thou follow'st, I will pay thy graces                     70
Home both in word and deed.—Most cruelly
Didst thou, Alonso, use me and my daughter.
Thy brother was a furtherer in the act.—
Thou art pinched for't now, Sebastian.—
[*To Antonio*] Flesh and blood,
You, brother mine, that entertained ambition,                    75
Expelled remorse and nature, whom, with Sebastian
(Whose inward pinches therefore are most strong)
Would here have killed your king, I do forgive thee,
Unnatural though thou art.—Their understanding
Begins to swell, and the approaching tide                        80
Will shortly fill the reasonable shore
That now lies foul and muddy. Not one of them
That yet looks on me, or would know me.—Ariel,
Fetch me the hat and rapier in my cell.

> [ARIEL *exits and returns immediately.*]

I will discase me, and myself present                            85
As I was sometime Milan. Quickly, spirit!
Thou shalt ere long be free.

> ARIEL *sings, and helps to attire him.*

[ARIEL]
Where the bee sucks, there suck I;
In a cowslip's bell I lie;
There I couch when owls do cry;                                  90
On the bat's back I do fly
After summer merrily.
Merrily, merrily shall I live now,
Under the blossom that hangs on the bough.

---

67. **mantle:** cloud.
70–71. **pay . . . Home:** reward your favors fully.
73. **furtherer:** accomplice.
74. **pinched:** punished; suffering.
76. **nature:** human, and brotherly, feelings.
81. **reasonable shore:** that is, the edges of their reason.
85. **discase:** undress.
86. **As . . . Milan:** as when I was Duke of Milan.
90. **couch:** lie down; **when owls do cry:** that is, at night.
92. **After summer:** that is, pursuing it from climate to climate.

PROSPERO
  Why, that's my dainty Ariel! I shall miss                 95
  Thee, but yet thou shalt have freedom. So, so, so.
  To the King's ship, invisible as thou art,
  There shalt thou find the mariners asleep
  Under the hatches. The Master and the Boatswain
  Being awake, enforce them to this place;             100
  And presently, I prithee.
ARIEL
  I drink the air before me, and return
  Or ere your pulse twice beat.               *Exit.*
GONZALO
  All torment, trouble, wonder, and amazement
  Inhabits here. Some heavenly power guide us       105
  Out of this fearful country!
PROSPERO               Behold, sir King,
  The wrongèd Duke of Milan, Prospero.
  For more assurance that a living prince
  Does now speak to thee, I embrace thy body,

    [*He embraces* ALONSO.]

  And to thee and thy company I bid             110
  A hearty welcome.
ALONSO            Whe'er thou beest he or no,
  Or some enchanted trifle to abuse me,
  As late I have been, I not know. Thy pulse
  Beats as of flesh and blood; and since I saw thee,
  Th' affliction of my mind amends, with which,     115
  I fear, a madness held me. This must crave
  (An if this be at all) a most strange story.
  Thy dukedom I resign and do entreat
  Thou pardon me my wrongs. But how should Prospero
  Be living, and be here?
PROSPERO    [*To* GONZALO] First, noble friend,     120
  Let me embrace thine age, whose honor cannot
  Be measured or confined. [*Embraces him.*]
GONZALO           Whether this be
  Or be not, I'll not swear.

---

96. **So . . . so:** Prospero is either arranging his attire or approving the final look.
100. **Being awake:** once they are awake; **enforce:** compel; lead.
103. **Or ere:** before.
111. **Whe'er:** whether.
112. **trifle:** trick; illusion; **abuse:** deceive; torment.
115. **amends:** improves.
116. **crave:** require.
117. **An . . . all:** if this is real.

PROSPERO                    You do yet taste
  Some subtleties o' th' isle, that will not let you
  Believe things certain. Welcome, my friends all.          125
  [*Aside to Sebastian and Antonio*] But you, my brace of lords,
      were I so minded
  I here could pluck his highness' frown upon you
  And justify you traitors. At this time
  I will tell no tales.
SEBASTIAN            The devil speaks in him!
PROSPERO                              No.
  For you, most wicked sir, whom to call brother          130
  Would even infect my mouth, I do forgive
  Thy rankest fault—all of them; and require
  My dukedom of thee, which perforce I know
  Thou must restore.
ALONSO            If thou beest Prospero,
  Give us particulars of thy preservation;          135
  How thou hast met us here, whom three hours since
  Were wracked upon this shore, where I have lost
  (How sharp the point of this remembrance is!)
  My dear son Ferdinand.
PROSPERO                    I am woe for't, sir.
ALONSO
  Irreparable is the loss, and Patience          140
  Says it is past her cure.
PROSPERO                    I rather think
  You have not sought her help, of whose soft grace
  For the like loss I have her sovereign aid
  And rest myself content.
ALONSO                    You the like loss?
PROSPERO
  As great to me, as late; and supportable          145
  To make the dear loss have I means much weaker
  Than you may call to comfort you; for I
  Have lost my daughter.
ALONSO                    A daughter?
  O heavens, that they were living both in Naples,

124. **subtleties:** magical illusions (playing on the additional sense of "elaborate pastries").
126. **brace:** pair (usually applied to animals).
127. **pluck:** pull.
128. **justify:** prove.
132. **rankest:** foulest.
133. **perforce:** necessarily.
139. **woe:** sorry.
142. **soft:** gentle; compassionate.
143. **sovereign:** supreme; potent.
145. **late:** recent.
145–46. **supportable . . . loss:** to make the grievous loss bearable.

The king and queen there! That they were, I wish                    150
Myself were mudded in that oozy bed
Where my son lies. When did you lose your daughter?
PROSPERO
   In this last tempest. I perceive these lords
At this encounter do so much admire
That they devour their reason, and scarce think                    155
Their eyes do offices of truth, their words
Are natural breath. But, howsoe'er you have
Been jostled from your senses, know for certain
That I am Prospero, and that very duke
Which was thrust forth of Milan, who most strangely                    160
Upon this shore (where you were wracked) was landed
To be the lord on't. No more yet of this,
For 'tis a chronicle of day by day,
Not a relation for a breakfast, nor
Befitting this first meeting. Welcome, sir;                    165
This cell's my court. Here have I few attendants,
And subjects none abroad. Pray you look in.
My dukedom since you have given me again,
I will requite you with as good a thing.
At least bring forth a wonder to content ye                    170
As much as me my dukedom.

    *Here* PROSPERO *discovers* FERDINAND *and* MIRANDA *playing*
    *at chess.*

MIRANDA
   Sweet lord, you play me false.
FERDINAND                    No, my dearest love,
   I would not for the world.
MIRANDA
   Yes, for a score of kingdoms you should wrangle,
And I would call it fair play.

---

150. **That they were:** in order to make it possible.
151. **mudded:** buried in the mud.
154. **admire:** wonder.
156. **do . . . truth:** perform truthfully.
160. **of:** from.
163. **chronicle:** narrative; **day by day:** either requiring several days to tell or involving the details of every day's events.
164. **relation:** report.
167. **abroad:** elsewhere.
171 **SD. discovers:** reveals (probably by pulling back a curtain across a door or recess at the back of the stage).
172. **play me false:** that is, you are cheating.
174. **score . . . wrangle:** that is, even if we were playing for twenty (*a score of*) kingdoms, which is less than *the world*, you would still contend with me (*wrangle*, with a possible implication of cheating).

ALONSO                    If this prove                    175
   A vision of the island, one dear son
   Shall I twice lose.
SEBASTIAN              A most high miracle!
FERDINAND
   Though the seas threaten, they are merciful.
   I have cursed them without cause.
ALONSO                          Now all the blessings
   Of a glad father compass thee about!              180
   Arise, and say how thou cam'st here.     [FERDINAND *rises.*]
MIRANDA                        O, wonder!
   How many goodly creatures are there here?
   How beauteous mankind is! O brave new world
   That has such people in't!
PROSPERO                    'Tis new to thee.
ALONSO    [*To* FERDINAND]
   What is this maid with whom thou wast at play?     185
   Your eld'st acquaintance cannot be three hours.
   Is she the goddess that hath severed us
   And brought us thus together?
FERDINAND                    Sir, she is mortal;
   But by immortal providence, she's mine.
   I chose her when I could not ask my father          190
   For his advice, nor thought I had one. She
   Is daughter to this famous Duke of Milan,
   Of whom so often I have heard renown
   But never saw before; of whom I have
   Received a second life; and second father           195
   This lady makes him to me.
ALONSO                    I am hers.
   But O, how oddly will it sound that I
   Must ask my child forgiveness!
PROSPERO                    There, sir, stop.
   Let us not burden our remembrances with
   A heaviness that's gone.
GONZALO              I have inly wept,                    200
   Or should have spoken ere this. Look down, you gods,
   And on this couple drop a blessèd crown.
   For it is you that have chalked forth the way

---

176. **of the island:** of the kind this island produces.
180. **compass thee about:** surround you.
183. **brave:** excellent, but also beautiful and finely dressed.
186. **eld'st:** longest.
194. **of:** from.
200. **heaviness:** sadness; **inly:** inwardly.
203. **chalked . . . way:** marked the path (as with a piece of chalk).

Which brought us hither.

ALONSO                    I say "Amen," Gonzalo.

GONZALO

Was Milan thrust from Milan that his issue                    205
Should become kings of Naples? O, rejoice
Beyond a common joy, and set it down
With gold on lasting pillars: in one voyage
Did Claribel her husband find at Tunis,
And Ferdinand her brother found a wife                    210
Where he himself was lost; Prospero his dukedom
In a poor isle; and all of us ourselves
When no man was his own.

ALONSO    [To FERDINAND *and* MIRANDA] Give me your hands.
Let grief and sorrow still embrace his heart
That doth not wish you joy.

GONZALO                    Be it so. Amen.                    215

Enter ARIEL, *with the* MASTER *and* BOATSWAIN *amazedly
following.*

O look, sir, look, sir: here is more of us.
I prophesied, if a gallows were on land
This fellow could not drown. [*To the* BOATSWAIN] Now, blasphemy,
That swear'st grace o'erboard, not an oath on shore?
Hast thou no mouth by land? What is the news?                    220

BOATSWAIN

The best news is that we have safely found
Our King and company; the next, our ship,
Which, but three glasses since we gave out split,
Is tight and yare and bravely rigged as when
We first put to sea.

ARIEL    [*To* PROSPERO] Sir, all this service                    225
Have I done since I went.

PROSPERO    [*To* ARIEL]        My tricksy spirit!

ALONSO

These are not natural events; they strengthen
From strange to stranger. Say, how came you hither?

BOATSWAIN

If I did think, sir, I were well awake,

---

205. **issue:** descendants.
213. **his own:** in possession of his senses or identity.
214. **still:** always.
215 SD. **amazedly:** with confusion or wonder.
218. **blasphemy:** that is, blasphemer.
223. **glasses:** hours; **gave out:** reported.
224. **tight:** watertight; **yare:** ready to sail.
226. **tricksy:** playful; ingenious.
227. **strengthen:** increase.

I'd strive to tell you. We were dead of sleep          230
And—how we know not—all clapped under hatches,
Where, but even now, with strange and several noises
Of roaring, shrieking, howling, jingling chains,
And more diversity of sounds, all horrible,
We were awaked, straightway at liberty,          235
Where we, in all her trim, freshly beheld
Our royal, good, and gallant ship, our Master
Cap'ring to eye her. On a trice, so please you,
Even in a dream were we divided from them
And were we brought moping hither.

ARIEL     [*To* PROSPERO]                    Was't well done?          240
PROSPERO     [*To* ARIEL]
Bravely, my diligence. Thou shalt be free.
ALONSO
This is as strange a maze as e'er men trod,
And there is in this business more than nature
Was ever conduct of. Some oracle
Must rectify our knowledge.
PROSPERO                         Sir, my liege,          245
Do not infest your mind with beating on
The strangeness of this business. At picked leisure,
Which shall be shortly, single I'll resolve you,
Which to you shall seem probable, of every
These happened accidents. Till when, be cheerful          250
And think of each thing well. [*To* ARIEL] Come hither, spirit.
Set Caliban and his companions free:
Untie the spell.                              [*Exit* ARIEL.]
[*To* ALONSO]     How fares my gracious sir?
There are yet missing of your company
Some few odd lads that you remember not.          255

Enter ARIEL, *driving in* CALIBAN, STEPHANO, *and* TRIN-
CULO *in their stolen apparel.*

230. of sleep: that is, asleep.
231. clapped under hatches: stowed under the deck.
232. several: diverse.
238. Cap 'ring . . . her: dancing with joy at the sight of her; On a trice: in an instant.
240. moping: in a daze.
244. conduct: guide.
245. rectify: put right.
246. infest: trouble; beating on: incessantly worrying about.
247. picked: chosen.
248. single: privately; by my own power; resolve: explain to.
249. every: all of.
250. happened accidents: things that have happened.
251. think . . . well: look positively on things; meditate on things.
255. some . . . lads: a couple of stray servants.

STEPHANO   Every man shift for all the rest, and let no man
take care for himself; for all is but fortune. *Coraggio*, bully-
monster, *coraggio*!

TRINCULO   If these be true spies which I wear in my head,
Here's a goodly sight!                                                                   260

CALIBAN
O Setebos, these be brave spirits indeed!
How fine my master is! I am afraid
He will chastise me.

SEBASTIAN
Ha, ha! What things are these, my lord Antonio?
Will money buy 'em?

ANTONIO                    Very like. One of them                                 265
Is a plain fish, and no doubt marketable.

PROSPERO
Mark but the badges of these men, my lords,
Then say if they be true. This misshapen knave,
His mother was a witch, and one so strong
That could control the moon, make flows and ebbs,                      270
And deal in her command without her power.
These three have robbed me, and this demi-devil
(For he's a bastard one) had plotted with them
To take my life. Two of these fellows you
Must know and own; this thing of darkness I                                275
Acknowledge mine.

CALIBAN                    I shall be pinched to death.

ALONSO
Is not this Stephano, my drunken butler?

SEBASTIAN
He is drunk now: where had he wine?

ALONSO
And Trinculo is reeling-ripe: where should they
Find this grand liquor that hath gilded 'em?                                 280
How cam'st thou in this pickle?

256. **shift:** look out for.
256–57. **Every . . . himself:** Stephano drunkenly reverses the usual phrases.
257. **Coraggio:** courage; **bully:** a term of friendly admiration (here probably used ironically).
259. **If . . . head:** that is, if my eyes do not deceive me.
265. **like:** likely.
267. **badges:** emblems worn by servants to identify their masters. The insignia on their clothing would probably be Alonso's.
270. **That could:** that she could.
271. **deal . . . power:** exercise the moon's influence, without her authority or assistance.
273. **bastard:** born out of wedlock; of inferior qualities.
275. **own:** acknowledge; claim.
279. **reeling-ripe:** so drunk that he can hardly walk.
280. **gilded:** made them red-faced.
281. **in this pickle:** in such a sorry state (but Trinculo's reply picks up and continues the second meaning of "preserved in liquor"—that is, either drunk with wine or soaked in "horse-piss").

TRINCULO   I have been in such a pickle since I saw you last
that I fear me will never out of my bones: I shall not fear
flyblowing.

SEBASTIAN   Why, how now, Stephano?                              285

STEPHANO   O, touch me not! I am not Stephano, but a cramp.

PROSPERO   You'd be king o' the isle, sirrah?

STEPHANO   I should have been a sore one then.

ALONSO   [*indicating* CALIBAN]
This is a strange thing as e'er I looked on.

PROSPERO
He is as disproportioned in his manners                         290
As in his shape. Go, sirrah, to my cell;
Take with you your companions. As you look
To have my pardon, trim it handsomely.

CALIBAN
Ay, that I will; and I'll be wise hereafter,
And seek for grace. What a thrice-double ass                    295
Was I to take this drunkard for a god,
And worship this dull fool!

PROSPERO                             Go to, away.

ALONSO
Hence, and bestow your luggage where you found it.

SEBASTIAN   Or stole it rather.
                    [*Exeunt* CALIBAN, STEPHANO, *and* TRINCULO.]

PROSPERO
Sir, I invite your highness and your train                      300
To my poor cell, where you shall take your rest
For this one night; which, part of it, I'll waste
With such discourse as, I not doubt, shall make it
Go quick away: the story of my life,
And the particular accidents gone by                            305
Since I came to this isle. And in the morn
I'll bring you to your ship, and so to Naples,
Where I have hope to see the nuptial
Of these our dear-belovèd solemnized,
And thence retire me to my Milan, where                         310
Every third thought shall be my grave.

ALONSO                                    I long
To hear the story of your life, which must
Take the ear strangely.

284. **flyblowing:** having fly eggs laid on him.
288. **sore:** aching; sorry.
292. **as you look:** if you hope.
293. **trim:** prepare.
302. **waste:** consume.
310. **retire me:** return.
313. **Take:** strike.

PROSPERO                    I'll deliver all,
And promise you calm seas, auspicious gales,
And sail so expeditious that shall catch                                315
Your royal fleet far off.—My Ariel, chick,
That is thy charge. Then to the elements
Be free, and fare thou well.—Please you draw near.

*Exeunt omnes [except* PROSPERO].

*Epilogue*

*Spoken by* PROSPERO.

Now my charms are all o'erthrown,
And what strength I have's mine own,
Which is most faint. Now 'tis true
I must be here confined by you,
Or sent to Naples. Let me not,                                           5
Since I have my dukedom got
And pardoned the deceiver, dwell
In this bare island by your spell,
But release me from my bands
With the help of your good hands.                                       10
Gentle breath of yours my sails
Must fill, or else my project fails,
Which was to please. Now I want
Spirits to enforce, art to enchant;
And my ending is despair,                                               15
Unless I be relieved by prayer
Which pierces so, that it assaults
Mercy itself and frees all faults.
As you from crimes would pardoned be,
Let your indulgence set me free.                    [*Exit.*]  20

---

313. deliver: explain; set free.
315–16. sail . . . fleet: such speed that you will be able to rejoin the rest of the ships in your party.
318. draw near: Although Prospero may be addressing the audience in preparation for his epilogue, he is probably inviting the courtiers into his cell.
9. bands: bonds.
10. help . . . hands: that is, by clapping.
11. Gentle breath: approving words, or perhaps whistles (probably in a nautical rather than theatrical context: sailors traditionally "whistled after the wind" when stalled in calm seas).
13. want: lack.
14. enforce: command.
17. pierces: moves; assaults: petitions.
18. Mercy itself: that is, God; frees: frees from.
20. indulgence: favor, but also official release from punishment for sin.

# A Note on the Text

No Shakespearean text is simple, but that of *The Tempest* is simpler than most. The play was first entered in the Stationers' Register on November 8, 1623, and first printed in the First Folio later that year. There is thus only one text with any claim to authority, and it seems to have been produced more carefully than most of the texts in the Folio. We have followed all other modern editors in basing our edition upon this text.

That said, readers should be under no illusion that the words they are reading in this or any other modern edition are exactly those that flowed from Shakespeare's pen. As is the case with all of Shakespeare's plays, we do not have a text in Shakespeare's hand; furthermore, as with roughly half of them, we do not have one printed during his lifetime. As always with the works of Shakespeare and his contemporaries, there were a number of intermediaries between the playwright and the printed text, and the process of making the text accessible to modern readers necessarily introduces further modifications (and further distance from Shakespeare's hand).

The text used by the printers of the Folio *Tempest* was evidently prepared by Ralph Crane, a professional scrivener who produced both legal and theatrical manuscripts. Although the copy therefore was almost certainly clean, it also would have incorporated some of Crane's scribal characteristics—which, from surviving copies of his other transcripts, seem to have included a fondness for parentheses and a tendency to insert descriptive stage directions (quite possibly based on what he saw at early productions of the play). The printers who set the Folio text—and there were at least three of them—would have introduced their own habits of spelling and punctuation, and (being both human and unable to consult the author directly) they would undoubtedly have made mistakes.

In modernizing the text, we have been guided by a goal that is straightforward in theory, if often difficult in practice. We have tried to provide an edition of the play that makes the text as accessible to modern readers as possible without sacrificing the linguistic and rhetorical complexity of the original. We have also tried to anticipate the needs of a wide range of readers (from those new to the play to scholars who have edited the text for themselves), and to be as flexible as possible in matters of staging.

The format and length of this Norton Critical Edition do not allow us to document, much less discuss, all of the ambiguities and uncertainties in the text. As mentioned above, some of the stage directions are probably Crane's rather than Shakespeare's. There are also confusions in the Folio's distinctions between prose and verse and, occasionally, in its line divisions (the layout of the songs is particularly muddled in this play). The spelling and punctuation have been adapted throughout to conform to current conventions, but in some places this has involved a decision between several possible meanings in the Folio text—that is, between multiple meanings that Shakespeare may well have wanted to keep in play. And there are some famous cruxes that require the intervention of editors: Is it Prospero or Miranda who condemns Caliban as an "abhorrèd slave" (1.2.350)? Does Ferdinand refer to "so rare a wondered father and a wise" or ". . . a wife" (4.1.123)? Do his female acquaintances in 3.1.46 "put it to the foil" or "put it to the soil"? Why is Sycorax described as "blue-eyed" (1.2.269)? And what are the "scamels" that Caliban promises to fetch for Stephano and Trinculo (in 2.2.167, the *Oxford English Dictionary*'s only citation for the word)? All readers interested in these details should turn both to the essays of Stephen Orgel and Leah Marcus in this volume and to the fuller discussions of such matters in David Lindley's "Textual Analysis" in his New Cambridge Edition of *The Tempest* (Cambridge University Press, 2002), pp. 219–50, and John Jowett's notes on the play in Stanley Wells and Gary Taylor, with John Jowett and William Montgomery, *William Shakespeare: A Textual Companion* (Oxford: Clarendon Press, 1987), pp. 612–17.

We also encourage readers to examine the primary texts for themselves: comparing even a short passage in the Folio with the text in this or other modernized editions will immediately reveal how many choices editors make without their readers' knowledge or consent. But even in reading our text alone it will be clear that we have made a few choices that resist the drift of modernization without (we hope) making the text harder to read and use. While the heavy and idiosyncratic punctuation in the Folio text may owe as much to Crane as to Shakespeare, it does present some rhetorical and poetic effects worth retaining. We have been particularly attracted to the conspicuous practice in *The Tempest* of using hyphens to create compound words, and we have tried to retain them wherever possible—in part to convey the sense of compression given by the play's language and plot, and in part to recover connections between words that have since been separated (most notably, perhaps, in our preference for "dark-backward and abysm" over the usual "dark backward and abysm" in 1.2.50).

## Textual Notes

The table below lists all significant departures from our copy text (the First Folio). Our readings appear to the left of the square bracket; the original reading from the Folio is on the right, with any explanation by the editors in italics. SD is the standard abbreviation for stage direction, SH for speech heading.

Because this is a modernized edition, we have not listed straightforward changes in punctuation and spelling. We have, however, tried to include words and phrases when the Folio text suggests possibilities of sound or sense that are simplified or edited out in the process of modernization. This decision is no substitute for examining the Folio text directly, but it will allow readers to see at a glance which acts of translation have been especially difficult or interesting. Words added to the text by the editors always appear within square brackets, and they are not collated here. Finally, although some of our readings derive from other editions of the play (ranging from the Second Folio of 1632 to the New Cambridge Shakespeare of 2002), a more detailed collation is beyond the scope and purpose of this edition.

**List of characters**
List of Characters] Names of the Actors; *At end of text*
PROSPERO] *sometimes* Prosper;
Milan] Millaine *throughout*
savage] saluage
ARIEL] Ariell *throughout*
The Scene] *at end of text*


**1.1**
**5** cheerly] cheerely
**8 SD** Ferdinand] Ferdinando
**25** Cheerly] cheerely
**42** from] for
**50** I'm] I'am
**62** furze] firrs


**1.2**
**1** art] *capitalized here and throughout*
**112** with th' King] with King
**173** princes] Princesse
**200** bowsprit] Bore-spritt
**201** lightnings] lightning
**229** Bermudas] Bermoothes
**248** made no] made thee no
**261** Algiers] Argier
**282** she] he
**357** vile] vild
**382 SD**] Burthen dispersedly *at 380*
**394 SD**] Ariell Song
**402 SD**] Burthen: ding dong.
**429** wert] wer't

**2.1**
0 **SD**] and others *after* Francisco.
5 master] Masters
18 dollar] dollor
36] *assigned to Sebastian*
37] *assigned to Antonio*
61 gloss] glosses
90 Ay] I
159 its] it
276 brother] Brothet

**2.2**
3 **SD**] *at head of scene*
46 Moll] Mall
143 o' th'] 'oth
176 **SH**] *omitted*
179 trencher] trenchering

**3.1**
2 sets] set
15 busilest] busie lest
47 peerless] peetlesse

**3.2**
3 'em] em'
25 debauched] debosh'd
118 **SD** *They sing*] Sings
119 scout] cout
120 scout] skowt

**3.3**
2 ache] aches
17 SEBASTIAN . . . more] *after SD Solemn . . . depart*
19 **SD** *Enter . . . depart*] *after 17 SD*
29 islanders] Islands
33 human] humaine
65 plume] plumbe
99 bass] base

**4.1**
9 of] off
13 gift] guest
17 rite] right
52 rein] raigne
53 abstemious] abstenious

61 vetches] fetches
68 poll-clipped] pole-clipt
75 her] here
83 short-grassed] short gras'd
101 SD] *in right margin next to 73–74*
106 marriage-blessing] marriage, blessing
106 SD *Singing*] They sing *opposite 106*
110 and] *omitted*
146 movèd] mou'd
169 Lest] Least
180 gorse] gosse
193 them on] on them
223 Let it] Let's

5.1
20 human] humane
39 midnight-mushrooms] midnight-mushrumps
46 strong-based] strong-bass'd
60 boiled] boile
75 entertained] entertaine
82 lies] ly
111 Whe'er] where
124 not] nor
149 Naples] Nalpes
185 wast] was't
236 her] our
248 shortly, single] shortly single)
257 *Coraggio*] *Corasio*
309 dear-belovèd solemnized] deere-belou'd, solemnized
313 strangely] starngely

# SOURCES AND CONTEXTS

# Magic and Witchcraft

## OVID

## [Medea]†

Before the moon should circlewise close both her horns in one
Three nights were yet as then to come. As soon as that she shone
Most full of light, and did behold the earth with fulsome face,
Medea with her hair not trussed so much as in a lace,
But flaring on her shoulders twain, and barefoot, with her gown
Ungirded, got her out of doors and wandered up and down
Alone the dead time of the night. Both man and beast and bird
Were fast asleep; the serpents sly in trailing forward stirred
So softly as you would have thought they still asleep had been.
The moisting air was whist; no leaf ye could have moving seen.
The stars alonely fair and bright did in the welkin shine.
To which she lifting up her hands did thrice herself incline,
And thrice with water of the brook her hair besprinkled she,
And gasping thrice she oped her mouth, and bowing down her knee
Upon the bare, hard ground she said, 'O trusty time of night
Most faithful unto privities, O golden stars whose light
Doth jointly with the moon succeed the beams that blaze by day,
And thou three-headed Hecatè, who knowest best the way
To compass this our great attempt and art our chiefest stay;
Ye charms and witchcrafts, and thou earth, which both with herb
     and weed
Of mighty working furnishest the wizards at their need;
Ye airs and winds; ye elves of hills, of brooks, of woods alone,
Of standing lakes, and of the night, approach ye every one,
Through help of whom (the crooked banks much wond'ring at the
     thing)
I have compellèd streams to run clean backward to their spring.
By charms I make the calm seas rough and make the rough seas
     plain,

† From *Ovid's Metamorphosis*, trans. Arthur Golding (London: William Seres, 1567), pp. 263–77.

And cover all the sky with clouds and chase them thence again.
By charms I raise and lay the winds and burst the viper's jaw,
And from the bowels of the earth both stones and trees do draw.
Whole woods and forests I remove; I make the mountains shake,
And even the earth itself to groan and fearfully to quake.
I call up dead men from their graves; and thee, O lightsome
    moon,
I darken oft, though beaten brass abate thy peril soon;
Our sorcery dims the morning fair and darks the sun at noon.
The flaming breath of fiery bulls ye quenchèd for my sake,
And causèd their unwieldy necks the bended yoke to take.
Among the earth-bred brothers you a mortal war did set,
And brought asleep the dragon fell whose eyes were never shet,
By means whereof deceiving him that had the golden fleece
In charge to keep, you sent it thence by Jason into Greece.
Now have I need of herbs that can by virtue of their juice
To flowering prime of lusty youth old withered age reduce.
I am assured ye will it grant; for not in vain have shone
These twinkling stars, ne yet in vain this chariot all alone
By draught of dragons hither comes.' With that was from the sky
A chariot softly glancèd down, and stayèd hard thereby.

# GIOVANNI PICO DELLA MIRANDOLA

## Oration on the Dignity of Man†

[Pico argues that God has granted mankind unlimited powers of self-determination and suggests that this is what God said to Adam at the moment of creation.]

I have read in the records of the Arabians that Abdul the Saracen, on being asked what thing on, so to speak, the world's stage, he viewed as most greatly worthy of wonder, answered that he viewed nothing more wonderful than man. And Mercury's, "a great wonder, Asclepius, is man!" On thinking over the reason for these sayings, I was not satisfied by the many assertions made by many men concerning the outstandingness of human nature: that man is the messenger between creatures, familiar with the upper and king of the lower; by the sharpsightedness of the senses, by the hunting-power of reason, and by the light of intelligence, the interpreter of nature; the part in between the standstill of eternity and the flow of time;

---

† From *On the Dignity of Man* (1486), trans. Charles Glenn Wallis (Indianapolis: Bobbs-Merrill, 1940).

and, as the Persians say, the bond tying the world together, nay, the nuptial bond.

\* \* \*

God the master-builder \* \* \* took up man, a work of indeterminate form; and, placing him at the midpoint of the world, He spoke to him as follows: "We have given to thee, Adam, no fixed seat, no form of thy very own, no gift peculiarly thine, that thou mayest feel as thine own, have as thine own, possess as thine own the seat, the form, the gifts which thou thyself shalt desire. A limited nature in other creatures is confined within the laws written down by Us. In conformity with thy free judgment, in whose hands I have placed thee, thou art confined by no bounds; and thou wilt fix limits of nature for thyself. I have placed thee at the center of the world, that from there thou mayest more conveniently look around and see whatsoever is in the world. Neither heavenly nor earthly, neither mortal nor immortal have We made thee. Thou, like a judge appointed for being honorable, art the molder and maker of thyself; thou mayest sculpt thyself into whatever shape thou dost prefer. Thou canst grow downward into the lower natures which are brutes. Thou canst again grow upward from thy soul's reason into the higher natures which are divine."

\* \* \* Let a certain holy ambition invade the mind, so that we may not be content with mean things but may aspire to the highest things and strive with all our forces to attain them: for if we will to, we can. Let us spurn earthly things; let us struggle toward the heavenly. Let us put in last place whatever is of the world; and let us fly beyond the chambers of the world to the chambers nearest the most lofty divinity.

\* \* \*

By rivaling the life of a cherub upon the earth, by confining the onslaughts of the affections by means of moral science, and by shaking off the mist of reason by means of dialectic, as if washing off the filth of ignorance and vice, let us purge the soul, that the affections may not audaciously run riot, nor an imprudent reason sometime rave. Then, over a soul which has been set in order and purified, let us pour the light of natural philosophy, that lastly we may perfect it with the knowledge of divine things.

\* \* \*

[Later Pico makes a distinction between two kinds of magic, one good and one bad.]

Magic has two forms, one consists entirely in the operations and powers of demons . . . which appears to me to be a distorted and monstrous business; and the other \* \* \* is nothing other than the highest realization of natural philosophy \* \* \* . No philosopher of merit, eager in the study of the beneficial arts, has ever devoted himself to the first. For just as that first form of magic makes man a slave or pawn of evil powers, so the second form makes him their ruler and lord. The first form cannot lay claim to being either an art or a science; while the second, filled as it is with mysteries, comprehends the most profound contemplation of the deepest secrets of things, and ultimately, the knowledge of the whole of nature.

*    *    *

# ANONYMOUS

## [Friar Bacon's Magical Exploits]†

### [Friar Bacon Performs before the King and Queen]

There presently, to their great amazement, ensued the most melodious music they had ever heard in their lives * * * another kind of music was heard, and presently dancers in antic shapes at a masquerade [were seen] * * * louder music was heard, and whilst that played, a table was placed by an invisible hand, and richly covered with all the dainties that could be thought on; then he bid the King and Queen draw their seats near, and partake of the provisions he had provided for their Highnesses; which they did and all thereupon vanished * * * [and] the place was perfumed with all the sweets of Arabia * * *

### [Bacon's Servant Miles Plays the Tabor and Pipe]

[Bacon] slipped an enchanted pipe into Miles's hand [and] Miles began to play, and [the three thieves began] to dance * * * they followed him dancing, as before, so that he led them through the quagmires * * *

### [Bacon Abjures His Magic]

[Bacon] burnt his books [and] shut himself up in a cell, where he lived two years lamenting for his sins, and dug the grave he was buried in with his own nails * * * at two years' end he died a true penitent * * *

---

† From "The Most Famous History of the Learned Friar Bacon" (c. 1590), possibly a common source for both *The Tempest* and Robert Greene's play *Friar Bacon and Friar Bungay*. See John Henry Jones, ed., *The English Faust Book* (Cambridge: Cambridge University Press, 1994), Appendix 4B.

# WILLIAM BIDDULPH

## [An English Conjuror on the High Seas]†

The Master of the ship, called Andrea, and his brother Stephano (being both owners of the ship) said that surely the English Doctor was a conjuror, for they never saw him without a book in his hand, but still reading until (by his learning) he had raised a storm upon them; and thought it best to make a Jonas out of him, and to cast both him and his books into the sea, which they had done indeed, if God (in mercy towards him) had not prevented them.

# REGINALD SCOTT

## [How to Enclose a Spirit]‡

O Sitrael, Malantha, Thamaor, Falaur, and Sitrami, written in these circles, appointed to this work, I do conjure and I do exorcise you, by the father, by the son, and by the holy ghost, by him which did cast you out of paradise, and by him which spoke the word and it was done, and by him which shall come to judge the quick and the dead and the world by fire, that all you five infernal masters and princes do come unto me, to accomplish and to fulfil all my desire and request, which I shall command you. * * * Also I conjure you, and every one of you, you infernal kings, by heaven, by the stars, by the ☉ and by the ☽ and by all the planets, by the earth, fire, air, and water, and by the terrestrial paradise, and by all things in them contained, and by your hell, and by all the devils in it, and dwelling about it, and by your virtue and power, and by all whatsoever, and with whatsoever it be, which may constrain and bind you. Therefore by all these foresaid virtues and powers, I do bind you and constrain you into my will and power, that you being thus bound may come unto me in great humility, and to appear in your circles before me visibly, in fair form and shape of mankind kings, and to obey unto me in all things, whatsoever I shall desire, and that you may not depart from me without my licence. And if you do against my precepts, I will promise unto you that you shall descend into the profound deepness of the sea, except that you do obey unto me,

† From *The Travels of Certain Englishmen into Africa, Asia, Troy, Bythinia, Thracia, and to the Black Sea* (London: Thomas Haveland, 1609), sigs. B2v–B3r.
‡ From *The Discovery of Witchcraft* (London: W. Brome, 1584), pp. 412–13. See Barbara A. Mowat, "Prospero's Book," *Shakespeare Quarterly* 52 (2001): 1–33.

in the part of the living form of God, which lives and reigns in the unity of the holy ghost by all world of worlds, Amen.

\* \* \*

I conjure, charge, and command you, and every one of you, Sitrael, Malantha, Thamaor, Falaur, and Sitrami, you infernal kings, to put into this crystal stone one spirit learned and expert in all arts and sciences, by virtue of this name of God Tetragrammaton, and by the cross of our Lord Jesus Christ, and by the blood of the innocent lamb, which redeemed all the world, and by all their virtues and powers I charge you, you noble kings, that the said spirit may teach, show, and declare unto me, and to my friends, at all hours and minutes, both night and day, the truth of all things both bodily and ghostly in this world whatsoever I shall request or desire, declaring also to me my very name. And this I command in your part to do, and to obey thereunto, as unto your own lord and master.

# Politics and Religion

## Isaiah XXIX†

1   Woe unto thee, o Ariel, Ariel, thou city that David dwelt in: go on from year to year, and let the lambs be slain.

I will lay siege unto Ariel, so that there shall be heaviness and sorrow in it: and it shall be unto me even an altar of slaughter.

I will besiege thee round about, and will fight against thee through a bulwark, and will rear up ditches against thee.

2   *Thou shalt be brought down, and shalt speak out of the ground, and thy speech shall go low out of the dust:*

*Thy voice also shall come up out of the ground, like the voice of a witch, and thy talking shall whisper out of the dust.*

Moreover, the noise of the strange enemies shall be like thin dust, and the multitude of tyrants shall be as dry straw that cannot tarry: even suddenly and in haste shall their blast go.

3   *Thou shalt be visited of the Lord of hosts, with thunder, earthquake, and with a great noise, with storm and tempest, and with the flame of a consuming fire.*

4   *And the multitude* of all nations that fight against Ariel, *shall be as a dream seen by night:* even so shall they be that make war against it, and strong holds to overcome it, and that lay any siege unto it.

5   In conclusion, *it shall be even as when an hungry man dreameth that he is eating, and when he awaketh, his soul is empty, or as when a thirsty man dreameth that he is drinking, when he awaketh, he is yet faint, and his soul hath appetite:* even so shall the multitude of all nations be that fight against Mount Zion.

6   Ponder these things once in your minds, and wonder: *Blinded are they themselves, and the blind guides of other, they are drunken, but not with wine: they are unstable, but not through strong drink:*

*For the Lord hath covered you with a slumbering spirit, and hath closed your eyes:* your prophets also and rulers that should see,

† Translated in *The Bishops' Bible* (1568). See Ann Pasternak Slater, "Variations within a Source: From Isaiah XXIX to *The Tempest,*" *Shakespeare Survey* 25 (1972): 125–35; and Anthony M. Esolen, " 'The isles shall wait for His law': Isaiah and *The Tempest,*" *Studies in Philology* 94.2 (1997): 221–47.

them hath he covered. And the vision of all the prophets, is become unto you as the words of a book that is sealed up, which men deliver to one that is learned, saying, Read thou in it: and he sayeth, I cannot, for it is sealed.

And the book is given to him that is not learned, saying, Read thou in it: and he sayeth, I am not learned.

Therefore thus hath the Lord said, For as much as this people, when they be in trouble, do honor me with their mouth, and with their lips, but their heart is far from me, and the fear which they have unto me, proceedeth of a commandment that is taught of men.

7    Therefore I will do marvels among this people, even marvellous things I say and a wonder: for *the wisedome of their wise men shall perish, and the understanding of their witty men shall hide itself.*

8    *Woe unto them that keep secret their thoughts, to hide their counsel from the Lord, and to do their works in darkness, saying, Who seeth us? and who knoweth us?*

9    *Doubtless your destruction is in reputation as the potter's clay: and doth the work say of him that made it, He made not me? And doth an earthen vessel say of him that fashioned it, He had no understanding?*

Is it not hard at hand that Libanus shall be turned into a low field, and that the low field shall be taken as the wood?

10    And in that day shall deaf men hear the words of the book, and *the eyes of the blind shall see even out of the cloud, and out of darkness. The meek spirited also shall be merry in the Lord, and the poor among them that be lowly shall rejoice* in the holy one of Israel:

*For he that did violence is brought to nought, and the scornful man is consumed, and they rooted out that made haste early to unrighteousness,* Making a man to sin in the world, and that took him in a snare, which reproved them in the open place, *and they that have turned the cause of the righteous to nought.*

Therefore thus sayeth the Lord to the house of Jacob, even thus sayeth he that redeemed Abraham, Jacob shall not now be confounded, nor his face pale. *But when he seeth his children the work of my hands in the midst of him, they shall sanctify my name,* and praise the holy one of Jacob, and fear the God of Israel.

*They also that have been of an erroneous spirit, shall come to understanding, and they that have been scornful shall learn doctrine.*

# SAMUEL PURCHAS

## Virginia's Verger†

This should be, and in most adventurers I hope is the scope of the
Virginian plantation, not to make savages and wild degenerate men
of Christians, but Christians of those savage, wild, degenerate men,
to whom preaching must needs be vain if it begins with public latro-
ciny.[1] And this is sufficient to prevent scruple of the Pope's Bull
which (if Basan Bulls roaring were evidence) makes as well against
England, this being no less questionable than Virginia, with Paul,
Pius, Gregory the Sixth breathing as much fire against the former
as Alexander against the latter. But what right can England then
challenge to Virginia? I answer that we would be loathe to begin
our right at wrong, either to ethnic or Christian; nor need we, having so manifold and just interests. First, as men, we have a natural
right to replenish the whole earth; so that if any country be not
possessed by other men (which is the case of the Summer Islands,
and has been of all countries in their first habitations) every man by
law of nature and humanity has right of plantation and may not by
other after-comers be dispossessed, without wrong to human nature. And if a country be inhabited in some parts, other parts remaining unpeopled, the same reason gives liberty to other men who
want convenient habitations to seat themselves, where (without
wrong to others) they may provide for themselves. For these have
the same right to these latter parts which the former had to the
former, especially where the people are wild and hold no settled
possession in any parts. Thus the holy patriarchs removed their
habitation and pasturages when those parts of the world were not
yet replenished; and thus the whole world has been planted and
peopled with former and later colonies; and thus Virginia has room
enough for her own (were their numbers a hundred times as many)
and for others also who, wanting at home, seek habitations there in
vacant places, with perhaps better right than the first who (being
like Cain, both murderers and vagabonds in their whatsoever and
howsoever own) I can scarcely call inhabitants. To question this
right would be to accuse almost all nations, which were rocked (for
the most part) in no other cradle; and to disappoint also that Divine
Ordinance of replenishing the earth, whose habitations otherwise

---

† From *Haklytus Posthumus or Purchas His Pilgrimes* (1625) (Glasgow: James MacLehose
and Sons, 1906), XIX: 222–25.
1. Robbery.

would be scattered islands in the seas or, like the present Spanish plantations in the Indies, so dispersed and disjoined that one cannot in any distress succour another and therefore are made an easier prey to every invader. Another right is that of merchandise: Non omnia possumus omnes, Nec vero terrae ferre omnes omnia possunt,[2] God in manifold wisdom has diversified every country's commodities, so that all are rich and all poor; not that one should be hungry and another drunken, but that the whole world might be as one body of mankind, each member communicating with others for public good. He has made this immutable decree in the mutability of the winds, commodities, and commodiousness of seas and harbours, variety of bays and rivers, multiplicity of all men's both necessities and superfluities, and their universal desire for novelties. This Solomon and Hiram had right to sail over the ocean and to negotiate with the Ophirians for gems, gold, ivory, and other commodities serviceable for his people's necessities, for pompous magnificence and for the Temple's holies. And if he did not plant colonies there, you must remember that the Jewish Pale was then standing, which prohibited voluntary remote dwellings, where each man was thrice a year to appear before the Lord in Jerusalem. Besides, it is a question whether the country peopled so long before had room for such neighbours.

It is therefore ungodly, and inhuman also, to deny the world to men, or like manger-dogs (neither to eat hay themselves nor to suffer the hungry ox) to prohibit that for others' habitation of which they themselves can make no use; or for merchandise, whereby much benefit accrues to both parts. They who do this, tollunt e vita vitae societatem, to use Tully's phrase, & hominem ex homine tullunt, to borrow St Jerome in another matter.[3] The barbarians themselves by light of nature saw this, and gave our people kind entertainment in mutual cohabitation and commerce; and they having not the law were a law unto themselves, practically acknowledging this law of nature written by him, which is natura naturans, in their hearts; from which if they since have declined, they have lost their own natural and given us another national right, their transgression of the law of nature which ties men to men in the right of nature's commons, exposing them (like a forfeited bond) to the chastisement of that common law of mankind; and also on our parts to the severity of the law of nations, which ties na-

2. All cannot do all (Virgil, *Eclogues*); Nor indeed can all soils bear all things (Virgil, *Georgics*).
3. Cicero's (Tully) phrase is actually *Quid est aliud tollere ex vita vitae societatem, tollere amicorum conloquia absentium?* (What is this but removing from life the social exchanges of life, to remove the communion of friends in absence?—*Phillipics*). St Jerome's words convey a similar sentiment.

tion to nation. And if they be not worthy of the name of a nation, being wild and savage, yet as slaves, bordering rebels, excommunicants, and outlaws are liable to the punishments of law, and not to the privileges, so is it with these barbarians, borderers, and outlaws of humanity. Arma tenenti, omnia dat qui justa negat,[4] If the arms be just, as in this case of vindicating unnatural, inhuman wrongs to a loving and profitable nation, entertained voluntarily in time of greatest pretended amity. On this quarrel David conquered all the kingdoms of the Ammonites and left it to his successors in many generations, notwithstanding Moses had otherwise left a special caution for their security, testifying that God had given it the sons of Lot, and prohibiting invasion to Israel. That natural right of cohabitation and commerce we had with others, this of just invasion and conquest, and many others previous to this, we have above others; so that England may both by law of nature and nations challenge Virginia for her own peculiar propriety, and that by all right and rites usual among men, not those mentioned alone but by others also, first discovery, first actual possession, prescription, gift, cession, and livery of seisin, sale for price, that I mention not the natural inheritance of the English there naturally born, and the unnatural outcries of so many unnaturally murdered, for just vengeance of rooting out the authors and actors of such prodigious injustice.

# GABRIEL NAUDÉ

## [Master Strokes of State]†

Oh what a despicable thing is man, unless he raises himself above human things; that is, unless he have a strong and fixed eye, and, as if he were placed upon some high tower, looks down upon the world, which appears to him as a theatre, ill regulated, and full of confusion, where some act comedies, and other tragedies, and where he may intervene; "Tanquam Deus aliquis ex Machina", like some divinity from a machine, as often as he pleases or the variety of occasions shall persuade him to do it.

 * * * In these master strokes of state, the thunderbolt falls before the noise of it is heard in the skies * * * , prayers are said be-

---

4. He who refuses what is just, gives up everything to him who is armed (Lucan, *Pharsalia*).
† From *Political Considerations upon Refin'd Politicks, and the Master-Strokes of State* (1653), trans. William King (London, 1711), pp. 24, 59–60.

fore the bell is rung for them; the execution precedes the sentence; he receives the blow that things he himself is giving it; he suffers who never expected it, and he dies that looked upon himself to be the most secure; all is done in the night and obscurity, amongst storms and confusion * * * .

# Geography and Travel

## ANONYMOUS

### Primaleon of Greece†

[The Lord of the Island sends one of his sons, Palantine, to greet Primaleon, and courtesies are exchanged. Asking about the island, Primaleon is told about a terrible giant, whom he insists on going to see and then engaging in combat. The giant is captured and proves susceptible to the charms of the Lord's daughter.]

*       *       *

'I come', quoth Palantine, 'on my father's behalf, who is Lord of this Island, to tell you that if you seek nothing else, he is content to let you have whatsoever you need, desiring yourself to come on shore while your people have gotten together your provision.' Primaleon thanked him, saying, for his sake, he would go with him. So, calling Torques and five other knights in his company, he went on land with Palantine, where they were very much gazed on because they had seldom seen any such knights. The Lord of the Isle courteously welcomed them, and while the ships were providing for victuals, Primaleon and the rest spent the time merrily, conferring on many matters with the Lord's son; of whom he demanded the island's spaciousness, and whether it were throughout inhabited or no, because it seemed so fertile and pleasant. 'Sir', answered Palantine, 'the most inhabitant part of this island, is on the sea-side, for the rest is very mountainy, where (no long time since, and yet at this present likewise) hath been seen a people far differing from other, because they are cruel and barbarous, feeding on raw flesh and clothed in wild beasts' skins; beside so ill-favored and deformed as it was a thing right marvellous to behold them, [of] which most usually is seen [he] whom we call Patagon, said to be engendered by a beast in the

---

† From *The Famous and Renowned History of* Primaleon *of Greece, Son to the great and mighty Prince Palmerin d'Oliva, Emperor of Constantinople*, translated into English by A[nthony] M[unday] (London: Thomas Snodham, 1619), Book 2, chap. 32, p. 254; chap. 35, p. 279; Book 3, chap. 32, pp. 169–71; chap. 33, pp. 171–72. See Gary Schmidgall, "*The Tempest* and *Primaleon*: A New Source," *Shakespeare Quarterly* 37 (1986): 423–39. While Books 1 and 2 were published in English in 1595–96, Book 3 did not appear until 1619. Schmidgall suggests that there may well have been an earlier (and now lost) edition.

woods, being the strangest misshapen and counterfeit creature in the
world. He hath good understanding, is amorous of women, * * *
hath the face of a dog, great ears which hang down upon his shoulders, his teeth sharp and big, standing out of his mouth very much;
his feet are like a hart's, and he runneth wondrous lightly.

*    *    *

*Zerphira* * * * went boldly to *Patagon*, bidding him go along with
her, stroking his head and using him very kindly; which made him
forget his former stubbornness and fall at her feet, for he greatly
delighted to gaze fair ladies in the face; so taking his chain in her
hand, he followed after her as gently as if he had been a spaniel.

*    *    *

When dinnertime drew near, they were sent for to come into the
hall, where they sat down every man in his order, as they did
the day before. And after dinner began the Revels, at which time
the Emperor called his daughter *Flerida* and *Prince Edward*, and
said unto them, 'Seeing we are now here assembled in great joy, I
will presently have you espoused together, that my heart may be
wholly satisfied and contented, and the feast complete.' At which
words the Archbishop rose out of his seat, and suddenly espoused
them together, by the means whereof, the joy was so great that all
men thought upon nothing else but upon pleasure and delight. And
at night, after supper, as every man beheld the sports and pastimes
that were made in the hall, suddenly there appeared before them
two wild men, as big as giants, with each of them a shield on his
arm and a great club in his hand, which began so furious a combat
that every man was abashed thereat, especially the ladies, which
had so great fear that they had thought to fly out of the hall if the
knights had not stayed them. * * * Meantime, the wild man and
the serpent fought a most fierce combat, which made a great noise
and rumor to rise in the hall amongst the knights that were there
and knew not what to think thereof. And as they all beheld the
combat, suddenly the serpent vanished away, and there was nothing
seen but a knight apparelled in a rich cloak, that went toward the
Emperor and, kneeling down before him, offered to kiss his hand.
But the Emperor that presently knew him to be the Knight of the
Enclosed Island, rose up joyfully to receive him and said, 'You are
heartily welcome, I am glad to see you in health.' 'My Lord', said
he, 'I am your humble servant, and therefore I was by great reason
bound to do something at so great a feast.' At the sight of this
knight, every man began to be quiet and appeased, all men being
glad of his coming, especially *Maiortes*, for the good that he and all
his friends hoped to receive at his hands, which was to be wholly
delivered out of the long enchantment where he had lived.

The Emperor caused the Knight of the Enclosed Island to be
lodged in the Palace, to honor him the more (for he loved and es-

teemed him much) and then went to his chamber, and every man likewise unto his. *Maiortes* desired *Prince Edward* the next day to solicit the Knight of the Enclosed Island to disenchant him, which he did; and having received the book of the Emperor, gave it unto him, wherewith *Maiortes* left the sword, and presently returned into the shape of a dog, as he was before. Then the Knight, reading in [the] book, knew how to disenchant him; and presently *Maiortes* received the shape of a man again, feeling himself to be in better disposition than he was before, when he had the Sword, and for that cause gave to the Knight many thanks for the great good that he had done unto him.

\* \* \*

# GASPAR GIL POLO

## [A Mediterranean Storm]†

The shepherdess, thou must know, that after my unfortunate marriage was agreed upon, the King's licence being now come, her old Father Eugerius, who was a widower, his son Polydorus, and his two daughters Alcida and Clenarda, and the hapless Marcelius, who is telling thee his grievous accidents, having committed the charges left us by the King to sufficient and trusty gentlemen, embarked ourselves in the port of Ceuta to go by sea to the noble city of Lisbon, there to celebrate (as I said) the marriage rites in presence of the King. The great content, joy, and pleasure which we all had, made us so blind that in the most dangerous time of the year, we feared not the tempestuous waves which did then naturally swell and rage, nor the furious and boisterous winds which in those months with greater force and violence are commonly wont to blow; but committing our frail bark to fickle fortune, we launched into the deep and dangerous sea, heedless of their continual changes and of innumerable misfortunes incident unto them. For we had not sailed far, when angry Fortune chastised us for our bold attempt, because before night came on, the wary Pilot discovered apparent signs of an imminent and sudden tempest. For the thick and dark clouds began to cover the heavens all over, the waves to roar and murmur, and contrary windes to blow on every side. "Oh what sorrowful and menacing signs", said the troubled and timorous pilot: "Oh luckless ship, what perils assail thee, if God of his great goodness and pity do not succour thee?" He had no sooner

† From *The Enamoured Diana*, trans. Bartholomew Yong, included with his translation of George of Montmayor's *Diana* (finished in 1583, published in London: 1598), pp. 393–95. See Peter Bilton "Another Island, Another Story: A Source for Shakespeare's *The Tempest*," *Renaissance Forum* 5/1 [www.hull.ac.uk/renforum/v5no1/bilton.htm].

spoken these words, when there came a furious and violent blast of
wind, that puffed and shook the whole body of the ship, and put it
in so great danger, that the rudder was not able to govern it, but
that tossed up and down by this mighty fury, it went where the
force of the angry waves and winds did drive it. The tempest by little and little with greater noise began to increase, and the raving
billows, covered over with a foamy froth, mightily to swell. The
skies poured down abundance of rain with throwing out of every
part of it fearful lightnings, & threatened the world with horrible
thunders. Then might there be heard a hideous noise of sea monsters, lamentable outcries of passengers, and flapping of the sails
with great terror. The wind on every side did beat against the ship,
and the surges with terrible blows shaking her unsteady sides, rived
and burst asunder the strong and soundest planchers. Sometimes
the proud billow lifted us up to the skies, and by and by threw us
down again into deep gulfs. * * * The Pilot being appalled with so
cruel Fortune, and his skill confounded by the countenance and
terror of the tempest, could now no more govern the tottered rudder. He was also ignorant of the nature and beginning of the winds,
and in a moment devised a thousand different things. The mariners
likewise aghast with the agony of approaching death, were not able
to execute the Master's command, nor (for such lamentations,
noise and outcries) could heare the charge & direction of their
hoarse and painful Pilot. Some strike sail, others turn the mainyard; some make fast again the broken shrouds; others mend and
caulk the riven planks; some ply the pump apace, and some the
rudder; and in the end, all put their helping hands to preserve
the miserable ship from inevitable loss. * * * In the meanwhile, the
forlorn and tossed ship, by the force and violence of the fierce western winds, which by the straits of Gibraltar came blowing as if they
were mad, sailed with greater speed than was expedient for our
safety, and being battered on every side with the cruel blows of en-
vious fortune by the space of a day and a night * * * ran many
leagues in the long Mediterranean sea, wheresoever the force of
the waves & winds did carry her. * * * In the end a fierce and
mighty tempest came so suddenly upon us, that the ship driven on
by the force of a boisterous blast that smit her on the starboard,
was in so great danger of turning bottom up, that she had now her
forepart hidden under the water: whereupon I undid my rapier
from my side (spying the manifest and imminent danger), so that it
might not hinder me and, embracing my Alcida, leaped with her
into the skiff that was fastened to the ship. * * * The next morning,
finding ourselves near to land, we made towards it amain. The two
mariners that were very skilfull in swimming, went not alone to the
wished shore, but taking us out of the boat carried us safely thither.

After we were delivered from the perils of the sea, the mariners drew their skiff to land, and viewing that coast where we arrived, knew that it was the island Formentera. * * *

# WALTER RALEGH

## A Map of Tunis and Carthage†

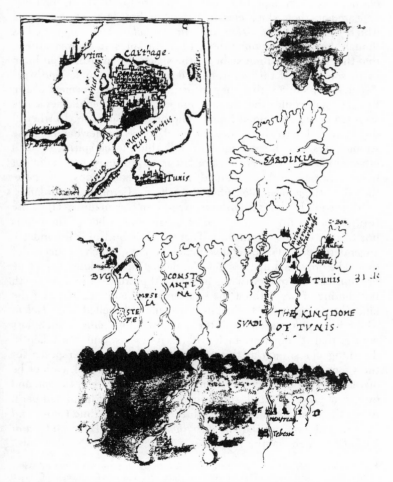

† Illustration from Sir Walter Ralegh's "Notebook" [1606–1608]. Add Ms 57555, f. 20v. Courtesy of The British Library.

# RICHARD EDEN

## [A Voyage to the Patagonians]†

The voyage made by the Spaniards round about the world, is one of the greatest and most marvellous things that have been known to our time.

\* \* \*

In this voyage they saw many strange fishes, & monsters of the sea, beside another strange thing which appeared unto them; for there appeared in their ships certain flames of fire, burning very clear, which they call *Saint Helen, & Saint Nicholas*. These appeared as though they had been upon the mast of the ships, in such clearness, that they took away their sight for the space of a quarter of an hour, by reason whereof they so wandered out of their course, and were dispersed in sunder, that they in manner despaired to meet again. But (as God would) the sea and tempest being quieted, they came safely to their determined course. And before I speak any further of the voyage, I have here thought good to say somewhat of these strange fires, which some ignorant folk think to be spirits, or such other fantasies, whereas they are but natural things, proceeding of natural causes, and engendered of certain exhalations. Of these, therefore, the great Philosopher of our time Hieronymus Cardanus, in his second book *De Subtilitate*, writeth in this manner. There are two manner of fires engendered of exhalations, whereof the one is hurtful, the other without hurt. That which is hurtful is fire indeed, engendered of malicious and venomous vapors, which in success of time take fire as apt matters to be kindled. The other kind is not true fire, but like the matter that is in such old putrefied wood, as giveth the shining of fire without the substance or quality thereof. Of the kind of true fire is the fireball or star commonly called *Saint Helen*, which is sometime seen about the masts of ships, being of such fiery nature, that it sometime melteth brazen vessels, and is a token of drowning, forasmuch as this chanceth only in great tempests; for the vapor or exhalation whereof this fire is engendered, cannot be driven together or compact in form of fire, but of a gross vapor, and by a great power of wind, and is therefore a token of imminent peril. As on the contrary part, the like fires called in old time *Castor and Pollux*, and now named *the two lights of Saint Peter and Saint Nicholas*, which for the most part fall on the cables of the ships,

---

† From *The History of Travel in the West and East Indies*, augmented by Richard Willes (London: Richard Jugge, 1577), pp. 429–36. Eden here draws on the account of Magellan's early-sixteenth-century circumnavigatory voyage written by the Italian nobleman Antonio Pigafetta.

leaping from one to another with a certain fluttering noise like birds, are a token of security, and of the tempest overpassed; for they are but vapors cleaving to the cables, which in success of time, the fire passing from one to another, appear in the similitude of a light candle. They are a token of security because they are little, not slow or gross, whereby they might have joined altogether in one and been thereby more malicious, and lasted longer. . . . But let us now return to the voyage.

When they had sailed past the Equinoctial line, they lost the sight of the North Star, and sailed by the southwest, until they came to a land named the land of *Bressil*, which some call *Brasilia*, being 22 degrees and a half toward the South Pole or Pole Antarctic. This land is continuate and one firm land with the cape of Saint Augustine, which is 8 degrees from the Equinoctial. In this land they were refreshed with many good fruits of innumerable kinds, and found here also very good sugar canes, and divers kinds of beasts and other things which I omit for brevity. They entered into this haven on Saint Lucy's bay, where the sun being their zenith (that is, the point of heaven directly over their heads) they felt greater heat that day than when they were under the Equinoctial line. This land of Brasile is very large and great, and bigger than all Spain, Portugal, France, and Italy, and is most abundant in all things. The people of this country pray to no manner of thing, but live by the instinct of nature, and to the age of 120 and 140 years. Both the men and women go naked, and dwell in certain long houses. They are very docile, and soon allured to the Christian faith.

Thirteen days after that they arrived at the said port, they departed from this land and sailed to the 34th degree and a half toward the Pole Antarctic, where they found a great river of fresh water and certain *cannibals*. Of these they saw one out of their ships of stature as big as a giant, having a voice like a bull. Our men pursued them, but they were so swift of foot that they could not overtake them.* * *

After other 15 days were past, there came four other giants without any weapons, but had hid their bows and arrows in certain bushes. The Captain retained two of these, which were youngest and best made. He took them by a deceit, in this manner, that giving them knives, shears, looking-glasses, bells, heads of crystal, & such other trifles, he so filled their hands that they could hold no more; then caused two pair of shackles of iron to be put on their legs, making signs that he would also give them those chains, which they liked very well, because they were made of bright and shining metal. And whereas they could not carry them because their hands were full, the other giants would have carried them, but the Captain would not suffer them. When they felt the shackles fast about their legs, they began to doubt; but the Captain did put them in comfort, and bade them stand still. In fine, when they saw how they were deceived, they roared like bulls, & cried upon their great devil *Setebos* to help them. Being thus taken, they were immediately separated and put in sundry ships. They could never bind the hands of the other two, yet was one of them with much difficulty overthrown by 9 of our men, & his hands bound; but he suddenly loosed himself and fled, as did also the other that came with them. In their fleeing, they shot of their arrows and slew one of our men. They say that when any of them die, there appear 10 or 12 devils, leaping and dancing about the body of the dead, and seem to have their bodies painted with divers colors, and that among other, there is one seen bigger than the residue, who maketh great mirth and rejoicing. This great devil they call *Setebos*, and call the less *Cheleule*. One of these giants which they took declared by signs that he had seen devils with two horns about their heads, with long hair down to their feet, and that they cast forth fire at their throats both before and behind. The Captain named these people *Patagoni*. The most part of them wear the skins of such beasts whereof I have spoken before; and have no houses of continuance, but make certain cottages, which they cover with the said skins and carry them from place to place. They live off raw flesh, and a certain sweet root which they call *Capar*. One of these which they had in their ships did eat at one meal a basket of biscuit, and drunk a bowl of water at a draught.

They remained five months in this port of *Saint Julian*, where certain of the under-captains conspiring the death of the General were hanged and quartered, among whom the Treasurer *Luigo* of *Mendoza* was one. Certain of the other conspirators he left in the said land of *Patagoni*.* * *

They found that in this strait, in the month of October, the night was not past four hours long. They found in this strait, at every three miles, a safe haven and excellent water to drink; wood also, and fish, and great plenty of good herbs. They think that there is not a fairer strait in the world. Here also they saw certain flying fishes. The other giant which remained with them in the ship named bread *Capar*, water *Oli*, red cloth *Cherecai*, red color *Cheiche*, black color *Amel*; and spoke all his words in the throat. On a time, as one made a cross before him and kissed it, showing it unto him, he suddenly cried *Setebos*, and declared by signs that if they made any more crosses *Setebos* would enter into his body and make him burst. But when in fine he saw no hurt come thereof, he took the cross, and embraced and kissed it oftentimes, desiring that he might be a Christian before his death. He was therefore baptised and named Paul.

*    *    *

# CAPT. WYATT

## [An Atlantic Storm]†

So sailing along by the coast of Virginia we came by the 12th of April, being Friday, so far to the north that we fell with the height of the Bermudas, a climate so far differing from the nature of all others which we had already passed that we might then think ourselves most happy when we were farthest from it. For had I as many tongues as my head has ears, yet might I come too short of the true description of the extremity of the outrageous weather which this place continually affords without any intermission. Often before we have had dangerous gusts, which vanished as suddenly as they happened; but these were always ordinary and their dangers still extraordinary, their dreadful flashing of lightning, the horrible claps of thunder, the monstrous raging of the swelling seas forced up into the air by the outrageous winds, all together conspiring in a moment our destruction, and breathing out, as it were, in one breath the very last blast of our confusion, so that—this being a general axiom of all seafaring men delivered for a verity, both by our English and the Spanish, French, and Portuguese, that hell is no hell in comparison to this, or that this itself is hell without any comparison—all this together did betoken greater grief to us than can be spoken. But these were but preparations for further dangers.

\* \* \*

And although, Right Honourable,[1] the remembrance of our earlier sorrows will be little less than a present death to our daunted spirits, which we did then endure not without great anguish of soul, neither can I resist without bitterness of passion nor your honour hear without pity. For this was our only comfort that, being mortified and resolved to die, of sinful and earthly creatures we were, by yielding nature her due debt, to be made saints for God, truly believing then to be made partakers of His heavenly happiness and every one giving his last farewell to his best and most dearest friends, desirous to see the last end of this sorrowful stratagem. But at last, when through the foggs that rise out of the seas, the blackness of the sky could not be seen for the darkness of the air, when we expected nothing less than splitting of sails, breaking of shrouds, spending of masts, springing of planks—in a word the dreadful devouring of us all by some

---

† From "Robert Dudley's Voyage to the West Indies" [1595], in *The Voyage of Robert Dudley to the West Indies*, ed. George F. Warner (London: Hakluyt Society, 1899), pp. 52–56. See Richard Wilson, "Voyage to Tunis: New History and the Old World of *The Tempest*," *English Literary History* 64 (1997): 333–57.

1. There is nothing to show who is addressed; probably Sir Robert Cecil.

sea-swallowing whirlpool—we were most miraculously delivered. For this fog being converted into so monstruous a shower of rain that it should seem the very windows of heaven were set open that it might with the more speed work our deliverance, fell with such vehemence that it not only allayed the raging of the fearful seas grown and swollen up into an incredible bigness, but broke the heart of that most bitter storm. Thus, while we were all so mated and amazed that, neither hearing what the master said for the whistling and buzzing of the winds, not knowing for fear what to amend, we were most miraculously by the mighty hand of God, past man's capacity and altogether unlooked for of ourselves, delivered.

And before it pleased God to inflict upon us this punishment, he foretold us by his warning messenger, a most rare accident, which the mariners called Santelmo or Corposantie,[2] which appear before any tempestuous weather as a sign of a most dangerous storm. And although the opinions of all writers are variable concerning its true essence, I am persuaded there can be no certain truth delivered about it. The Greeks call it Poliduces, the Latins Castor and Pollux; Pliny writes that it is as much seen on land among a great army of men as at sea among mariners; Virgil seems to confirm this in the second book of the Aeneid, saying that it appeared at the head of Julius Ascanius; and Titus Livius affirms that such a thing appeared on the head of Servius Tullius, the sixth King of the Romans. But however it is variably censured in sundry writers, this is certainly agreed upon: that it foretells some great thing to come, and if it appears in two lights, the goodness comes, and if but one, then some eminent danger is at hand to ensue; for, if just one fire is seen, it presages a most cruel, dangerous, and tempestuous storm, hazarding both ship, goods, and lives of all those who happen to be in it. This is not only confirmed by all sorts of nations which are navigators, like the Spaniards, French, Portuguese, Turks, Moors, indeed all kinds of sea-faring men, but we, to our great peril, were made eyewitnesses, which in my opinion was and is more authentic for us than if we received the reports of thousands of others. It is a fearful tale to tell, and a discourse dreadful to the hearer to have delivered as a truth, that in the night a substance of fire resembling the shape of a fiery dragon should fall into our sails and there remain some quarter of an hour, afterwards falling onto the deck and passing from place to place, ready to set everything on fire, since fire most commonly converts all things into the same substance as itself, which is fire, being the true confirmation of that axiom of Aristotle that *omne tale efficit maius tale*.[3] This, I say, might seem

---

2. Corpo Santo and St. Elmo's Fire are names given to the balls of electric light seen on the masts and yardarms of a ship in stormy weather.
3. Properly *Quod efficit tale, illud est magistale* (What makes another such is more such itself).

dreadful to the hearer, but it was much more dreadful for us, who beheld it with our eyes. This was strange, but the event much more strange, for this fiery dragon, having continued halfway over to the astonishment of us all, vanished without any harm done either to our shipping or to any of our company, except the most strange sequel, as you have already heard in the description of this last storm, and yet not so strange as true.

\* \* \*

# MICHEL DE MONTAIGNE

## [The Cannibals of Brazil]†

I find (as far as I have been informed) there is nothing in that nation that is either barbarous or savage, unless men call that barbarism which is not common to them. As indeed, we have no other aim of truth and reason than the example and idea of the opinions and customs of the country we live in. There is ever perfect religion, perfect policy, perfect and complete use of all things. They are even savage, as we call those fruits wild which nature of herself and of her ordinary progress has produced, whereas indeed they are those which ourselves have altered by our artificial devices and diverted from their common order we should rather term savage. In those are the true and most profitable virtues, and natural properties most lively and vigorous, which in these we have bastardised, applying them to the pleasure of our corrupted taste. And if, notwithstanding, in divers fruits of those countries that were never tilled, we shall find that in respect of ours they are most excellent, and as delicate unto our taste, there is no reason art should gain the point of honour over our great and puissant mother Nature. We have so much by our inventions surcharged the beauties and riches of her works that we have altogether overchoked her; yet wherever her purity shines, she makes our vain and frivolous enterprises wonderfully ashamed.

> *Et veniunt hederæ sponte sua melius,*
> *Surgit et in solis formosior arbutus antris,*
> *Et volucres nulla dulcius arte canunt.*

> Ivies spring better of their own accord,
> Unhaunted plots much fairer trees afford.
> Birds by no art much sweeter notes record.[1]

† From "Of the cannibals" [1580], in *The Essays*, trans. John Florio (London: V. Sims for E. Blount, 1603), pp. 101–2, 104, 106–7.
1. Propertius.

All our endeavour or wit cannot so much as reach to represent the nest of the least birdlet, its contexture, beauty, profit and use, no, nor the web of a silly spider. "All things," says Plato, "are produced either by nature, by fortune, or by art. The greatest and fairest by one or other of the first two, the least and imperfect by the last." Those nations seem therefore so barbarous to me because they have received very little fashion from human wit, and are yet near their original naturalness. The laws of nature do yet command them, which are but little bastardised by ours. And that with such purity as I am sometimes grieved the knowledge of it came no sooner to light at what time there were men who better than we could have judged of it. I am sorry Lycurgus and Plato had it not, for it seems to me that what in those nations we see by experience does not only exceed all the pictures with which licentious Poetry has proudly embellished the golden age and all her quaint inventions to feign a happy condition of man, but also the conception and desire of philosophy. They could not imagine a genuity[2] so pure and simple as we see it by experience, nor ever believe our society might be maintained with so little art and human combination. It is a nation, I would answer Plato, that has no kind of traffic, no knowledge of letters, no intelligence of numbers, no name of magistrate, nor of political superiority, no use of service, of riches or of poverty, no contracts, no successions, no partitions, no occupation but idle, no respect of kindred, but common, no apparel but natural, no manuring of lands, no use of wine, corn, or metal. The very words that import lying, falsehood, treason, dissimulations, covetousness, envy, detraction, and pardon were never heard of amongst them. How dissonant would he find his imaginary commonwealth from this perfection!

> Hos natura modos primum dedit.

> Nature at first uprise
> These manners did devise.[3]

Furthermore they live in a country of so exceeding pleasant and temperate situation that as my testimonies have told me, it is very rare to see a sick body amongst them, and they have further assured me they never saw any man there either shaking with the palsy, toothless, with eyes dropping, or crooked and stooping through age.

\* \* \*

[Discusses their cannibalism]

I am not sorry we note the barbarous horror of such an action, but grieved that prying so narrowly into their faults we are so

2. Simplicity.
3. Virgil, Georgics.

blinded in ours. I think there is more barbarism in eating men alive than to feed upon them being dead, to mangle by tortures and torments a body full of lively sense, to roast him in pieces, to make dogs and swine gnaw and tear him in mammocks[4] (as we have not only read, but seen very lately, yes and in our own memory, not amongst ancient enemies, but our neighbours and fellow-citizens; and what is worse, under pretence of piety and religion) than to roast and eat him after he is dead.

\*     \*     \*

[Remembers speaking to three cannibals who had been brought to Rouen]

Afterward some demanded their advice and would needs know what things of note and admirable they had observed amongst us. They answered three things, the last of which I have forgotten, and am very sorry for it, the other two I still remember. They said first they found it strange that so many tall men with long beards, strong and well-armed, as were about the King's person (it is likely they meant the Switzers of his guard) would submit themselves to obey a beardless child, and that we did not rather choose one amongst them to command the rest. Secondly (they have a manner of phrase whereby they call men but a moiety of men from others),[5] they had perceived there were men amongst us full-gorged with all sorts of commodities, and others who, hunger-starved and bare with need and poverty, begged at their gates; and found it strange these moities so needy could endure such an injustice and that they took not the others by the throat, or set fire to their houses. I talked a good while with one of them, but I had so bad an interpreter, and who did so ill apprehend my meaning, and who through his foolishness was so troubled to conceive my imaginations, that I could draw no great matter from him. Touching that point, wherein I demanded of him what good he received by the superiority he had amongst his countrymen (for he was a captain and our mariners called him king), he told me it was to march foremost in any charge of war. Further I asked him how many men did follow him, he showed me a distance of place, to signify they were as many as might be contained in so much ground, which I guessed to be about 4 or 5,000 men. Moreover, I demanded if, when the wars were ended, all his authority expired; he answered that he had only this left him, which was that when he went on progress and visited the villages depending of him, the inhabitants prepared paths and highways athwart the hedges of their woods for him to pass through at ease. All that is not very ill, but what of that? They wear no kind of breeches or hose.

4. Shreds.
5. They speak of men as halves of each other, that is, in two groups.

# WILLIAM STRACHEY

## [Storms and Strife in Bermuda]†

We were within seven or eight days at the most by Capt. Newport's reckoning of making Cape Henry upon the coast of Virginia, when on St James's day, July 24, being Monday (preparing for no less all the black night before), the clouds gathering thick upon us, and the winds singing and whistling most unusually, which made us cast off our pinnace, towed till then astern, a dreadful storm and hideous began to blow from out of the north-east, which swelling and roaring as it were by fits, some hours with more violence than others, at length it did beat all light from heaven, which, like a hell of darkness turned black upon us, so much the fuller of horror, as in such cases horror and fear are used to overrun the troubled and overmastered senses of us all. Our eyes lay so sensible to the terrible cries and murmurs of the winds, and to the distraction of our company since even the most armed and best prepared among us was not a little shaken. * * *

For four and twenty hours the storm in a restless tumult had blown so exceedingly that we could not apprehend in our imaginations any possibility of greater violence, yet we did still find it, not only more terrible but more constant, fury added to fury, and one storm urging a second more outrageous than the former, whether it so wrought upon our fears, or indeed met with new forces. Sometimes strikes in our ship amongst women and passengers, not used to such hurly and discomforts, made us look upon each other with troubled hearts and panting bosoms; our clamours drowned in the winds, and the winds in thunder. Prayers might well be in the heart and lips, but drowned in the outcries of the officers: nothing was heard that could give comfort, nothing seen that might encourage hope. It is impossible for me, had I the voice of Stentor,[1] and the expression of as many tongues as his throat of voices, to express the outcries and miseries, not languishing, but wasting his spirits, and art constant to his principles but not prevailing. Our sails lay wound up without use and if at any time we bore but a hollocks, or half forecourse, to guide her before the sea, six and sometimes eight men were not enough to hold the whipstaff in the steerage and the tiller below in the gunners' room, by which may be imagined the strength of the storm. The sea swelled above the clouds

---

† From *A True Repertory of the Wreck and Redemption of Sir Thomas Gates, Knight, upon and from the Islands of the Bermudas*, in Samuel Purchas, *Haklytus Posthumas or Purchas His Pilgrimes* (1625) (Glasgow: James MacLehose and Sons, 1906), xix: 5–72.
1. A Greek herald of loud voice, as described by Homer in *The Iliad*.

and gave battle unto heaven. It could not be said to rain, the waters like whole rivers did flood the air. And this I still did observe, that whereas upon the Land, when a storm has poured itself forth once in drifts of rain, the wind has thereby been beaten down and vanquished, and has not lasted long after, here the glut of water (as if it were meanwhile throttling the wind) was no sooner a little emptied and qualified, than instantly the winds (as having now gotten their mouths free and at liberty) spoke louder and grew more tumultuous and malignant. What shall I say? Winds and seas were as mad as fury and rage could make them. For my own part, I had been in some storms before, on the coast of Barbary and Algiers as well as in the Levant, and one even worse in the Adriatic gulf, in a bottom off Candy, so I may well say: Ego quid sit ater Adriae novi sinus, & quid albus Peccet Iapex.[2] Yet all that I had ever suffered gathered together might not hold comparison with this. There was not a moment in which the sudden splitting or instant overturning of the ship was not expected.

\*    \*    \*

During all this time, the heavens look'd so black upon us that it was not possible to observe the elevation of the pole: not a star by night nor a sunbeam by day was to be seen. Only upon the Thursday night Sir George Sommers, being upon the watch, had an apparition of a little round light, like a faint star, trembling and streaming along with a sparkling blaze, half the height of the main mast, and shooting sometimes from shroud to shroud, tempting to settle as it were upon any of the four shrouds. And for three or four hours together, or rather more, half the night it kept with us, running sometimes along the mainyard to the very end, and then returning. At which, Sir George Sommers called several people about him and showed it them: they observed it with much wonder and carefulness, but all of a sudden, towards the morning watch, they lost sight of it, and knew not which way it went. The superstitious seamen make many constructions of this sea-fire, which nevertheless is usual in storms; the same (it may be) which the Greeks were wont in the Mediterranean to call Castor and Pollux, of which, if one only appeared without the other, they took it for an evil sign of great tempest. The Italians and such, who lie open to the Adriatic and Tyrrene Sea, call it Corpo Santo (a sacred body); the Spaniards call it Saint Elmo and have an authentic and miraculous legend for it. Be it what it will, we laid other foundations of safety or ruin than in the rising or falling of it, could it have served us now miraculously to have taken our height by it, it might have stricken amazement and a reverence in our devotions, according to the due of a miracle.

2. Ah! well I know / How Hadria glooms, how falsely clear / The west-winds blow (Horace, Odes).

But it did not light us any whit the more to our known way, as we now ran (as do hoodwinked men) at all adventures, sometimes north and north-east, then north and by west, and in an instant again varying two or three points, and sometimes half the compass. East and by south we steered away as much as we could to bear upright, which was no small carefulness nor pain to do, although we much unrigged our ship, threw overboard much luggage, many a trunk and chest (in which I suffered no mean loss) and stave many a butt of beer, hogsheads of oil, cider, wine, and vinegar, and heaved away all our ordinance on the starboard side, and had now purposed to have cut down the main mast, the more to lighten her, for we were much spent, and our men so weary that their strength altogether failed them, with their hearts, having travailed now from Tuesday till Friday morning, day and night, without either sleep or food, for the leakage taking up all the hold, we could neither come by beer nor fresh water, fire we could keep none in the cook-room to dress any meat, and carefulness, grief, and our turn at the pump or bucket were sufficient to hold sleep from our eyes.

*   *   *

We found it to be the dangerous and dreaded island, or rather islands, of the Bermuda; whereof let me give your Ladyship a brief description before I proceed to my narration. And that the rather, because they be so terrible to all that ever touched on them, and such tempests, thunders, and other fearful objects are seen and heard about them, that they be called commonly, The Devil's Islands, and are feared and avoyded of all sea travellers alive, above any other place in the world. Yet it pleased our merciful God to make even this hideous and hated place, both the place of our safetie, and meanes of our deliverance.

And hereby also, I hope to deliver the world from a foul and general error: it being counted of most, that they can be no habitation for men, but rather given over to devils and wicked spirits; whereas indeed we find them now by experience to be as habitable and commodious as most countries of the same climate and situation; in so much as if the entrance into them were as easy as the place itself is contenting, it had long before this been inhabited, as well as other islands. Thus shall we make it appear that truth is the daughter of time, and that men ought not to deny everything which is not subject to their own sense.

*   *   *

[There are mutinies and rebellions among the company]

In these dangers and devilish disquiets (whilst the almighty God wrought for us, and sent us miraculously delivered from the calamities of the sea, all blessings upon the shore, to content and bind us to gratefulness) thus enraged amongst ourselves, to the destruction each of the others, into what a mischief and misery had we been given up, had we not had a Governor with his authority to have suppressed the same? Yet was there a worse practice, faction, and conjuration afoot, deadly and bloody, in which the life of our Governor, with many others were threatened, and could not but miscarry in his fall. But such is ever the will of God (who, in the execution of his judgments, breaks the firebrands upon the head of him who first kindled them) that there were those who conceived that our Governor indeed neither dared, nor had authority to put into execution, or pass the act of justice upon any one, however treacherous or impious. Their own opinions deceived them so much about the unlawfulness of any act which they would execute, as they dared to justify among themselves that if they should be apprehended before the performance, they should happily suffer as martyrs. They therefore persevered not only to draw in as many associates as they could persuade to the abandoning of our governor and the inhabiting of this island. They had now proposed to have made a surprise of the store-house, and to have forced from thence what was therein either of meal, cloth, cables, arms, sails, oars or what else it pleased God that we had recovered from the wreck, and was to serve our general necessity and needs, either for the relief of us while we stayed here, or for the carrying of us from this place again, when our pinnace should have been furnished.

But as all giddy and lawless attempts have always something of imperfection, and that as well by the property of the action, which holds disobedience and rebellion (both full of fear), as through the ignorance of the devisers themselves; so in this (besides those defects) there were some of the association who, not strongly enough fortified in their own conceits, broke from the plot itself, and (before the time was ripe for its execution) discovered the whole order and every agent and actor of it, who nevertheless were not suddenly apprehended, because the confederates were divided and separated in place, some with us, and the chief with Sir George Summers on his island (and indeed all his company). But good watch was placed upon them, every man from then on was commanded to wear his weapon, without which previously we had freely walked from quarter to quarter and conversed among ourselves, and every man was advised to stand upon his guard, his own life not being in safety, whilst his next neighbour was not to be trusted. The sentinels and nightwatchmen doubled, the passages of both the quarters were carefully observed, by which means nothing was further attempted; until a gentleman among them, one Henry Paine, on the thirteenth of March, full of mischief and every hour preparing something or other, stealing swords, adises, axes, hatchets, saws, augers, planes, mallets, etc to make good his own bad end, his watch night coming about, and being called by the captain of the same to be upon the guard, did not only give his said commander evil language, but struck at him, doubled his blows, and when he was not allowed to close with him, went off the guard, scoffing at the double diligence and attendance of the watch, appointed by the governor for much purpose, as he said: upon which, the watch telling him, if the governor should hear of his insolence, it might turn him to much blame and happily be as much as his life was worth. The said Paine replied with a settled and bitter violence, and in such irreverent terms as I should offend the modest ear too much if I expressed it in his own phrase; but the contents were, how the governor had no authority of that quality to justify upon anyone (however mean in the colony) an action of that nature, and therefore let the governor (said he) kiss etc. Which words, being with the omitted additions brought the next day into every common and public discourse, at length they were delivered over to the governor, who, examining well the fact (the transgression so much the more exemplary and odious, as being in a dangerous time, in a confederate, and the success of the same wishtly[3] listened after, with a doubtful conceit, what might be the issue of so notorious a boldness and impudence) calling the said Paine before him, and the whole company, where (being soon convinced both by the witness of the commander and many who were on the watch with him), our governor, who had now the eyes of the whole colony fixed upon him, condemned him to be instantly hanged; and the ladder being ready, after he had made many confessions, he earnestly desired, being a gentleman, that he might be shot to death, and towards the evening he had his desire, the sun and his life setting together.

\* \* \*

Likewise we buried five of our company, Jeffery Briars, Richard Lewis, William Hitchman, and my god-daughter Bermuda Rolfe, and one untimely Edward Samuell, a sailor, being villainously killed by the foresaid Robert Waters (also a sailor) with a shovel, who struck him therewith under the ear, for which he was apprehended and appointed to be hanged the next day (the fact being done in the twilight), but being bound fast to a tree all night, with many ropes and a guard of five or six to attend him, his fellow sailors (watching the advantage of the sentinels sleeping), in despite and disdain that justice should be showed on a sailor, and that one of their crew should be an example to others, not taking into consideration the unmanliness of the murder, nor the horror of the sin, they cut his

3. Intently.

bands and conveyed him into the woods, where they fed him nightly, and closely. Afterwards, by the mediation of Sir George Summers, upon many conditions, he had his trial respited by our governor.

\* \* \*

# SIR HENRY MAINWARING

## The Seaman's Dictionary†

**Blow.** Every one knows when the wind blows, but there are some speeches used at sea, which are not generally understood, as the wind *blows home*, or *blows through*; that is, when the wind doth not cease, or grow less till it come past that place: also *blow through* is sometimes used, when they think the wind will be so great that it will blow asunder the sails.

**A Butt.** By this word taken indefinitely is meant a vessel or cask, as a butt of wine, etc., but in sea language, thus: a *butt* is properly the end of a plank joining to another, on the outward side of the ship under water.

**Course** is taken for that point of the compass which the ship is to sail upon. . . . *Alter the course*, that is, sail upon another point of the compass; *mistake the course*, that is, not to know how the land lies or which way to go. Also *main course* and *fore course*, *mizen course* are the sails without the bonnets. Not all ships of great burden have *double courses* to hold more wind and give the ship more way in a fresh gale, but in an easy gale they hinder, as do all things that are weighty overhead.

**Fathom.** A fathom is six foot; which, though every one know, I set down to give notice that we measure the length of all our ropes by fathoms, and not by any other measure, as we do the compass of the ropes by inches, for we say a cable or hawser of so many fathom long or so many inches about; also we reckon in sounding by fathoms.

**Split.** When the wind hath blown a sail to pieces, we say the sail is split.

† From *The Seaman's Dictionary* (c. 1623), edited by G. E. Manwaring and W. G. Perrin for The Navy Records Society, 1922.

A **Tempest.** When it overblows so exceedingly that it is not possible to bear any sail, and that it is a wind mixed with rain or hail, they call it a tempest, which they count a degree above a storm.

To **Try.** Trying is to have no more sail forth but the mainsail, the tack aboard, the bowline set up, the sheet close aft, and the helm tied down close aboard. Some try with their mizen only, but that is when it blows so much that they cannot maintain the mainsail. A ship *a-try* with her mainsail (unless it be an extraordinary grown sea) will make her way two points afore the beam; but with a mizen not so much.

# CRITICISM

# JOHN DRYDEN

## [The Character of Caliban]†

To return once more to Shakespeare; no man ever drew so many characters, or generally distinguished them better from one another, excepting only Jonson. I will instance but in one, to show the copiousness of his invention; it is that of Caliban, or the monster, in *The Tempest*. He seems there to have created a person which was not in nature, a boldness which, at first sight, would appear intolerable; for he makes him a species of himself, begotten by an incubus on a witch; but this, as I have elsewhere proved, is not wholly beyond the bounds of credibility, at least the vulgar still believe it. We have the separated notions of a spirit, and of a witch; (and spirits, according to Plato, are vested with a subtle body; according to some of his followers, have different sexes;) therefore, as from the distinct apprehensions of a horse, and of a man, imagination has formed a centaur; so, from those of an incubus and a sorceress, Shakespeare has produced his monster. Whether or no his generation can be defended, I leave to philosophy; but of this I am certain, that the poet has most judiciously furnished him with a person, a language, and a character, which will suit him, both by father's and mother's side: he has all the discontents, and malice of a witch, and of a devil, besides a convenient proportion of the deadly sins; gluttony, sloth, and lust, are manifest; the dejectedness of a slave is likewise given him, and the ignorance of one bred up in a desert island. His person is monstrous, and he is the product of unnatural lust; and his language is as hobgoblin as his person; in all things he is distinguished from other mortals.

# NICHOLAS ROWE

## [The Magic of *The Tempest*]‡

But certainly the greatness of this author's genius nowhere so much appears as where he gives his imagination an entire loose, and raises his fancy to a flight above mankind and the limits of the visible world. Such are his attempts in *The Tempest, Midsummer*

---

† From the Preface to *Troilus and Cressida, or, Truth found too late* (1679), in *Dryden: The Dramatic Works*, ed. Montague Summers (London: Nonesuch Press, 1932), V:21–22.
‡ From *The Works of Mr. William Shakespear* (London: for Jacob Tonson, 1709), 1: xxiii–xxvi.

*Night's Dream, Macbeth* and *Hamlet*. Of these *The Tempest*, however it comes to be placed the first by the former publishers of his works, can never have been the first written by him: it seems to me as perfect in its kind as almost anything we have of his. One may observe that the unities are kept here with an exactness uncommon to the liberties of his writing; though that was what, I suppose, he valued himself least upon, since his excellencies were all of another kind. I am very sensible that he does, in this play, depart too much from that likeness to truth which ought to be observed in these sort of writings; yet he does it so very finely that one is easily drawn in to have more faith for his sake than reason does well allow of. His magic has something in it very solemn and very poetical; and that extravagant character of Caliban is mighty well sustained, shows a wonderful invention in the author, who could strike out such a particular wild image, and is certainly one of the finest and most uncommon grotesques that was ever seen. The observation, which I have been informed three very great men concurred in making upon this part, was extremely just. That Shakespeare had not only found out a new character in his Caliban, but had also devised and adapted a new manner of language for that character. Among the particular beauties of this piece, I think one may be allowed to point out the tale of Prospero in the first act; his speech to Ferdinand in the fourth, upon the making of the masque of Juno and Ceres; and that in the fifth, where he dissolves his charms and resolves to break his magic rod. This play has been altered by Sir William Davenant and Mr Dryden; and though I won't arraign the judgement of those two great men, yet I think I may be allowed to say that there are some things left out by them that might, and even ought, to have been kept in. Mr Dryden was an admirer of our author and, indeed, he owed him a great deal, as those who have read them both may very easily observe. And, I think, in justice to them both, I should not on this occasion omit what Mr Dryden has said of him.

> Shakespeare, *who, taught by none, did first impart*
> *To* Fletcher *wit, to lab 'ring* Johnson *art.*
> *He, monarch-like, gave those his subjects law,*
> *And is that Nature which they paint and draw.*
> Fletcher *reach'd that which on his heights did grow,*
> *Whilst* Johnson *crept and gather'd all below:*
> *This did his love, and this his mirth digest,*
> *One imitates him most, the other best.*
> *If they have since out-writ all other men,*
> *'Tis with the drops which fell from* Shakespeare's *pen.*
> *The storm which vanish'd on the neighb'ring shore,*
> *Was taught by* Shakespeare's Tempest *first to roar.*

*That innocence and beauty which did smile*
*In* Fletcher, *grew on this enchanted isle.*
*But* Shakespeare's *magic could not copied be,*
*Within that circle none dared walk but he.*
*I must confess 'twas bold, nor would you now*
*That liberty to vulgar wits allow,*
*Which works by magic supernatural things;*
*But* Shakespeare's *pow'r is sacred as a king's.*
     Prologue to *The Tempest,* as it is altered
     by Mr Dryden.

It is the same magic that raises the fairies in *Midsummer Night's Dream,* the witches in *Macbeth,* and the ghost in *Hamlet,* with thoughts and language so proper to the parts they sustain, and so peculiar to the talent of this writer. But of the two last of these plays I shall occasion to take notice, among the tragedies of Mr Shakespeare. If one undertook to examine the greatest part of these by those rules which are established by Aristotle, and taken from the model of the Grecian stage, it would be no very hard task to find a great many faults; but as Shakespeare lived under a kind of mere light of nature, and had never been made acquainted with the regularity of those written precepts, so it would be hard to judge him by a law he knew nothing of. We are to consider him as a man that liv'd in a state of almost universal licence and ignorance. There was no established judge, but every one took the liberty to write according to the dictates of his own fancy.

# SAMUEL TAYLOR COLERIDGE

## Notes on *The Tempest*†

\*   \*   \*

*The Tempest* is a specimen of the purely romantic drama, in which the interest is not historical, or dependent upon fidelity of portraiture, or the natural connexion of events,—but is a birth of the imagination, and rests only on the coaptation and the union of the elements granted to, or assumed by, the poet. It is a species of drama which owes no allegiance to time or space, and in which, therefore, errors of chronology and geography—no mortal sins in any species—are venial faults, and count for nothing. It addresses itself entirely to the imaginative faculty; and although the illusion may be assisted by the effect on the senses of the complicated scenery and decorations

† From *The Literary Remains of Samuel Taylor Coleridge,* collected and ed. Henry Nelson Coleridge (London: W. Pickering, 1836), 2: 92–102.

of modern times, yet this sort of assistance is dangerous. For the principal and only genuine excitement ought to come from within,—from the moved and sympathetic imagination; whereas, where so much is addressed to the mere external senses of seeing and hearing, the spiritual vision is apt to languish, and the attraction from without will withdraw the mind from the proper and only legitimate interest which is intended to spring from within.

The romance opens with a busy scene admirably appropriate to the kind of drama, and giving, as it were, the key-note to the whole harmony. It prepares and initiates the excitement required for the entire piece, and yet does not demand any thing from the spectators, which their previous habits had not fitted them to understand. It is the bustle of a tempest, from which the real horrors are abstracted;—therefore it is poetical, though not in strictness natural—(the distinction to which I have so often alluded)—and is purposely restrained from concentering the interest on itself, but used merely as an induction or turning for what is to follow.

In the second scene, Prospero's speeches, till the entrance of Ariel, contain the finest example, I remember, of retrospective narration for the purpose of exciting immediate interest, and putting the audience in possession of all the information necessary for the understanding of the plot. Observe, too, the perfect probability of the moment chosen by Prospero (the very Shakespeare himself, as it were, of the tempest) to open out the truth to his daughter, his own romantic bearing, and how completely anything that might have been disagreeable to us in the magician, is reconciled and shaded in the humanity and natural feelings of the father. In the very first speech of Miranda the simplicity and tenderness of her character are at once laid open;—it would have been lost in direct contact with the agitation of the first scene. The opinion once prevailed, but, happily, is now abandoned, that Fletcher alone wrote for women;—the truth is, that with very few, and those partial, exceptions, the female characters in the plays of Beaumont and Fletcher are, when of the light kind, not decent; when heroic, complete viragos. But in Shakespeare all the elements of womanhood are holy, and there is the sweet, yet dignified feeling of all that *continuates* society, as sense of ancestry and of sex, with a purity unassailable by sophistry, because it rests not in the analytic processes, but in that sane equipoise of the faculties, during which the feelings are representative of all past experience,—not of the individual only, but of all those by whom she has been educated, and their predecessors even up to the first mother that lived. Shakespeare saw that the want of prominence, which Pope notices for sarcasm, was the blessed beauty of the woman's character, and knew that it arose not from any deficiency, but from the more exquisite harmony

of all the parts of the moral being constituting one living total of
head and heart. He has drawn it, indeed, in all its distinctive energies of faith, patience, constancy, fortitude,—shown in all of them
as following the heart, which gives its results by a nice tact and
happy intuition, without the intervention of the discursive faculty,—sees all things in and by the light of affections, and errs, if it
ever err, in the exaggerations of love alone. In all the Shakespearian
women there is essentially the same foundation and principle; the
distinct individuality and variety are merely the result of the modification of circumstances, whether in Miranda the maiden, in Imogen the wife, or in Katharine the queen.

But to return. The appearance and characters of the super or
ultra-natural servants are finely contrasted. Ariel has in every thing
the airy tint which gives the name; and it is worthy of remark that
Miranda is never directly brought into comparison with Ariel, lest
the natural and human of the one and the supernatural of the other
should tend to neutralize each other; Caliban, on the other hand, is
all earth, all condensed and gross in feelings and images; he has the
dawnings of understanding without reason or the moral sense, and
in him, as in some brute animals, this advance to the intellectual
faculties, without the moral sense, is marked by the appearance of
vice. For it is in the primacy of the moral being only that man is
truly human; in his intellectual powers he is certainly approached
by the brutes, and, man's whole system duly considered, those powers cannot be considered other than means to an end, that is, to
morality.

In this scene, as it proceeds, is displayed the impression made by
Ferdinand and Miranda on each other; it is love at first sight;—

> at the first sight
> They have chang'd eyes:—

and it appears to me, that in all cases of real love, it is at one moment that it takes place. That moment may have been prepared by
previous esteem, admiration, or even affection,—yet love seems to
require a momentary act of volition, by which a tacit bond of devotion is imposed,—a bond not to be thereafter broken without vio-
lating what should be sacred in our nature. How finely is the true
Shakespearian scene contrasted with Dryden's vulgar alteration of
it, in which a mere ludicrous psychological experiment, as it were,
is tried—displaying nothing but indelicacy without passion. Prospero's interruption of the courtship has often seemed to me to have
no sufficient motive; still his alleged reason—

> lest too light winning
> Make the prize light—

is enough for the ethereal connexions of the romantic imagination, although it would not be so for the historical. The whole courting scene, indeed, in the beginning of the third act, between the lovers is a masterpiece; and the first dawn of disobedience in the mind of Miranda to the command of her father is very finely drawn, so as to seem the working of the Scriptural command, *Thou shalt leave father and mother*, &c. O! with what exquisite purity this scene is conceived and executed! Shakespeare may sometimes be gross, but I boldly say that he is always moral and modest. Alas! in this our day decency of manners is preserved at the expense of morality of heart, and delicacies for vice are allowed, whilst grossness against it is hypocritically, or at least morbidly, condemned.

In this play are admirably sketched the vices generally accompanying a low degree of civilization; and in the first scene of the second act Shakespeare has, as in many other places, shown the tendency in bad men to indulge in scorn and contemptuous expressions, as a mode of getting rid of their own uneasy feelings of inferiority to the good, and also, by making the good ridiculous, of rendering the transition of others to wickedness easy. Shakespeare never puts habitual scorn into the mouths of other than bad men, as here in the instances of Antonio and Sebastian. The scene of the intended assassination of Alonzo and Gonzalo is an exact counterpart of the scene between Macbeth and his lady, only pitched in a lower key throughout, as designed to be frustrated and concealed, and exhibiting the same profound management in the manner of familiarizing a mind, not immediately recipient, to the suggestion of guilt, by associating the proposed crime with something ludicrous or out of place,—something not habitually matter of reverence. By this kind of sophistry the imagination and fancy are first bribed to contemplate the suggested act, and at length to become acquainted with it. Observe how the effect of this scene is heightened by contrast with another counterpart of it in low life,—that between the conspirators Stephano, Caliban, and Trinculo in the second scene of the third act, in which there are the same essential characteristics.

In this play and in this scene of it are also shown the springs of the vulgar in politics,—of that kind of politics which is inwoven with human nature. In his treatment of this subject, wherever it occurs, Shakespeare is quite peculiar. In other writers we find the particular opinions of the individual; in Massinger it is rank republicanism; in Beaumont and Fletcher even *jure divino* principles are carried to excess;—but Shakespeare never promulgates any party tenets. He is always the philosopher and the moralist, but at the same time with a profound veneration for all the established institutions of society, and for those classes which form the permanent elements of the state—especially never introducing a professional character, as such, otherwise than as respectable. If he must have any name, he should be styled a philosophical aristocrat, delighting in those hereditary institutions which have a tendency to bind one age to another, and in that distinction of ranks, of which, although few may be in possession, all enjoy the advantages. Hence, again, you will observe the good nature with which he seems always to make sport with the passions and follies of a mob, as with an irrational animal. He is never angry with it, but hugely content with holding up its absurdities to its face; and sometimes you may trace a tone of almost affectionate superiority, something like that in which a father speaks of the rogueries of a child. See the good-humoured way in which he describes Stephano passing from the most licentious freedom to absolute despotism over Trinculo and Caliban. The truth is, Shakespeare's characters are all *genera*[1] intensely individualized; the results of meditation, of which observation supplied the drapery and the colors necessary to combine them with each other. He had virtually surveyed all the great component powers and impulses of human nature,—had seen that their different combinations and subordinations were in fact the individualizers of men, and showed how their harmony was produced by reciprocal disproportions of excess or deficiency. The language in which these truths are expressed was not drawn from any set fashion, but from the profoundest depths of his moral being, and is therefore for all ages.

# LUDWIG TIECK

## Shakespeare's Treatment of the Marvellous†

Admiration has often been expressed for Shakespeare's genius, which in so many of his artistic works leaves the common course behind and seeks out new pathways, following the passions now into their most subtle nuances, now to their uttermost bounds, now initiating the spectator into the mysteries of the night, transporting him into the company of witches and ghosts, then again surrounding him with fairies wholly different from those terrible apparitions. Given the boldness with which Shakespeare offends against the customary rules of the drama, we too often overlook the immeasur-

1. Types.
† From "Shakespeare's Treatment of the Marvellous" [1793], trans. Louise Adey, in Jonathan Bate, ed., *The Romantics on Shakespeare* (Harmondsworth: Penguin, 1992), pp. 60–66. Copyright © 1992 Louise Adey. Reprinted by permission of the Penguin group.

ably greater artistry with which he conceals from our notice such want of regularity: for the touchstone of true genius is to be found in the fact that, for every audacious fiction, every unusual angle of depiction, it is able to predispose the mind of the spectator to the acceptance of illusion; that the poet does not presume on our good-will but so excites our imagination, even against our wishes, that we forget the rules of aesthetics, together with all the notions of our enlightened century, and abandon ourselves completely to the lovely delusions of the poet; that after its intoxication the soul will-ingly yields to fresh enchantments and the playful imagination is not awoken from its dreams by any sudden, unpleasant surprise.

In this highest achievement of dramatic art Shakespeare will per-haps remain forever inimitable—that great alchemy which trans-formed everything he touched into gold seems to have died with him. For however much his masterpieces are imitated by his con-temporaries and by later poets, by the English and the Germans, not one of them has ventured to follow him into that magic circle in which he appears so great and so terrible. Those few who have tried to rival him in this appear in comparison to him like conjurors whom no spirit will obey, despite their mysterious spells, their mys-tic circles and all their magical apparatus, and who in the end arouse only boredom because they do not possess the artistry to lull to sleep our powers of reason and judgement.

At the time when he lived, Shakespeare, more than any other writer, was the poet of his people; he did not write for the rabble but for his nation, and so, whether he knew the masterpieces of an-tiquity or not, they were not the tribunal to which he brought his plays, on the contrary, he had learnt what produces an effect on people's minds by studious observation of mankind, and he created his works of art according to his own instinct and the rules which he had derived from experience. This is the reason why most of his plays are so generally effective in performance and when read, and why they must necessarily be effective, for perhaps there is no poet who has calculated the theatrical effect of his works as carefully as Shakespeare, though without treating his audience to hollow *coups de théâtre*, or entertaining them with feeble surprises. He holds their attention rapt to the very end without recourse to the artifices dear to many a calculating poet and without any appeal to curiosity, and he moves them intensely, even to the point of terror, with his bold strokes of genius.

*     *     *

It is primarily through the characters of Ariel and Caliban that Shakespeare creates this whole marvellous world around us; they are, so to speak, the guardians who never permit our minds to re-turn to the realm of reality; in every serious scene we are reminded by the presence of Ariel of where we are, in every comic scene, by that of Caliban. Prospero's magical contrivances, which occur one after the other without interruption, do not for a single moment permit our eyes to return to the reality which would instantly reduce all the chimeras of the poet to dust and ashes. Even the strange contrast between Ariel and Caliban enhances our faith in the marvellous. The creation of that exotic figure was a most felicitous idea on the part of the poet; in this figure he shows us the strangest mixture of absurdity and abomination; this monster is so remote from humanity and is portrayed with such extreme plausibility and conviction that Caliban's presence alone would persuade us that we had been transported to an utterly strange, as yet unknown world * * *

## FANNY KEMBLE

### [Some Notes on *The Tempest*]†
* * *

The opening of this play is connected with my earliest recollections. In looking down the 'dark backward and abysm of time,' [1.2.50] to the period when I was but six years old, my memory conjures up a vision of a stately drawing-room on the ground-floor of a house, doubtless long since swept from the face of the earth by the encroaching tide of new houses and streets that has submerged every trace of suburban beauty, picturesqueness, or rural privacy in the neighbourhood of London, converting it all by a hideous process of assimilation into more London, till London seems almost more than England can carry * * *

[In the drawing-room a lovely-looking lady] used to tell me the story of the one large picture which adorned the room. Over and over again, at my importunate beseeching, she told it,—sometimes standing before it, while I held her hand, and listened with upturned face, and eyes rounding with big tears of wonder and pity, to a tale which shook my small soul with a sadness and strangeness * * * In the midst of a stormy sea, on which night seemed fast settling down, a helmless, mastless, sailless bark lay weltering giddily, and in it sat a man in the full flower of vigorous manhood. His attitude was one of miserable dejection, and, oh, how I did long to remove the hand with which his eyes were covered, to see what manner of look in them answered to the bitter sorrow which the speechless lips expressed! His other hand rested on the fair curls of a girl-baby of three years old,

† From *Notes upon some of Shakespeare's Plays* (London: Richard Bentley & Sons, 1882), pp. 123, 126–28, 131, 132–36, 155–57, 159–61. Line numbers to the play have been added.

who clung to his knee, and, with wide, wondering blue eyes and laughing lips, looked up into the half-hidden face of her father.— 'And that,' said the sweet voice at my side, 'was the good Duke of Milan, Prospero,—and that was his little child, Miranda.'

There was something about the face and figure of the Prospero that suggested to me those of my father; and this, perhaps, added to the poignancy with which the representation of his distress affected my childish imagination. But the impression made by the picture, the story, and the place where I heard the one and saw the other, is among the most vivid that my memory retains. And never, even now, do I turn the magic page that holds that marvellous history, without again seeing the lovely lady, the picture full of sad dismay, and my own six-year-old self listening to that earliest Shakespearian lore that my mind and heart ever received. I suppose this is partly the secret of my love for this, above all other of the poet's plays:—it was my first possession in the kingdom of unbounded delight which he has since bestowed upon me * * *

*The Tempest* is, as I have already said, my favourite of Shakespeare's Dramas. The remoteness of the scene from all known localities allows a range to the imagination such as no other of his plays affords * * *

But chiefly I delight in this play, because of the image which it presents to my mind of the glorious supremacy of the righteous human soul over all things by which it is surrounded. Prospero is to me the representative of wise and virtuous manhood, in its true relation to the combined elements of existence—the physical powers of the external world, and the varieties of character with which it comes into voluntary, accidental, or enforced contact.

Of the wonderful chain of being, of which Caliban is the densest and Ariel the most ethereal extreme, Prospero is the middle link. He—the wise and good man—is the ruling power, to whom the whole series is subject.

First, and lowest in the scale, comes the gross and uncouth but powerful savage, who represents both the more ponderous and unwieldy natural elements (as the earth and water), which the wise Magician by his knowledge compels to his service; and the brutal and animal propensities of the nature of man, which he, the type of its noblest development, holds in lordly subjugation.

Next follow the drunken, ribald, foolish retainers of the King of Naples, whose ignorance, knavery, and stupidity represent the coarser attributes of those great unenlightened masses, which in all communities threaten authority by their conjunction with brute force and savage ferocity; and only under the wholesome restraint of a wise discipline can be gradually admonished into the salutary subserviency necessary for their civilization.

Ascending by degrees in the scale, the next group is that of
the cunning, cruel, selfish, treacherous worldlings—Princes and Po-
tentates—the peers in outward circumstances of high birth and
breeding of the noble Prospero—whose villanous policy (not un-
aided by his own dereliction of his duties as a governor in the pur-
suit of his pleasure as a philosopher) triumphs over his fortune,
and, through a devilish ability and craft, for a time gets the better
of truth and virtue in his person.

From these, who represent the baser intellectual as the former
do the baser sensual properties of humanity, we approach by a most
harmonious moral transition, through the agency of the skilfully in-
terposed figure of the kindly gentleman, Gonzalo, those charming types of youth and love, Ferdinand and Miranda—the fervent
chivalrous devotion of the youth, and the yielding simplicity and
sweetness of the girl, are lovely representations of those natural
emotions of tender sentiment and passionate desire which,
watched and guided and guarded by the affectionate solicitude and
paternal prudence of Prospero, are pruned of their lavish luxuri-
ance and supported in their violent weakness by the wise will that
teaches forbearance and self-control as the only price at which
these exquisite flowers of existence may unfold their blossoms in
prosperous beauty, and bear their rightful harvest of happiness as
well as pleasure.

Next in this wonderful gamut of being, governed by the sovereign
soul of Prospero, come the shining figures of the Masque—beautiful bright apparitions, fitly indicating the air, the fire, and all the
more smiling aspects and subtler forces of nature * * *

Last—highest of all—crowning with a fitful flame of lambent
brightness this poetical pyramid of existence, flickers and flashes
the beautiful Demon, without whose exquisite companionship we
never think of the royal Magician with his grave countenance of
command—Ariel seems to me to represent the keenest perceiving
intellect—apart from all moral consciousness and sense of responsibility. His power and knowledge are in some respects greater than
those of his master—he can do what Prospero cannot—he lashes
up the Tempest round the Island—he saves the King and his
companions from the shipwreck—he defeats the conspiracy of Sebastian and Antonio, and discovers the clumsy plot of the beast
Caliban—he wields immediate influence over the elements, and
comprehends alike without indignation or sympathy—which are
moral results—the sin and suffering of humanity. Therefore, because he is only a spirit of knowledge, he is subject to the spirit of
love—and the wild, subtle, keen, beautiful, powerful creature is
compelled to serve with mutinous waywardness and unwilling subjection the human soul that pitied and rescued it from its harsher

slavery to sin—and which, though controlling it with a wise severity
to the fulfilment of its duties, yearns after it with the tearful eyes of
tender human love when its wild wings flash away into its newly-
recovered realm of lawless liberty * * *

Brought up in all but utter solitude, under no influence but that
of her wise and loving father on earth, and her wise and loving
Father in Heaven, Miranda exhibits no more coyness in her acceptance of Ferdinand's overtures than properly belongs to the
instinctive modesty of her sex, unenhanced by any of the petty
pretty arts of coquetry and assumed shyness, which are the express
result of artificial female training . . . [She] offers her life to her
lover with the perfect devotion and humility of the true womanly
nature:—

> To be your fellow
> You may deny me, but I'll be your servant
> Whether you will or no.
> [3.1.84–6]

In the purity and simplicity of this 'tender of affection,' Ferdinand
made acquaintance with a species of modesty to which assuredly
none of those ladies of the Court of Naples, 'whom he had eyed
with best regard,' [3.1.40] had ever introduced him; and indeed to
them Miranda's proceeding might very probably have appeared
highly unlady-like, as I have heard it pronounced more than once
by—ladies * * *

But Prospero was after all a mere man, and knew no better than
to bring up Miranda to speak the truth, and the fair child had been
so holily trained by him, that her surrender of herself to the man
she loves is so little feminine after the approved feminine fashion,
that it is simply angelic.

That Shakespeare, who indeed knew all things, knew very well
the difference between such a creature as Miranda and a well-
brought-up young lady, is plain enough, when he makes poor Juliet,
after her passionate confession of love made to the stars, and over-
heard by Romeo, apologise to him with quite pathetic mortifica-
tion for not having been more 'strange' [Romeo and Juliet,
II.ii.101]. She regrets extremely her unqualified expressions of affection,—assures Romeo that nothing would have induced her to
have spoken the truth, if she had only known he heard her, and
even offers * * * to 'frown and be perverse and say him nay,'
[II.ii.96]—and in short has evidently shocked her own conventional
prejudices quite as much as she fears she has his * * * But then
Juliet was the flower of Veronese young ladies, and her good
mother, and gossiping nurse, were not likely to have neglected her
education to the tune of letting her speak the truth without due

preparation. Miranda is to be excused as a savage—probably Ferdinand thought her excusable.

# HENRY JAMES

## [Surrendering to *The Tempest*]†

\* \* \* Everything has thus been attributed to the piece before us, and every attribution so made has been in turn brushed away; merely to glance at such a monument to the interest inspired is to recognise a battleground of opposed factions, not a little enveloped in sound and smoke. Of these copious elements, produced for the most part of the best intention, we remain accordingly conscious; so that to approach the general bone of contention, as we can but familiarly name it, for whatever purpose, we have to cross the scene of action at a mortal risk, making the fewest steps of it and trusting to the probable calm at the centre of the storm. There in fact, though there only, we find that serenity; find the subject itself intact and unconscious, seated as unwinking and inscrutable as a divinity in a temple, save for that vague flicker of derision, the only response to our interpretative heat, which adds the last beauty to its face.

\* \* \*

One can speak, in these matters, but from the impression determined by one's own inevitable standpoint; again and again, at any rate, such a masterpiece puts before me the very act of the momentous conjunction taking place for the poet, at a given hour, between his charged inspiration and his clarified experience: or, as I should perhaps better express it, between his human curiosity and his aesthetic passion. Then, if he happens to have been, all his career, with his equipment for it, more or less the victim and the slave of the former, he yields, by way of a change, to the impulse of allowing the latter, for a magnificent moment, the upper hand. The human curiosity, as I call it, is always there—with no more need of making provision for it than use in taking precautions against it; the surrender to the luxury of expertness may therefore go forward on its own conditions. I can offer no better description of *The Tempest* as fresh re-perusal lights it for me than as such a surrender, sublimely enjoyed; and I may frankly say that, under this impression of it, there is no refinement of the artistic consciousness that I do not see my way—or feel it, better, perhaps, since we but grope,

† From *The Complete Works of William Shakespeare*, ed. Sidney Lee, Vol. 16 (New York: George D. Sproul, 1907), pp. ix–xxxii.

at the best, in our darkness—to attribute to the author. It is a way that one follows to the end, because it is a road, I repeat, on which one least misses some glimpse of him face to face. If it be true that the thing was concocted to meet a particular demand, that of the master of the King's revels, with his prescription of date, form, tone and length, this, so far from interfering with the Poet's perception of a charming opportunity to taste for *himself*, for himself above all, and as he had almost never so tasted, not even in *A Midsummer Night's Dream*, of the quality of his mind and the virtue of his skill, would have exceedingly favoured the happy case. Innumerable one may always suppose these delicate debates and intimate understandings of an artist with himself. 'How much *taste*, in the world, may I conceive that I have?—and what a charming idea to snatch a moment for finding out! What moment could be better than this— a bridal evening before the Court, with extra candles and the handsomest company—if I can but put my hand on the right "scenario"?' We can catch, across the ages, the searching sigh and the look about; we receive the stirred breath of the ripe, amused genius; and, stretching, as I admit I do at least, for a still closer conception of the beautiful crisis, I find it pictured for me in some such presentment as that of a divine musician who, alone in his room, preludes or improvises at close of day. He sits at the harpsichord, by the open window, in the summer dusk; his hands wander over the keys. They stray far, for his motive, but at last he finds and holds it; then he lets himself go, embroidering and refining: it is the thing for the hour and his mood. The neighbours may gather in the garden, the nightingale be hushed on the bough; it is none the less a private occasion, a concert of one, both performer and auditor, who plays for his own ear, his own hand, his own innermost sense, and for the bliss and capacity of his instrument. Such are the only hours at which the artist *may*, by any measure of his own (too many things, at others, make heavily against it); and their challenge to him is irresistible if he has known, all along, too much compromise and too much sacrifice.

The face that beyond any other, however, I seem to see *The Tempest* turn to us is the side on which it so superlatively speaks of that endowment for Expression, expression as a primary force, a consuming, an independent passion, which was the greatest ever laid upon man. It is for Shakespeare's power of constitutive speech quite as if he had swum into our ken with it from another planet, gathering it up there, in its wealth, as something antecedent to the occasion and the need, and if possible quite in excess of them; something that was to make of our poor world a great flat table for receiving the glitter and clink of outpoured treasure. The idea and the motive are more often than not so smothered in it that they scarce know themselves, and the resources of such a style, the provision of images, emblems, energies of every sort, laid up in advance, affects us as the storehouse of a king before a famine or a siege—which not only, by its scale, braves depletion or exhaustion, but bursts, through mere excess of quantity or presence, out of all doors and windows. It renders the poverties and obscurities of our world, as I say, in the dazzling terms of a richer and better. It constitutes, by a miracle, more than half the author's material; so much more usually does it happen, for the painter or the poet, that life itself, in its appealing, overwhelming crudity, offers itself as the paste to be kneaded. Such a personage works in general in the very elements of experience; whereas we see Shakespeare working predominantly in the terms of expression, *all* in the terms of the artist's specific vision and genius; with a thicker cloud of images to attest his approach, at any point than the comparatively meagre given case ever has to attest its own identity. He points for us as no one else the relation of style to meaning and of manner to motive; a matter on which, right and left, we hear such rank ineptitudes uttered. Unless it be true that these things, on either hand, are inseparable; unless it be true that the phrase, the cluster and order of terms, *is* the object and the sense, in as close a compression as that of body and soul, so that any consideration of them as distinct, from the moment style is an active, applied force, becomes a gross stupidity: unless we recognise this reality the author of *The Tempest* has no lesson for us. It is by his expression of it exactly as the expression stands that the particular thing is created, created as interesting, as beautiful, as strange, droll or terrible—as related, in short, to our understanding or our sensibility; in consequence of which we reduce it to naught when we begin to talk of either of its presented parts as matters by themselves.

\* \* \*

So it is then; and it puts into a nutshell the eternal mystery, the most insoluble that ever was, the complete rupture, for our understanding, between the Poet and the Man. There are moments, I admit, in this age of sound and fury, of connections, in every sense, too maddeningly multiplied, when we are willing to let it pass as a mystery, the most soothing, cooling, consoling too perhaps, that ever was. But there are others when, speaking for myself, its power to torment us intellectually seems scarcely to be borne; and we know these moments best when we hear it proclaimed that a comfortable clearness reigns. I have been for instance reading over Mr. Halliwell-Phillipps, and I find him apparently of the opinion that it is all our fault if everything in our author's story, and above all in this last chapter of it, be not of a primitive simplicity. The complexity arises from our suffering our imagination to meddle with the

Man at all; who is quite sufficiently presented to us on the face of the record. For critics of this writer's complexion the only facts we are urgently concerned with are the facts of the Poet, which are abundantly constituted by the Plays and the Sonnets. The Poet is *there*, and the Man is outside: the Man is for instance in such a perfectly definite circumstance as that he could never miss, after *The Tempest*, the key of his piano, as I have called it, since he could play so freely with the key of his cash-box. The supreme master of expression had made, before fifty, all the money he wanted; therefore what was there more to express? This view is admirable if you can get your mind to consent to it. It must ignore any impulse, in presence of Play or Sonnet (whatever vague stir behind either may momentarily act as provocation) to try for a lunge at the figured arras. In front of the tapestry sits the immitigably respectable person whom our little slateful of gathered and numbered items, heaven knows, does amply account for, since there is nothing in him to explain; while the undetermined figure, on the other hand—undetermined whether in the sense of respectability or of anything else—the figure who supremely interests us, remains as unseen of us as our Ariel, on the enchanted island, remains of the bewildered visitors. Mr. Halliwell-Phillipp's theory, as I understand it—and I refer to it but as an advertisement of a hundred others—is that we too are but bewildered visitors, and that the state of mind of the Duke of Naples and his companions is our proper critical portion.

* * * We stake our hopes thus on indirectness, which may contain possibilities; we take that very truth for our counsel of despair, try to look at it as helpful for the Criticism of the future. That of the past has been too often infantile; one has asked one's self how it *could*, on such lines, get at him. The figured tapestry, the long arras that hides him, is always there, with its immensity of surface and its proportionate underside. May it not then be but a question, for the fulness of time, of the finer weapon, the sharper point, the stronger arm, the more extended lunge?

# LYTTON STRACHEY

## Shakespeare's Final Period†

Is it not thus, then, that we should imagine him in the last years of his life? Half enchanted by visions of beauty and loveliness, and half bored to death; on the one side inspired by a soaring fancy to

† From *Books and Characters* (London: Chatto & Windus, 1922), pp. 60–64. Line numbers to the play have been added.

the singing of ethereal songs, and on the other urged by a general disgust to burst occasionally through his torpor into bitter and violent speech? If we are to learn anything of his mind from his last works, it is surely this.

And such is the conclusion which is particularly forced upon us by a consideration of the play which is in many ways most typical of Shakespeare's later work, and the one which critics most consistently point to as containing the very essence of his final benignity—*The Tempest*. There can be no doubt that the peculiar characteristics which distinguish *Cymbeline* and *The Winter's Tale* from the dramas of Shakespeare's prime, are present here in a still greater degree. In *The Tempest*, unreality has reached its apotheosis. Two of the principal characters are frankly not human beings at all; and the whole action passes, through a series of impossible occurrences, in a place which can only by courtesy be said to exist. The Enchanted Island, indeed, peopled, for a timeless moment, by this strange fantastic medley of persons and of things, has been cut adrift for ever from common sense, and floats, buoyed up by a sea, not of waters, but of poetry. Never did Shakespeare's magnificence of diction reach more marvellous heights than in some of the speeches of Prospero, or his lyric art a purer beauty than in the songs of Ariel; nor is it only in these ethereal regions that the triumph of his language asserts itself. It finds as splendid a vent in the curses of Caliban:

> All the infection that the sun sucks up
> From bogs, fens, flats, on Prosper fall, and make him
> By inch-meal a disease!        [2.2.1–3]

and in the similes of Trinculo:

> Yond' same black cloud, yond' huge one, looks like a foul bombard that would shed his liquor.        [2.2.20–21]

The *dénouement* itself, brought about by a preposterous piece of machinery, and lost in a whirl of rhetoric, is hardly more than a peg for fine writing.

> O, it is monstrous, monstrous!
> Methought the billows spoke and told me of it;
> The winds did sing it to me; and the thunder,
> That deep and dreadful organ-pipe, pronounced
> The name of Prosper; it did bass my trespass.
> Therefore my son i' th' ooze is bedded, and
> I'll seek him deeper than e'er plummet sounded,
> And with him there lie mudded.        [3.3.95–102]

And this gorgeous phantasm of a repentance from the mouth of the pale phantom Alonzo is a fitting climax to the whole fantastic play.

A comparison naturally suggests itself, between what was perhaps
the last of Shakespeare's completed works, and that early drama
which first gave undoubted proof that his imagination had taken
wings. The points of resemblance between *The Tempest* and *A Midsummer Night's Dream*, their common atmosphere of romance and
magic, the beautiful absurdities of their intrigues, their studied contrasts of the grotesque with the delicate, the ethereal with the
earthy, the charm of their lyrics, the *verve* of their vulgar comedy—
these, of course, are obvious enough; but it is the points of difference which really make the comparison striking. One thing, at any
rate, is certain about the wood near Athens—it is full of life. The
persons that haunt it—though most of them are hardly more than
children, and some of them are fairies, and all of them are too
agreeable to be true—are nevertheless substantial creatures, whose
loves and jokes and quarrels receive our thorough sympathy; and the
air they breathe—the lords and the ladies, no less than the mechanics and the elves—is instinct with an exquisite good-humour, which
makes us as happy as the night is long. To turn from Theseus and
Titania and Bottom to the Enchanted Island, is to step out of a
country lane into a conservatory. The roses and the dandelions have
vanished before preposterous cactuses, and fascinating orchids too
delicate for the open air; and, in the artificial atmosphere, the gaiety
of youth has been replaced by the disillusionment of middle age.
Prospero is the central figure of *The Tempest*; and it has often been
wildly asserted that he is a portrait of the author—an embodiment
of that spirit of wise benevolence which is supposed to have thrown
a halo over Shakespeare's later life. But, on closer inspection, the
portrait seems to be as imaginary as the original. To an irreverent
eye, the ex-Duke of Milan would perhaps appear as an unpleasantly
crusty personage, in whom a twelve years' monopoly of the conversation had developed an inordinate propensity for talking. These
may have been the sentiments of Ariel, safe at the Bermoothes; but
to state them is to risk at least ten years in the knotty entrails of an
oak, and it is sufficient to point out, that if Prospero is wise, he is
also self-opinionated and sour, that his gravity is often another name
for pedantic severity, and that there is no character in the play to
whom, during some part of it, he is not studiously disagreeable. But
his Milanese countrymen are not even disagreeable; they are simply
dull. 'This is the silliest stuff that e'er I heard,' remarked Hippolyta
of Bottom's amateur theatricals; and one is tempted to wonder what
she would have said to the dreary puns and interminable conspiracies of Alonzo, and Gonzalo, and Sebastian, and Antonio, and
Adrian, and Francisco, and other shipwrecked noblemen. At all
events, there can be little doubt that they would not have had the
entrée at Athens.

The depth of the gulf between the two plays is, however, best measured by a comparison of Caliban and his masters with Bottom and his companions. The guileless group of English mechanics, whose sports are interrupted by the mischief of Puck, offers a strange contrast to the hideous trio of the 'jester,' the 'drunken butler,' and the 'savage and deformed slave,' whose designs are thwarted by the magic of Ariel. Bottom was the first of Shakespeare's masterpieces in characterisation, Caliban was the last: and what a world of bitterness and horror lies between them! The charming coxcomb it is easy to know and love; but the 'freckled whelp hag-born' moves us mysteriously to pity and to terror, eluding us for ever in fearful allegories, and strange coils of disgusted laughter and phantasmagorical tears. The physical vigour of the presentment is often so remorseless as to shock us. 'I left them,' says Ariel, speaking of Caliban and his crew:

> I' the filthy-mantled pool beyond your cell,
> There dancing up to the chins, that the foul lake
> O'erstunk their feet.                    [4.1.182–84]

But at other times the great half-human shape seems to swell, like the 'Pan' of Victor Hugo, into something unimaginably vast.

> You taught me language, and my profit on't
> Is, I know how to curse.                    [1.2.362–63]

Is this Caliban addressing Prospero, or Job addressing God? It may be either; but it is not serene, nor benign, nor pastoral, nor 'On the Heights.'

# G. WILSON KNIGHT

## [Prospero's Lonely Magic]†

\* \* \*

Now on the island of *The Tempest* Prospero is master of his lonely magic. He has been there for twelve years. Two creatures serve him: Ariel, the 'airy nothing' of poetry; and the snarling Caliban, half-beast, half-man; the embodiment of the hate-theme. These two creatures are yoked in the employ of Prospero, like Plato's two steeds of the soul, the noble and the hideous, twin potentialities of the human spirit. Caliban has been mastered by Prospero and Ariel. Though he revolts against his master still, the issue is not in doubt,

---

† From "Myth and Miracle" [1929], in his *The Crown of Life* (London: Methuen, 1947), pp. 25–28. By kind permission of Francis Berry. Line numbers to this Norton Critical Edition appear in brackets when they differ from the author's original citation.

and the tunes of Ariel draw out his very soul in longing and desire, just as the power of poetry shows forth the majesty of Timon, whose passion makes of universal hate a noble and aspiring thing. These three are the most vital and outstanding figures in the play: for Shakespeare had only to look inward to find them. But there are other elements that complete the pattern of this self-revelation.

Prospero's enemies are drawn to the magic island of great poetry by means of a tempest raised by Prospero with the help of Ariel. In Alonso, despairing and self-accusing, bereft of his child, we can see traces of the terrible end of *Lear*; in Antonio and Sebastian, the tempter and the tempted, plotting murder for a crown, we can see more than traces of *Macbeth*. But, driven by the tempest-raising power of tragic and passionate poetry within the magic circle of Prospero and Ariel, these hostile and evil things are powerless: they can only stand spell-stopped. They are enveloped in the wondrous laws of enchantment on the island of song and music. Caliban, who has been mastered by it, knows best the language to describe the mystic tunes of Ariel:

> Be not afeard; the isle is full of noises,
> Sounds and sweet airs that give delight and hurt not.
> Sometimes a thousand twangling instruments
> Will hum about mine ears, and sometimes voices,
> That, if I then had waked after long sleep,
> Will make me sleep again; and then, in dreaming,
> The clouds methought would open and show riches
> Ready to drop upon me, that, when I waked,
> I cried to dream again.     (III.ii.147[135–43])

The protagonists of murder and bereavement are exquisitely en-trapped in the magic and music of Prospero and his servant Ariel. So, too, were the evil things of life mastered by the poetry of the great tragedies, and transmuted into the vision of the myths. The spirit of the Final Plays also finds its perfected home in this last of the series. Here the child-theme is repeated in Miranda, cast adrift with her father on the tempestuous seas; here the lost son of Alonso is recovered, alive and well, and the very ship that was wrecked is found to be miraculously 'tight and yare and bravely rigg'd' as when it 'first put out to sea.' (V.i.224[223–24]). Prospero, like Cerimon over Thaisa, revives, with music, the numbed con-sciousness of Alonso and his companions; and, as they wake, it is as though mortality were waking into eternity. And this thought makes necessary a statement and a distinction as to the dual possible ap-proaches to the significance of *The Tempest*.

First, we can regard it as the poet's expression of a view of hu-man life. With the knowledge of Shakespeare's poetic symbolism in

memory, we will think of the wreck as suggesting the tragic destiny
of man, and the marvellous survival of the travellers and crew as
another and more perfectly poetic and artistic embodiment of the
thought expressed through the medium of anthropomorphic theology in *Cymbeline* that there exists a joy and a revival that makes
past misery, in Pericles' phraseology, 'sport.' According to this reading Prospero becomes in a sense the 'God' of the *Tempest*-universe,
and we shall find compelling suggestion as to the immortality of
man in such lines as Ariel's when Prospero asks him if the victims
of the wreck are safe:

> Not a hair perish'd;
> On their sustaining garments not a blemish,
> But fresher than before.         (I.ii.217[217–19])

So, too, thinking of sea-storms and wreckages as Shakespeare's
symbols of human tragedy, we shall find new significance in Ariel's
lines:

> Nothing of him that doth fade,
> But doth suffer a sea-change
> Into something rich and strange.  (I.ii.397[398–400])

Especially, if we remember that the soul's desire of love in Shakespeare is consistently imaged as a rich something set far across
tempestuous seas, we shall receive especial delight in the song:

> Come unto these yellow sands,
>   And then take hands:
> Curtsied when you have, and kiss'd
>   The wild waves whist.          (I.ii.375[374–77])

Commentators divide into two camps and argue long as to the syn-
tax and sense of those last two lines: is 'whist,' or is it not, they say,
a nominative absolute? And if not, how can waves be kiss'd? A
knowledge of Shakespeare's imagery, however, is needed to see the
triumphant mysticism of the dream of love's perfected fruition in
eternity stilling the tumultuous waves of time. This is one instance
of many where the imaginative interpretation of a poet, and a
knowledge of his particular symbolism, short-circuits the travails
and tribulations of the grammarian or the commentator who in
search for facts neglects the primary facts of all poetry—its suggestion, its colour, its richness of mental association, its appeal, not to
the intellect, but the imagination.

  The second approach is this, which I have already indicated. *The
Tempest* is a record, crystallized with consummate art into a short
play, * * * of the spiritual progress from 1599 or 1600 to the year
1611, or whenever, exactly, *The Tempest* was written. According to

this reading Prospero is not God, but Shakespeare—or rather the controlling judgement of Shakespeare, since Ariel and Caliban are also representations of dual minor potentialities of his soul. From this approach three incidents in the play reveal unique interest. First, the dialogue between Prospero and Ariel in 1.2. where Ariel is tired and cries for the promised freedom, and is told that there is one last work to be done—which is in exact agreement with my reading of the faltering art of *Cymbeline*; second, Prospero's well-known farewell to his art, where commentators have seldom failed to admit what Professor Saintsbury calls a 'designed personal allegory,' and where I would notice that Prospero clearly regards his art as pre-eminently a tempest-raising magic, and next refers to the opening of graves at his command, thereby illustrating again the sequence from tragedy to myth which I have described; and third, Prospero's other dialogue with Ariel in 5.1 where Ariel pities the enemies of his master and draws from Prospero the words:

Hast thou, which art but air, a touch, a feeling
Of their afflictions, and shall not myself,
One of their kind, that relish all as sharply,
Passion as they, be kindlier moved than thou art? (V.i.21[21–24])

In poetic creation 'all is forgiven, and it would be strange not to forgive'; but the partial and fleeting flame of the poet's intuition may light at last the total consciousness with the brilliance of a cosmic apprehension. This speech suggests the transit from the intermittent love of poetic composition to the perduring love of the mystic.

Now these two methods of approach considered separately and in sequence are not so significant as they become when we realize that they are simultaneously possible and, indeed, necessary. Together they are complementary to *The Tempest*'s unique reality. For it will next be seen that these two aspects when considered together give us a peculiar knowledge of this act of the poet's soul in the round: so that the usual flat view of it which reads it as an impersonal fairy story—corresponding to my reading of it as an objective vision of life—becomes a three-dimensional understanding when we remember the implicit personal allegory. Only by submitting our faculties to both methods can we properly understand the play to the full. *The Tempest* is at the same time a record of Shakespeare's spiritual progress and a statement of the vision to which that progress has brought him. It is apparent as a dynamic and living act of the soul, containing within itself the record of its birth: it is continually re-writing itself before our eyes. Shakespeare has in this play so become master of the whole of his own mystic universe that that universe, at last perfectly projected in one short play into the forms and shapes of objective human existence, shows us, in the wreck of *The Tempest*, a complete view of that existence, no longer as it normally appears to man, but as it takes reflected pattern in the still depths of the timeless soul of poetry. And, since it reveals its vision not as a statement of absolute truth independently of the author, but related inwardly to the succession of experiences that condition and nurture its own reality, it becomes, in a unique sense beyond other works of art, an absolute. There is thus now no barrier between the inward and the outward, expression and imitation. God, it has been said, is the mode in which the subject-object distinction is transcended. Art aspires to the perfected fusion of expression with imitation. *The Tempest* is thus at the same time the most perfect work of art and the most crystal act of mystic vision in our literature.

# G. WILSON KNIGHT

## A Chart of Shakespeare's Dramatic Universe†

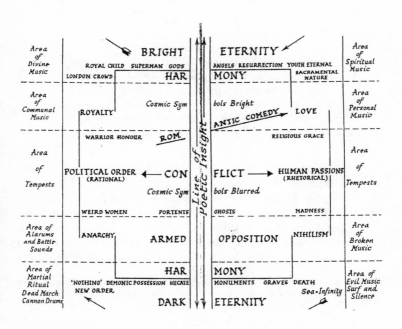

† From *The Shakespearean Tempest, with a Chart of Shakespeare's Dramatic Universe* (Oxford: Oxford University Press, 1932). By kind permission of Francis Berry.

# FRANK KERMODE

## [Art vs. Nature]†

1. *Buds of Nobler Race.* The civilized castaways of *The Tempest* are brought into close contact with a representative of Nature uncontrolled by Art. How do they differ from Caliban, and how is this difference expressed?

It is useful to compare Spenser's treatment of two salvage men in *The Faerie Queene*. The one who carries off Amoret in Book IV is an unamiable personification of greedy lust—"For he liv'd all on ravin and on rape" (IV. vii. 5). The full description leaves no doubt that this is the wild man of the entertainments, and that his arethe "natural" activities of lust and cannibalism. The salvage[1] man who treats Serena so gently in the sixth book is quite different; though he cannot speak he shows a tenderness which is, apparently, against his nature. The reason is, that "he was borne of noble blood" (VI. v. 2); we do not hear how he came to be languageless and salvage, but we know he owes his gentleness to his gentle birth.

> O what an easie thing is to descry
> The gentle bloud, how ever it be wrapt
> In sad misfortunes foule deformity
> And wretched sorrowes, which have often hapt!
> For howsoever it may grow mis-shapt,
> Like this wyld man being undisciplynd,
> That to all virtue it may seeme unapt,
> Yet will it shew some sparkes of gentle mynd,
> And at the last breake forth in his owne proper kynd.
>
> (VI. v. 1.)

That gentle birth predisposed a man to virtue, even if it was not absolutely necessary to virtue, was part of the lore of courtesy. *Fortes creaniur fortibus . . .*[2]—argument as to the mode of inheriting, and of cultivating, *nobilitas*, runs through the history of moral philosophy from Aristotle through Dante to the Renaissance. It is true that, with evidence to the contrary continually before their eyes, philosophers could not uniformly maintain that where there

---

† From *The Tempest* (London: Arden Editions, 1954), pp. xxiv–lix. Reprinted by permission of The Arden Shakespeare, an imprint of Thompson Learning. Line numbers to this Norton Critical Edition of the play appear in brackets when they differ from the author's original citation.

1. "Salvage" is the First Folio description of Caliban in the list of characters, usually now modernized to "savage," although the earlier form is closer to its Latin origin in *silva*, a wood [*Editors*].

2. The brave beget the brave (Horace) [*Editors*].

was high birth there was virtue, taking nobility to mean the *non vile*, "the perfection of its own nature in each thing";[3] and in Italy there was a growing tendency to judge of nobility by actual manners and merit, rather than by family. As early as the *Convito* the conditions of its development are described as much more complex than the racial theory of its provenance allows;[4] but more commonplace thought constantly recurs to the biological analogy; *est in juvencis, est in equis, patrum Virtus*[5]—as Polixenes conceived that there were "buds of nobler race".

The question is debated in the first book of Castiglione's *Courtier* by Canossa and Pallavicino. The arguments are conventional, but they serve to illustrate the theory of natural nobility which animates Spenser's portrait of the salvage man. Nature makes the work of greatness easier, and the penalties of failure heavier, for the high-born; "because nature in every thing hath deepely sowed that privie seed, which giveth a certaine force and propertie of her beginning, unto whatsoever springeth of it, and maketh it like unto herselfe. As we see by example . . . in trees, whose slippes and grafts alwaies for the most part are like unto the stock of the tree they cam from: and if at any time they grow out of kinde, the fault is in the husbandman";[6] which is to say, in the individual nobleman—a fault of nurture, not of nature. Thus Canossa, though not to the satisfaction of Pallavicino, accounts also for the Antonios of the world. He allows an important place to education, believing, with Prospero and against Socrates, that pedagogues could be found capable of nursing the seed:

> Therefore even as in the other artes, so also in the vertues, it is behofefull to have a teacher, that with lessons and good exhortations may stirre up and quicken in us those moral vertues, whereof wee have the seede inclosed and buried in the soule.[7]

If the seed is not there (and here Prospero's experience confirms him) the husbandman loses his labour, and brings forth only "the briers and darnell of appetites" which he had desired to restrain. Canossa omits all the other factors which might be brought into consideration—"the complex nature of the seed", "the disposition of the dominant Heaven"—which Dante two centuries before had attempted to calculate, and takes account only of nature and of nurture. This leaves an opening for Pallavicino's reply, and Castiglione had, of course, to arrange matters to suit his dialectic scheme. But

---

3. *Il Convito. The Banquet* of Dante Alighieri, trans. E. P. Sayer (1887), p. 226. See the curtain-lecture in Chaucer's *Wife of Bath's Tale*.
4. *ibid.*, see *e.g.* p. 241.
5. In steers and in horses is to be found the excellence of their sire (Horace) [*Editors*].
6. *The Courtier* (1528), trans. Hoby (1561), ed. of 1928 (Everyman), p. 31.
7. Castiglione, *The Courtier, ibid.*

for Spenser moral virtues inhabit the simpler, the ideal, world of romance, and his salvage man differs from his kind in that he has the seed implanted by nature, though not husbanded by nurture.

There is a striking version of the theory by Edward Phillips, the nephew of Milton. Phillips, in a passage so much above his usual manner that critics have seen in it the hand of his uncle, identifies two forces which distinguish the better part of mankind from the more brutish:

> . . . the first is that *Melior natura* which the Poet speaks of, with which whoever is amply indued, take that Man from his Infancy, throw him into the Desarts of *Arabia*, there let him converse some years with Tygers and Leopards, and at last bring him where civil society & conversation abides, and ye shall see how on a sudden, the scales and dross of his barbarity purging off by degrees, he will start up a Prince or Legislator, or some such illustrious Person: the other is that noble thing call'd *Education*, this is, that Harp of *Orpheus*, that lute of *Amphion*, so elegantly figur'd by the Poets to have wrought such Miracles among irrational and insensible Creatures, which raiseth beauty even out of deformity, order and regularity out of Chaos and confusion, and which, if throughly and rightly prosecuted, would be able to civilize the most savage natures, & root out barbarism and ignorance from off the face of the Earth: those who have either of these qualifications singly may justly be term'd *Men*; those who have both united in a happy conjunction, *more* than *Men*; those who have neither of them in any competent measure . . . *less* than *Men* . . .[8]

Phillips here takes the view expressed by Dante, Pallavicino, and many others, that the want of nature can be partially supplied by Education, and in this respect differs from those who, like Canossa and, as we shall see, the romance-writers, held more rigidly to the notion of the seed without which all husbandry is not only wasted but even harmful, since it promotes the growth of undesirable weed-like qualities. The unknown poet's *melior natura* provides an excellent label for all the ideas associated with "buds of nobler race", and his "Education" enables us to see Prospero's "nurture" in its proper context. Miranda, as Prospero early informs us, is endowed not only with the *melior natura*, but with education:

> here
> Have I, thy schoolmaster, made thee more profit
> Than other princess' can, that have more time
> For vainer hours, and tutors not so careful. (I. ii. 171–4.)

8. Preface to *Theatrum Poetarum* (1675); in *Critical Essays of the Seventeenth Century*, ed. J. E. Spingarn (1908), III. 257.

She has both these qualities of nobility "united in a happy conjunction". Caliban has neither, and there is in the structure of the play a carefully prepared parallel between the two characters to illustrate this point; Caliban's education was not only useless—on *his* nature, which is nature *tout court*, nurture would never stick—but harmful. He can only abuse the gift of speech; and by cultivating him Prospero brings forth in him "the briers and darnell of appetites"—lust for Miranda, discontent at his inferior position, ambition, intemperance of all kinds, including a disposition to enslave himself to the bottle of Stephano. And there is in his "vile race" that "which *good* natures Could not abide to be with";[9] in other words there is a repugnance between the raw, unreclaimed nature which he represents, and the courtier-stock with which he has to deal, endowed as it is with grace, and nurtured in refinement through the centuries, in the world of Art.[1]

II. *Prospero's Art.* At the risk of introducing "distincts" where there is no "division" it may be said that Prospero's Art has two functions in *The Tempest.* The first is simple; as a mage he exercises the supernatural powers of the holy adept. His Art is here the disciplined exercise of virtuous knowledge, a "translation of merit into power",[2] the achievement of "an intellect pure and conjoined with the powers of the gods, without which we shall never happily ascend to the scrutiny of secret things, and to the power of wonderfull workings".[3] This Art is contrasted with the natural power of Sycorax to exploit for evil purposes the universal sympathies. It is a technique for lib-

9. I.ii.361–62[357–59]. My italics.
1. "Nature" and its compounds are used in a wide range of meanings in *The Tempest*, as they always are in literature. I have shown how it is used in connexion with Caliban (his "vile race" opposed to the race *non vile*—the stock etymology of *nobile*) and there is also some play on the idea that this nature is "monstrous"—i.e. un-natural—a paradox which involves the concept of another and higher nature. "Lord, that a monster should be such a natural" (III.ii.30–31) where the pun depends upon the colloquial "natural" (= "idiot"). Miranda puts the paradox the other way round when she sees Ferdinand, and thinks he is a spirit, "For nothing natural I ever saw so *noble*" (I.ii.421–22[416–17], where the *Melior natura* is contrasted with the *vile* she recognized in Caliban. There is here of course a strong admixture of "natural" meaning "not supernatural". This meaning recurs in the last Act, when Alonso, hearing that the ship is safe, says, "These are not natural events" (V.i.227) where we think at once that they are due to Prospero's Art. In V.i.157 "natural breath" is of courses imply "human" breath, though the reading "These words Are natural breath" (N.S.) modifies it slightly. There are three other meanings (though it should be pointed out that this schematization inevitably entails over-simplification): Antonio, who is of noble race, and should have the better nature, exhibits "an evil nature" (I.ii.93) in his ambition. This is a disposition to do evil which can inhere in good stock for reasons given below. He is called "unnatural" (V.i.79) by Prospero as he forgives him; the primary meaning here is "unfraternal, neglecting the ties of blood", but there is also the sense of "degenerate, a betrayer of his race and of the better nature". See also V.i.78–79. Finally, *natura naturans* occurs in a form we have learned to recognize, in Gonzalo's "all things in common nature should produce" and "nature should bring forth of it own kind . . ." (*i.e.* without culture) II.i.155, 158–59.
2. R. H. West, *The Invisible World* (1939), pp. 41–5.
3. Cornelius Agrippa, *Occult Philosophy*, translated by J. F. (1651), III. iii.

erating the soul from the passions, from nature; the practical application of a discipline of which the primary requirements are learning and temperance, and of which the mode is contemplation.
When Prospero achieves this necessary control over himself and
nature he achieves his ends (reflected in the restoration of harmony
at the human and political levels) and has no more need of the instrument, "rough magic".

The second function is symbolic. Prospero's Art controls Nature;
it requires of the artist virtue and temperance if his experiment is to
succeed; and it thus stands for the world of the better natures and
its qualities. This is the world which is closed to Caliban (and Co-
mus); the world of mind and the possibilities of liberating the soul,
not the world of sense, whether that be represented as coarsely natural or charmingly voluptuous. Art is not only a beneficent magic in
contrast to an evil one; it is the ordination of civility, the control of
appetite, the transformation of nature by breeding and learning; it
is even, in a sense, the means of Grace.

Prospero is, therefore, the representative of Art, as Caliban is of
Nature. As a mage he controls nature; as a prince he conquers the
passions which had excluded him from his kingdom and overthrown law; as a scholar he repairs his loss of Eden; as a man he
learns to temper his passions, an achievement essential to success
in any of the other activities.

Prospero describes his efforts to control his own passion in V. i.
25–7—

> Though with their high wrongs I am struck to th' quick,
> Yet with my nobler reason 'gainst my fury
> Do I take part.

In an age when "natural" conduct was fashionably associated with
sexual promiscuity, chastity alone could stand as the chief function
of temperance, and there is considerable emphasis on this particular restraint in *The Tempest*. The practice of good magic required it;
but in this it is again merely the practical application of civility.
Prospero twice, and Juno again, warn Ferdinand of the absolute necessity for it, and Ferdinand's ability to make pure beauty "abate
the ardour of his liver" is in the strongest possible contrast to Caliban's straightforward natural lust for it. The unchaste designs of
Stephano arouse Prospero's anger also; it is as if he were conduct-
ing, with magically purified book and rod, the kind of experiment
which depended for its success on the absolute purity of all concerned; and indeed, in so far as his aims were a dynastic marriage
and the regeneration of the noble, this was so.

This is characteristic of the way in which the magic of Prospero
translates into more general terms. The self-discipline of the magi-

cian is the self-discipline of the prince. It was the object of the good ruler to make his people good by his own efforts; and that he might do so it was considered necessary for him to acquire learning, and to rid himself "of those troublous affections that untemperate mindes feele".[4] The personal requirements of mage and prince are the same, and Prospero labours to regain a worldly as well as a heavenly power. Like James I in the flattering description, he "standeth invested with that triplicitie which in great veneration was ascribed to the ancient *Hermes*, the power and fortune of a *King*, the knowledge and illumination of a Priest, and the Learning and universalitie of a Philosopher".[5]

Learning is a major theme in the play; we learn that Miranda is capable of it and Caliban not, and why this should be so; but we are also given a plan of the place of learning in the dispositions of providence. Prospero, like Adam, fell from his kingdom by an inordinate thirst for knowledge; but learning is a great aid to virtue, the road by which we may love and imitate God, and "repair the ruins of our first parents",[6] and by its means he is enabled to return. The solicitude which accompanied Adam and Eve when "the world was all before them" went also with Prospero and Miranda when they set out in their "rotten carcass of a butt".

> By foul play, as thou say'st, were we heav'd thence,
> But blessedly holp hither. (I. ii. 62–3.)

They came ashore "by Providence divine"; and Gonzalo leaves us in no doubt that Prospero's fault, like Adam's, was a happy one:

> Was Milan thrust from Milan, that his issue
> Should become kings of Naples? O rejoice
> Beyond a common joy! . . . (V. i. 205–7.)

He had achieved the great object of Learning, and regained a richer heritage.[7] But he is not learned in only this rather abstract sense; he is the learned prince. Like Boethius, he had been a natural philosopher, and had learnt from Philosophy that "to hate the wicked were against reason." He clearly shared the view that "no wise man had rather live in banishment, poverty, and ignominy, than prosper in his own country. . . For in this manner is the office of wisdom performed with more credit and renown, where the governors' happiness is participated by the people about them." And Philosophy, though ambiguously, taught both Boethius and Prospero "the way by which thou mayest return to thy country".[8]

4. Castiglione, *op. cit.* p. 277.
5. Cleland, *The Institution of a Young Noble Man*, II. i.
6. Milton, *Of Education*, in *Prose Works*, ed. Hughes, p. 31.
7. For a somewhat similar reading, though different in detail, see N. Coghill, "The Basis of Shakespearian Comedy", *Essays and Studies* (1950), pp. 1–28.
8. *The Consolation of Philosophy*, IV Prose 5, V Prose 1 (Loeb edition, pp. 335, 365).

There is nothing remarkable about Prospero's ambition to regain his own kingdom and strengthen his house by a royal marriage. To be studious and contemplative, but also to be able to translate knowledge into power in the active life, was the object of his discipline; the Renaissance venerated Scipio for his demonstration of this truth, and Marvell's Horatian Ode speaks of Cromwell in the same terms.

> The chiefe Use then in man of that he knowes,
> Is his paines taking for the good of all . . .
> Yet *Some seeke knowledge, merely but to know,*
> And idle Curiositie that is . . .[9]

Prospero is not at all paradoxical in presenting himself at the climax as he was "sometime Milan". Yet he does not intend merely to look after his worldly affairs; every third thought is to be his grave. "The end of the active or doing life ought to be the beholding; as of war, peace, and as of paines, rest."[1] The active and contemplative lives are complementary.

In all respects, then, Prospero expresses the qualities of the world of Art, of the *non vile*.

# GEORGE LAMMING

## A Monster, a Child, a Slave†

> Eia for those who never invented anything
> Eia for those who never conquered anything
> But who in awe give themselves to the essence of things
> Ignorant of the shell, but seized by the rhythm of things
> Not intent on conquest, but playing the game of the world
> True and truly the first born of this world
> Receptive to every breath of the world
> Brotherly enclosure for all the winds of the world
> Bed and not gutter for all the waters of the world
> Sparks of the holy fire of the world, trembling in the world's tremble
> AIMÉ CÉSAIRE

*The Tempest* is a drama which grows and matures from the seeds of exile and paradox. Through a process of poetic schematisation, it contains and crystallises all the conflicts which have gone before. It

---

9. Fulke Greville, *A Treatie of Humane Learning* (1603–5), St. 144–5; ed. G. Bullough (1938), I. 190.
1. Castiglione, *op. cit.* p. 280. See also Bacon, *Advancement of Learning*, World's Classics ed., pp. 11–12, 15–16, 42. The theme is a humanist commonplace.
† From *The Pleasures of Exile* [1960] (London: Allison & Busby, 1984), pp. 95–117. Amended by the author. Reprinted by permission of the author. Line numbers to the play have been added.

is the poet's last will and testament; but the details of the legacy
read like an epitaph: an apology for any false dividends which Art—
meaning all method and experience of transformation—may have
brought home.

> Now my charms are all o'erthrown,
> And what strength I have's mine own,
> Which is most faint: now, 'tis true,
> I must be here confin'd by you,
> Or sent to Naples. Let me not,
> Since I have my dukedom got,
> And pardon'd the deceiver, dwell
> In this bare island by your spell;
> But release me from my bands
> With the help of your good hands:
> Gentle breath of yours my sails
> Must fill, or else my project fails,
> Which was to please. Now I want
> Spirits to enforce, Art to enchant;
> And my ending is despair,
> Unless I be reliev'd by prayer,
> Which pierces so, that it assaults
> Mercy itself, and frees all faults.
>   As you from crimes would pardon'd be,
>   Let your indulgence set me free. [*Epilogue*, 1–20]

It is the Epilogue which reminds us that the Voyage is not over. Indeed, we are right back where we started:

### ACT I. *Scene* I
(On a ship at sea a tempestuous noise of thunder and lightning
heard)

Will the magic of prayer help Prospero and his crew safely towards Milan where the marriage of Miranda and Ferdinand may remind them that Innocence and Age are two sides of the same coin;
that there are no degrees of forgiveness; that compassion will not
exclude any? Will Prospero, no longer interested in temporal success, enter his grave without admitting that his every third thought
remains alive? For where, we wonder, is our excluded Caliban? And
what fearful truth will Caliban discover now the world he prized
has abandoned him to the solitude of his original home: the Island
which no act of foreign appropriation ever could deprive him of.

It is not only aesthetic necessity, but the *facts* of lived experience
which demanded that the territory of the drama had to be an island. For there is no landscape more suitable for considering the
Question of the sea, no geography more appropriate to the study of
exile. And it is that ruthless, though necessary wreck, which warns

us that we are all deeply involved in the politics of intrigue. The tides have turned treacherous. Thunder is talking a language which everyone understands; and in this moment of peril we are reminded by the loyal that there are very important people on board: a King and his heir, the King's brother, a Duke who has important connections not far away. There is panic among the great; and the old counsellor, Gonzalo—loyal even to his mistakes, Gonzalo the perfect embodiment of servitude, thinks not of himself but of his master's safety:

> GONZALO: Nay, good, be patient.
> BOATS: When the sea is. Hence! What cares these roarers for the name of King? To cabin: silence! trouble us not.
> GONZALO: Good, yet remember whom thou hast aboard.
>                                                   [1.1.15–18]

It is an expression of the perfect colonial concern: what will happen if the edifice of one man's presence crumbles? But these sailors have always sojourned with danger. Their harbour is no more than a postponement of peril. The sea is their kingdom, and they don't give a damn about the King who is essentially a land-crab. That's how they think; and confidence demands that they should say so:

> BOATS: None that I more love than myself. You are a counsellor; if you can command these elements to silence, and work the peace of the presence, we will not hand a rope more; use your authority: if you cannot, give thanks you have lived so long, and make yourself ready in your cabin for the mischance of the hour, if it so hap. Cheerly, good hearts! Out of our way, I say. [1.1.19–25]

It is a fine piece of straight talking and is in direct contrast to the forgivable stammering which comes from dear, old Gonzalo. We shall draw attention to another contrast when we encounter Ariel and Caliban in a similar situation of servant and master. But this wreck strikes terror in every heart; for it was Nature combined with Art which brought it about. Men seem to think that it is their last chance to call a spade a spade; and there is a good deal of bad language as the ship surrenders its sails to the total embrace of the sea. But the sea in conspiracy with the Art which also created these characters has returned them to safety.

According to plan they will reach shore; for it's on land and among the living that the awkwardness of the past must be resolved. Yet there must have been an interval of absolute hell: the purgatorial journey from origins to some landmark which reminds that you are always in transit. Ariel, in a spirit of pure and diabolical delight, gives a first-hand account of their suffering:

ARIEL:                                      Not a soul
But felt a fever of the mad, and play'd
Some tricks of desperation. All but mariners
Plung'd in the foaming brine, and quit the vessel,
Then all afire with me: the King's son, Ferdinand,
With hair up-staring,—then like reeds, not hair,—
Was the first man that leap'd; cried, 'Hell is empty,
And all the devils are here.' [1.2.208–15]

To which Prospero replies: 'Why, that's my spirit!'

A most appropriate parallel in contemporary history is the unfor-
gettable transport of slaves from Africa to the Caribbean . . .

> 'On ship the slaves were packed in the hold on galleries one
> above the other. Each was given only four or five feet in length
> and two or three feet in height, so that they could neither lie at
> full length nor sit upright . . . In this position they lived for the
> voyage, coming up once a day for exercise and to allow the
> sailors "to clean the pails." But when the cargo was rebellious
> or the weather bad, then they stayed below for weeks at a time.
> The close proximity of so many naked human beings, their
> bruised and festering flesh, the foetid air, the prevailing dysen-
> tery, the accumulation of filth, turned these holds into a hell.
> During the storms the hatches were battened down, and in the
> close and loathsome darkness they were hurled from one side
> to another by the heaving vessel, held in position by the chains
> on their bleeding flesh. No place on earth, observed one writer
> of the time, concentrated so much misery as the hold of a
> slave ship.'[1]

That purgatory of the Middle Passage lasted six thousand miles;
and like Prospero commending his 'brave spirit,' there was the captain of the slave ship with so clear a conscience that one of them,
in the intervals of waiting to enrich British capitalism with the profits of another valuable cargo, enriched British religion by composing the hymn:

'How sweet the name of Jesus sounds!'

But these 'savage and deformed slaves' arrived; and like the character
who or which fits this description in *The Tempest*, they worked, and
were rebellious often went wild with the spirit of freedom, and were
imprisoned, and yet, like Caliban, they survived as though there were
some divinity which made them unique in their capacity to last.

We are back, then, to the Island, once the birthright of Caliban,
and now the Kingdom of a Duke who lives in exile.

---

1. From C. L. R. James, *The Black Jacobins* [1938] (New York: Vintage Books, 1963), 8
[*Editors*].

If we consider the politics of the Island, the size of its population as well as its relation to the world beyond its shores, we are left with a remarkable example of a State which is absolutely run by one man. Absolute is the only word for a power which does not even require an army. Prospero has no need of bureaucrats. Caliban is his slave, which means, among other things, his physical survival:

> But, as 'tis,
> We cannot miss him: he does make our fire,
> Fetch in our wood, and serves in offices
> That profit us. What, ho! slave! Caliban!
> Thou earth, thou! speak. [1.2.310–14]

We are trying to suggest the way in which Prospero saw himself in relation to the immediate neighbourhood around him. It is in his relation to Caliban, as a physical fact of life that we are allowed to guess some of Prospero's needs. He needs this slave. Moreover, he must be cautious in his dealings with him, for Caliban contains the seed of revolt.

After the slaves were encamped in Haiti, torture became a common method of persuading them to work. In some cases, they were roasted; others were buried alive up to the neck, their heads smeared with sugar that the flies might devour them; they were fastened to nests of wasps, made to eat their excrement, drink their urine, and lick the saliva of other slaves. A great pastime too, was to fill them with gunpowder and strike a match somewhere near the hole of the arse. There is a similar sadism in Prospero whenever he is moved to threaten Caliban for his rebellion:

> PROSPERO: For this, be sure, tonight thou shalt have cramps,
> Side-stitches that shall pen thy breath up; urchins
> Shall, for that vast of night that they may work,
> All exercise on thee; thou shalt be pinch'd
> As thick as honeycomb, each pinch more stinging
> Than bees that made 'em. [1.2.325–30]

But Prospero dare not dynamite Caliban; for there is one slave only, one pair of hands that labour. To murder Caliban would be an act of pure suicide. But Caliban is more than his source of food as we shall see. Caliban haunts him in a way that is almost too deep and too intimate to communicate.

But we must return to the politics of the island, to Ariel's function in this drama of intrigue. For Ariel, like Caliban, serves Prospero; but Ariel is not a slave. Ariel has been emancipated to the status of a privileged servant. In other words: a lackey. Ariel is Pros-

pero's source of information; the archetypal spy, the embodiment—
when and if made flesh—of the perfect and unspeakable secret police. It is Ariel who tunes in on every conversation which the
degradation of his duty demands that he report back to Prospero.
Of course, he knows what's going on from the very beginning. Ariel
is on the inside. He knows and serves his master's intention, and
his methods are free from any scruples:

> ARIEL: All hail, great master! grave sir, hail! I come
> To answer thy best pleasure; be 't to fly,
> To swim, to dive into the fire, to ride
> On the curl'd clouds, to thy strong bidding task
> Ariel and all his quality. [1.2.189–93]

But it is a dangerous partnership, and Prospero never hesitates to
remind him of his servitude. Like some malevolent old bitch with a
bad conscience, Prospero's habit is to make you aware of his power
to give. He is an expert at throwing the past in your face. And Ariel
is no exception:

> PROSPERO:              Dost thou forget
> From what torment I did free thee?
> ARIEL: No.
> PROSPERO: Thou dost, and think'st it much to tread the ooze
> Of the salt deep,
> To run upon the sharp wind of the north,
> To do me business in the veins o' th' earth
> When it is bak'd with frost.
> ARIEL:                    I do not, sir.
> PROSPERO: Thou liest, malignant thing! Hast thou forgot
> The foul witch Sycorax, who with age and envy
> Was grown into a hoop? hast thou forgot her?
> ARIEL: No, sir.
>                     *    *    *
> PROSPERO:                   Thou best know'st
> What torment I did find thee in; thy groans
> Did make wolves howl, and penetrate the breasts
> Of ever-angry bears: it was a torment
> To lay upon the damn'd, which Sycorax
> Could not again undo: it was mine Art,
> When I arriv'd and heard thee, that made gape
> The pine, and let thee out.
> ARIEL:              I thank thee, master. [1.2.250–59, 286–93]

It is at this point that we can offer the contrast between Ariel and
Caliban in a similar encounter with Prospero. Caliban is a victim of
mental torture. It weakens him; and sometimes it seems that his

confidence is lost. But the spirit of freedom never deserts him. When he makes his first appearance in the play, it is at the order of Prospero.

PROSPERO: Thou poisonous slave, got by the devil himself
Upon thy wicked dam, come forth!

*Enter* CALIBAN

CALIBAN: As wicked dew as e'er my mother brush'd
With raven's feather from unwholesome fen
Drop on you both! a south-west blow on ye
And blister you all o'er!
PROSPERO: For this, be sure, tonight thou shalt have cramps,
Side-stitches that shall pen thy breath up; urchins
Shall, for that vast of night that they may work,
All exercise on thee; thou shalt be pinch'd
As thick as honeycomb, each pinch more stinging
Than bees that made 'em.
CALIBAN:                          I must eat my dinner.
This island's mine, by Sycorax my mother,
Which thou tak'st from me. When thou cam'st first,
Thou strok'st me, and made much of me; wouldst give me
Water with berries in't; and teach me how
To name the bigger light, and how the less,
That burn by day and night: and then I lov'd thee,
And show'd thee all the qualities o' th' isle,
The fresh springs, brine-pits, barren place and fertile
Curs'd be I that did so! All the charms
Of Sycorax, toads, beetles, bats, light on you!
For I am all the subjects that you have,
Which first was mine own King: and there you sty me
In this hard rock, whiles you do keep from me
The rest o' th' island. [1.2.319–44]

Caliban has not lost his sense of original rootedness, and for this reason Prospero must deal with him harshly. The rock imprisonment is, in our time, a form of the emergency regulation which can forbid a son of the soil to travel outside a certain orbit; marked out and even made legal by a foreign visitor. But Caliban keeps answering back, and it is his refusal to be silent which now bullies Prospero into the crucial charge:

PROSPERO:                          Thou most lying slave,
Whom stripes may move, not kindness! I have us'd thee,
Filth as thou art, with human care; and lodg'd thee
In mine own cell, till thou didst seek to violate
The honour of my child.
CALIBAN: O ho, O ho! would't had been done!

Thou didst prevent me; I had peopled else
This isle with Calibans. [1.2.344–50]

What an extraordinary way for a slave to speak to his master and in the daughter's presence. But there is a limit to accepting lies and it was the Lie contained in the charge which the man in Caliban could not allow. 'I wish it were so.' But he does not wish it for the mere experiment of mounting a piece of white flesh. He goes further and imagines that the consequence of such intercourse would be a fabulous increase of the population.

I had peopled else
This isle with Calibans.

Is there a political intention at work? Does he mean that he would have numbers on his side; that he could organise resistance against this obscene, and selfish monster. But why, we wonder, does Caliban think that the population would be Calibans? Why would they not be Mirandas? Does he mean that they should carry the father's name? But these children would be bastards and should be honoured no less with their mother's name. Or were there other possibilities?

Did Caliban really try to rape her? This is a case where the body, in its consequences, is our only guide. Only the body could establish the truth; for if Miranda were made pregnant, we would know that someone had penetrated her. We might also know whether or no it was Caliban's child; for it is most unlikely that Prospero and his daughter could produce a brown skin baby. Could Prospero really have endured the presence and meaning of a brown skin grandchild. It would not be Miranda's own doing. It would not be the result of their enterprise. It would be Miranda's and Caliban's child. It would be *theirs*: the result and expression of some fusion both physical and other than physical: a fusion which, within himself, Prospero needs and dreads!

Prospero is a Duke who has been deprived of his kingdom. Through the logical treachery of his brother, Antonio, and the conspiracy of the neighbouring King of Naples, Alonso, Prospero was thrown out of his kingdom. Miranda, his heir, was then no more than three years old. Father and child were hurried on a bark, taken out to sea and then dumped on

A rotten carcass of a butt, not rigg'd
Nor tackle, sail, nor mast; [1.2.146–47]

But all this happened twelve years before the wreck which brings some visitors on to the island, and Miranda, now grown into a virtuous beauty, is hearing about these events for the first time. She is at the ripe and provocative age of fifteen, a virgin and, like her father, curious about the facts of life. She had witnessed or had some vision of the wreck which has just taken place; and it is an appeal on behalf of those, presumably dying at sea, which leads to her father's recapitulation of the times before they were expelled from Milan. She tries to explain what of the wreck she has seen; and her vision of their suffering is also the measure of the pain she feels on their behalf.

> MIRANDA: O, I have suffered
> With those I saw suffer! A brave vessel
> (Who had, no doubt, some noble creature in her,)
> Dashed all to pieces. O, the cry did knock
> Against my very heart!
> PROSPERO: Be collected:
> No more amazement: tell your piteous heart
> There's no harm done. [1.2.5–15]

It is this contrast of attitude towards a common disaster which introduces the noble and compassionate nature of Miranda on the one hand, and the supernatural power of her father on the other. Equally noble in their origins, Father and Child are different only in the degrees of their knowledge. What comes between them is the distance which separates Age that apprehends, from Innocence which can only see. Prospero who is also her first and only teacher now gives Miranda a lesson in their domestic history. She learns that the wrecked crew will land safely on this island; and she learns, stage by fastidious stage, the circumstance and purpose of the happy misfortune. And so her curiosity, an essential logic of the drama, forces Prospero to give a hurried lesson in domestic history. He begins, as his custom with all people, by drawing her attention to her limitations:

> PROSPERO: I have done nothing but in care of thee,
> Of thee, my dear one; thee, my daughter, who
> Art ignorant of what thou art; nought knowing
> Of whence I am, nor that I am more better
> Than Prospero, master of a full poor cell,
> And thy no greater father. [1.2.16–21]

Now the search for time lost has begun. He traces the orbit of memory in which she will travel back to find some image of her infancy. And the first landmark, the first anchor which comes to mind is a memory of her maids. She can remember three or four. Prospero assures her there were many more. He coaxes her to dig up some more evidence of that lost infancy; but she can't get much further.

PROSPERO: What seest thou else
In the dark backward and abysm of time?
If thou rememberest aught ere thou cam'st here,
How thou cam'st here thou mayst.
MIRANDA: But that I do not. [1.2.49–52]

What impresses us here is the fact that she has, it seems, absolutely no recollection of her mother. Nor does she raise the question until Prospero's ambiguous way of explaining relations forces
her to ask:

MIRANDA: Sir, are you not my father?

To which he gives a reply characteristic of his method of rendering information:

PROSPERO: Thy mother was a piece of virtue, and
She said thou wast my daughter; and thy father
Was Duke of Milan; and his only heir
And princess, no worse issued. [1.2.55–59]

It is the first and, if I am not mistaken, the very last reference we
have to Miranda's mother who was, presumably, Prospero's wife. Is
she alive? Or did she die in the treacherous *coup d'état* which led to
Prospero's exile? But Prospero does not mention her again; for he is
busy giving his daughter a summary account of events which led to
his brother's conspiracy with the King of Naples, who, with his son,
Ferdinand, is among the survivors destined for this Island. So is the
old counsellor Gonzalo who was given the job of designing Prospero's downfall. The whole gang are alive and well, but ignorant of
what's in store for them.

Resurrected from the water, innocent and guilty, offer a striking
parallel with the Haitian ceremony of Souls. Prospero is the bitter
reality which they cannot avoid; and Miranda is no more than an
initiate who is being briefed at lightning speed about the necessary
facts. These are carefully chosen, for the techniques of propaganda
are not unknown to Prospero; and he emerges swiftly, but surely, as
the outraged martyr: the embodiment of an original nobility, a criterion of virtue which bears witness to the disgrace of his degenerate adversaries.

This is the only light in which Miranda can see him; for she has
no experience of the world beyond this island, no instruments for
making a comparative judgment. Caliban is the only other man she
has seen; but his whole relation to the condition meant by Man is
gravely in doubt. Her father's account of history—which is no more
than a schematic arrangement of necessary and self-protective emphasis—fills her with an admiration which she can only express

through regret. She regrets that she should have been so much trouble to him.

MIRANDA: Your tale, sir, would cure deafness. [1.2.106]

Her case is perhaps not unrelated to what, in our time, is called brain-washing. Virtue, nobility, chastity and beauty, degeneracy, bestiality, lust, and physical deformity are the antitheses which she has thoroughly absorbed and which will, in the course of time, be exemplified by those she meets. Caliban, her first experience of a stranger, is already the black temple of every tendency that characterises the beast, and he serves as a reminder to any noble spirit which may be tempted to overreach the laws of its nature. It is against this moral background of opposites that Miranda learns how it came about that her father could have lost his dukedom.

> PROSPERO: I pray thee, mark me.
> I, thus neglecting worldly ends, all dedicated
> To closeness and the bettering of my mind
> With that which, but by being so retir'd,
> O'er-priz'd all popular rate, in my false brother
> Awak'd an evil nature; and my trust,
> Like a good parent, did beget of him
> A falsehood in its contrary, as great
> As my trust was; which had indeed no limit,
> A confidence sans bound. . . .
>         Me, poor man, my library
> Was dukedom large enough: of temporal royalties
> He thinks me now incapable; confederates,
> So dry he was for sway, wi' th' King of Naples
> To give him annual tribute, do him homage,
> Subject his coronet to his crown, and bend
> The dukedome, yet unbow'd,—alas, poor Milan!—
> To most ignoble stooping.
> MIRANDA: O the heavens!
> PROSPERO: Mark his condition, and th' event; then tell me
> If this might be a brother.
> MIRANDA: I should sin
> To think but nobly of my grandmother:
> Good wombs have borne bad sons. [1.2.88–97, 109–20]

And when she asks the pertinent question:

MIRANDA: Wherefore did they not
That hour destroy us? [1.2.137–38]

he congratulates her on the acuity of her attention, and proceeds to explain that his survival was due entirely to the love his people— meaning the common herd of men and women—bore him.

His absence could probably be explained in much the same way that the political exile of African chiefs could be given 'some rational interpretation.' The present Asantehene, Otumfuo Sir Osei Agyeman Prempeh II, K.B.E., suffered a similar fate when he was banished by a British Administration to the Seychelles. . . . It was some years before he was returned. So also did King Jaja of Nigeria, who, for some odd reason, was removed to Barbados, the island of the author's birth. The latter episode enriched the almost absent folk music with a tune about Jaja.

Prospero is not only a ruler, but a philosopher as well; and we can assume that this combination: the Philosopher-King—the hereditary right to rule people and the spiritual need to organise reality—is directly related to that creative will to conquer the absolute: a will which finds its most perfect vessel in the infinitely expanding powers of transformation that characterise the timeless frontiers of the Poetic Vision. This is the total atmosphere of expectation in which Miranda lives. Her father will arrange her future; and all will be well provided the references of truth are not disturbed by some fearful contingency. Sooner or later the wrecked crew will come safely to shore; ignorance will be dispelled by Prospero's light. Like the miraculous discovery of one's empty purse, the guilty will find their conscience. The magic of birth will sail Miranda, young, beautiful and a virgin, into the arms of a King's only son. Her eye will show her at one glance who is her heart's desire. The rest is forgiveness and preparation for a marriage whose future must remain promising and absent as paradise.

> Was Milan thrust from Milan, that his issue
> Should become Kings of Naples? O, rejoice
> Beyond a common joy! [5.1.205–7]

Caliban cannot be revealed in any relation to himself; for he has no self which is not a reaction to circumstances imposed upon his life. He is not seen as a possibility of spirit which might fertilise and extend the resources of any human vision. Caliban is the very climate in which men encounter the nature of ambiguities, and in which, according to his desire, each man attempts a resolution by trying to slay the past. Caliban's history—for he has a most turbulent history—belongs entirely to the future. It is the wind which reminds us that trouble has gone into hiding. In all his encounters with his neighbours—whether they be Kings or drunken clowns— Caliban is never accorded the power *to see*. He is always the measure of the condition which his physical appearance has already defined. Caliban is the excluded, that which is eternally below possibility, and always beyond reach. He is seen as an occasion, a state of existence which can be appropriated and exploited for the purposes of another's own development. Caliban is a reminder of lost virtue or the evil vigour of the Beast that is always there: a magnetic temptation, and an eternal warning against the contagion of his daemon ancestry.

The difficulty is to take from Caliban without suffering the pollution innate in his nature. To yield to Caliban's natural generosity is to risk the deluge: for his assets—such as they are—are dangerous, since they are encrusted, buried deep in the dark. It is not by accident that his skin is black; for black, too, is the colour of his loss; the absence of any soul. If he shows an aptitude for music, it is because the perfection of harmonies can strike some chord in his nervous system.

> CALIBAN: Be not afeard; the isle is full of noises,
> Sounds and sweet airs, that give delight, and hurt not.
> Sometimes a thousand twangling instruments
> Will hum about mine ears; and sometimes voices,
> That, if I then had wak'd after long sleep,
> Will make me sleep again: and then, in dreaming,
> The clouds methought would open, and show riches
> Ready to drop upon me: that, when I wak'd,
> I cried to dream again. [3.2.133–41]

Caliban is in his way a kind of Universal. Like the earth he is always there, generous in gifts, inevitable, yet superfluous and dumb. And like the earth which draws attention to age and therefore to the past, he cannot be devoured. Caliban is, therefore, the occasion to which every situation, within the context of the Tempest, must be related. No Caliban no Prospero! No Prospero no Miranda! No Miranda no Marriage! And no Marriage no Tempest! He confronts Prospero as a possibility; a challenge; and a defeat.

> This thing of darkness
> I acknowledge mine. [5.1.275–76]

He confronts the drunken butler Stephano, and the jester Trinculo, as a commercial speculation, a promising investment:

> STEPHANO:                    If I can recover him, and keep him
> tame, I will not take too much for him; he shall pay for him
> that hath him and that soundly. [2.2.72–75]

But it is the difference in these intentions which suggest the difference between Prospero and Trinculo; it is a difference which has to do with birth and the inescapable law of heredity. Caliban's incapacity to see that Trinculo and Stephano are crooks, his readiness to accord them the worship he had once given Prospero, are proof of his condition. And it is this condition which Prospero, in the role of philisopher, would like to experiment with. The problem of learning is now firmly stated. Education, meaning the possession of the Word—which was in the beginning or not at all—is the tool which Prospero has tried on the irredeemable nature of his savage and deformed slave. We are brought to the heart of the matter by the cantankerous assertion, spoken by Miranda, but obviously the thought and vocabulary of her father.

> MIRANDA: Abhorred slave,
> Which any print of goodness wilt not take,
> Being capable of all ill! I pitied thee,
> Took pains to make thee speak, taught thee each hour
> One thing or other: when thou didst not, savage,
> Know thine own meaning, but wouldst gabble like
> A thing most brutish, I endow'd thy purposes
> With words that made them known. But thy vile race,
> Though thou didst learn, had that in't which good natures
> Could not abide to be with; therefore wast thou
> Deservedly confin'd into this rock,
> Who hadst deserv'd more than a prison. [1.2.350–61]

There is no escape from the prison of Prospero's gift. This example of deformity was a challenge to Prospero's need to achieve the impossible. Only the application of the Word to the darkness of Caliban's world could harness the beast which resides within this cannibal. This is the first important achievement of the colonising process. This gift of Language is the deepest and most delicate bond of involvement. It has a certain finality. Caliban will never be the same again. Nor, for that matter, will Prospero.

Prospero has given Caliban Language; and with it an unstated history of consequences, an unknown history of future intentions. This gift of Language meant not English, in particular, but speech and concept as a way, a method, a necessary avenue towards areas of the self which could not be reached in any other way. It is this way, entirely Prospero's enterprise, which makes Caliban aware of possibilities. Therefore, all of Caliban's future—for future is the very name for possibilities—must derive from Prospero's experiment which is also his risk.

Provided there is no extraordinary departure which explodes all of Prospero's premises, then Caliban and his future now belong to Prospero. Caliban is Prospero's risk in the sense that Adam's awareness of a difference was a risk which God took with Man. Prospero believes—his belief in his own powers demands it—that Caliban can learn so much and no more. Caliban can go so far and no farther. Prospero lives in the absolute certainty that Language which is his gift to Caliban is the very prison in which Caliban's achievements will be realised and restricted. Caliban can never reach perfection, not even the perfection implicit in Miranda's privileged ignorance.

For Language itself, by Caliban's whole relation to it, will not allow his expansion beyond a certain point. This kind of realisation, this kind of expansion, is possible only to those who reside in that state of being which is the very source and ultimate of the language that bears them always forward. The difference between Caliban and the sinner is this. A sinner remains a child of God, and redemption is not so much an order as a natural duty. Grace is the sinner's birthright. But Caliban is not a child of anything except Nature. To be a child of Nature, in this sense, is to be situated in Nature, to be identified with Nature, to be eternally without the seed of a dialectic which makes possible some *emergence* from Nature.

Such is Caliban, superfluous as the weight of the earth until Prospero arrives with the aid of the Word which might help him to clarify the chaos which shows its true colours all over his skin. But he can never be regarded as an heir of that Language, since his use of Language is no more than his way of serving Prospero; and Prospero's instruction in this Language is only his way of measuring the distance which separates him from Caliban. If it were possible for Caliban to realise Language as his perfect inheritance, and if, in spite of this new power, Prospero could still appropriate and imprison him at will; then Prospero would have achieved the triplicity which he is pursuing: 'The Power and Fortune of a King, the knowledge and illumination of a priest, and the learning and the universality of a philosopher.' The seeds of this triplicity are within Prospero; but there is one disqualification which hounds him slowly to despair. Prospero is getting old, and the powers he would claim are associated in his mind with youth. Caliban at twenty-four is certainly young. But he has no *sight*. He is without that necessary light which is the very origin of Language, the light which guides Prospero, and which, at the same time, Prospero is trying to surpass.

Caliban may become Man; but he is entirely outside the orbit of Human. It is not Prospero who keeps him there; nor is it his own fault that he is there. It is some original Law which exists even beyond Prospero's seeing. It is this Law which has ordained the state of existence we call Caliban. If Caliban turns cannibal, it is not because human flesh may appear a necessary substitute for food which is absent. It is rather because he is incapable of differentiating between one kind of reality and another. His hunger is too large—not his greed but his hunger—too large to be harnessed by any process of selection. He cannot distinguish between Man, the object, and Human, the form and ideal which auras that object. He could not recognise the difference of quality between Prospero and Trinculo or between Stephano and Ferdinand. Language may help him to describe the physical attributes which nobility calls beautiful; but language will not help him to distinguish between separate personalities. Word and concept may be part of his vocabulary; but they are no part of his way of seeing.

Caliban is not allowed to distinguish, for the eyes that register personality must belong to, must derive from a consciousness which could be regarded as person. And Caliban is a condition.

Hence the charge of rape. Caliban would think no more of raping Miranda than he might of eating her if she were alone, and he was hungry or feeling too idle to go swimming.

This is precisely Miranda's view of Caliban also; for her father and only teacher throughout her life is Prospero. It would not be difficult for Miranda to accuse Caliban also of having actually raped her; for she probably dreams about him, and does not trust his heredity when she is asleep. If she dreamt that Caliban had raped her, she would not be able to tell whether it had happened or not; for Caliban, as the descendant of a Devil, may have inherited that traditional power which allowed Devils to put their female victims asleep while they had their pleasure. It is through Miranda, the product of Prospero's teaching, that we may glimpse the origin and perpetuation of myth coming slowly but surely into its right as fact, history, absolute truth.

Throughout the play we are impressed by the affinities, the likeness of circumstance between Miranda and Caliban. Like many an African slave child, Miranda has no recollection of her mother. The actual Caliban of *The Tempest* has the advantage—regrettable as he makes it sound—of having known the meaning and power of his mother Sycorax.

But Miranda has a deeper affinity than this likeness of circumstance. She was no more than an infant when she and her father met Caliban on the island. Prospero says she was scarcely three. Caliban would have been about twelve. As time passed, and Prospero grew more and more occupied with his Book, Caliban and the child, Miranda, must have grown closer by the necessary contact of servant and mistress. Before the emergency regulation which imprisoned him in a rock, Caliban must have taken this child for walks about the island. He probably had to carry her on his back, the way we have seen African servants showing their affection to European children. Between the age of three and five Miranda must have spent a lot of time playing with Caliban, the way European children, during their parents' absence, monopolise the African servant's rest hour.

Miranda and Prospero may be equal in their assumed superiority
of origins over Caliban. But Caliban and the Duke's daughter have
a bond that is not easily broken. They are alike in their ignorance;
and there are parallels in their response to strangers from the world
beyond these shores. The moment Miranda sets eyes on Ferdinand—handsome, noble and a prince—she suffers a genuine attack
of lovesickness.

> MIRANDA:                          I might call him
> A thing divine; for nothing natural
> I ever saw so noble. [1.2.415–17]

And Ferdinand who is her equal in vigour and her other half in
chastity lets her know exactly his intentions.

> FERDINAND: O, if a virgin,
> And your affection not gone forth, I'll make you
> The Queen of Naples. [1.2.445–47]

Ferdinand does not yet know that his father is alive; hence his
promise to Miranda that she will be queen. It is at this point that
Prospero intervenes to supply us again with the kind of stuff he is
made of: an imperialist by circumstance, a sadist by disease; and,
above all, an old man in whom envy and revenge are equally
matched. Immediately after Ferdinand's offer of marriage, Prospero
says:

> PROSPERO:                        Soft, sir! one word more.
> (Aside) They are both in either's pow'rs: but this swift business
> I must uneasy make, lest too light winning
> Make the prize light. (To Ferdinand) One word more; I charge
>       thee
> That thou attend me: thou dost here usurp
> The name thou ow'st not; and hast put thyself
> Upon this island as a spy, to win it
> From me, the lord on't. [1.2.447–54]

It is possible that Prospero envies and admires the passion which
is an essential part of the couple's youth. It is likely that he had
never experienced any such feeling towards his wife. His imperialism is like an illness, not only in his personal relationships, but in
his relation to the external and foreign world. This island belongs to
Caliban whom he found there; yet some privilege allows Prospero
to assert—and with an authority that is divine—that he is lord of
the island.

Sadism is characteristic of this type. He approves of the union
of Ferdinand and his daughter. Indeed, it is a part of his overall
arrangement; but youth and innocence must be punished before

they can partake of the pleasures and paradox of love. He accuses
Ferdinand of being a spy when he knows that the shipwrecked boy
is occupied with sorrow for the imagined death of his father. He
tells Miranda that she must not rush these things; and again that
loathsome habit of cutting people down to size is revealed:

> PROSPERO: Thou think'st there is no more such shapes as he,
> Having seen but him and Caliban: foolish wench!
> To th' most of men this is a Caliban,
> And they to him are angels. [1.2.476–79]

His accusation of espionage is also intended to test Ferdinand's
nobility. Enraged, the boy draws his sword, and is immediately
charmed into immobility by Prospero's magic. Even Miranda, who
has not long heard what an excellent specimen of nobility and wisdom her father is, even she is shaken by the appearance of the
monster in Prospero. Torn between her love for the young prince
and her tribal allegiance to Prospero, she tries to cheer Ferdinand
up:

> Be of comfort;
> My father's of a better nature, sir,
> Than he appears by speech: this is unwonted
> Which now came from him. [1.2.493–96]

An opinion which we know to be in direct contradiction with the
facts; for the obscenity of Prospero's rage knows no bounds in his
dealings with Ariel and Caliban: the two agents of labour and public relations without whom he would be helpless. It is this innocence and credulity in Miranda which—were it not for a difference
in their degrees of being—would have made her and Caliban almost identical.

For Caliban also has this tendency to take people at their face
value. Whereas Prospero's fear springs from a need to maintain his
power—for to lose his power is to lose face—and it is only through
power that the world knows him; Caliban is the epitome of a pure
and uncalculated naïveté. Having been deprived of his freedom, it
seems that Caliban has nothing to lose but his goodwill; and one
meaning we can extract from this is that the suspension of a man's
freedom can have the effect of returning him to the fundamental
sources of integrity. Temporary imprisonment is the greatest service
an imperialist can do to a nationalist leader. It is in the solitude of
the cell that he gets a chance, free from the indulgence of his followers, to think things out. When he is freed—as we shall see with
Caliban—he returns to the streets with a formidable power born of
suffering and reflection. But it is this original tendency to welcome
which gets Caliban into trouble. We recall what he tells Prospero:

CALIBAN: This island's mine, by Sycorax my mother
Which thou tak'st from me. [1.2.331–32]

And later, in his state of utter displacement brought about by
Prospero's betrayal of love, Caliban makes the same mistake again.
Trinculo is a jester, a man who lives at the mercy of a successful
joke. Stephano is a butler and an irresponsible and adventurous
drunk. In their original home, they bear much the same relation to
royalty that Caliban here bears to Prospero. They are scum. It is to
these innocent bandits that Caliban turns for help. He is plotting
revolution with them; but they have absolutely no idea what it
means for Caliban that he should get Prospero out of the way. To
them, it is no more than cutting another throat. To Caliban it is an
enterprise of colossal importance. Yet it is to these men that Caliban will surrender his secrets:

CALIBAN: I prithee, let me bring thee where crabs grow;
And I with my long nails will dig thee pig-nuts;
Show thee a jay's nest, and instruct thee how
To snare the nimble marmoset; I'll bring thee
To clustering filberts, and sometimes I'll get thee
Young scamels from the rock. Wilt thou go with me?
[2.2.162–67]

In some real, though extraordinary way, Caliban and Miranda are
seen side by side: opposite and contiguous at the same time. They
share an ignorance that is also the source of some vision. It is, as it
were, a kind of creative blindness.

In different circumstances, they could be together in a way that
Miranda and her father could not. For Prospero is alone. He hates
and fears and needs Caliban. The role of father demands that he
should pay Miranda some attention, equip her with a few basic prejudices; but he is not really interested in her as a person. The education he bestows is in the nature of a formality. Miranda herself has
told him that he was always postponing to tell her certain things.

It has taken him twelve years to tell the child one or two things
which any decent parent of his intelligence would have passed on
long ago. When she asked him: Are you not my father? he talks
about the chastity of her mother; and we realise—with some knowledge of this type—that he is taking refuge in the lesson of chastity
in order to evade or obscure any talk about the woman who is
supposed to be his wife. Who, we are left to wonder, was really
Miranda's mother? And what would she have had to say about this
marvellous monster of a husband who refuses us information?

An interesting contrast is seen in his dealing with Caliban on the
same subject. For some reason or other, the memory of Sycorax,

Caliban's mother, arouses him to rage that is almost insane. For all that he is a Duke and noble, Prospero can't conquer that obscene habit of throwing the past, turning your origins into a weapon of slander. In Caliban's case it takes the form of his mother being a so-and-so.

We ask ourselves why a Duke should debase himself to speak in such a way. The tone suggests an intimacy of involvement and concern which encourages speculation. But we could not speak with authority on the possibilities of this defect until we had heard from Sycorax and Miranda's mother. They are both dead; and so our knowledge must be postponed until some arrangement comparable to the Haitian Ceremony of Souls returns them to tell us what we should and ought to know.

We begin to distrust this Duke. Why should we believe, in the light of all that has happened now, that the people of Milan really loved him. For it's a difficult love: the love of a dispossessed crowd for a rich and absent idol. Prospero contributed in no uncertain terms to his brother's treachery. If he wanted to retain the honour and privilege of Duke, then he should have been prepared to undertake the responsibilities. If the Book dominated his deepest interest; then he should have told the people that in the interest of learning which would be to their benefit, he would have to abdicate. It was the only decent thing to do.

Antonio can be forgiven for usurping the rights and privileges that were not his. Prospero sees this as another occasion of ingratitude. When he hears of Caliban's conspiracy to overthrow him, he is again plunged into rage. For this is seen as ingratitude of a most bestial nature. Caliban whom he had given Language conspiring with men not much better than himself to sabotage the divine hierarchy of which he is the most privileged on earth!

> PROSPERO: He is as disproportion'd in his manners
> As in his shape. Go, sirrah, to my cell;
> Take with you your companions; as you look
> To have my pardon, trim it handsomely. [5.1.290–93]

One wonders whether it is ingratitude that bothers Prospero. Could it not be a shattering kind of self-knowledge, the knowledge that he really deserves such ingratitude? Prospero's gifts are no part of his concern for those who receive. Could it be that Prospero didn't really care any more about the people of Milan than he cared about his wife? Is it that age and the pressure of a simple honesty had forced him to see his total indifference to his neighbour as a perfect example of human degradation? For the real sin is not hatred, which implies an involvement, but the calculated and habitual annihilation of the person whose presence you can ignore but never

exclude. What can he feel when he recalls the statement which
tells us what Caliban truly felt?

> CALIBAN:                                    When thou cam'st first,
> Thou strok'dst me, and made much of me; wouldst give me
> Water with berries in't; and teach me how
> To name the bigger light, and how the less,
> That burn by day and night: and then I loved thee.
>     [1.2.332–36]

Will the Lie upon which Prospero's confident authority was built
be discovered? For tomorrow they will take to sea, rehearsing again
the distance and purgatory which have always separated them from
their forgotten slave.

We can assume that they are gone. Dawn has rigged their sails;
the clouds have dispersed; and the sun is loud as wedding bells.
But no one bade them farewell.

Tonight, in his deformity and his solitude, Caliban, like Ishmael,
is left alone.

# BARBARA A. MOWAT

## Prospero, Agrippa, and Hocus Pocus†

> If by your Art (my deerest father) you have
> Put the wild waters in this Rore; alay them.
> (*The Tempest*, I. ii. 1–2)

After years of discounting Prospero's magic Art as simply a
metaphor for the creative imagination, critics of *The Tempest* since
the 1930s have been making serious efforts to come to terms with
Prospero as a Renaissance magician, a mortal with spirits at his
command and with power over the natural and supernatural
worlds.[1] In the 1960s, new interest in Renaissance attitudes toward
the occult led to an outpouring of attempts to place Prospero as a
magician and to discover the shape and parameters of his magic.[2]

---

† From *English Literary Renaissance* 11 (1981): 281–303. Reprinted by permission of the
  editors. Line numbers to this Norton Critical Edition of the play appear in brackets
  when they differ from the author's original citation.
1. The seminal work on Prospero's magic was Walter Clyde Curry's "Sacerdotal Science in
   Shakespeare's *The Tempest*," *Archiv*, 90, Bd. 168 (1935), 25–36, 185–96, rpt. in *Shakespeare's Philosophical Patterns* (Baton Rouge, 1959; orig. prtd. 1937), pp. 163–99. See
   also C. J. Sisson, "The Magic of Prospero," *Shakespeare Survey*, 11 (1958), 70–77; and
   Frank Kermode, "Introduction," *The Tempest*, Arden edition (Cambridge, Mass., 1954),
   pp. xlvii ff.
2. On Renaissance attitudes toward the occult, see especially D. P. Walker, *Spiritual and
   Demonic Magic from Ficino to Campanella* (London, 1958); Frances Yates, *Giordano
   Bruno and the Hermetic Tradition* (New York, 1969; orig. prt., 1964); Eugenio Garin,

Today, the issue is not that Prospero's Art is likely to be discounted, but that it is likely to be taken far too seriously and treated in far too ponderous a manner. In recent journals, one actually senses a battle shaping between those who follow Curry, Sisson, Kermode, and Yates in seeing Prospero as the quintessential Renaissance philosopher-magus or theurgist, who "exercises the supernatural powers of the holy adept" (Kermode, p. xlvii) and those who say, instead, that since all magic is evil, Prospero is actually "a type of the potentially damned sorcerer" who shows "in his actions something infinitely more malevolent" than the positive magic claimed for the magus.[3] The problem here is two-fold. In the first place, Prospero's magic is far more complex than such an easy dichotomy would suggest. Robert West has long since demonstrated that Prospero cannot be safely ensconced in either of these magic traditions, black or white, and his essay linking *The Tempest* to Shakespeare's world of "outer mystery" is a fine corrective to those who would attempt to so limit Prospero's Art.[4] In the second place, those who argue about Prospero as magus or Prospero as witch tend to ignore the fact that these are only two of the many images of magicians current in Renaissance England, and thus tend to overlook aspects of Prospero's Art which radically affect audience response to him and to his creations of illusion and transformation. Prospero is, I would argue, more various and more fascinating than the insubstantial, all-too-solemn magus or the vengeful, finally repentant witch now being preferred by critics for our contemplation. By examining the language, and, to a lesser extent, the actions which reveal Prospero's magic to us, I hope to make clear the complexity of his image and of the response which he summons from

---

"Magic and Astrology in the Civilisation of the Renaissance," *Science and Civic Life in the Italian Renaissance*, trans. Peter Munz (Garden City, New York, 1969), pp. 145–65; Keith Thomas, *Religion and the Decline of Magic* (New York, 1971); and Wayne Shumaker, *The Occult Sciences in the Renaissance* (Berkeley, 1972).

   Among recent studies of Prospero's magic, see, e.g., D. G. James, *The Dream of Prospero* (Oxford, 1967), pp. 45–71; Hardin Craig, "Magic in *The Tempest*," *Philological Quarterly*, 47 (1968), 8–15; Harry Levin, "Two Magian Comedies: 'The Tempest' and 'The Alchemist'," *Shakespeare Survey*, 22 (1969), 47–58; Kurt Tetzeli von Rosador, *Magic im Elisabethanischen Drama* (Braunschweig, 1970), pp. 164–86; Elizabeth Sewell, "'As I was sometime Milan': Prospects for a Search for Giordano Bruno, through Prospero, Coleridge, and the Figure of Exile," *Mosaic*, 8 (1974), 127–37; David Woodman, *White Magic and English Renaissance Drama* (Cranbury, N.J., 1973), pp. 64 ff.; Robert Egan, "This Rough Magic: Perspectives of Art and Morality in *The Tempest*," *Shakespeare Quarterly*, 23 (1972), 171–82; Frances Yates, *Shakespeare's Last Plays: A New Approach* (London, 1975), pp. 87–106; D'Orsay Pearson, "'Unless I be Relieved by Prayer': *The Tempest* in Perspective," *Shakespeare Studies*, VII (1974), 253–82; and David Young, *The Heart's Forest: A Study of Shakespeare's Pastoral Plays* (New Haven and London, 1972), pp. 146–91, and "Where the Bee Sucks: A Triangular Study of *Doctor Faustus*, *The Alchemist*, and *The Tempest*, in *Shakespeare's Romances Reconsidered*, ed. Carol McGinnis Ray and Henry E. Jacobs (Lincoln and London, 1978), pp. 149–66.

3. D'Orsay Pearson, p. 256.
4. Robert West, "Ceremonial Magic in *The Tempest*," *Shakespeare and the Outer Mystery* (Lexington, Kentucky, 1968), pp. 80–95.

his audience. My hope is to open us up once again to the blend of
seriousness and jest, of belief and skepticism, which is the climate
of Shakespeare's magic island.

I

Let me begin with a portion of Prospero's long narrative to
Miranda about his life in Milan. He is explaining to her the coup
d'état which hurled them from their palace into a "full poor cell" on
an unnamed island. The lines, although familiar deserve our close
attention:

> The Government I cast upon my brother,
> And to my State grew stranger, being transported
> And rapt in secret studies . . . .
>
> I thus neglecting worldly ends, all dedicated
> To closenes, and the bettering of my mind
> with that, which but by being so retir'd
> Ore-priz'd all popular rate: in my false brother
> Awak'd an evill nature . . . .
>
> . . . hence his Ambition growing:
> . . . . . . . . . . . . . . . .
> . . . he needes will be
> Absolute *Millaine*, Me (poore man) my Librarie
> Was Dukedome large enough: of temporall roalties
> He thinks me now incapable . . . .
>
> [Gonzalo,] of his gentlenesse
> Knowing I lov'd my bookes, . . . furnishd me
> From mine owne Library, with volumes, that
> I prize above my Dukedome.
>
> . . . by my prescience
> I finde my *Zenith* doth depend upon
> A most auspitious starre, whose influence
> If now I court not, but omit; my fortunes
> Will ever after droope . . .[5]

Within this narrative, those who see Prospero as a magus could
find solid evidence to support their stand. Separate from the text or
replaced within the larger narrative, these lines give us a recognizable Hermetic magus, a Prospero much like Agrippa, Trithemius,
and John Dee, men who linked magic to intellectual study, who
said with Ficino and with Pico that magic is the greatest of the

5. All quotations from Shakespeare's plays are taken from the *Norton Facsimile First Folio*.
   The line numberings, in place of the through-line numbering of the Facsimile, are those
   of the Riverside edition of the plays (1974). The passage here quoted is from I, ii,
   75–77, 89–93, 105–11, 165–68, 180–84.

philosophies, the greatest of the sciences, taking the magus away from the pettiness of this world and drawing him close to the gods. Look carefully at Prospero's words: "transported and rapt in secret studies." This is the kind of language used by Agrippa and Trithemius in their correspondence about *The Occult Philosophy*, where they speak of "that ancient Magick, the discipline of all wise men" as "sublime and sacred"; Agrippa refers to Trithemius's knowledge as "transcending" and to Trithemius himself as a "man very industrious after secret things"; Trithemius commends Agrippa for having "penetrate[d] into such secrets as have been hide from most learned men," and exhorts him to keep these secret things hidden from the "vulgar." Agrippa later celebrates Ceremonial Magic as the "divine science" by which, if one is "alwaies busied," contemplating it "every moment . . . by a sage and diligent inquisition," one ascends "by all the degrees of the creatures . . . even to the Archetype himself."[6] John Dee, too, uses language of rapture and transport when he writes of his "studies and studious exercises." He defends his magical endeavors from charges of sorcery, describing them as, instead, the means by which he sought the truth "by the true philosophicall method and harmony: proceeding and ascending (as it were) *gradatim*, from thinges visible to consider of thinges invisible: from thinges bodily, to conceive of thinges spirituall: from thinges transitorie, & momentanie, to meditate of things permanent. . . ."[7] For Prospero, as for the real-life magus, studies of secret things stand in contradistinction to mundane concerns, to Trithemius's "vulgar" and Dee's "transitorie & momentanie." Similarly when Prospero a moment later talks of "neglecting worldly ends," he reflects the language of these same men, to whom things "worldly" and "temporal" meant precisely things of this world, transitory rewards acquired through ambition and love of wealth and power. "Worldly ends" and "temporal roialties" are the goals of Prospero's brother, who, "drie . . . for Sway," turns traitor both to Prospero and to Milan.

Prospero's dedication to "closenes" (i.e., to solitude or perhaps to secrecy) and to the "bettering of [his] mind" likewise recalls the real-life magus, as does his prizing of his books above his dukedom. For the magus—even an emperor-magus like Rudolf II—the magic books which open to the adept the secrets of the universe are prop-

6. The letters between Cornelius Agrippa and Johannes Trithemius, Abbot of Saint James of Herbipolis, written in 1510, are printed in Agrippa's *Three Books of Occult Philosophy*, trans. J. F. (1651), pp. A2–A5. The later letter from Agrippa, "To the most Renowned & Illustrious Prince, Hermannus of Wyda" (written, as indicated by internal evidence, in 1531), prefaces Book III of *Occult Philosophy* ("Ceremonial Magic"), pp. 341–42.

7. "A Letter Containing a most brief discourse Apologetical . . ." (1599), p. A2v. See also Dee's "Monas Hieroglyphica" (Antwerp, 1564), trans. and introduced by C. H. Josten, *Ambix* xii, 1964, pp. 102, 197.

erly valued above mere mortal power and station.[8] Note that in the
famous lines "he furnished me / From mine own Library, with volumes, that / I prize above my Dukedome," Shakespeare has Prospero use the present tense verb *prize*, an indication that the
Prospero we meet on the island is even yet, "twelve yere since,"
very much the Hermetic magus. The reiteration of the phrase "my
Library" is also of interest, echoing as it does some of the more passionate statements of John Dee about his treasured volumes.[9]

In Prospero's long narrative to Miranda, there are only two points
at which the language seems potentially at odds with that used by
the magus. The first is the phrase, "and to my State grew stranger,"
with its hint of self-recrimination foreign to the language of the
magus; the second is the phrase "but by being so retir'd," which
again attaches guilt to magic studies, and is thus unlike the language used by maguses in their writings. One final passage deserves
our close attention, inasmuch as it is usually read as Prospero's
apology, his admission that his studies, his retreat into magic, were
morally wrong. "I thus neglecting worldly ends," he says, "all dedicated / To closenes . . . in my false brother / Awak'd an evill nature."
Were Prospero here saying that he had neglected his duty and that
he was therefore blameworthy, then this passage would place him
outside the world of the magus. But, as I noted earlier, Prospero
does not here say that he neglected his duty; he says, rather, that he
neglected "worldly ends"—a virtue for neo-Platonist and Christian
alike; and though his giving over of "temporal sway" to his brother
did allow Antonio's worldly ambitions to grow, the analogy that
Prospero uses in his own defense suggests no sense of self-
condemnation. "My trust," he says, "Like a good parent, did beget
of him / A falsehood in it's contrarie, as great / As my trust was,
which had indeede no limit, / A confidence sans bound." To para-
phrase, using Miranda's words: "Good wombes have borne bad
sonnes."

Further, within this supposed apology, Prospero give us his most
affirmative evaluation of his secret studies. He was, he said, "all
dedicated / To . . . the bettering of my mind / with that which . . . /
Ore-priz'd all popular rate," or, as David Horne glosses it in the Yale

8. Rudolf, King of Bohemia and Holy Roman Emperor from 1576 to 1612, was described
   by a contemporary, Melchior Goldast (1612) as an "intelligent and sagacious Prince"
   who "contemned all vulgar things, loving only the rare and miraculous." He was, according to his biographer R. J. W. Evans, "a notorious patron of occult learning who trod
   the paths of secret knowledge with an obsession bordering on mania." *Rudolf II and His
   World: A Study in Intellectual History, 1576–1612* (Oxford, 1973), esp. pp. 196–242,
   where Evans quotes Goldast and discusses "Rudolf and the Occult Arts."
9. See, e.g., John Dee, "A Letter, Nine Yeeres Since, written and first published: Containing a most brief discourse Apologeticall . . ." (1603), p. B3, where he refers to the "volumes . . . which by Gods providence, have been preserved from the spoile made of my
   Librarie . . . here . . . Anno 1583. In which Librarie, were about 400 bookes: whereof,
   700 were ancientlie written by hand . . ."

Shakespeare, "surpassed in value everything the world rates highly." Such a description of dark and secret studies echoes Hermetic magi from Agrippa to John Dee.

In Prospero's early narrative about his magic, then, he speaks almost entirely in the vein of the Renaissance philosopher-magus. The image given of him here, drawn throughout from the magus tradition, is sharpened by the contrasting image drawn in the same scene of Sycorax, the witch who copulated with the devil, who whelped Caliban, who worshipped the god Setebos, and whose sorceries were "terrible to enter human hearing."

## II

Thus far, then, those who would see Prospero as quintessential magus would seem justified in their reading of his character. Yet move with me to another set of lines, where Prospero is again speaking of his magic, of himself as magician. "I have," he says,

> bedymn'd
> The Noone-tide Sun, call'd forth the mutenous windes,
> And twixt the greene Sea, and the azur'd vault
> Set roaring warre: To the dread ratling Thunder
> Have I given fire, and rifted *Joves* stowt Oke
> With his owne Bolt: The strong bass'd promontorie
> Have I made shake, and by the spurs pluckt up
> The Pyne, and Cedar. Graves at my command
> Have wak'd their sleepers, op'd, and let 'em forth
> By my so potent Art. (V. i. 41–50)

Such claims, such diction, lift us suddenly into a world quite antithetical to Hermetic magic, into a world of Medeas, of Thessalian witches, of such "old enchantresses" as Lyly's Dipsas or such enchanters as Owen Glendower, who kept poor Hotspur awake with many such skimble-skamble tales of earthquakes and fiery cressets, curious arts and deep experiments.

Both West and Sisson note the incongruity of having a speech derived from Ovid's Medea coming from the lips of a theurgist or magus. But they fail to note the larger significance of Shakespeare's use of these lines: namely, that this speech links Prospero to a tradition as venerable as that of the magus, a tradition which was seen in the Renaissance as the antithesis of Hermetic magic. Ovid's Medea is an enchanter, a magician who, unlike the magus, does not seek spiritual growth, but seeks instead godlike control over the natural and supernatural worlds. Apuleius's enchantress, Meroe, is another figure from this tradition; she has "power to rule the heavens, to bring down the sky, to bear up the earth, to turn the waters into hills and the hills into running waters, to lift up the terrestrial

spirits into the air, and to pull the gods out of the heavens, to ex-
tinguish the planets and to lighten the deep darkness of hell."
Agrippa, writing in 1510, quotes this passage as an example of the
outrageous claims, the "cursed and detestable fooleries," which had
brought the sacred discipline of magic as practised by himself and
other Hermetic magi into disrepute.[1] Medea and Meroe are not
alone in making such claims. Lyly's Dipsas can, she says, "darken
the sun by my skill and remove the moon out of her course, . . . restore youth to the aged and make hills without bottoms." Glendower can summon spirits, command the devil, raise tempests.
Reginald Scot scoffed at such claims: only God and Jesus had, he
said, such powers. Hotspur, too, scoffed, as did Trithemius, who
warned friends to beware of such braggarts as Faustus, the kind of
conjuror who gave good magic a bad name.[2]

When Prospero extols his magic control over the sun, the winds,
the sea; when he claims that, through his "potent Art," graves have
"op'd" and let forth their sleepers, he stands before us briefly as a kind
of pagan enchanter. The moment is a powerful one, with Prospero
alone onstage *"in his Magicke robes,"* celebrating in potent language
his enchanter's Art. Yet the moment is also a brief one. As he reaches
the culmination of his "hybrisrede"[3] he immediately dismisses it, and
dismisses the magic that it celebrates. "My so potent Art" becomes,
within a single line, "this rough Magicke," and Prospero's language
takes him into yet another world, another magic tradition:

> But this rough Magicke
> I heere abjure: and when I have requir'd
> Some heavenly Musicke (which even now I do)
> To worke mine end upon their Sences, that
> This Ayrie-charme is for, I'le breake my staffe,
> Bury it certaine fadomes in the earth,
> And deeper then did ever Plummet sound
> Ile drowne my booke. (V. i. 50–57)

This speech of abjuration, with its dismissal of magic Art as "rough"
and its promise to destroy both staff and book, is not the language

---

1. West, pp. 92–93; Sisson, pp. 75–76. *The Golden Ass of Lucius Apuleius*, trans. William
   Adlington (orig. pub. 1566), ed. F.J. Harvey Darton (London, 1924), p. 49. Agrippa,
   *Three Books of Occult Philosophy*, p. A3. Agrippa himself complicates this whole issue,
   however, by later claiming that sometimes the magus "receiveth this miraculous power"
   to "command the Elements, drive away Fogs, raise the winds . . . raise the dead" (*Occult
   Philosophy*, p. 357).
2. John Lyly, *Endymion, The Man in the Moon*, I, iv. Although Glendower, in *1 Henry IV*,
   does not actually claim the ability to raise tempests, he implies that he has control over
   the weather, and he is credited by Holinshed with tempest-raising powers. Reginald
   Scot, *The Discoverie of Witchcraft* (1584), pp. 1–2. Trithemius's letters about Faustus
   are quoted by William Rose in his introduction to *The Historie of the Damnable Life and
   Deserved Death of Doctor John Faustus, 1592* (South Bend, Indiana, 1963), pp. 3–5.
3. The term "hysbrisrede" is used by Tetzeli von Rosador to describe such bragging
   speeches by magicians; see his *Magie im Elisabethanischen Drama*, pp. 65–71.

of the great enchanters, who tend to remain proud of their powers, disappearing like Ovid's Medea in a cloud "as dark as the music chanted in her spells" (Book VII). Nor is this speech suggestive of the Hermetic magus. John Dee, called upon to recant, went to his pauper's death still composing passionate letters to the King and Parliament defending his Hermetic beliefs and practices, though his library had been destroyed by irate citizens lashing out at his necromancy, his magic glass, and his converse with spirits. Trithemius never admitted to any conflict between his Hermetic practices and his position as a Christian abbot. If Agrippa recanted, he did so only within the context of a total recantation and a cry of "all is vanity."

I would suggest that Prospero's recantation, his use of the term "abjure" (with its links to the Christian church through association with the word "heresy"), and his promise to drown his book, place him in yet a third tradition. This is the tradition of the wizard—the pagan enchanter brought into the Christian world, the magician with the magus's pride in his secret knowledge, the enchanter's power over the elements, the sorcerer's control over spirits, and, finally, the Christian's concern over the fate of his soul. Those who fall into the camp of the wizard are a diverse lot; we find them in medieval legend, in commedia dell'arte *scenari*, in Renaissance prose "histories"—like those, for example, about "Fryer Bacon" and about "J. Faustus"—and in the elaborate wizard dramas of the 1590s.[4]

We recognize the wizard wherever we find him by his dual role. He is a magician who uses what D. P. Walker calls "transitive magic"[5] to

4. For a complete study of this tradition, one would want to begin with legends of wizards in *The Golden Legend*, and to examine carefully the relationship between Merlin and the various figures of the wizard which one finds in sixteenth century narrative and drama. One can find typical legends about wizards in J. Payne Collier's Introduction to *John a Kent and John a Cumber*, by Anthony Munday (London, 1851), especially pp. xxii–xxvi; in John William Ashton's "A Critical Edition of Anthony Munday's *John a Kent and John a Cumber*" (University of Chicago unpublished dissertation, 1928), pp. 61 ff.; in William Godwin's *Lives of the Necromancers, or an account of the most eminent persons in successive ages, who have claimed for themselves, or to whom has been imputed by others, the exercise of magical power* (1834); and in E. M. Butler's *The Myth of the Magus* (Cambridge, Eng., 1948).

Commedia dell'arte magicians are mentioned by K. M. Lea in her *Italian Popular Comedy: A Study in the Commedia dell'arte, 1560–1620, with special reference to the English Stage*, II (Oxford, 1934), pp. 444–45; she also includes several *scenari* which involve magicians in the same volume, pp. 555–674.

The prose "histories" to which I here refer are, specifically, *The Famous History of Fryer Bacon: Contayning the wonderfull things he did in his Life. Also the manner of his death, with the Lives and Deaths of the two Conjurors, Bungay and Vandermast* (1640[?]) and *The Historie of the damnable life, and deserved death of Doctor John Faustus . . .* , trans. by P. F. (1592).

Recent editions of wizard dramas are Robert Greene's *Friar Bacon and Friar Bungay*, ed. Daniel Seltzer, Regents Renaissance Drama Series (Lincoln, Neb., 1963), and Christopher Marlowe's *Doctor Faustus*, in *Christopher Marlowe, The Complete Works*, II, ed. Fredson Bowers (Cambridge, Eng., 1973).

5. Walker, *Spiritual and Demonic Magic*, p. 82 ff.

affect other people and to effect wondrous happenings; at the same
time, he is a human being with moral concerns. He delights in
his magic powers; however, as a human in a Christian world, he
must eventually admit the "roughness" of his magic. This moral imperative sets him apart not only from his pagan predecessors and
his Hermetic contemporaries (who thought that they had reconciled magic and the Christian moral world) but also from such figures as Shakespeare's Oberon, who, contemporary with the stage
versions of Faust and Bacon, shares many of the characteristics of
the wizard, but, not being mortal, need not recant and give over his
power.

The line separating the wizard from the enchanter is not a rigid
one. Shakespeare, for example, following Holinshed, chooses to
treat Owen Glendower as an enchanter, and omits from his portrait
the wizard-legends that tell of his repentance and his years of her-
mit life.[6] The real-life Friar Roger Bacon never admitted that his
"magic" studies were evil, and is thus more like a magus or an enchanter than a wizard; but the legends, narratives, and dramas
about him show him as repentant and self-condemnatory.[7] In *The
Famous Historie*, for example, the Friar "cries out upon himself"
for neglecting divine studies and, in a passage very reminiscent of
Acts 19.19, where the "practicers of curious arts" are forced to
burn their books, he decides to remove the cause of the "heavie
burthen" of his knowledge of magic by publicly burning his books,
and thenceforward devotes his life to pious meditation as an an-
chorite (G2v–G3v). Greene's Bacon also recants, of course, repent-
ing "that Bacon ever meddled in this art." Faustus, too, although
pictured by his contemporary Trithemius as a conjuror-sorcerer, de-
velops in legend into a powerful wizard figure with the wizard's
guilty conscience. Marlowe's Faustus, like his model in the *Faust-
buch*, seriously attempts to repent, ending his final soliloquy with
"Come not, Lucifer, / I'll burn my books . . . !" Lyly's Dipsas, described as "an old enchantress" and pictured as one throughout
most of *Endymion*, suddenly moves into the Christian moral world
at the end of the play, and as a reward for renouncing the filthy
trade of magic, regains her lost husband.

Prospero is like his wizard predecessors in a variety of ways.
First, he has the noted duality of the wizard. Like the magician-

---

6. See Collier's Introduction to *John a Kent and John a Cumber*, pp. xxiv–xxv, for two such
legends about Owen.
7. On the historical Bacon, see, e.g., S. C. Easton, *Roger Bacon and His Search for a Universal Science* (Oxford: Oxford University Press, 1952). Waldo F. McNeir, in his "Traditional Elements in the Character of Greene's Friar Bacon," *Studies in Philology* 45
(1948), 172–79, gives some attention to the "growth of the Bacon legend." See especially fn. 2, pp. 172–73.

hero of such *scenari* as "Pantaloonlet,"[8] he is a father concerned for his daughter as well as a worker of beneficent magic; like Faustus and Bacon, he is both a maker of spectacles and a man with "a beating mind." Prospero, *"on the top, invisible,"* performing magic acts, is at the same time Prospero, the wronged Duke of Milan.

Second, Prospero's magic acts follow the tradition of those acts performed by wizards in earlier plays. While the acts of wizards in legends are grand and magnificent, those performed by commedia dell'arte magicians are more limited in scope, and they form a pattern which carries over into the more elaborate wizard dramas. Commedia dell'arte wizards use charms to interfere in the lives of others, they produce and destroy food magically, and they use "spirits" to cudgel and torment their enemies. The wizard dramas of Greene and Marlowe include this same set of magic acts and add to it the summoning of spirits in the guise of famous persons or gods to entertain noble patrons and to give evidence of the magician's power. The magic acts which we see Prospero perform—the placing of charms on Miranda and Ferdinand, the summoning of spirits to present shows, the use of magic to aid friends and punish enemies, the creation and dissolution of a magic banquet—these acts are predictable stage-wizard magic: as Prospero says of the Masque of Spirits, "they expect it from me."

But it is the renunciation of magic, the return to the conventional world, and the concern with his own mortality, that most clearly link Prospero to the wizard tradition. The suddenness of his renunciation is reminiscent of such commedia dell'arte magicians as the magician-hero of "Pantaloonlet" who, after having used his magic to bring about a happy ending for himself, his friends and his daughter, abruptly declares that "he does not wish to practice his magic art any longer but instead he will live with [the ordinary mortals]; [and] he throws away his rod and his book" (Lea. ii. 642). But the language with which Prospero abjures his magic reminds us strongly of the Bacons and Faustuses of narrative and drama. The pattern established by Prospero's magic acts and the duality of Prospero's role as both a worker of transitive magic and as a man whose fate concerns us, place him among the wizards, and lead directly to his repudiation of magic, phrased in the language of the wizard: "Ile drown my book," and "retire me to my Millaine, where / Every third thought shall be my grave."

III

Thus far, we have seen reflected in Prospero's language several familiar worlds of magic—the lofty, proud world of the magus, the

8. Lea, II, 636–42.

thrasonical, hyperbolic world of the enchanter, the ambiguous world of the wizard who, at the end, turns his back on magic books and wands. In the final bit of dialogue which I will consider, we will seem, at first, to have left the recognizable traditions behind. This dialogue begins when Prospero summons Ariel: "Come away, Servant, come. . . ." Ariel approaches: "All haile, great Master, grave Sir, haile: I come / To answer thy best pleasure . . ." (I. ii. 198–200) [1.2.189–90]. The lines which most interest me occur a bit later, but we should pause and attempt to place ourselves linguistically.

Although the magician is here summoning a spirit, we are clearly not in the world of spirit-summonings inhabited by "callers and conjurors of wicked and damned Sprites"—to use John Dee's phrase. Shakespeare had twice before shown us that world, and it is one far removed from Prospero and his summoning of Ariel. The witches' conjurations in *Macbeth* we can immediately dismiss as irrelevant; the spirits are not the witches' servants but their masters, who "will not be commanded." Bolingbroke's conjuration of a spirit in *2 Henry VI* is only slightly more reminiscent of Prospero and Ariel. Instead of Prospero's open, daylight world, Bolingbroke's conjuring is done at night: "Deepe Night, darke Night, the silent of the Night / . . . The time when Screech-owles cry, and Bandogs howle, / And Spirits walke, and Ghosts breake up their Graves; / That time best fits the worke we have in hand" (I. iv. 15–19). A witch grovels on the ground, the spirit appears under the temporary compulsion of the magic rites, speaks cryptically, and surrounded by thunder and lightning, quickly returns to his true master in the infernal realms below. Prospero has little in common with such conjury. He is Ariel's "great Master"; Ariel is Prospero's industrious "Servant," "correspondent to command."

The language of Prospero and Ariel also seems foreign to the world of the Hermetic magi and their *daemons*. Curry saw Ariel as a neo-Platonic *daemon* under Prospero's control; Kittredge and others follow Curry; and many critics explain Ariel by citing recondite sources: Plato's reference to spirits who act as messengers, Iamblichus's description of the various spirits who inhabit the air and act as guardians of man, Hermes Trismegistus's lines and Agrippa's passages discussing the higher forms of invisible life which link man to the demi-urge.[9] Yet nowhere in such writings can I find evidence that the magus may take as his servant a *daemon*

9. Curry, *Shakespeare's Philosophical Patterns*, pp. 186–194; George Lyman Kittredge, Introduction to *The Tempest*, in *Sixteen Plays of Shakespeare* (Boston, 1946), p. 11. On Ariel as a *daemon*, see also A. Koszul, "Ariel," *English Studies*, XIX (1937), 200–4, and W. Stacey Johnson, "The Genesis of Ariel," *Shakespeare Quarterly*, II (1951), 205–10. For Plato on *daemons*, see "The Symposium," trans. W. Hamilton (Baltimore, Md., 1951), p. 81; for Iamblichus's discussion of *daemons*, see Section IV, pp. 203–24 (note 3, above). In the Hermetic writings see *Hermetica*, ed. and trans. by Walter Scott, 4 vols. (Oxford, 1924), 1,293; Agrippa, *Three Books of Occult Philosophy*, pp. 390 ff.

who will come at his command, call him master, and present himself as a willing, obedient servant. Iamblichus and Agrippa come
closest to suggesting that the magus eventually "controls" *daemons*.
Yet Iamblichus gives us, at best, a rather murky picture in which divine energy flows and power is mystically exerted between the
"priest" and various levels of *daemons* (IV. i–ii). Agrippa, though
claiming that "the understanding of Divine things . . . compels even
good Angels . . . unto our service" (*Occult Philosophy*, p. 342) states
unequivocally that although the magus may "call up good spirits,"
these spirits "can by no bonds . . . be allayed by us"; rather, they
must be beseeched "by some sacred things" (p. 447). Spirits thus
beseeched through religious signs "sometimes apply themselves to
humane uses" yet "not as being compelled by any kind of necessity,
but of their own accord . . . being overcome by the prayers of them
that called on them." It is the "good spirits" that overcome and control the more useful "evil spirits" for the magus (pp. 447–48).

The relationship of Prospero, Ariel, and the lesser spirits (the
"rabble," as Shakespeare at one point calls them) could suggest a
kind of translation of Agrippa's three-fold grouping of the magus,
the "good spirit" whom he beseeches and the "evil spirits" whom
the good spirit can control. But if we consider the tone in which
Prospero addresses Ariel, remember the larger context of Agrippa's
discussion of Ceremonial Magic, and consider such phrases from
*The Tempest* as Prospero's command to Ariel—"Goe bring the rabble / (Ore whom I give thee powre)"—we are unlikely to see the
Prospero-Ariel relationship in Agrippan terms, unless we conclude
that Shakespeare was being fanciful, either tongue-in-cheek or
through a rather monumental kind of dramatic license. John Dee's
accounts of his summoning of spirits is much more in line with the
Agrippan model, and seems far afield from Prospero's "Come away,
Servant," or from Ariel's "Grave Sir, haile: I come / To answer thy
best pleasure." Dee claims to have been successful in calling into
his chambers a succession of spirits who grudgingly speak with
him, but he must beseech them continually (as Agrippa had
warned) and never are they under his command. Dee's rather piti-
ful attempts to get from the spirits any of their secrets or to persuade them to stay once their real master in the world beyond calls
them are quite unlike Prospero's peremptory commands and Ariel's
quick obedience.[1]

In the traditions of magic which we have thus far examined,
there are, of course, magicians who have spirits at their command.
These are the enchanters and the wizards. Glendower holds Hotspur "at least nine howres, / In reckning up the severall Devils

1. See *A True and Faithful Relation of What passed for many yeers between Dr. John Dee and
Some spirits* (1659).

Names, / That were his Lacqueyes." The historical Faustus, we are
told, had a familiar spirit in the guise of a black dog who did his
magic work for him; the legends surrounding John a Kent always
included a familiar spirit who accompanied and served him; and
James I wrote that the devil himself will often act as a familiar, and
will, to some magicians, "be a continual attender, in forme of a
Page."[2] The master-servant relationship that we hear at Prospero's
meeting with Ariel would therefore be appropriate to the enchanter
and wizard traditions, but only if we were willing to see Ariel as
Prospero's "familiar"—i.e., a demon under Prospero's command. If
we look further into the Prospero-Ariel dialogue, though, we realize
that we need not be driven to that extremity, for their language
leads us to yet another world of magic in which Ariel's position is
far less sinister than that of a "familiar," and in which Prospero appears as neither conjuror nor enchanter:

Prospero:     *Ariel*, thy charge
              Exactly is perform'd; but there's more worke:
              What is the time o'th'day?

Ariel:        Past the mid season.

Pro:          At least two Glasses: the time 'twixt six & now
              Must by us both be spent most preciously.

Ar.           Is there more toyle? Since ÿ dost give me pains,
              Let me remember thee what thou hast promis'd,
              Which is not yet perform'd me.

Pro.                    How now? moodie?
              What is't thou canst demand?

Ar.                     My Libertie.

Pro.          Before the time be out? no more;

Ar.                     I prethee,
              Remember I have done thee worthy service,
              Told thee no lyes, made thee no mistakings, serv'd
              Without or grudge, or grumblings; thou did promise
              To bate me a full yeere.

Pro.                    Do'st thou forget
              From what a torment I did free thee?
                      . . . . .
              If thou more murmur'st, I will rend an Oake
              And peg-thee in his knotty entrailes, till
              Thou hast howl'd away twelve winters.

---

2. *1 Henry IV*, III. i; the "historical personage" of Faust is discussed by William Rose, *The
Damnable Life*, pp. 3–22; for legends about John a Kent, see Collier, pp. xxii–xxv; *Dae-
monologie, in Forme of a Dialogue* (Edinburgh, 1597), p. 20.

Ar.                     Pardon, Master,
            I will be correspondent to command
            And doe my spryting, gently.

Pro.                    Doe so: and after two daies
            I will discharge thee.

Ar.                     That's my noble Master:
            What shall I doe? say what? what shall I doe?

Pro.        Goe make thy selfe like a Nymph o'th'Sea,
            Be subject to no sight but thine, and mine: invisible
            To every eye-ball else: goe take this shape
            And hither come in't: goe: hence
            With diligence. (I. ii. 237–304)

Several aspects of Prospero's relationship to Ariel become clear
in this dialogue. First, there are obvious resemblances between
their "contract of servitude" and that of Faustus and Mephistoph-
ilis: the charge to be invisible "to every eye-ball else," to take the
whimsical form commanded by his master, is almost an echo of the
Faust-Mephistophilis contract. As in the Faust story, Prospero's
contract binds the spirit to "at all times appear at his command"
and "doe for him whatsoever." Ultimately the contracts are quite
different, inasmuch as Prospero's terminates not with his own
damnation but with Ariel's freedom. Nevertheless it is possible that
the relationship between Faustus and his "swift-flying Spirit" may
have helped shape Prospero and Ariel.

More important, though, is that aspect of the relationship which
emerges in their use of words such as "discharge thee" and "before
the time be out," and in the emphasis throughout the passage on
Ariel's proper behavior. According to the terms of the contract as
implied in the dialogue, Ariel must be diligent, must be obedient,
must be truthful. In the face of Prospero's anger, Ariel insists that
he has indeed been diligent, "told . . . no lyes, made . . . no mistakings, [and] serv'd / Without or grudge, or grumblings." "Remember," he says, "thou did promise / To bate me a full yeere." This kind
of language occurs repeatedly between Prospero and Ariel, and it
leads us to that other world of magic reflected in *The Tempest* (and,
to some extent, in *A Midsummer Night's Dream* and *John a Kent
and John a Cumber* as well). I would suggest that Ariel's language is
not that of a demon, nor of a *daemon*, but of a servant boy ready for
his freedom, and further, that the language with which he and
Prospero haggle over a few more hours of service belongs more to
the mundane world of the streetcorner "art-Magician" or "Jugler"
(these are Reginald Scot's terms for Houdini-type illusionists) than
to the arcane, terrifying Hermetic or demonic spheres.

The tradition of the Jugler is, like that of the magus and the enchanter, an ancient one. Cornelius Agrippa, writing in 1527, traces "this Arte of delusions or juglinges" back into antiquity. "There are bookes extant," he notes, "of the delusions or juglinges of Hermes touchinge this skill," and he gives examples of tricks of legerdemaine done by Numa Pompilus and Pythagorus. Through illusions, he says "the Magitiens doo shewe vaine visions, and with Juglinge castes doo plaie many miracles, & cause dreams, which thinge is not so much done by Geoticall inchauntmentes . . . [as] with a readie subteltie and nimblenesse of the handes, as wee dayly see stage players and Juglers doo. . . ." "The ende of this skil," he says, is "to stretche out imaginations even unto apperaunce, of which there shall afterwarde no signe appeare." And in a statement of particular relevance to readers of *The Tempest*, he notes that "we have reade also that one Pasetes a Jugler was wonte to shew to straungers a very sumptuouse banket, & when it pleased him to cause it vanishe awaie, all they whiche sate at the table beinge disappointed both of meate & drinke."[3]

Performing magicians of the kind described by Agrippa were familiar figures in Elizabethan and Jacobean England. They played on street corners, in "Fayres and Markets," in the provinces, and in London theaters.[4] In his *Discovery of Witchcraft*, Reginald Scot names several prominent illusionists: "one Kingsfield of London" who performed the difficult "decollation of John Baptist" with his boy assistants at "a Bartholomewtide, An. 1582, in the sight of diverse that came to view this spectacle" (p. 349); one "John Cautares," in S. Martins, "who getteth not his living thereby, but . . . nevertheless hath the best hand and conveiance (I thinke) of anie man that liveth this daie" (pp. 351–52). There are, in Jacobean documents, many references to one William Vincent, licensed "to exercise and practize the Arte of legerdemaine . . . in any Convenient place within any his Ma[ts] Dominions" (Bentley, II, 612–13). And probably most famous of all the illusionists, appearing in provincial and mentioned twice by Ben Jonson in his plays, "one man more excelling in that craft than others, that went about in King *James* his time, and long since, who called himself, *The Kings Majesties most excellent Hocus Pocus*."[5]

That these performing magicians were "conjurors" of the "I have

3. Cornelius Agrippa, *Of the Vanitie and uncertaintie of Artes and Sciences*, translated by Ja. San [ford] (1569), pp. 62–63.
4. Frank Aydelotte, *Elizabethan Rogues and Vagabonds* (Oxford Historical and Literary Studies. Under the direction of C. H. Firth and Walter Raleigh) Vol. I (Oxford, 1913), pp. 49–52.
5. Thomas Ady, *A Candle in the Dark: or A Treatise Concerning the Nature of Witches and Witchcraft* (1656), pp. 28–29. For a discussion of Hocus Pocus as a professional conjuror during James' and Charles' reign, see Trevor H. Hall, *Old Conjuring Books: A Bibliographical and Historical Study* (London, 1972), pp. 126–29.

no tricks up my sleeve" variety is clear from the description given of their devices in Scot's *Discovery of Witchcraft* (many of which are still part of the stage magician's repertoire) as well as from an interesting phrase which appears in George Abbott's attack on Giordano Bruno. Bruno, during his famous visit to Oxford in 1583, preparing to give his public lecture on Copernicus and Hermetic magic, is described by Abbott as an "Italian Didapper" who "more boldly than wisely got up into the highest place of our best and most renowned schoole, stripping up his sleeve like some Jugler. . . ."[6] And that the juglers were proficient in the creation of illusions is also clear. S[amuel] R[id], in 1612, notes not only that "Jugling is now become common, I mean the professors who make an occupation and profession of the same" but also that "I must needs say that some deserve commendation for the nimbleness and agility of their hands, & might be thought to performe as excellent things by their Legerdemaine, as any of your wizards witches or magitians whatsoever."[7] Scot, in 1584, Rid, in 1612, and "Hocus Pocus Junior," in 1634, all wrote detailed explanations of how the Juglers' tricks worked in order to clear them of the imputation that they were witches. Thomas Cooper, writing in 1617, insisted nevertheless that Juglers worked with the devil's aid.[8] As Thomas Ady put it: "the craft of Jugling, to them that are not acquainted with it, breedeth great admiration in the beholders, and seemeth, to silly people, to be miraculous, and yet being known is but deceit and foolery" (pp. 28–29). Even in the days of Cromwell, notes Ady, people "will stand like Pharaoh and his Servants, and admire a Jugling Imposture," thinking the Jugler is working "true miracles," or "will stand affrighted, or run out of the room scared like fools, saying, The Devil is in the room, and helpeth him to do such Tricks; and some saying absolutely, He is a Witch, and ought to be hanged" (p. 29).

Since it is Prospero's master-servant talk with Ariel which first led us to the Jugler tradition, it is important to note that Juglers did indeed have young servants who aided them in the creation of illusions. The Juglers carried small animals in their pockets who they pretended were their "familiars," and they led their astounded audiences to believe that the "familiar" created supernatural events. But it was the illusionist's boy who was the confederate in the creation of the illusion: the boy who hid behind the post and blew wine "miraculously" through the wall by means of a pipe; the boy who allowed himself to be "decapitated" and "healed"; the boy who fetched, who carried, who obediently served his master.

6. Quoted by Frances Yates, *Giordano Bruno and the Hermetic Tradition*, pp. 208–09.
7. Rid, *The Art of Jugling, or Legerdemaine* (1614), p. 82.
8. "Hocus Pocus Junior," *The Anatomie of Legerdemaine, or the Art of Jugling set forth in his proper colours . . .* (1634); Thomas Cooper, *The Mysterie of Witchcraft* (1617).

In one description of a Jugler (probably Hocus Pocus himself), we read about their "boys," and we hear how their masters spoke to them:

> then the Jugler calleth to his Boy, and biddeth him bring him a glass of Claret Wine . . . ; the silly Spectators thinking [they see] the same wine which he drank to come again out of his fore-head; then he saith, If this be not enough, I will draw good Claret Wine out of a post . . . and then is one of his boys on the other side of the wall, with a Bladder and a pipe . . . conveyeth the Wine to his Master thorow the Post . . . and being all drunk up but one small glass at the last, he calleth to his Boy, saying, Come, sirrah, you would faine have a cup, but his Boy maketh answer in a disdainful manner saying, No Master not I, if that be good Wine that is drawn out of a Post I will lose my head; yea sirrah saith his Master, then your head you shall lose; come sirrah, you shall go to pot for that word; then he layeth his Boy down upon the Table . . . commanding him to lye still.
>
> (Ady, pp. 37–38)

The language of this passage, with its "Come, sirrah," and its "No, master, not I," its emphasis on the master's control and the boy's cooperation, suggests that the Jugler's assistant is one of those servants described in Renaissance handbooks for servants, a boy bound by contract to serve his master for certain years, and bound as well to be diligent, to be obedient, and to be truthful:

> [Servants] must be obedient at a worde, at a call, and at a becke . . . : they must say and doe as the lad *Samuell* did who served under *Eli* . . . : when the voyce called him, *Samuell, Samuell*, he answered by and by, heere I am, and ranne quickly to *Eli* and sayd, *behold heere I am, for thou callest me*.[9]

In Prospero's dialogues with Ariel we hear strong echoes of the master magician and his "boy," and we see in Ariel (except for his moments of moodiness, of "malignant" rebelliousness) the good servant who, like Samuel, comes at a beck, a call.

It is perhaps shocking to hear between Prospero and Ariel the language of Elizabethan master and servant. Even more disturbing

---

9. Thomas Fosset, *The Servants Dutie or the Calling and Condition of Servants. Serving for the instruction, not only of Servants, but of Masters and Mistresses* (1612), pp. 22–23. See also pp. 18–19, and pp. 25 ff. Equally interesting is *The Cities Advocate* . . . (1629), which discusses the contracts of bondage and of apprenticeship; J. Fit John, *A Diamonde Most Precious, worthy to be marked: Instructing All Maysters and Servauntes, how they ought to leade their lyves* . . . (1577), esp. pp. 47 ff.; and *St. Paul's Threefold Cord: wherewith are severally combined; the mutuall Oeconomicall Duties, Betwixt . . . Master-Servant* (1635), p. 273.

is to note the relationship of Prospero to the illusionists, the master Hocus Pocuses of Stuart England. Yet I find that Louis B. Wright, in 1927, noted the resemblance of Prospero and Ariel to the magician and his assistant, and pointed out that, in *The Tempest*, "in one scene, at least, there appears to have been a trick of legerdemain by Ariel, who makes a banquet disappear."[1] There are other tricks of legerdemain in the play. The Jugler's assistant, disguised as a Harpy, himself vanishes in thunder and lightning; the entire cast of the pre-nuptial masque "to a strange, hollow, and confused noise . . . heavily vanish." Many of the illusions Prospero creates—the omnipresent music, the magically appearing banquet, the masque of spirits, the hunt with the spirit dogs—these would be known in the Jugler's trade as "acts done through confederacie" (i.e., with the help of assistants arranged in advance), just as the various disappearing acts would be called "acts done through 'deceptio visus.' "[2] Even the tempest itself, as we hear Ariel describe it in I. ii, seems as much the result of "deceptio visus" and trickery as of supernatural control over Jove's own lightning.

## IV

I noted earlier that Prospero is a product of several magic traditions; interestingly and significantly, each of these traditions brings with it into the play a different set of attitudes toward man and toward marvels. In spite of their differences, it is possible to conflate the magus, the enchanter, and the wizard into one figure, the "serious magician" who believes in supernatural powers, who believes that he is in touch with those powers, and that through those powers he can bring about genuine transformations. This figure stands in stark contrast to the juggler-illusionist or "art-Magician," a figure who pretends to use spirits to bring about transformations, but who is only a trickster.

It would seem an impossible feat to combine within a single hero the dichotomous images of the serious magician and the carnival illusionist, the magician as Agrippa and the magician as Hocus Pocus. Yet I would argue that Shakespeare has done just that, that Prospero's own transformations between the poles of "serious magician" and "Jugler" can be traced through scene after scene of the play, and that those transformations and the shifts in tone and in our attitude toward the magician which accompany the transformations are at the heart of the play, and of the questions the play poses about reality and illusion, about creativity and theatrical fak-

---

1. Wright, "Juggling Tricks and Conjury on the English Stage before 1642," *Modern Philology*, 24 (1927), 276.
2. See Reginald Scot, *Discovery of Witchcraft* (1584), pp. 307 ff., and Rid, p. B3.

ery, and about disturbing resemblances between the dramatist and the magician.[3]

If we can entertain the idea that Prospero is as much Hocus Pocus as he is Agrippa, then we can look at key moments in *The Tempest* with a fresh eye: at Prospero, "on the top," congratulating Ariel on his Harpy-performance and vanishing act; at Prospero explaining to Ferdinand the relationship between the masque-illusion and the illusion that we call life, the "revel" which, as a creator himself of insubstantial shows, the master jugler suspects of equal insubstantiality; at Prospero, in the epilogue, "stripping up his sleeve like some Jugler" to reveal the tricks, to let us know, finally that his magician's project, which Ariel has been at such pains to keep alive, is finally the Jugler's project: "to please."

Annie Dillard compares the illusions to which we are treated by Nature to a kind of carnival show. She watches the light change in late afternoon, watches clouds and mountains turn from pink to gray, disappear, appear again in new forms, until finally "the show pull[s] out." "Nothing is left," she says, "but an unreal blue and a few banked clouds low in the north."

> Some sort of carnival magician has been here, some fast-talking worker of wonders who has the act backwards. "Something in this hand," he says, "something in this hand, something up my sleeve, something behind my back . . ." and abracadabra, he snaps his fingers, and it's all gone. Only the bland, blank-faced magician remains, in his unruffled coat, barehanded, acknowledging a smattering of baffled applause. When you look again the whole show has pulled up stakes and moved on down the road. It never stops. New shows roll in from over the mountains and the magician reappears unannounced from a fold in the curtain you never dreamed was an opening. Scarves of clouds, rabbits in plain view, disappear into the black hat forever. Presto chango. The audience, if there is an audience at all, is dizzy from head-turning, dazed.[4]

The blending of seriousness with jest, of revelation with bewilderment, which Miss Dillard suggests is the kind of tone which *The Tempest* achieves. Nature presents spectacles which we perceive as best we can through our easily deluded senses. Presto chango, the racks vanish; the globe itself will one day vanish like a carnival show, an Inigo Jones masque, Prospero's revels or Shakespeare's play. Prospero's magic powers slide into fakery; Ceres and Iris are "really" only spirits who are in turn "really" only actors. The "real-

---

3. See, e.g., B. A. Mowat, " 'And that's true, too': Structures and Meanings in *The Tempest*," *Renaissance Papers 1976*, pp. 37–50.
4. Annie Dillard, *Pilgrim at Tinker's Creek* (New York, 1974), p. 11.

ity" or fakery of the magician's power and our inability to fix this power as supernatural or as sleight-of-hand are central to the play and its vision of life, just as they point to the central ambiguities in our own vision of man in the natural and supernatural worlds.

In Prospero's role we can read the story of a man's personal growth from vengeance to mercy, and from rough magic to deep spirituality; or we can simply enjoy the magician's struggles to bring about the play's remarkable happy ending. But however we view him, the final image of Prospero which lingers in our minds is of the mortal creature of the epilogue—the magus who has learned to think of his mortality, the Faustus who successfully destroyed his book, the illusionist who stands before us revealing the tricks of his trade. The applause for which he begs we give to end his play and to free him from his island, but we give it also to celebrate the wonder of Prospero himself.

# DAVID LINDLEY

## Music, Masque, and Meaning in *The Tempest*†

*The Tempest* employs more music than any other Shakespeare play. It is also the play that most insistently echoes the manner of the masque. Both these aspects of the work have been much commented upon, but in the general revaluation of *The Tempest* which has seen the older view of it as a celebration of reconciliation replaced by a critical consensus stressing its inconclusiveness, ambiguity, and doubt, the music has consistently been accepted as imaging and enacting ideals of harmony and concord, whether or not those ideals are finally attained.[1]

This attitude to the play's music rests upon the view that Shakespeare was employing the standard Renaissance theory that earthly music reflected the celestial harmony of the spheres, and by that analogy was empowered to affect and influence humankind. There can indeed be no mistaking the fact that the power of Ariel's music to allay the fury of the elements and to calm Ferdinand's passions in Act I or to heal the perturbed minds of the noble lords in Act V

---

† From *The Court Masque* (Manchester: Manchester University Press, 1984), pp. 47–59. Reprinted by permission of the author. Line numbers to this Norton Critical Edition of the play appear in brackets when they differ from the author's original citation.

1. One of the most persuasive comments on the play's darknesses is W. H. Auden's poetic descant, *The Sea and The Mirror*. A characteristic early statement of changing attitudes is Rose Zimbardo, 'Form and Disorder in *The Tempest*', *Shakespeare Quarterly*, 16 (1963), pp 49–65. A traditional view of the music is articulated by John P. Cutts, 'Music in *The Tempest*', *Music and Letters*, 39 (1958), pp. 347–58. A less straightforwardly symbolic reading informs Theresa Coletti, 'Music and *The Tempest*', in *Shakespeare's Late Plays*, ed. Richard C. Tobias and Paul G. Zolbrod (Athens, Ohio, 1974), pp. 185–99.

are fully comprehensible only in a context where an audience might
readily supply this symbolic significance to the music they hear.
Nor can one doubt that the failure of Antonio and Sebastian to
hear and respond to the music that lulls the other lords to sleep in
Act II, Scene i is emblematic of the moral disharmony of their natures.

But music in the theatre need not summon up this kind of symbolic significance, for, as Duke Vincentio recognises, 'music oft
hath such a charm / To make bad good and good provoke to harm'.[2]
We have to recognise that music may delude or spur illicit passions
as well as cure, heal, and restore. We do not applaud Orsino's indulgence of appetite with music's moody food, for example.

In the experience of a theatre audience music is much too varied
in its stimulus and dramatic significance to be tidily packaged in a
neo-Platonic wrapper. But in the world of the court masque the
power of music and its emblematic significance is much more
firmly controlled and directed. Part of the argument of this essay is
precisely that *The Tempest* exploits and explores the tensions between these different dramatic possibilities.

Some of these tensions are apparent in the play's final song,
'Where the bee sucks'. Critics have been moved to eloquence by it.
'Ariel's song is pure lyric and pure joy', writes Mary Chan, while
Seng claims: 'For the brave new world of redeemed man which is to
succeed on the old one of crime and punishment there could
hardly be a better hymn of praise than Ariel's song of summer and
freedom.'[3] But these and many other determined efforts to bestow
symbolic significance on this song fail to attend to its actual effect
in its dramatic context.

Prospero has called for a 'solemn air' to restore the unsettled
minds of the nobles. As the charm begins to work he resumes the
mantle of his lost dukedom. This is the climatic moment of the
story that *The Tempest* narrates. Prospero has successfully courted
his 'most auspicious star', has regained the lost dukedom, ensured
political harmony by betrothing his daughter to the son of his former opponent, and yet to accompany the gesture that signals this
triumphant conclusion we are offered no ceremonious fanfare but
a song about lying in cowslips.

The disparity between the song and the dramatic action it ac-
companies forces the audience into reflection. At first the close juxtaposition of the song with the curative heavenly music suggests
that they both belong to the same symbolic realm, but as the words
of the song register, the difference between them is sharply estab-

---

2. *Measure for Measure*, IV.i.14–15.
3. Mary Chan, *Music in the Theatre of Ben Jonson* (Oxford, 1980), p. 328; Peter Seng, *The Vocal Songs in the Plays of Shakespeare* (Cambridge, Mass., 1967), p. 271.

lished. One is the impersonal sonority of the heavens, the other entirely personal and spontaneous song. This is the first time that Ariel has sung his own words, and their self-indulgence links it with other 'unscripted' songs in the play, Stephano's 'The master, the swabber, the bosun and I' and, more obviously, Caliban's song of freedom, 'No more dams I'll make for fish'.

For all the differences between these singers, the fundamental similarity of the songs cannot be ignored. They alert us to a different musical possibility from that allowed by a neo-Platonic theory. Music here is an outburst of individual feeling, a gesture whose expression is entirely circumscribed by the individuality of the singer. Such song, as Mark Booth has pointed out, invites us as audience to submerge ourselves in an identification with the singing voice, hence the appeal of the simple, quasi-pastoral lyric that Ariel sings. But at the same time, the failure of the song to support the action for which it is the incidental music confirms the truth of Booth's observation: 'A song, set in a play, but set out of the play too by its music, facilitates our indulgence in feelings that may be undercut before and after the music plays'.[4] Here it is not so much the feeling itself that is undercut, as the disparity between Prospero's abandonment of magic and return to the real world and Ariel's fugitive fantasy that is highlighted. When one adds to this the fact that Ariel, the singer whose feelings we have briefly been persuaded by their musical utterance to take as our own, is an insubstantial figure (quite unlike the obstinately corporeal Stephano and Caliban) then the unsettling elusiveness of this song is plain.

Uncertainty of response is a characteristic effect of most of the musical events in the play. The first song is 'Come unto these yellow sands'. Ferdinand concludes that its music 'waits upon / Some god o' th' island', and reinforces his attribution of celestial origin by his account of its power:

> This music crept by me on the waters
> Allaying both their fury and my passion
> With its sweet air: thence I have follow'd it
> Or it hath drawn me rather.  (I.ii.394–7) [1.2.390–93]

No neo-Platonist could wish for better demonstration of the potential of music, no Orpheus could work more marvellously than the singing Ariel. We are willing as an audience to consent to the power Prospero exercises through music precisely because we are able to supply for it the necessary conventional symbolic significance.

Yet there is an unease about the song. Though it sounds fine at first, the burden of the song, sung by 'watch-dogs' and 'Chanti-

---

4.  Mark Booth, *The Experience of Songs* (New Haven and London, 1981), pp. 14–23; 118.

cleer', jars with the lyric's romantic opening. A sense of discomfort is fully justified when, at the end of the play, the sprites who sang 'bow-bow' appear in doggy habit to chase Stephano and Trinculo from Prospero's cave. The refrain of the song hints at the capricious, even malevolent side of Prospero's magic and its instruments, demonstrated clearly when he orders his spirits to 'hunt soundly' the conspirators. The 'god o' th' island' can threaten as well as invite, as Ferdinand himself is soon to realise.

The celebrated 'Full fathom five' follows almost at once. Much can be said about this exquisite and potent lyric, its proleptic significance in imaging the 'sea-change' the characters experience, its immediate effectiveness in preparing Ferdinand for his meeting with Miranda, or the way its eerie transformations bespeak the power of the art which contrives it. But at the same time an audience must realise that at the simplest level the words of the song are untrue. Already assured that 'there's no harm done', we are uncomfortably aware that Ferdinand's statement, 'this ditty doth remember my drowned father' reflects an understanding of events entirely contrived by Prospero.

We are caught, therefore, in a double response to this song. Persuaded by Ferdinand's attitude, we accept the emblematic significance that music always possesses as a potential in Renaissance drama; but at the same time our superior awareness of the true narrative state of things makes us uneasily conscious of the compromise with truth that Prospero's designs necessitate.

In two other episodes later in the play there is a similar compromising of music's symbolic significance as it is subordinated to Prospero's designs.

Ariel's music charms Alonso, Gonzalo, and others to sleep in Act II, Scene i apparently only so that Antonio's and Sebastian's conspiracy might have space to declare itself. Prospero's magic arts thus create the conditions for the instigation of vice as well as for the harmonising of discordant passions. More significant is the episode in Act III, Scene ii, where the tune of the catch 'Flout 'em and scout 'em' is taken up by Ariel's pipe, much to the amazement of Stephano and Trinculo. They, like Ferdinand, follow the celestial music, only to be led into a bog.

However one might contain these episodes within a standard view of music's symbolic significance, by pointing out that where the virtuous Ferdinand is rewarded the base conspirators are duly punished, this should not obscure the fact that by responding to music Alonso and his followers are rendered vulnerable (though by music also they are preserved) and Stephano and Trinculo are reeking of horse-piss. For the audience, and indeed for the characters on stage, the music that lulls the nobles to sleep and the transformed music of the vulgar catch are the same as the music of Ferdinand's song. What distinguishes one from the other is not the nature of the musical harmony, nor the effects they have, but the consequence Prospero derives from his manipulative power.

As will become clear later this focussing on music as a means of power is of great significance for the play as a whole, and for its use of the masque genre in particular. For the moment we might turn from Ferdinand's wonder at the celestial music to Caliban's celebrated response to the island's sound. He tells Stephano and Trinculo:

> Be not afeard; the isle is full of noises,
> Sounds and sweet airs, that give delight, and hurt not.
> Sometimes a thousand twangling instruments
> Will hum about mine ears; and sometimes voices,
> That, if I then had wak'd after long sleep,
> Will make me sleep again; and then, in dreaming,
> The clouds methought would open, and show riches
> Ready to drop upon me; that, when I wak'd,
> I cried to dream again.          (III.ii.133–41) [133–41]

The fact that his response is so similar to Ferdinand's complicates the simple moral scale where sensitivity to music is a mark of virtue. It suggests a moral neutrality in music's effects. For if, in the myth most often used to support the neo-Platonic view of music, Orpheus made rocks, stones, and trees move, it says much for music's power, but indicates also the involuntariness of response to it, and therefore the potential danger of its effects in the hands of an unscrupulous manipulator. But the most important aspect of this speech is Caliban's account of the way music persuades him to sleep and to dream of innumerable riches, only to wake and, waking, to cry to dream again. For it is this pattern of response that underlies the two biggest set-pieces of the work, the two masques which immediately follow this speech.

In the first a banquet is laid before Alonso and his company. As Prospero watches, his spirits enter to 'solemn and strange music'. Unlike Stephano and Trinculo the nobles are not frightened, but respond to the sweetness of the sound. They, like the dreaming Caliban, are offered riches in the form of food that they desperately need. But just as Caliban can never capture his dream-treasure, so they are denied their banquet as it is taken away 'by a quaint device' and Ariel rebukes the 'three men of sin'.[5]

No sooner is this scene over than Prospero prepares for the next masque. He addresses Ariel:

---

5. For a study of the manifold implications of the banquet see Jacqueline E. M. Latham, 'The Magic Banquet in *The Tempest*', *Shakespeare Studies*, 12 (1979), pp. 215–27.

Thou and thy meaner fellows your last service
Did worthily perform; and I must use you
In such another trick. Go bring the rabble,
O'er whom I give thee power, here to this place:
Incite them to quick motion; for I must
Bestow upon the eyes of this young couple
Some vanity of mine Art: it is my promise,
And they expect it from me.          (IV.i.35–42)

The connection between this and the previous device is unambigu-
ously made; performed by the same spirits, it is 'such another trick'.
The oddity that Prospero introduces what should be one of the
play's central emblematic statements with such apparent contempt
may be left on one side for future consideration.

The masque proceeds. Iris, Ceres, and Juno gravely meet and
promise richness and fertility to the betrothed couple. Iris then
summons the 'Naiads of the windring brooks' and 'sunburn'd sicklemen' to dance before the couple. Since there are no courtiers
on Prospero's island, it is the spirits who must take the place of
masquers and perform the dance which, in Jonson's phrase, may
'make the beholders wise'.[6] The conjunction of watery female semi-
deities and fiery male reapers draws upon the conventional symbolism that Jonson, for example, uses in *Hymenaei*:

Like are the *fire*, and *water*, set;
That, ev'n as *moisture*, mixt with *heat*,
Helps everie naturall birth, to life;
So, for their Race, joyne *man* and *wife*.[7]

The dance, therefore, suits well with the promise of fertility that
the three goddesses make in their song to the couple.

Anthony Stafford's gloss on this symbol reveals a further appro-
priateness to the concerns of the masque. He writes:

To the same ende did the Romanes of old, carrie before the
married couple, fier, and water (the former representing the
man; the later, the woman,) what else signifying, then that
the woman should expect till heate bee infused into her by her
husband? it being as much against the nature of an honest
spouse, as of the coldest water, to boile of her selfe; and on the
contrarie side, that the bridegroom should distill warmth into
his own water and heate it, but not over-heate it.[8]

Prospero at the beginning of the act had warned the couple against
anticipation of the wedding night, and then returned to the theme
as he sternly rebukes Ferdinand:

6. Ben Jonson, ed. C.H. Herford and Percy Simpson (Oxford, 1925–52), 11 vols., 7,
   p. 489.
7. Herford and Simpson, 7, p. 215.
8. *Niobe* (1611) sig. C2–3.

> do not give dalliance
> Too much the rein: the strongest oaths are straw
> To th'fire in th' blood: be more abstemious,
> Or else, good night your vow!

Ferdinand replies:

> I warrant you, sir;
> The white cold virgin snow upon my heart
> Abates the ardour of my liver.        (IV.i.51–6)

This ideal control, imaged in snow and fire, is sustained throughout the masque (from which Cupid is excluded) and is symbolised in the graceful dance of the temperate nymphs and sunburned sicklemen.

Through this masque Prospero enforces upon Ferdinand and Miranda the difference between a chaste conjunction issuing in happy fertility and the beastly lust that would have peopled the isle with Calibans, or brought forth Stephano's 'brave brood'. The urgency of his warnings to the couple before the masque begins suggests that Prospero is by no means certain that, without the persuasive effect of his 'harmonious vision', he can trust them to understand the difference.

The entertainment, then, works according to the ideal prescription for the masque, leading the spectators to fuller understanding through their contemplation of an image which impresses itself upon them by the power music, dance, and word have to imitate the deeper harmonies of the universe. But though these spectators are of a morally unblemished nature, this show, like the lords' banquet, is snatched away as with 'a strange, hollow and confused noise' the spirits 'heavily vanish'. On their departure Prospero launches into the play's most famous speech, fusing the terminology of masque and reality to remind his audience that the vision, however harmonious, must fade, and they, like Caliban, may cry to dream again.

The pattern of these two scenes is further emphasised by the last trick of Prospero's devising, as Ariel loads a line with glistering apparel to distract Caliban and his fellow conspirators. This illusory richness (which has no real narrative necessity, since Prospero could simply have set his dogs on them when they arrived) is functionally the same as the two shows that precede it. This offering of the island also proves a false treasure.

The frustration common to all these scenes might indeed be held to form the 'deep structure' of the play (to borrow a linguistic term). It is realised in many of the surface incidents of the play. Ferdinand is offered Miranda, but then reduced to servitude; Caliban mistakes the promise first of Prospero and then of Stephano to his discomfiture; the villainous Antonio and Sebastian have Alonso presented to them as a victim, only for him to wake up before they can seize the prize. Most notably, Prospero himself has sought the goal of wisdom only to lose his dukedom in the process, and then, on regaining the dukedom must resign the art he has devoted his life to acquiring.

It is the omnipresence of this pattern that helps to account for the uncertainty of the play's effect upon an audience, since it belongs to tragedy rather than to romance. Unease is clarified in the emphasis the pattern receives in the three masque-like episodes, for masques are by their very nature affirmative offerings, made to a married couple, a patron or a monarch, and their standard pattern moves from inhibition to celebration. In standing on its head the masque genre that it employs *The Tempest* examines the problematic nature of the form, and articulates many of the difficulties and dilemmas that attended it throughout its life.[9]

The Jacobean court masque was continually under attack, most frequently on the grounds of its excessive expenses and vainglorious display. The standard defence was an appeal to the notion of princely magnificence: conspicuous consumption is a sign of the richness and importance of a court that would be demeaned by anything less than elaborate and costly show. In *The Tempest* there is the paradox that all its goodly visions issue not from the self-projection of a rich and stable court, but from the power of a magician who inhabits a 'full poor cell' on a desert island. The actors are not the lords and ladies of James's court, whose richness and magnificence might properly become them, but spirits. The play seems to insist that the true riches of the island are the quick freshes and the fruits that Caliban showed to Prospero, rather than the sumptuous banquet that the lords reach for in vain. One might, indeed, see the relationship between the first two set-pieces as antimasque and masque making precisely that point by their juxtaposition. But Prospero's masques are, from this point of view, vanities indeed, having no basis in economic and political reality. Their defence must be sought elsewhere.

Jonson saw the heart of the masque, and its most serious validation, in its capacity to 'lay hold on more remov'd mysteries'.[1] But making this claim raises further problems. In the first place the arcane hieroglyphs of the masque, since they are comprehensible only to the learned, could make little impression upon the actual

---

9. Ernest B. Gilman discusses the manipulation of the masque genre in his ' "All eyes": Prospero's Inverted Masque', *Renaissance Quarterly*, 33 (1980), pp. 214–30, though he sees the conspirators as an 'antimasque', and does not discuss the other shows.
1. Herford and Simpson, 7, 209.

audience of Jacobean courtiers, preoccupied with the elegant trappings of ostentation. Secondly, the ideal relationship of performer and role, where the noble personage became (in both senses of the word) the part that he played, was always vulnerable to the uncomfortable knowledge that the glorious surface only partly concealed a less than ideal reality.

As more and more people became disillusioned with the excesses and corruptions of James's court, the gap between the masque ideal and the reality it was supposed to reflect became ever harder to paper over, and the educational potential of the masque less and less easy to credit. Writers both for the court and for the public theatre were moved to explore that gap. Tragedians used the discontinuity between image and reality to bitter satirical ends; Daniel expressed increasing disquiet at the vanity of masques; Jonson attempted to take on critics directly in works like *Love Restored*, and Campion in *The Lords' Masque* anxiously insisted upon the necessity of the masquers remembering the significance of the roles they played as they returned to their normal world.[2]

*The Tempest* grows out of this general disquiet, and attempts itself to grapple with the problems it raises. While the characters in the play are not themselves participants in the masque, yet the final scene of the play does approach indirectly the question of the relationship between a masquer and the role he enacts. For Prospero arranges as the conclusion of his work of reconciliation a masque-like emblem as he discloses Ferdinand and Miranda playing chess. He promises to requite Alonso's restoration of his dukedom with 'as good a thing'; he will, in terms that echo masquing vocabulary, 'bring forth a wonder to content ye'. The emblematic use of the loving couple is very like Campion's later use of the figures of Princess Elizabeth and Frederick Elector Palatine as the concluding symbol of his *Lords' Masque*, but whereas in Campion's work the masquers and audience turn to do homage to the couple sitting in state, Shakespeare's lovers are preoccupied with each other, and their ideal status is immediately undermined by Miranda's challenge, 'Sweet lord, you play me false'. Whatever the precise significance of the exchange which follows, it is obvious that Ferdinand and Miranda resist the possibility of being subsumed into an iconic gesture.

2. See Inge-Stina Ewbank, ' "These pretty devices": A Study of Masques in Plays', in *A Book of Masques*, ed. T. J. B. Spencer and Stanley Wells (Cambridge, 1967), pp. 405–48; Ralph Berry, 'Masques and Dumb Shows in Webster's Plays', *The Elizabethan Theatre*, 7 (1981), pp. 124–46, and, in the same journal, pp. 111–23, Cyrus Hoy, 'Masques and the Artifice of Tragedy'; Jeffrey Fischer, '*Love Restored*: A Defense of Masquing', *Renaissance Drama*, 7 (1977), pp. 231–44; David Lindley, *Thomas Campion* (Leiden, 1986), Chapter 4.

This resistance accords with Miranda's own modest deflection of
Ferdinand's attempt to turn her into a masque-like goddess at
the beginning of the play. It also fits into the way the final scene
as a whole plays with the masque's climatic moment of disclosure.
When Alonso first sees Prospero he cries out:

> Whether thou be'st he or no,
> Or some enchanted trifle to abuse me,
> As late I have been, I do not know.               (V.i.111-3)

(The paradox of trifles that torment is itself a record of the play's
deeply ambiguous attitude to the status and effect of theatrical illusions.) But then Miranda herself looks at the 'goodly creatures' before her as if they were a masquing company. The ingenuousness of
her amazement is obvious to the audience, and ironically under-
lined by Prospero's ' 'Tis new to thee'. Thus, where the court
masque moves securely and triumphantly from the world of illusion
to the court reality it had translated, transcended, and imaged,
Shakespeare's dissolution involves a blurring of realms, and much
more uncertainty about the boundaries of the too easily opposed
worlds of illusion and reality. In so doing it unsettles the audience's
response. Are we to be glad that Ferdinand and Miranda are human
in a way that Campion's Frederick and Elizabeth are inhibited from
being, and do we therefore register this conclusion as a satirical
barb aimed at the insulations of the court masque? Or do we regret
that Miranda's naïveté, like the optimistic idealism of Gonzalo, is
bound to founder on the ambitious pragmatism of Antonio and
Sebastian? The problem is not merely an intellectual one, but a
dilemma of feeling and response, a dilemma that is most pressingly
active in our response to music. For music's capacity to work directly upon feeling is, in the masque, sanctified by its necessary
connection with the divinely harmonious universe. In *The Tempest*
we respond as fully to music's lure, but the rightness of our sub-
mission is continually questioned.

But though the ending of the play, with its ambiguous relationship
to a masque's dissolving, follows upon scenes which have asserted
the impossibility of a masque's converting the truly wicked and indicated the frailty of such visions even for the morally unblemished,
the play does not therefore retreat to the cynicism of Bacon's verdict;
'these things are but toys'.[3] For though Prospero had introduced his
betrothal masque as a vanity, yet he is concerned enough about its
effect to command the spectator's attention, 'Or else our spell is
marr'd'. He stresses, as Jonson so often does, the importance of the
spectator's conspiracy in enabling the masque to work.

3. Francis Bacon, 'Of Masques and Triumphs', in *Essays* (London, 1597).

It is through the presentation of the dilemmas of Prospero, the maker of masques and convenor of the company of musical sprites, that Shakespeare tests the importance and the limitations of the masque genre. For though the constant state of tension in which Prospero exists throughout the play may be explained by the narrative necessity he is under to seize this one opportunity to regain his dukedom, his emotional state can best be understood as arising from a desperate sense of the fragility of the power his art gives him, coupled with an equally urgent sense of the significance of that art.

The outbursts of anger that structure the long second scene of Act I are all aroused by the failure of others to observe a properly obedient attitude towards him. This is not mere despotism, but a precarious fear that those over whom he can or should exercise control resist or abuse the roles he fashions for them. Throughout the play Ariel, executant of Propero's designs, is continually checked up on, commanded to faithful reproduction of his script, overlooked in performance, commended for actorly success. Prospero is as anxious as Hamlet in his producer's guise, as nervous as any caricatured author on the first night of his play.

Prospero cares so intensely not primarily because he himself stands to gain from his magic (the lack of triumph at his resumption of the ducal mantle is, however disconcerting, in accord with the lack of real ambition in Prospero's character), not even because of his love for his daughter and hope for her future, but essentially because the efficacy of his art is itself to be the validation of a lifetime spent in acquiring it. This is the first and only time that his magic is put to the real rest of confronting the complexities of human wickedness, desire, and frailty. Compared to this his past magical exercises, retailed in Act V, are mere sideshows, and his Medean speech not the triumphant assertion of theatrical power that Kernan describes[4] but a frenzied effort to boost his own confidence before he turns to undo the charm upon the nobles and finds out whether his magic has actually worked upon stubborn human nature. Prospero's anxiety raises precisely the question of the capacity of masque image to work upon an audience that the masque itself resolutely sidestepped and contained.

But if it is the sense of the fragility of his powers that troubles Prospero, the audience's response is further complicated by the fact that they are unsure, during the course of the play, exactly what purpose Prospero intends to serve. At times he seems only to exult in revenge and to be persuaded to forgiveness by Ariel very late in the play. But yet he takes care for the future of his daughter

---

4. Alvin B. Kernan, *The Playwright as Magician* (New Haven and London, 1979), p. 143.

and troubles to attempt to induce repentance in the minds of the lords.

This is a highly significant complication since it establishes as a central issue in the play the responsibility of the poet in constructing his work to some purposeful end. Merely to exercise power, to perform tricks, would indeed be a vanity. Magic power exists to be harnessed, but it is the nature of the magician's designs that determines the moral value of that power. Under Prospero the island resounds to sweet noises, where for the witch Sycorax the only music was the shriek of the imprisoned Ariel. Prospero must liberate the lords from their charmed imprisonment as he had earlier released Ariel if we are not to condemn him as he condemns Sycorax.

In *The Tempest*, therefore, the masque genre is subjected to a double examination. On the one hand its moral effectiveness is determined (and circumscribed) by the nature and limitations of its beholders; but on the other hand it is also vitally dependent upon the nature and purposes of its contriver. It reflects the sensitivity of Ben Jonson both to the ignorance of his audiences and to the vanity of Inigo Jones, a contriver of masques who (in Jonson's view) saw no further than 'shows, shows, mighty shows'.[5]

The radical element in Shakespeare's work is the recognition, through the examination of Prospero's predicament, of the fundamentally rhetorical nature of the masque. It is an instrument of power, of coercion and manipulation, resistible and corruptible. It is not enough simply to lay hold on some neo-Platonic idea, and, by reproducing it claim that it will therefore 'work'.

This understanding corresponds very significantly with the new view of music and its effects that was at this time taking hold. For the older, idealist notion of music's correspondence with the music of the spheres was being replaced by a rhetorical model of its affects. Monody and declamatory song were the vehicles of this change, and it was especially in the masque with its professional virtuoso singers that the style flourished.[6] To see rhetoric and neo-Platonism as opposites is of course a far too crude distinction. Nonetheless it is the element of persuasion that rhetoric brings with it that threatens the security of the correspondence between ideal and human reality that sustained the masque and the theories of *musica speculativa*. It is our awareness that the songs Ferdinand hears are part of Prospero's rhetoric as well as the images of celestial harmony he takes them to be that opens up the play's enact-

---

5. 'An Expostulation with Inigo Jones', *The Complete Poems*, ed. George Parfitt (Harmondsworth, 1975), p. 346.
6. See John Hollander, *The Untuning of the Sky* (Princeton, N.J., 1961) *passim*; James Anderson Winn, *Unsuspected Eloquence* (New Haven and London, 1981), Chapter 4; and for the music, Ian Spink, *English Song, Dowland to Purcell* (London, 1974).

ment of the problems that attend the making of masque and music.

This does not, of course, deny the validity of masque or of music. Their power exists, and may be harnessed for good or for ill. The play as a whole interrogates a series of familiar Renaissance debating topics. Art versus nature, action versus contemplation, reality versus illusion are but some of the subjects the play considers, and for all of them no simple preference is established. Most significant for the question of the validity of transitory masque is the opposition between Caliban and Ariel, beast against spirit, earth and water versus air and fire, body against soul.

This last distinction is used by Jonson to characterise the masque, and to defend his part in it. The display is its body, the mystery the poet shadows is its soul, 'impressing and lasting'.[7] In a very similar analogy Renaissance musicians compared the words of a song to the soul, the musical notes to the body, for only through the words are the fluctuating and transitory impressions of sound given direction and lasting purpose.[8]

In *The Tempest* both these notions are severely tested. When the play ends it is not the spirit who remains, but the thing of darkness that Prospero must acknowledge his and transport back to Milan. In the final scene it is the instrumental music that is curative, and Ariel's last song that slips into solipsism.

Conventional justification of masque and of music is therefore questioned. The self-regarding, inconsequential beauty of 'Where the bee sucks' signals the basic fact that music, like the magic powers it enables Prospero to deploy and the masquing visions he creates with its aid, is of itself nothing and the riches it promises an illusion. Prospero's shaking of the earth is similarly a self-indulgence unless it is played to some purpose before an audience, just as Ariel's singing acquires a positive function only when scripted by Prospero and directed to human listeners.

But to recognise, as the play does, that it is the body we are stuck with, the life of action that must ultimately claim us, does not mean that music and the masque must be dumped, valueless, into the sea along with the books of magic. For the power of art is perenially available. Prospero denies himself the means of access to magical powers, not the validity of their exercise. For all their inadequacies music and masque have succeeded in bringing Alonso to repentance, and have imaged the love of Ferdinand and Miranda as something more than mere political convenience. Furthermore, as

---

7. Herford and Simpson, 7, 209.
8. See, for example, Monteverdi's observation that musical pieces without words were 'bodies without soul', in Oliver Strunk, *Source Readings in Music History* (New York, 1950), p. 406.

an audience we cannot deny the power of theatrical illusion when it is only through the masque-play that Prospero creates that we can encounter the meditation upon the limitations of masque and music that Shakespeare offers to us.

Stephen Orgel has rightly suggested that *The Tempest* is the 'most important Renaissance commentary' on 'court masques and plays'. Mary Chan claims that it 'shows the validity of the masque's conceptual basis', while, by contrast, Ernest Gilman calls it 'a delicately subversive maneuver staged in the enemy camp and hinting at the bedazzled, insulated self-regard of such entertainments'.[9] The truth is that *The Tempest* resists such simplification of its stance, presenting instead a multi-layered and deeply ambivalent attitude.

It does so because, though it reflects many of the substantial uncertainties about the masque genre current at the time of its composition, it actively involves the spectator in feeling, not merely contemplating the problems. Thus we, like the spectators on stage, are frustrated and disappointed as harmonious visions end in discord. We recognise the compromises that follow upon Prospero's manipulative aims, yet we respect the urgent desire that led him to a life of contemplation to secure the power he exercises. At the end of the play Prospero's wistful farewell to Ariel is echoed by our own regret as we tender the applause that releases Prospero from his island, but banishes us from the theatre. But perhaps most important of all in engendering the audience's complicity in the play's paradoxical statement is the music. Not only are the characters on stage pushed hither and thither by Prospero's music, but it works its end upon our senses also, with an undeniable insinuation. The symbolic view of music is comprehensible as an attempt to validate morally the experiential truth of music's power. *The Tempest*, by unpicking without ever quite denying that analogy does not merely reflect a historical moment, the time of 'the untuning of the sky', but forces us as an audience to go beyond a simple criticism of the fragility of the world of the stage. The Platonic theories that sustain a Sidneyan belief in art's golden world are crumbling, but we are left 'wishing it might be so'.

9. Orgel, *The Illusion of Power* (Berkeley, Los Angeles and London, 1975), p. 45; Chan, *Music in Ben Jonson*, p. 330; Gilman, ' "All eyes" ', p. 220.

# STEPHEN ORGEL

## Prospero's Wife†

This essay is not a reading of *The Tempest*. It is a consideration of five related moments and issues. I have called it *Prospero's Wife* because some of it centres on her, but as a figure conspicuous by her absence from the play, I take her as a figure of my larger subject: the absent, the unspoken, that seems to me the most powerful and problematic presence in *The Tempest*. In its outlines, the play seems a story of privatives: withdrawal, usurpation, banishment, becoming lost, shipwreck. As an antithesis, a principle of control, preservation, re-creation, the play offers only magic, embodied in a single figure, the extraordinary power of Prospero.

### FAMILY HISTORY

Prospero's wife is alluded to only once in the play, in Prospero's reply to Miranda's question, 'Sir, are you not my father?'

> Thy mother was a piece of virtue, and
> She said thou wast my daughter; and thy father
> Was Duke of Milan; and his only heir
> And princess: no worse issued.
>
> (I.ii.55–9)[1]

Prospero's wife is identified as Miranda's mother, in a context implying that although she was virtuous, women as a class are not, and that were it not for her word, Miranda's legitimacy would be in doubt. The legitimacy of Prospero's heir, that is, derives from her mother's word. But that word is all that is required of her in the play; once he is assured of it, Prospero turns his attention to himself and his succession, and he characterises Miranda in a clause that grows increasingly ambivalent: 'his only heir / And princess: no worse issued.'

Except for this moment, Prospero's wife is absent from his memory. She is wholly absent from her daughter's memory: Miranda can recall several women who attended her in childhood, but no mother. The attitudes implied toward wives and mothers here are confirmed shortly afterward when Prospero, recounting his brother Antonio's crimes, demands that Miranda 'tell me / If this might be

---

† From *Representations*, 8 (1985): 1–13. Amended by the author. Reprinted by permission of the author and The University of California Press. Line numbers to this Norton Critical Edition have been added in brackets when they differ from the author's original citation.
1. In this instance, I have restored the folio punctuation of line 59.

a brother', and Miranda takes the question to be a charge of adultery against Prospero's mother:

> I should sin
> To think but nobly of my grandmother:
> Good wombs have borne bad sons.
> (I.ii.118–20)

She immediately translates Prospero's attack on his brother into an attack on his mother (and the best she can produce in her grandmother's defence is a 'not proved'); and whether or not she has correctly divined her father's intentions, Prospero makes no objection.

The absent presence of the wife and mother in the play constitutes a space that is filled by Prospero's creation of surrogates and a ghostly family: the witch Sycorax and her monster child Caliban (himself, as becomes apparent, a surrogate for the other wicked child; the usurping younger brother), the good child/wife Miranda, the obedient Ariel, the violently libidinised adolescent Ferdinand. The space is filled, too, by a whole structure of wifely allusion and reference: widow Dido, model at once of heroic fidelity to a murdered husband and the destructive potential of erotic passion; the witch Medea, murderess and filicide; three exemplary goddesses, the bereft Ceres, nurturing Juno, and licentious Venus; and Alonso's daughter Claribel, unwillingly married off to the ruler of the modern Carthage and thereby lost to her father forever.

Described in this way, the play has an obvious psychoanalytic shape. I have learned a great deal from Freudian treatments of it, most recently from essays by David Sundelson, Coppélia Kahn, and Joel Fineman in the volume called *Representing Shakespeare*.[2] It is almost irresistible to look at the play as a case history—*whose* case history is a rather more problematic question and one that criticism has not, on the whole, dealt with satisfactorily: not, obviously, that of the characters. I want to pause first over what it means to consider the play as a case history.

In older psychoanalytic paradigms (say Ernest Jones's), the critic is the analyst, Shakespeare the patient, the plays his fantasies. The trouble with this paradigm is that it misrepresents the analytic situation in a fundamental way. The interpretation of analytical material is done in conjunction with, and in large measure by, the patient, not the analyst; what the analyst does is to *enable* the patient, to free the patient to interpret. An analysis done without the patient, like Freud's of Leonardo, will be revealing only about the analyst. A more recent paradigm, in which the audience's response

---

2. Murray M. Schwartz and Coppélia Kahn (eds), *Representing Shakespeare* (Baltimore, 1980).

is the principal analytic material, seems to me based on even more
fundamental misconceptions, first because it treats an audience as
an entity, a unit, and moreover a constant one; and more problematically, because it conceives of the play as an objective event, so
that the critical question becomes, 'This is what happened: how do
we respond to it?'

To take the psychoanalytic paradigm seriously, however, and treat
the plays as case histories, is surely to treat them *not* as objective
events but as collaborative fantasies and to acknowledge thereby
that we, as analysts, are implicated in the fantasy. It is not only the
patients who create the shape of their histories, and when Bruno
Bettelheim observes that Freud's case histories 'read as well as the
best novels',[3] he is probably telling more of the truth than he intends. Moreover, the crucial recent advances in our understanding
of Freud and psychoanalysis have been precisely critical acts of
close and inventive reading—there are, in this respect, no limits to
the collaboration. But if we accept this as our paradigm and think
of ourselves as Freud's or Shakespeare's collaborators, we must also
acknowledge that our reading of the case will be revealing, again,
chiefly about ourselves. This is why every generation, and perhaps
every reading, produces a different analysis of its Shakespearean
texts. In the same way, recent psychoanalytic theory has replaced
Freud's central Oedipal myth with a drama in which the loss of the
seducing mother is the crucial infant trauma. As men, we used to
want assurance that we could successfully compete with or replace
or supersede our fathers; now we want to know that our lost mothers will return. Both of these no doubt involve real perceptions, but
they also undeniably serve particular cultural needs.

Shakespeare plays, like case histories, derive from the observation of human behaviour, and both plays and case histories are
imaginative constructs. Whether or not either is taken to be an objective report of behaviour has more to do with the reader than the
reporter, but it has to be said that Shakespearean critics have more
often than not treated the plays as objective accounts. Without
such an assumption, a book with the title *The Girlhood of Shakespeare's Heroines* would be incomprehensible. We feel very far from
this famous and popular Victorian work now, but we still worry
about consistency and motivation in Shakespearean texts, and
much of the commentary in an edition like the Arden Shakespeare
is designed to explain why the characters say what they say—that
is, to reconcile what they say with what, on the basis of their previous behaviour, we feel they ought to be saying. The critic who wor-

3. Bruno Bettelheim, *The New Yorker*, 1 March 1982, p. 53.

ries about this kind of consistency in a Shakespeare text is thinking of it as an objective report.

But all readings of Shakespeare, from the earliest seventeenth-century adaptations through eighteenth-century attempts to produce 'authentic' or 'accurate' texts to the liberal fantasy of the old Variorum Shakespeare, have been aware of deep ambiguities and ambivalences in the texts. The eighteenth century described these as Shakespeare's errors and generally revised them through plausible emendation or outright rewriting. The argument was that Shakespeare wrote in haste and would have written more perfect plays had he taken time to revise; the corollary to this was, of course, that what we want are the perfect plays Shakespeare did not write rather than the imperfect ones that he did. A little later the errors became not Shakespeare's but those of the printing house, the scribe, the memory of the reporter or the defective hearing of the transcriber; but the assumption has always been that it is possible to produce a 'perfect' text: that beyond or behind the ambiguous, puzzling, inconsistent text is a clear and consistent one.

Plays, moreover, are not only—and one might argue, not primarily—texts. They are performances, too, originally designed to be read only in order to be acted out, and the gap between the text and its performance has always been, and remains, a radical one. There always has been an imagination intervening between the texts and their audiences, initially the imagination of producer, director, or actor (roles that Shakespeare played himself ), and since that time the imagination of editors and commentators as well. These are texts that have always had to be realised. Initially unstable, they have remained so despite all attempts to fix them. All attempts to produce an authentic, correct, that is, stable text have resulted only in an extraordinary variety of versions. Their differences can be described as minor only if one believes that the real play is a Platonic idea, never realised but only approached and approximately represented by its text.

This is our myth: the myth of a stable, accurate, authentic, legitimate text, a text that we can think of as Shakespeare's legitimate heir. It is, in its way, a family myth, and it operates with peculiar force in our readings of *The Tempest*, a play that has been, for the last hundred and fifty years, taken as a representation of Shakespeare himself bidding farewell to his art, as Shakespeare's legacy.

### THE MISSING WIFE

She is missing as a character, but Prospero, several times explicitly, presents himself as incorporating the wife, acting as both father and mother to Miranda, and, in one extraordinary passage, describes the voyage to the island as a birth fantasy:

> When I have decked the sea with drops full salt,
> Under my burden groaned, which raised in me
> An undergoing stomach, to bear up
> Against what should ensue.
>
> (I.ii.155–8)

To come to the island is to start life over again—both his own and Miranda's—with himself as sole parent, but also with himself as favourite child: he has been banished by his wicked, usurping, possibly illegitimate younger brother Antonio. This too has the shape of a Freudian fantasy: the younger child is indeed the usurper in the family, and the kingdom he usurps is the mother. On the island, Prospero undoes the usurpation, recreating kingdom and family with himself in sole command.

But not quite, because the island is not his alone—or if it is, then he has repeopled it with all parts of his fantasy, the distressing as well as the gratifying. When he arrives he finds Caliban, child of the witch Sycorax, herself a victim of banishment. The island provided a new life for her too, as it did literally for her son, with whom she was pregnant when she arrived. Sycorax died some time before Prospero came to the island; Prospero never saw her, and everything he knows about her he has learned from Ariel. Nevertheless, she is insistently present in his memory—far more present than his own wife—and she embodies to an extreme degree all the negative assumptions about women that he and Miranda have exchanged.

It is important, therefore, that Caliban derives his claim to the island from his mother: 'This island's mine, by Sycorax my mother' (I.ii.333) [1.2.331]. This has interesting implications to which I shall return, but here I want to point out that he need not make the claim this way. He could derive it from mere prior possession: he was there first. This, after all, would have been the sole basis of Sycorax's claim to the island, but it is an argument that Caliban never makes. And in deriving his authority from his mother, he delivers himself into Prospero's hands: Prospero declares him a bastard, 'got by the devil himself / Upon thy wicked dam' (I.ii.321–2) [1.2.319–20], thereby both disallowing any claim from inheritance and justifying his loathing for Caliban.

But is it true that Caliban is Sycorax's bastard by Satan? How does Prospero know this? Not from Sycorax: Prospero never saw her. Not from Caliban: Sycorax died before she could even teach her son to speak. Everything Prospero knows about the witch he knows from Ariel—her appearance, the story of her banishment, the fact that her pregnancy saved her from execution. Did Sycorax also tell Ariel that her baby was the illegitimate son of the devil? Or is this Prospero's contribution to the story, an especially creative piece of invective and an extreme instance of his characteristic assumptions about women? Nothing in the text will answer this question for us; and it is worth pausing to observe first that Caliban's claim seems to have been designed so that Prospero can disallow it, and second that we have no way of distinguishing the facts about Caliban and Sycorax from Prospero's invective about them.

Can Prospero imagine no good mothers, then? The play, after all, moves toward a wedding, and the most palpable example we see of the magician's powers is a betrothal masque. The masque is presided over by two exemplary mothers, Ceres and Juno; and the libidinous Venus with her destructive son Cupid has been banished from the scene. But the performance is also preceded by the most awful warnings against sexuality, male sexuality this time: all the libido is presumed to be Ferdinand's while Miranda remains Prospero's innocent child. Ferdinand's reassuring reply, as David Sundelson persuasively argues,[4] includes submerged fantasies of rape and more than a hint that when the lust of the wedding night cools, so will his marital devotion:

> the murkiest den,
> The most opportune place, the strong'st suggestion
> Our worser genius can, shall never melt
> Mine honor into lust, to take away
> The edge of that day's celebration . . .
>
> (IV.i.25–9)

This is the other side of the assumption that all women at heart are whores: all men at heart are rapists—Caliban, Ferdinand, and of course that means Prospero too.

### THE MARRIAGE CONTRACT

The play moves toward marriage, certainly, and yet the relations it postulates between men and women are ignorant at best, characteristically tense, and potentially tragic. There is a familiar Shakespearean paradigm here: relationships between men and women interest Shakespeare intensely, but not, on the whole, as husbands and wives. The wooing process tends to be what it is here: not so much a prelude to marriage and a family as a process of self-definition—an increasingly unsatisfactory process, if we look at the progression of plays from As You Like It, Much Ado about Nothing,

---

4. David Sundelson, 'So Rare a Wonder'd Father: Prospero's *Tempest*', in *Representing Shakespeare*, p. 48.

*Twelfth Night* through *All's Well that Ends Well*, *Measure for Measure*, *Troilus and Cressida* to *Antony and Cleopatra* and *Cymbeline*. If we want to argue that marriage is actually the point of the comic wooing process for Shakespeare, then we surely ought to be looking at how he depicts marriages; and here Petruchio and Kate, Capulet and Lady Capulet, Claudius and Gertrude, Othello and Desdemona, Macbeth and Lady Macbeth, Cymbeline and his queen, Leontes and Hermione will not persuade us that comedies ending in marriages have ended happily—or if they have, it is only because they have ended there, stopped at the wedding day.

What happens after marriage? Families in Shakespeare tend not to consist of husbands and wives and their offspring but of a parent and a child, usually in a chiastic relationship—father and daughter, mother and son. When there are two children, they tend to be presented as alternatives or rivals: the twins of *The Comedy of Errors*, Sebastian and Viola, infinitely substitutable for each other; or the good son–bad son complex of Orlando and Oliver, Edgar and Edmund. We know that Shakespeare himself had a son and two daughters, but that family configuration never appears in the plays. Lear's three daughters are quite exceptional in Shakespeare, and even they are dichotomised into bad and good. We may also recall Titus Andronicus's four sons and a daughter and Tamora's three sons, hardly instances to demonstrate Shakespeare's convictions about the comforts of family life.

The family paradigm that emerges from Shakespeare's imagination is a distinctly unstable one. Here is what we know of Shakespeare's own family: he had three brothers and three sisters who survived beyond infancy, and his parents lived into old age. At eighteen he married a woman of twenty-four by whom he had a daughter within six months, and a twin son and daughter a year and a half later. Within six more years he had moved permanently to London, and for the next twenty years—all but the last three years of his life—he lived apart from his wife and family. Nor should we stop here: we do not in the least know that Susanna, Hamnet, and Judith were his only children. He lived in a society without contraceptives, and unless we want to believe that he was either exclusively homosexual or celibate, we must assume a high degree of probability that there were other children. That they are not mentioned in his will may mean that they did not survive, but it also might mean that he made separate, non-testamentary provision for them. Certainly the plays reveal a strong interest in the subject of illegitimacy.

Until quite late in his career, he seems to have expressed his strongest familial feelings not toward children or wives but toward parents and siblings. His father dies in 1601, the year of *Hamlet*, his mother in 1608, the year of *Coriolanus*. And if we are thinking about unsurping bastard younger brothers, it cannot be coincidental that the younger brother who followed him into the acting profession was named Edmund. There are no dramatic correlatives comparable to these for the death of his son Hamnet in 1596. If we take the plays to express what Shakespeare thought about himself (an assumption that strikes me as by no means axiomatic) then we will say that he was apparently free to think of himself as a father— to his two surviving daughters—only after the death of both his parents: 1608 is the date of *Pericles* as well as *Coriolanus*.

One final biographical observation: Shakespearean heroines marry very young, in their teens. Miranda is fifteen. We are always told that Juliet's marriage at fourteen is not unusual in the period, but in fact it is unusual in all but upper-class families. In Shakespeare's own family, his wife married at twenty-four and his daughters at twenty-four and thirty-one. It was Shakespeare himself who married at eighteen. The women of Shakespeare's plays, of course, are adolescent boys. Perhaps we should see as much of Shakespeare in Miranda and Ariel as in Prospero.

### POWER AND AUTHORITY

The psychoanalytic and biographical questions raised by *The Tempest* are irresistible, but they can supply at best partial clues to its nature. I have described the plays as collaborative fantasies, and it is not only critics and readers who are involved in the collaboration. It is performers and audiences, too, and I take these terms in their largest senses, to apply not merely to stage productions but also to the theatrical dimension of the society that contains and is mirrored by the theatre. Cultural concerns, political and social issues, speak through *The Tempest*—sometimes explicitly, as in the open-ended discussion of political economy between Gonzalo, Antonio, and Sebastian in Act II. But in a broader sense, family structures and sexual relations become political structures in the play, and these are relevant to the political structures of Jacobean England.

What is the nature of Prospero's authority and the source of his power? Why is he Duke of Milan and the legitimate ruler of the island? Power, as Prospero presents it in the play, is not inherited but self-created: it is magic, or 'art', an extension of mental power and self-knowledge, and the authority that legitimises it derives from heaven—*Fortune* and *Destiny* are the terms used in the play. It is Caliban who derives his claim to the island from inheritance, from his mother.

In the England of 1610, both these positions represent available, and indeed normative, ways of conceiving of royal authority. James

I's authority derived, he said, both from his mother and from God. But deriving one's legitimacy from Mary Queen of Scots was ambiguous at best, and James always felt exceedingly insecure about it. Elizabeth had had similar problems with the sources of her authority, and they centred precisely on the question of her legitimacy. To those who believed that her father's divorce from Katherine of Aragon was invalid (that is, to Roman Catholics), Elizabeth had no hereditary claim; and she had, moreover, been declared legally illegitimate after the execution of her mother for adultery and incest. Henry VIII maintained Elizabeth's bastardy to the end; her claim to the throne derived exclusively from her designation in the line of succession, next after Edward and Mary, in her father's will. This ambiguous legacy was the sole source of her authority. Prospero at last acknowledging the bastard Caliban as his own is also expressing the double edge of kingship throughout Shakespeare's lifetime (the ambivalence will not surprise us if we consider the way kings are represented in the history plays). Historically speaking, Caliban's claim to the island is a good one.

Royal power, the play seems to say, is good when it is self-created, bad when it is usurped or inherited from an evil mother. But of course the least problematic case of royal descent is one that is not represented in these paradigms at all; it is one that derives not from the mother but in the male line from the father: the case of Ferdinand and Alonso, in which the wife and mother is totally absent. If we are thinking about the *derivation* of royal authority, then, the absence of a father from Prospero's memory is a great deal more significant than the disappearance of a wife. Some have dealt with this in a psychoanalytic framework, whereby Antonio becomes a stand-in for the father, the real usurper of the mother's kingdom.[5] Here again, however, the realities of contemporary kingship seem more enlightening, if not inescapable. James in fact had a double claim to the English throne, and the one through his father, the Earl of Darnley, was in the strictly lineal respects somewhat stronger than that of his mother. Both Darnley and Mary were direct descendants of Henry VII, but under Henry VIII's will, which established the line of succession, descendants who were not English-born were specifically excluded. Darnley was born in England, Mary was not. Indeed, Darnley's mother went from Scotland to have her baby in England precisely in order to preserve the claim to the throne.

King James rarely mentioned this side of his heritage, for per-

---

5. Coppélia Kahn makes this point, following a suggestion of Harry Berger, Jr, in 'The Providential Tempest and the Shakespearean Family', in *Representing Shakespeare*, p. 238. For an alternative view, see the exceptionally interesting discussion by Joel Fineman, 'Fratricide and Cuckoldry: Shakespeare's Doubles', in *Representing Shakespeare*, p. 104.

fectly understandable reasons. His father was even more disreputable than his mother; and given what was at least the public perception of both their characters, it was all too easy to speculate about whether Darnley was even in fact his father.[6] For James, as for Elizabeth, the derivation of authority through paternity was extremely problematic. Practically, James's claim to the English throne depended on Elizabeth's naming him her heir (we recall Miranda's legitimacy depending on her mother's word), and James correctly saw this as a continuation of the protracted negotiations between Elizabeth and his mother. His legitimacy, in both senses, thus derived from two mothers, the chaste Elizabeth and the sensual Mary, whom popular imagery represented respectively as a virgin goddess ('a piece of virtue') and a lustful and diabolical witch. James's sense of his own place in the kingdom is that of Prospero, rigidly paternalistic but incorporating the maternal as well: the king describes himself in *Basilicon Doron* as 'a loving nourish father' providing the commonwealth with 'their own nourishmilk'.[7] The very etymology of the word *authority* confirms the metaphor: *augeo*, increase, nourish, cause to grow. At moments in his public utterances, James sounds like a gloss on Prospero: 'I am the husband, and the whole island is my lawful wife; I am the head, and it is my body.'[8] Here the incorporation of the wife has become literal and explicit. James conceives himself as the head of a single-parent family. In the world of *The Tempest*, there are no two-parent families. All the dangers of promiscuity and bastardy are resolved in such a conception—unless, of course, the parent is a woman.

My point here is not that Shakespeare is representing King James as Prospero or Caliban or both, but that these figures embody the predominant modes of conceiving of royal authority in the period. They are Elizabeth's and James's modes, too.

### THE RENUNCIATION OF MAGIC

Prospero's magic power is exemplified, on the whole, as power over children: his daughter Miranda, the bad child Caliban, the obedient but impatient Ariel, the adolescent Ferdinand, the wicked younger brother Antonio, and indeed, the shipwreck victims as a whole, who are treated like a group of bad children. Many critics talk about Prospero as a Renaissance scientist and see alchemical metaphors in the grand design of the play. No doubt there is something in this; but what the play's action presents is not experiments

---

6. The charge that he was David Rizzio's child was current in England in the 1580s, spread by rebellious Scottish Presbyterian ministers. James expressed fears that it would injure his chance of succeeding to the English throne, and he never felt entirely free of it.
7. C. H. McIlwain, *Political Works of James I* (Cambridge, MA, 1918), p. 24.
8. From the 1603 speech to parliament; McIlwain, *Political Works*, p. 272.

and empiric studies but a fantasy about controlling other people's minds. Does the magic work? We are given a good deal of evidence of it: the masque, the banquet, the harpies, the tempest itself. But the great scheme is not to produce illusions and good weather: it is to bring about reconciliation, and here we would have to say that it works only indifferently well. 'They being penitent', says Prospero to Ariel, 'The sole drift of my purpose doth extend / Not a frown further' (V.i.28–30). The assertion opens with a conditional clause whose conditions are not met: Alonso is penitent, but the chief villain, the usurping younger brother Antonio, remains obdurate. Nothing, not all Prospero's magic, can redeem Antonio from his essential badness. Since Shakespeare was free to have Antonio repent if that is what he had in mind—half a line would have done for critics craving a reconciliation—we ought to take seriously the possibility that repentance is not what he had in mind. Perhaps, too, penitence is not what Prospero's magic is designed to elicit from his brother.

Why is Prospero's power conceived as magic? Why, in returning to Milan, does he renounce it? Most commentators say that he gives up his magic when he no longer needs it. This is an obvious answer, but it strikes me as too easy, a comfortable assumption cognate with the view that the play concludes with reconciliation, repentance, and restored harmony. To say that Prospero no longer needs his magic is to beg all the most important questions. What does it mean to say that he needs it? Did he ever need it, and if so, why? And does he in fact give it up?

Did he ever need magic? Prospero's devotion to his secret studies is what caused all the trouble in the first place—this is not an interpretation of mine; it is how Prospero presents the matter. If he has now learned to be a good ruler through the exercise of his art, that is also what taught him to be a bad one. So the question of his need for magic goes to the heart of how we interpret and judge his character: is the magic a strength or a weakness? To say that he no longer needs it is to say that his character changes in some way for the better; that by renouncing his special powers he becomes fully human. This is an important claim. Let us test it by looking at Prospero's renunciation.

What does it mean for Prospero to give up his power? Letting Miranda marry and leaving the island are the obvious answers, but they can hardly be right. Miranda's marriage is *brought about* by the magic; it is part of Prospero's plan. It pleases Miranda, certainly, but it is designed by Prospero as a way of satisfying himself. Claribel's marriage to the King of Tunis looks less sinister in this light: daughters' marriages, in royal families at least, are designed primarily to please their fathers. And leaving the island, reassuming the dukedom, is part of the plan, too. Both of these are presented as acts of renunciation, but they are in fact what the exercise of Prospero's magic is intended to effect, and they represent his triumph.

Prospero renounces his art in the great monologue at the beginning of Act V, 'Ye elves of hills, brooks, standing lakes and groves', and for all its valedictory quality, it is the most powerful assertion of his magic that the play gives us. It is also a powerful literary allusion, a close translation of a speech of Medea in Ovid,[9] and it makes at least one claim for Prospero that is made nowhere else in the play, that he can raise the dead. For Shakespeare to present this as a *renunciation* speech is upping Prospero's ante, to say the least.

In giving up his magic, Prospero speaks as Medea. He has incorporated Ovid's witch, prototype of the wicked mother Sycorax, in the most literal way—verbatim, so to speak—and his 'most potent art' is now revealed as translation and impersonation. In this context, the distinction between black magic and white magic, Sycorax and Prospero, has disappeared. Two hundred lines later, Caliban too is revealed as an aspect of Prospero: 'This thing of darkness I acknowledge mine.'

But Caliban is an aspect of Antonio, the evil child, the usurping brother. Where is the *real* villain in relation to Prospero now? Initially Antonio had been characterised, like Caliban and Sycorax, as embodying everything that is antithetical to Prospero; but in recounting his history to Miranda, Prospero also presents himself as deeply implicated in the usurpation, with Antonio even seeming at times to be acting as Prospero's agent: 'The government I cast upon my brother'; '[I] to him put the manage of my state'; 'my trust . . . did beget of him / A falsehood', and so forth. If Prospero is accepting the blame for what happened, there is a degree to which he is also taking the credit. Antonio's is another of the play's identities that Prospero has incorporated into his own; and in that case, what is there to forgive?

Let us look, then, at Prospero forgiving his brother in Act V. The pardon is enunciated—'You, brother mine, that entertain ambition . . . I do forgive thee' (ll.75–8)[1]—and qualified at once ('unnatural though thou art'), reconsidered as more crimes are remembered, some to be held in reserve ('at this time I will tell no tales' [ll.128–9]), all but withdrawn ('most wicked sir, whom to call brother / Would even infect my mouth' [ll.130–1]), and only then confirmed through forcing Antonio to relinquish the dukedom, an

---

9. *Metamorphoses*, 7:197–209, apparently at least partly refracted through Golding's English version.
1. Kermode and most editors read 'entertained', but I have restored the folio reading, which seems to me unexceptionable.

act that is presented as something he does unwillingly. The point is
not only that Antonio does not repent here but also that he is not
allowed to repent. Even his renunciation of the crown is Prospero's
act: 'I do . . . require / My dukedom of thee, which perforce, I
know, / Thou must restore' (ll. 131–4). In Prospero's drama, there
is no room for Antonio to act of his own free will.

The crime that Prospero holds in reserve for later use against his
brother is the attempted assassination of Alonso. Here is what happened: Prospero sends Ariel to put all the shipwreck victims to
sleep except Antonio and Sebastian. Antonio then persuades Sebastian to murder Alonso—his brother—and thereby become king of
Naples. Sebastian agrees, on the condition that Antonio kill Gonzalo. At the moment of the murders, Ariel reappears and wakes
Gonzalo:

> My master through his art foresees the danger
> That you his friend are in; and sends me forth—
> For else his project dies—to keep them living.
> (II.i.293–5) [293–95]

This situation has been created by Prospero, and the conspiracy
is certainly part of his project—this is why Sebastian and Antonio
are not put to sleep. If Antonio is not forced by Prospero to propose
the murder, he is certainly acting as Prospero expects him to do
and as Ariel says Prospero 'through his art foresees' that he will.
What is clearly taking place is Prospero restaging his usurpation
and maintaining his control over it this time. Gonzalo is waked
rather than Alonso so that the old courtier can replay his role in
aborting the assassination.

So at the play's end, Prospero still has usurpation and attempted
murder to hold against his brother, things that still disqualify Antonio from his place in the family. Obviously there is more to Prospero's plans than reconciliation and harmony—even, I would think,
in the forthcoming happy marriage of Ferdinand and Miranda. If
we look at that marriage as a political act (the participants are, after all, the children of monarchs) we will observe that in order to
prevent the succession of his brother, Prospero is marrying his
daughter to the son of his enemy. This has the effect of excluding
Antonio from any future claim on the ducal throne, but it also effectively disposes of the realm as a political entity: if Miranda is the
heir to the dukedom, Milan through the marriage becomes part of
the kingdom of Naples, not the other way round. Prospero recoups
his throne from his brother only to deliver it over, upon his death,
to the King of Naples once again. The usurping Antonio stands
condemned, but the effects of the usurpation, the link with Alonso
and the reduction of Milan to a Neapolitan fiefdom are, through

Miranda's wedding, confirmed and legitimised. Prospero has not re-gained his lost dukedom; he has usurped his brother's. In this con-text, Prospero's puzzling assertion that 'every third thought shall be my grave' can be seen as a final assertion of authority and control: he has now arranged matters so that his death will remove Anto-nio's last link with the ducal power. His grave is the ultimate tri-umph over his brother. If we look at the marriage in this way, giving away Miranda is a means of preserving his authority, not of relin-quishing it.

A BIBLIOGRAPHICAL CODA

The significant absence of crucial wives from the play is curiously emphasised by a famous textual crux. In Act IV Ferdinand, over-whelmed by the beauty of the masque being presented by Prospero, interrupts the performance to say,

> Let me live here ever.
> So rare a wondered father and a wise
> Makes this place Paradise.
> (ll.122–4)

Critics since the eighteenth century have expressed a nagging worry about Ferdinand's celebrating his betrothal by including Prospero but not Miranda in his paradise. In fact, what Ferdinand said, as Jeanne Addison Roberts demonstrated only in 1978, reads in the earliest copies of the folio, 'So rare a wondered father and a wife', but the crossbar of the f broke early in the print run, turning it to a long s and thereby eliminating Miranda from Ferdinand's thoughts of wonder.[2] The odd thing about this is that Rowe and Malone in their eighteenth-century editions emended wise to wife on logical grounds, the Cambridge Shakespeare of 1863 lists wife as a variant reading of the folio, and Furnivall's 1895 photographic facsimile was made from a copy that reads wife, and the reading is preserved in Furnivall's parallel text. Nevertheless, after 1895 the wife became invisible: bibliographers lost the variant, and textual critics consistently denied its existence until Roberts pointed it out. Even Charlton Hinman with his collating machines claimed that there were no variants whatever in this entire forme of the folio. And yet when Jeanne Roberts examined the Folger Library's copies of the book, including those that Hinman had collated, she found that two of them have the reading wife, and two more clearly show the crossbar of the f in the process of breaking. We find only what we are looking for or are willing to see. Obviously in 1978, this was

2. ' "Wife" or "Wise"—*The Tempest* 1. 1786', *University of Virginia Studies in Bibliography*, 31 (1978).

a reading whose time had come. And whose time, at the beginning of the twenty-first century, may already be past. Peter Blayney, observing that the physical construction of a piece of type surely precludes the crossbar of an *f* breaking and migrating, examined the "wife" copies under a high-powered microscope. What Jeanne Roberts was seeing, he believes, was probably the effects of ink on a piece of lint, caught, for the time it took to print off a few copies, between the *s* and *e* of "wise," after which it was dislodged and made its leisurely way out of the text.[3] Once again, we find what we are looking for and are willing to see. Typography, it now appears, will not rescue Shakespeare from patriarchy and male chauvinism after all. Prospero's wife—and Ferdinand's—remain invisible.

# JOHN GILLIES

## Shakespeare's Virginian Masque†

It is probably no more than coincidence that Shakespeare's spectacular and exotic play *The Tempest* was performed at court with Chapman's similarly exotic *Memorable Masque* for the marriage, in February 1613, of the princess Elizabeth to the Elector Palatine. But coincidence is sometimes hospitable to design, and we can imagine how interestingly these particular entertainments might have complemented each other. In the first place, each must have seemed to mirror what Jonson would have called their "present occasion," and also, conceivably, its political implications. This would have gratified Chapman, who is careful to assert that "all these courtly and honouring inventions . . . should expressively arise out of the places and persons for and by whom they are presented."[1] Curiously, much the same assertion is regularly made on behalf of Shakespeare, who is sometimes supposed to have inserted the betrothal masque as his own "courtly and honouring invention" into act 4 of *The Tempest*.[2] It is easier, however, to imagine the two

3. Introduction to the 2nd ed. of *The First Folio of Shakespeare*, ed. Charlton Hinman (New York: W. W. Norton, 1996), p. xxxi.
† From *English Literary History* 53 (1986): 673–707. Copyright © The Johns Hopkins University Press. Reprinted by permission of The Johns Hopkins University Press. Line numbers to this Norton Critical Edition have been added in brackets when they differ from the author's original citation.
1. George Chapman, *The Memorable Masque of the two honourable houses, or Inns of Court, the Middle Temple and Lincoln's Inn* (lines 178–82), Stephen Orgel and Roy Strong, eds., *Inigo Jones: The Theatre of The Stuart Court*, vol. 1 (Sotheby Parke Bernet: Univ. of California Press, 1973), 253–63. Further citations of *Memorable Masque* are included parenthetically in the text.
2. For various reasons the following all regard the masque as either occasional or an interpolation (or both): W. A. Wright, ed., *The Cambridge Shakespeare*, vol. 1 (1863; reprint,

entertainments having excited notice for the sheer novelty of
their Virginian imagery. This might have had the interesting
consequence of heightening the audience's response to the Virginian dimension of *The Tempest*, because what is understated and
seemingly peripheral in Shakespeare is bolder and more substantial
in Chapman.

The *Memorable Masque* is self-consciously Virginian. A company
of "Virginian knights . . . altogether estrangeful and Indian-like"
(36), arrive at Britain on a floating island under the conduct of Plutus, the god of riches. At first glance, Plutus seems a little out of
place in the company of Indians, but as George Sandys (translator
of Ovid and resident treasurer of the Virginia Company) was to explain: "Those Westerne climats abounded with gold and silver,
wrapt in the secret bowels of the earth."[3] Hence the Western Indies
could be as fitting a home for Plutus as the Indies of Donne's "eastern riches." Looked at another way, the domain of Plutus might be
either east or west: "both the indias, of spice and mine."[4] Mines, of
course, are subterranean. Hence Chapman's Plutus is also an
"earthy deity"—but one who wishes to cast off his earthy Virginian
ways and become reconciled with "the celestial goddess Honour"
(81), who resides in Britain.

The action of the masque proper follows from a satirical anti-
masque on the misuse of riches. A company of sun-worshiping
"Virginian priests . . . therefore called the Phoebades" (13–14), command "an artificial rock" to open, at which "the upper part of
the rock was suddenly turned to a cloud, discovering a riche and
refulgent mine of gold" (150–52), and the company of Virginian
"princes" seated inside. The Phoebades then sing praises to the sun
(which is shown setting behind the cloud), when their voices are answered by "other music and other voices, directing their observance
to the King" (543–44), the British Phoebus who is forever rising.

London: Macmillan, 1891), 99; F. G. Fleay, *A Chronicle History of the Life and Work of
William Shakespeare* (1886; reprint, New York: AMS Press, 1970), 249–50; J. M.
Robertson, *Shakespeare and Chapman* (1917; reprint London: Unwin, 1971), 210–15;
W. J. Lawrence, "The Masque in *The Tempest*," *The Fortnightly Review* 107 ( June 1920):
941–46; J. Dover Wilson, ed., *The Tempest* (1921; reprint Cambridge; Cambridge Univ.
Press 1969), 80–82; Irwin Smith, "Ariel and the Masque in *The Tempest*," *Shakespeare
Quarterly* 21 (1970): 213–22; Glynne Wickham, "Masque and Anti-masque in *The Tempest*," *Essays and Studies*, New Series 28 (1975): 1–14. Whereas all of these assume or at
least imply that the masque has a special relationship with its occasion, Wickham alone
is bold enough to provide a detailed reading of the masque as a key to the political un-
dercurrents.

3. George Sandys, *Ovid's Metamorphosis Englished, Mythologized, and Represented in Figures* (1632; reprint, Karl K. Hulley and Stanley T. Vandersall, eds., Lincoln: Univ. of Ne-
braska Press, 1970), 253. This has been called "the first major literary work produced in
the New World" (Christopher Grose, *Ovid's Metamorphoses: An Index to the 1632 Commentary of George Sandys* [Malibu: Udena Publications, 1981], vii).

4. John Donne, "A Hymn to God my God, in my Sickness," and "The Sun Rising," in
A. J. Smith, ed., *John Donne: The Complete English Poems* (Harmondsworth: Penguin,
1971), 347, 80.

Eventually this potentially inharmonious contest is resolved by "Eunomia" or Law, who orders the Virginians to renounce their "superstitious worship of these suns subject to cloudy darkenings and descents" (595–96), and worship instead the rising sun of Britain.

In this context *The Tempest* must have seemed almost parodic. Where Chapman's masque is about law, Shakespeare's play is about power. Where Chapman's Britain is visited by a suitably opulent delegation of Virginian priests and knights, Shakespeare's only Virginian intourist is Trinculo's "dead indian." Where Chapman's native knights obligingly hand over their gold-mine, Shakespeare's intractably "salvage and deformed slave" curses his disinheritors with the gift of language. Even when benevolently inclined, Caliban is able to offer nothing more marketable than "young scamels from the rock" or, perhaps, himself, "a plain fish, and no doubt marketable" (5.1.264–66).[5] Riches may conjoin briefly with honour in the blessing of Shakespeare's Juno, but more usually in *The Tempest* they inspire evil courtiers to murder and drunken servants to rebel. Shakespeare even seems to parody Chapman's cloudy gold mine with its El Doradoesque mythology of Indian riches, in Caliban's dream that

> The clouds methought would open, and show riches
> Ready to drop upon me; that, when I wak'd,
> I cried to dream again.
>
> (3.2.139–41)

Finally, the storm imagery of *The Tempest* contrasts starkly with the placidity of the *Memorable Masque*. If the play was staged with scenic machinery at court, Shakespeare's shipwreck scene must have been spectacularly realistic compared with the dreamy fantasy of Chapman's floating island. In short, beside Chapman's utopian masque, the dystopian mood of Shakespeare's play must have seemed especially pointed.

Shakespeare's idea of Virginia should also have seemed far more contemporary than Chapman's. D. J. Gordon has argued that Chapman's celebration of Virginia reflects Raleigh's promotion of Guiana in 1596 more than it reflects the Virginia Council's promotion of Virginia in 1613.[6] The theme of conversion may be common to both but the gold mine and the notion of Indian opulence are certainly Guianan,[7] as is the theme of reconciling honour with riches. Moreover, as Gordon suggests, the sun worship is probably

---

5. All references are to the Arden edition, Frank Kermode, ed., *The Tempest* (1954; reprint London: Methuen, 1966).
6. See D. J. Gordon, "Chapman's *Memorable Masque*," in Stephen Orgel, ed., *The Renaissance Imagination: Essays and Lectures by D. J. Gordon* (Berkeley: Univ. of California Press, 1975), 194–202.
7. In his *The Discoverie Of The Large, Rich, and Bewtiful Empire of Guiana* (London, 1596).

more Peruvian than Virginian. It does seem then, that the *Memorable Masque* is essentially an adaptation of Chapman's earlier celebration of the Guianan venture in *De Guiana* (1595), which is also inspired by the idea of reconciling English honour with Indian riches. For all its Virginian imagery, it is a little anachronistic for 1613—more Elizabethan than Jacobean.

*The Tempest* is not only more topical, but more truly engaged with its historical moment. The shipwreck scene, the accompanying scenarios of providential deliverance, and indeed the very title of the play, clearly allude to the wreck of the *Sea Adventure* in 1609.[8] And, as this event was of more than just topical interest, so the interest of the allusions is more than simply topical. The wreck marked a nadir in the affairs of the Virginia Company and, in the following year, became a focus for debate about the wisdom of the Plantation. It brought to a head "the tide of vulgar opinion"[9] which had been gathering against Virginia. Even before the wreck, events had not been going well. The colonists were starving, disease was rampant, order was disintegrating and the natives were unaccommodating. Now it appeared that the much heralded direct transatlantic route (north of the devil-ridden Bermudas rather than south of them, via the Caribbean) was demonstrably suicidal.[1] Most serious of all, it was

---

8. The *Sea-Adventure* was one of a fleet of ships which set out in May 1609 for the relief of the colony at Jamestown. But it was wrecked off the Bermudas, with the governors of the expedition, Sir Thomas Gates and Sir George Summers aboard, causing great consternation. Finally, when it was known that Gates and Summers had reached Virginia, the company was able to use their apparently miraculous deliverance as propaganda. Some of the resulting documents are now accepted as sources of *The Tempest*. These are: Sylvester Jourdan's *Discovery Of The Barmudas, Otherwise called the Isle of Divels* (1610); the Council of Virginia's *True Declaration of the Estate of the Colonie in Virginia, with a confutation of such scandalous reports as have tended to the disgrace of so worthy an enterprise* (1610); the derivative *True and Sincere Declaration Of The Purpose And Ends Of The Plantation Begun In Virginia* (1610); and a manuscript by the secretary to the expedition, William Strachey, *A True Reportory of the Wracke And Redemption Of Sir Thomas Gates, Knight . . .* , dated 15 July 1610 and first published in *Purchas His Pilgrimes* (1625). See Kermode, xxvi–xxx; and, Geoffrey Bullough, ed., *Narrative And Dramatic Sources Of Shakespeare* vol. 7 (London: Routledge & Kegan Paul, 1975): 237–300. A *True and Sincere Declaration* and *A Discovery of the Barmudas* can be found in the microfilm collection *Early English Books 1475–1640, Selected from Pollard and Redgrave's Short-Title Catalogue* (Ann Arbor, Michigan: University Microfilms International).

9. *A True Declaration of the Estate of the Colonie in Virginia* (D. B. Quinn, ed., *New American World* vol. 5 [London: Macmillan, 1979], 248–62, 248. Further page references in the text are to this edition). The general tendency of "vulgar opinion" is evident in the *True Declaration* itself, where the opinion formers are identified as balladists, "they that roared out the tragicall historie of the man eating of his dead wife in Virginia," sundry authors of "clamorous and tragicall narrations," rumour-mongering defectors ("that scum of men") from the colony, and players (256).

1. The idea of a new transatlantic route to Virginia, bypassing the Caribbean, appears to have been such a tempting response to the accusation "that the countrey is *farre off*, and the *passage* long and dangerous," that William Crashaw advances it even though acknowledging "that our last fleete was dispersed and foreshaken by a *storme*" (*A Sermon Preached in London Before the Right Honourable the Lord Lawarne* [1610], E, E2). According to Crashaw, "this passage into *Virginea . . .* is *. . .* so faire, so safe, so secure, so easie, as though God himselfe had built a bridge for men to passe from *England* to *Virginea*" (E 2).

becoming clear that "riches," either in the form of gold mines or a quick return on investments, were not to be had from Virginia. The starving and demoralised colonists would need more than Elizabethan "honour" to survive, they would need an iron will, or failing that, the iron discipline embodied in the Company's second charter and its draconian "Lawes divine, morall, and martiall."[2]

With its emphasis on self-discipline, its apparent endorsement of absolute power as a necessary means to general prosperity, and its no-nonsense attitude towards savagery, *The Tempest* can be seen to reflect not only the events of 1609, but the mood which gave them significance. Initially, therefore, the play may well have been perceived primarily in terms of the polemical milieu of the wreck, rather than the other way around. By 1610, when news of the deliverance of the ship's company had reached England, the Virginia Counsel sought to portray the wreck as providential. Hence, the wreck generated its own canon of texts, and indeed, became a text itself because the Company had ensured that (and how) it would be read: "If any man shall accuse these reports of partiall falsehood . . . let him now reade with judgement, but let him not judge before he hath read" (255). We can easily imagine, therefore, that the Virginian subtext of *The Tempest* was legible to contemporary audiences even without the special context of the *Memorable Masque*.

But to later readers unattuned to contemporary events, and later audiences denied what I have imagined as ideal opportunities to experience the Virginian dimension of *The Tempest*, that dimension has been all but invisible. It would not even be suspected until 1808, when Edmund Malone discovered the Bermuda documents and proposed them as sources.[3] Even today, the exact nature and significance of the Virginian influence remains an open question.[4] What I will explore here is the possibility that *The Tempest* is both more profoundly, and more specifically Virginian than is commonly allowed—more so indeed than Chapman's anachronistic celebration of Indian riches. In particular, I want to suggest two things. First, that two important Shakespearean motifs, the ideas of temperance and fruitfulness, are identifiably Virginian. This is to say that the play translates into poetic and dramatic terms a pair of rhetorical *topoi* that are crucial in forming the official portrait of Virginia. Second, I want to show that these Virginian motifs, culmi-

2. The Company's second charter of May 23, 1609 (*New American World*, 205–12) embodied the authoritarian ideology of the "governor," and was in the possession of Gates when he left for Virginia on the *Sea Adventure*. The "Lawes divine, morall, and martiall," a reaction to the experiences of 1607–1609, were promulgated by Sir Thomas Dale on June 22, 1611 (*New American World*, 221–25).

3. Edmund Malone, *Account of the Incidents from Which the Title and Part of the Story of Shakespeare's Tempest Were Derived* (London: 1808).

4. A useful summary of the debate is given by Charles Frey, "*The Tempest* and the New World," *Shakespeare Quarterly* 30 (1979): 29–41.

nating in the masque of Ceres, take on a distinctly Ovidian form. Here, I will argue that though Ovid may seem to lead us away from Virginia, he really leads us back to the informing principle of her discursive being—the principle of the moralised landscape.

In the first place, then, I am suggesting that the Shakespearean motifs of temperance and fruitfulness derive from standard *topoi* in the discourse of Virginia. That discourse began in 1594, when Raleigh successfully petitioned Elizabeth to allow him to rename as "Virginia" an indeterminate area of North America then known as "Wingandacoa." The christening was more than a courtly gesture—more even than a shrewd promotion—for it created a potent figure, and therewith a way of imaginatively possessing an area that was virtually unknown but for its Indian name and its compass coordinates. The figure allowed a savage geography to be read as a moral geography (much as the nymph "Irena" in book 5 of *The Faerie Queene* allows the reader to imagine Ireland as a willing candidate for the civilizing attentions of Artegall and Talus). "Virginia" was a "beautiful daughter of the creation . . . whose virgin-soile was never yet polluted by any Spaniards lust."[5] She conjured up visions of a land of pristine newness and incredible fertility. She was a *tabula rasa* awaiting inscription by the bearers of the true word; a savage, yet nubile nymph who longed for the English embrace. In 1609, the Reverend William Crashaw, who "was serving as a sort of director of publicity for the company,"[6] imagined "Virginea" as a young woman being schooled by an older and male "England" in the course of a scriptural dialogue appended to the published version of an important sermon to the Counsel.[7] In 1632, Thomas Morton likened Virginia to "a faire virgin, longing to be sped, / And meete her lover in a Nuptiall bed."[8] In 1625, the Reverend Samuel Purchas exhorted his readership of "Christian suters" to

> looke upon Virginia; view her lovely lookes (howsoever like a modest Virgin she is now vailed with wild Coverts and shadie Woods, expecting rather ravishment then marriage from her Native Savages) survay her . . . so goodly and well proportioned limmes and members; her Virgin portion nothing empaired, . . . and in all these you shall see, that she is worth the wooing and loves of the best Husband.[9]

5. George Donne's *Virginia Reviewed* in T. H. Breen, "George Donne's *Virginia Reviewed*: A 1638 Plan to Reform Colonial Society," *William and Mary Quarterly* (Third Series) 30 (1973): 449–66, 454.
6. Louis B. Wright, *Religion and Empire: The Alliance between Piety and Commerce in English Expansion 1558–1625* (Chapel Hill: Univ. of North Carolina Press, 1943), 100.
7. *A Sermon*, L.
8. *The New English Canaan*, cited in Annette Kolodny, *The Lay Of The Land: Metaphor as Experience and History in American Life and Letters* (Chapel Hill: Univ. of North Carolina Press, 1975), 12.
9. Samuel Purchas, *Virginias Verger* (1625), in *Hakluytus Posthumus or Purchas His Pilgrimes*, (Glasgow: James MacLehose & Sons; 1905), xix:232, 242.

Such nuptial, not to say prurient, imagery is typical of Virginian apologists from Raleigh to Purchas. The *nomen* bespoke a kind of coy allure which the propagandists were not slow to exploit. Of course, Virginia's hospitality to wordplay could also be abused (as, for example in the satirical *Eastward Ho!* of 1605, where the rapacious Captain Seagull rallies his band of adventurers with the cry: "Come boys, Virginia longs til we share the rest of her maidenhead" [3.3.14–15]), but generally it seems to have worked in her favour. Raleigh's choice of name was an inspired act of myth-making, suggesting an attractive combination of innocence, docility and quasi-erotic availability.

But whatever sub- or semi-conscious signals were implicit in her name, Virginia also suggested a more conscious and acknowledged symbolic stratum. The whole elaborate edifice of Elizabeth's mythology of state had rested on the attribute that Virginia celebrated. The American nymph was a fresh sprig of old and familiar stock, which may be why she bears more than a passing resemblance to Elizabeth's favorite mythological identity. This was Astraea, the virgin goddess of justice and patroness of the Golden Age, who on her departure from earth became identified with the heavenly sign, Virgo. During her golden reign, Astraea had reconciled virginity with fruitfulness, spring (the golden season) with August (the month of Virgo), and heaven with earth. On her departure, these contraries split apart and would not be reconciled again until her return, either in the guise of another golden reign (such as Elizabeth's) or of a golden country such as Virginia. (It is worth noting here that the masque of act 4 reconciles spring with August). Conceivably, it may be this figure who is the root of Virginia's virginal character, the messianic hopes she inspired and her golden attributes of temperance and fruitfulness.

Whether Astraean or not, however, temperance and fruitfulness appear as important features of Virginia very early in her history. But they are not coeval. The earliest and most influential of the Virginia voyage narratives, by Arthur Barlowe, stresses fruitfulness rather than temperance. Printed in Hakluyt's *Principal Navigations* of 1589, it describes the formal possession of "the countrey Wingandacoa, (and nowe by her Majestie, Virginia),"[1] under Raleigh's new patent in 1584. With the probable help of Raleigh and Hakluyt, Barlowe tells of a paradise in which: "the earth bringeth foorth all things in abundance, as in the first creation, without toile or labour" (8). The soil effortlessly yielded three crops in five months,

---

1. In David B. Quinn and Alison M. Quinn, eds., *Virginia Voyages from Hakluyt* (London: Oxford Univ. Press, 1973), 1–12, 4. Further references to Barlowe's narrative and to Thomas Harriot's (cited below and collected in Quinn and Quinn, 46–76) appear parenthetically in the text.

miraculous draughts of fish were there for the taking. A wide range
of useful (if not precious) commodities were to be had in plenty.
The inhabitants were "most gentle, loving, and faithfull, void of all
guile, and treason, and such as lived after the manner of the golden
age" (8). Similarly, the narratives of Thomas Harriot, Ralph Lane
and John White, also printed in Hakluyt (and also showing signs of
editorial guidance) consistently give the impression of a virgin
paradise.

Temperance first appears as a Virginian feature in Thomas Harriot's *A briefe and true report of the new found land of Virginia.* Har-
riott praised "the excellent temperature of the aire . . . at all
seasons," and "the holsomenesse thereof" (75), which preserved
the colonists of 1588 in good health—in spite of a shortage of
clothing and lack of shelter during the winter. He then links the
two features in what tends to become a rhetorical formula in later
accounts: "Seeing therefore the ayre there is so temperate and hol-
some, the soile so fertile . . . I hope there remains no cause
whereby the action should be misliked" (75–76). The action, however, was "misliked" even as Harriot wrote. His Virginian apologia is
intended, at least in part, as a rebuttal of "slaunderous and shame-
full speaches bruited abroad by many that returned from thence"
(47). Tales of hardship, mismanagement, hostile natives and a
dawning awareness that Virginia was no El Dorado were so effective in dispelling the myth of Virginia as to deprive Raleigh of funds
for a major venture in 1587 (xiii). The same threat hung over the
heads of the Jacobean patentees, the Virginia Company of London;
and their propaganda (like Raleigh's) was obliged to disable the
counter-mythology. What was needed was a rhetorical strategy that
would confirm the original myth of Virginia while instilling a new
and more realistic mood of forbearance in inevitable hardship—
along with a (less realistic) willingness to postpone profits indefinitely. Temperance was one answer to this promotional problem
because (unlike fruitfulness) it could avail itself of a moral, as well
as a geographical, dimension.

Nowhere is the use of temperance as a polemical strategy so evident as in the *True Declaration* (1610), the most authoritative
printed justification of the wreck of the *Sea Adventure.* The author
of this document faced formidable difficulties. To begin with, the
problem of disease at Jamestown threatened to disable the myth of
a temperate climate, while the experience of "the starving time" in
1609 posed a challenge to the myth of fruitfulness. In a passage
thought to be echoed in *The Tempest,*[2] the issues are put as a
rhetorical question: "How is it possible, that such a virgin and tem-

2. See Kermode, ed., *The Tempest,* 45. Page numbers refer to the text of *True Declaration*
appearing in Quinn, *New American World.*

perat aire, should work such contrarie effects," and again, how can "plentie and famine, a temperate climate, and distempered bodies, felicities and miseries . . . be reconciled together" (255)? The answers are as rhetorically ingenious as they are logically absurd. While admitting that "our fort . . . is most part invironed with an ebbing and flowing salt water, the owze of which sendeth forth an unwholsome and contagious vapour," the writer prefers to blame the disease on the "intemperate idlenes" of the afflicted rather than on the site of Jamestown. This is proved by "*Sir Thomas Gates* his experiment: he professeth that in a fortnights space he recovered the health of most of them by moderat labour, whose sickness was bred in them by intemperate idlenes" (255). We are left with the impression that infection from the fens is somehow optional, depending on one's moral fibre and work-rate. In view of the mortality rate and the chronic labour problem at Jamestown, the idea is (to put it mildly) wishful thinking. Nevertheless it is typical of a strategy which found rhetorical solutions for real difficulties; there is no suggestion that Jamestown be resited or the "owze" drained.

As with the problem of disease, the embarrassing topics of shipwreck and starvation are parlayed into the more manageable *topos* of intemperance. Figuratively speaking, the intemperance of the colonists at Jamestown represents a "tempest of dissension" more dire than the storm that wrecked the *Sea Adventure*:

> The broken remainder of those supplies made a greater shipwrack on the continent of *Virginia*, by the tempest of dissension: every man overvaluing his own worth, would be a Commander . . . when therefore licence, sedition, and furie, are the fruits of a headie, daring, and unruly multitude, it is no wonder that so many in our colony perished: it is a wonder that all were not devoured. *Omnis inordinatus animus sibi ipsi fit poena*, every inordinate soul becomes his owne punishment.
>
> (255)

As well as the idea of intemperance, we might notice the figurative use of the word "fruits" to convey the outcome of intemperance. In spite of the starving time, Virginia had not ceased to be fruitful: the colonists had simply become too lazy to avail themselves of the abundance that surrounded them. The writer relates: "An incredible example of their idlenes . . . that . . . some of them eat their fish raw, rather than they would go a stones cast to fetch wood and dresse it" (255).

As this last anecdote implies, Barlowe's idea of Virginia as an earthly paradise could be potentially subversive in its suggestion that "the earth bringeth forth all things . . . without toile or labour."

Hence, if the myth of the earthly paradise was to remain viable for the Jamestown colony, it would require modification, which it duly received: "God sels us all things for our labour, when *Adam* himselfe might not live in paradice without dressing the garden" (255). In this more market-oriented version of the myth, fruitfulness is linked to temperance by the necessity for labour. The formula took, and from this point onward becomes a fully assimilated and necessary element of the colonial idea of Virginia.

Planting and cultivation would bring forth good fruits while dissent, "dreames of mountaines of gold, and happy robberies" (256), would bring forth evil fruits. There is an intriguing hint that gold-hunger led to the formation of factions, and even mutiny. A "viperous generation" seems to have broken away from the main colony in Raleighesque hopes of finding "mountaines of gold," or of thriving by piracy. It is interesting to note that the Guianan incentive ("Golde is our Fate," *De Guiana*) is now perceived as deviant and that the Guianan imagery of riches becomes a foil to the more agriculturally oriented imagery of Virginia. Both the *True Declaration* and its companion pamphlet, *A True and Sincere Declaration of the purpose and ends of the Plantation begun in Virginia* (1610), suggest that by neglecting "the opportunity of seed-time" there is a danger of "everything returning from civill Propryety to Naturall, and Primary Community" (11). Gold-diggers would not only go hungry but would go native as well, and the civilisation they stand for will crumble into the wilderness. If left unsown, the garden ("Virginia's Verger") would not feed the colonists; if left unweeded, the metaphoric garden of "civill Propryety" would grow to seed. Fruitfulness would become rankness: "the fruits of a headie, daring, and unruly multitude."

In all four of the Bermuda documents that Shakespeare is supposed to have drawn on, the influence of these *topoi* is profound. *A True and Sincere Declaration* explains that the "distemper" of Virginia proceeds from "such as are the weeds and rancknesse" (25) of England, the original garden from which they have been transplanted. However, it also urges "the fruitfulness and wholesomenesse of this Land, and . . . the recompense it shall in time bring" (21). The *topoi* are also to be found in the two documents by, respectively, Sylvester Jourdan and William Strachey, which concentrate on the Bermuda adventure rather than the state of the colony at Jamestown, and do not appear to have been under the direct control of the company. Jourdan's *A Discovery of the Barmudas* (1610) describes those islands in terms of the Virginian *topoi*: "yet did we find there the ayre so temperate and the Country so aboundantly fruitful of all fit necessaries, for the sustentation and preservation of man's life" (9). Strachey's *A True Reportory Of The*

*Wracke And Redemption Of Sir Thomas Gates, Knight* (1610),[3] though by far the most reliable account of the Bermuda sojourn, relies entirely on the *True Declaration* for its account of Virginia, and as a consequence duplicates its rhetorical strategy. The colonists are "men of such distempered bodies and infected mindes" (294), that their gardens lie unsown while they themselves grow rank with "neglect and sensuall surfet" (293).

For contemporary London audiences who would have known Virginia primarily in terms of her moral geography, the following passage must have been richly ironic:

| Adr. | Though this island seem to be desert, |
|------|---------------------------------------|
|      | . . . . . . . . . . . . . . . . . . . . . . . . . . . . . |
|      | Uninhabitable, and almost inaccessible,— |
| Seb. | Yet,— |
| Adr. | Yet,— |
| Ant. | He could not miss't. |
| Adr. | It must needs be of subtle, tender and delicate temperance. |
| Ant. | Temperance was a delicate wench. |
| Seb. | Ay, and a subtle; as he most learnedly deliver'd. |
| Adr. | The air breathes upon us here most sweetly. |
| Seb. | As if it had lungs, and rotten ones. |
| Ant. | Or as 'twere perfum'd by a fen. |
| Gon. | Here is everything advantageous to life. |
| Ant. | True; save means to live. |
| Seb. | Of that there's none, or little. |
| Gon. | How lush and lusty the grass looks! how green! |
| Ant. | The ground, indeed, is tawny. |
| Seb. | With an eye of green in't. |
| Ant. | He misses not much. |
| Seb. | No; he doth but mistake the truth totally. |

(2.1.34–55) [35–56]

Characteristically Virginian paradoxes—"plentie and famine," the lush paradise which is also a desert, the temperate land of pestilential fens, the inaccessible place which is just around the corner— are wonderfully parodied. So is the credibility gap: "he doth but mistake the truth totally." The "fen" parody is the wittier for also being a theatrical joke at the expense of the audience who "breathe" upon the stage castaways with their collectively "rotten lungs." I am suggesting that what we have here is more than a happily random series of Virginian echoes, but a conscious parody of the discursive portrait of Virginia. This would imply, in turn, that a

3. In Bullough, *Narrative and Dramatic Sources*, 275–94.

Virginian subtext was legible as parody to a degree of depth and precision that we have not been used to contemplate. But the importance of Virginia in The Tempest goes far beyond parody. Temperance and fruitfulness provide the play with fundamental structural and thematic motifs—the bedrock of its own moral land-scape.

Temperance describes the trajectory of the play's "rarer action," its symbolic axis. The Shakespearean "tempest of dissension" initi-ates (and is the effect of) a "rage" which is first tempered and then chastised in a pair of masque-like displays. To begin with, Ferdinand's intemperate grief is allayed by the song of Ariel as a sea-nymph (1.2.377–406) [374–402], with its masque-like invita-tions to curtseying and dancing. Then, the greed and rapacity of the courtier group, the "men of sin," is confronted with its own image in the harpy snatching away the "banquet" offered by the "living drollery." These two devices are complemented by a third, the betrothal masque of act 4 that celebrates the temperate love of Ferdinand and Miranda and stands at the apex of the symbolic tra-jectory. It celebrates where the previous devices temper or chastise; its "harmonious vision" counters the disharmony of the storm and the varieties of intemperance it generated.

If the logic of The Tempest were as straightforward as that of the Memorable Masque, we might expect the masque of Ceres to con-clude (as well as complete) the symbolic design, but it does not. When it dissolves to "a strange hollow and confused noise," the sea comes back. Prospero is "touch'd" by its rage; his mind "beating" with "anger, so distemper'd" (4.1.138–45). The dialectic of temper-ance and intemperance continues. As a punishment for their intru-sion, Caliban, Trinculo and Stephano are soused

> I' th' filthy-mantled pool beyond your cell,
> There dancing up to th' chins, that the foul lake
> O'erstunk their feet.
>
> (4.1.182–84)

They are then hunted by hounds. (In the Ovidian story of Actaeon, hounds typify intemperate desires.) Finally, it is clear that stormy weather and rotten vapours will be just as much the portion of the "brave new world" as they were of the sad old one. Nevertheless, the masque of Ceres stands as the principal symbol of what the play affirms—that renewal can come out of destruction if the in-fected mind is tempered and the fruitful soil of virtue is cultivated.

We may notice in the "foul lake" an echo of the "fen" imagery mentioned earlier. This cannot be accidental, for fen imagery ap-pears throughout the play and might be thought of as a motif—a ubiquitous mirror of intemperance. The "filthy-mantled pool" mirrors the intemperate language of Caliban, who curses Prospero with "All the infections that the sun sucks up / From bogs, fens, flats" (2.2.60–61) [2.2.1–2]. Indeed, fens seems curiously inspirational to Caliban:

> As wicked dew as e'er my mother brush'd
> With raven's feather from unwholesome fen
> Drop on you both.
> 
> (1.2.323–25) [321–23]

They would also appear to have been of some importance in Sycorax's magic. In a strictly metaphoric sense, they feature in the spells of Prospero, who imagines the dispelling of the brain-boiled courtiers both as a new dawn of awareness in which "the ignorant fumes that mantle / Their clearer reason" (5.1.67–68) are dispersed, and as a returning tide of understanding that "Will shortly fill the reasonable shore, / That now lies foul and muddy" (5.1.81–82). Thus, fens are present not only as imagined places but also as metaphors, in which form they contribute to a general idiom of disease and distemper. In Prospero's advice to the newly healthy Alonso, "Do not infest your mind with beating on / The strangeness of this business" (5.1.246–47), the fen imagery of disease is linked to the "beating" of "sea-sorrow," thereby combining in one image the two most important symbolic *loci* of intemperance in the play—fens and sea.

If temperance is the principal means of regeneration, fruitfulness, or "foison," is its symbolic image. The play offers several versions of fruitfulness corresponding to the moral and imaginative capacities of its characters. The degenerate courtiers, Antonio and Sebastian, see only barrenness. They find the island's air foul and its ground "tawny." The island is a mirror, reflecting their sterility; in the ghostly banquet and the ravenous harpy it also reflects their greed. By the same token, the well-tempered courtiers find the desert fruitful. For Adrian and Gonzalo, the air is temperate and the grass astonishingly "lusty" and "green." Just as Arthur Barlowe had imagined Virginia, so Gonzalo imagines the island as an earthly paradise where:

> Nature should bring forth,
> Of it own kind, all foison, all abundance,
> To feed my innocent people.
> 
> (2.1.158–60)

But Gonzalo's temperance does not save him from naivety. Nor does the sterility of Antonio and Sebastian keep them from commenting shrewdly on his utopian "plantation." With some justice, they see his earthly paradise as fruitfulness gone to seed:

| *Gon.* | Had I plantation of this isle, my lord,— |
| *Ant.* | He'd sow't with nettle-seed. |
| *Seb.* | Or docks, or mallows. |

(2.1.139–40)

As we shall see, the idea of rank growth—fruitfulness *in malo*—becomes a motif defining disordered desires, and thereby coincides with the fen motif. Indeed, in Prospero's forgiveness of Antonio, both motifs are audible in the one word:

> For you, most wicked sir, whom to call brother
> Would even infect my mouth, I do forgive
> Thy rankest fault.

(5.1.130–32)

The use of "rankest" in conjunction with "infect" conveys not only an image of the unweeded garden but a whiff of the diseased fen.

The dialectic is not exhausted yet. All these versions of classical "foison"—natural, "rank" and cultivated—are offset against a fourth kind of "foison," represented by Caliban's non-classical wilderness with its "clustering filberts," "pig nuts," "scamels" and "the nimble marmoset." The contrasts here are ambiguous rather than clear-cut. Caliban's delight in the fruits of his wild nature is one of several ways in which Shakespeare prefers his vitality over the weary cynicism of Antonio and Sebastian—even, perhaps, over the weary virtue of Prospero. Meanwhile, his association with "bogs" and "fens" allies him with the rankness that characterises the intemperate cynics.

Like temperance, then, fruitfulness is a quality that varies according to the character imagining it. Each kind of image is dialectically constituted as an important symbolic motif and is related to the other in a way that recalls their formation in the Virginia discourses of 1609. In both the play and the propaganda alike, temperance and fruitfulness provide the rhetorical basis of a "poetic geography"[4] comprising the sea, the weather, and kinds of landscape (the earthly paradise, fens, rank wilderness, tawny deserts). The topographical parallels between *The Tempest* and Virginia are more than simply random. The play is surprisingly insistent on certain specific features of landscape (such as fens) that transcend the commonplace and, especially when the moral significance is taken into account, suggest a unique parallel with Virginia. The difference is that whereas the Virginia discourses employ the *topoi* (and their derivative settings) as persuasive tropes in a colonial promotion, Shakespeare uses them to construct a dialectic of civilisation

---

4. The expression is Vico's. See Thomas Goddard Bergin and Max Harold Fisch, eds., *The New Science of Giambattista Vico* (Ithaca: Cornell Univ. Press, 1968), 285.

and savagery, of art and nature, and so explores the deeper issues implied by the Virginia colony.

We are now in a position to explore the iconography of the masque of Ceres, the symbolic entertainment in which the Virginian motifs of temperance and fruitfulness, along with various kinds of imagined weather and landscape, reach their culmination. The masque works on two levels. At the more literal, it is a celebration of the betrothal of Ferdinand and Miranda. But Juno, the marriage goddess, also presides over a metaphoric betrothal of the elements. Earth is reconciled with heaven, land with sea, hot with cold, wet with dry, spring with harvest. At both levels, literal and metaphoric, the reconciliations are achieved through temperance and result in fruitfulness. The harvest goddess who presides over a fertile and cultivated landscape represents both fruitfulness and the temperance necessary for the work of cultivation. The rainbow goddess is not only Juno's messenger, but a mythological personification of temperate weather. She also recapitulates and justifies the mythology of the earlier "masques of Ariel"[5] that comprise the structural axis of the motif of temperance. We may begin, then, by sketching the mythological identity of Iris, Shakespeare's personification of temperance.

Iris is an iconographic mirror of the entire symbolscape of temperance in *The Tempest*. As a winged figure who combines the elements of air and water in her rainbow, she epitomises the ambience of sea and weather imagery. She is weather *in bono* where the storm is weather *in malo*. Shakespeare cannot have been unaware of the pun on the Latin word for weather (*tempestas*) that lurks in the very title of his play, nor the fact that Iris is mythologically related to the *Tempestates* (the Winds) through her marriage to Zephyrus, the gentle wind of Spring. If Iris is thereby juxtaposed with the storm, she also suggests temperance where the shipwreck suggests intemperance. She invites "temperate nymphs" to the masque's "graceful dance" as if in answer to the shipwreck's rage— the conventional significance of which Shakespeare heightens by a suggestion of drunkenness on board: "We are merely cheated of our lives by drunkards" (1.1.55). Iris also has specifically mythological points of contact with earlier "masques of Ariel." As the daughter of Thaumas (son of Pontus, the sea) and Electra (daughter of Oceanus), she is the sister of the harpies, who are also creatures of the sea and the weather. In Hesiod, the harpies are given "speaking

5. See Henri Peyré, "Les 'Masques' D'Ariel: Essai d'interpretation de leur symbolisme," *Cahiers Elisabethains* 19 (1981): 53–71. This is by far the best purely iconographic study of the masque of Ceres and, E. K. Chambers notwithstanding ("The Integrity of *The Tempest*," *The Review of English Studies* 1 [1925]. 129–50), the most convincing defence of its organic interconnection with the rest of the play.

names" that identify them as violent winds.[6] In Homer, they are identified with "the spirits of the storm.[7] Shakespeare clearly underlines these ideas by introducing his harpy with storm effects: "Thunder and lightning" (3.3.52–53), and by imagining the harpy's judgement on Alonso as a masque-like storm scene:

> O, it is monstrous, monstrous!
> Methought the billows spoke, and told me of it;
> The winds did sing it to me; and the thunder,
> That deep and dreadful organ-pipe, pronounc'd
> The name of Prosper: it did bass my trespass.
>                                      (3.3.95–99)

If Iris is the calm sister of the raging Harpy, she is also temperamentally and functionally allied with the "nymph o'th'sea" who appears briefly (and in terms of plot motivation, inexplicably) when Prospero commands Ariel:

> Go make thyself like a nymph o'th'sea: Be subject to
> No sight but thine and mine; invisible
> To every eyeball else.
>                                      (1.2.301–304)

Ariel's invisible appearance and almost immediate exit has always been something of a mystery. Apart from underlining Caliban's first entry, it seems curiously functionless and messy. A plot motivation is both flaunted and withheld:

> (*Enter* ARIEL *like a water-nymph*)
> *Prosp.*    Fine apparition! my quaint Ariel,
>             Hark in thine ear.
> *Ari.*      My lord, it shall be done. (*Exit*)
>                                 (1.2.318–20) [317–18]

It is only when we think of the nymph in terms of the iconography linking Iris to the harpy that her function becomes clear. Ariel's entry as an "invisible" water-nymph prepares the audience for his next, and notionally invisible, entry with Ferdinand for the song "Come unto these yellow sands" (1.2.377–406) [374–402]. The stage direction for that entry ("*Re-enter* ARIEL, *invisible, playing and singing,*" 1.2.376–77 [374SD]), has led the Arden editor to suppose that Ariel must be dressed in a property gown "to go invisible" (29, 34). But if he enters as a sea-nymph he will still be "invisible" because the purpose of the earlier entry can only have been to signal the audience that sea-nymphs are invisible in this play and don't

---

6. See Peyré, 63, note 72. Most of the purely iconographical points about Iris can be found in Peyré.
7. See D. C. Allen, *Image and Meaning: Metaphoric Traditions in Renaissance Poetry* (Baltimore: Johns Hopkins Press, 1960), 58.

need conventional gowns "to go invisible." This should lead us to conclude that Shakespeare went to the trouble of the earlier and apparently unmotivated entry in order to prepare the ground for an appropriate mythological tableau in the sea-change song. Ariel would still be dressed as a nymph, thereby enhancing the imagery of nymphs in the song. The role of the nymph in tempering the rage of "sea-sorrow," will, in turn, underline the later appearance of the harpy who incites the billows, the wind and the thunder to madden Alonso. Both figures anticipate and are balanced by the rainbow goddess—pediments in an iconographic monument to temperance, of which Iris is the crown.

The "daugher of Thaumantes faire," as Spenser refers to her (*The Faerie Queene*, 5.3.25), also has a special affinity with Miranda in as much as both names signify "wonder." The mythographer Richard Lynche found that Iris means "wonder" both because "she was the daughter of Thaumante which signifieth admiration," and because of her rainbow, "the strange varietie of the colours [w]hereof possesseth the beholders minds, with a continuing wonder and admiring continuation.[8] Thus, Iris is not only Miranda's mythological double but stands in the same relation to her father (Thaumas) as Miranda stands in relation to hers—the thaumaturge, or wonderworker.

No sooner is Iris onstage than she summons Ceres with an elaborate evocation of her domain:

> Ceres, most bounteous lady, thy rich leas
> Of wheat, rye, barley, vetches, oats, and pease;
> Thy turfy mountains, where live nibbling sheep,
> And flat meads thatch'd with stover, them to keep;
> Thy banks with pioned and twilled brims,
> Which spongy April at thy hest betrims,
> To make cold nymphs chaste crowns; and thy broom-groves,
> Whose shadow the dismissed bachelor loves,
> Being lass-lorn, thy poll-clipt vineyard;
> And thy sea-marge, sterile and rocky-hard,
> Where thou thyself dost air.
>
> (4.1.60–75)

The function of this verbal landscape is more than merely decorative. As with the play's other symbolic landscapes that it echoes and inverts, the landscape of Ceres is precisely sited and articulated. To begin with, it is comprehensively opposed to Gonzalo's idea of an earthly paradise. Where Gonzalo dreams of a native "foison" exclusive of both agriculture and civilization:

8. *The fountaine of ancient fiction* (1599; reprint, New York: Garland, 1976), lii–liii.

> For no kind of traffic
> Would I admit, no name of magistrate.
> Letters should not be known. Riches, poverty,
> And use of service, none. Contract, succession,
> Bourn, bound of land, tilth, vineyard, none.
>                                        (2.1.151–55) [144–48]

Ceres (who in Golding's Ovid, "first made lawes"[9]) boasts just those varieties of industrial foison that Gonzalo forswears. Her "barns and garners," her "vines with clust'ring bunches growing," her "rich leas / Of wheat, rye, barley, vetches, oats and pease," all affirm agriculture, husbandry, and stewardship (if not direct ownership) of the land. Where Gonzalo's paradisal "plantation" is seen by uncharitable yet shrewd eyes, as choked by weeds ("nettle-seed. / Or docks, or mallows," 2.1.140), Ceres's "vineyard" is "poll-clipt," her "turfy mountains" are trimmed by "nibbling sheep." The husbandry of Ceres thus contrasts favorably with the incipient "rankness" of Gonzalo's ideal "plantation" in the same way that the *True Declaration* qualifies Barlowe's myth of a Virginian paradise with a plea for the necessity of labour: "God sels us all things for our labour, when Adam himselfe might not live in paradice without dressing the garden."

\*  \*  \*

\* \* \* I have argued that Shakespeare's masque of Ceres is the culmination of a dialectic between the Virginian motifs of temperance and fruitfulness. I have also argued that the masque is ultimately beholden to Ovid for the iconography of its moral landscape—both for the topographical detail and for the kind of morality that informs it. Can we go one step further and say that Ovid (who, after all, is the original of the Renaissance idea of the *paysage moralisé*) is also behind the moral topography of Virginia? Just possibly, though we could never be sure that the debt was conscious. But then Shakespeare's masque may not be *consciously* Ovidian either. The point is that once a landscape is imagined as temperate, fruitful and virginal, once its fruitfulness is supposed to depend somehow on temperance and virginity, then the logic can *only* be Ovidian. Both *The Tempest* and Virginia are inevitably Ovidian. \* \* \*

---

9. *Metamorphoses* 5.436, in Golding's 1567 translation of Ovid's account of Ceres and Proserpine (5.434–811), W. H. D. Rouse, ed., *Shakespeare's Ovid: Being Arthur Golding's Translation Of The Metamorphoses* (London: Centaur Press, 1961). Further citations of Ovid will be to Golding's translation, in this edition.

# PETER HULME

## Prospero and Caliban†

The traditional identification of Prospero with Shakespeare, though spurious, half grasps the crucial point that Prospero, like Shakespeare, is a dramatist and creator of theatrical effects. The analogies between the play he stages and *The Tempest* itself are close and important and for long stretches of the middle three acts the two are almost identical, at least as far as the audience is concerned, since the outer frame, the play *without* the play, becomes attenuated. Prospero's play is, at root, a project whose outcome depends upon his skill at presentation, his ultimate purpose being to manoeuvre Alonso physically and psychologically in such a way that the revelation of his son's seemingly miraculous return from the dead will be so bound up with Ferdinand's love for Miranda that Alonso will be in no position to oppose the union that guarantees the security of Prospero's Milanese dukedom, at least during the remainder of Prospero's lifetime.

The preparation for that climax involves suspense: the revelation must be delayed until the last possible minute in order to intensify Alonso's surprise, but also in order to accumulate as much humiliation as Alonso is thought capable of bearing. Prospero's plan involves taking at least a substantial bite out of the cake of revenge as well as keeping it intact so as to bestow a wholesome forgiveness on the parties who have offended him.[1] Where Prospero's play differs most from *The Tempest* is that its audience on stage does not, until the last moment, realize that it is a play at all. The final scene contains no such surprise for *The Tempest*'s audience: during that scene we simply witness, rather than share, the *anagnorisis* of the court party.

Just how far can Prospero's identification as a playwright be pushed? The minimal argument would be that he simply engineers the initial dispersal of the courtiers and the series of machines and devices while the characters themselves act absolutely according to their own will and volition, actors who, within certain physical limitations, improvise their own lines and behaviour. This would limit Prospero's role to that of stage-manager. If Prospero were properly

---

† From *Colonial Encounters: Europe and the Native Caribbean, 1492–1796* (London: Routledge, 1986), pp. 115–34. Amended by the author. Reprinted by permission of the author. Line numbers to this Norton Critical Edition of the play have been added in brackets when they differ from the author's original citation.
1. Coppélia Kahn, 'The Providential Tempest and the Shakespearean Family,' in Murray M. Schwartz and Coppélia Kahn, eds., *Representing Shakespeare: New Psychoanalytic Essays*, Baltimore: The Johns Hopkins University Press, 1980, p. 238.

playwright, on the other hand, he would have *total* control over the words and deeds of the other characters. This stronger version of the argument can hardly be supported. It would, to begin with, rob the play of any suspense; but there are internal points to be made against it too, such as Antonio's recalcitrance, which tends to sour Prospero's last scene and which therefore, if 'playwright', he would presumably have removed.

But seeing Prospero as simply stage-manager underestimates, if not his actual control, then at least the sense we are given of how he wants his play to proceed. In the thwarted attempt on Alonso's life, for example, the court party is put to sleep by Ariel's music, but with Sebastian and Antonio left deliberately awake. That this is no accident is made clear by their comments: '*Seb.*: What a strange drowsiness possesses them! . . . *Ant.*: They fell together all, as by consent' (II.i.194 and 198) [194, 199]. Prospero, one might say, gives Antonio and Sebastian the time and the opportunity for conspiracy; they oblige by acting according to type, and are suitably thwarted. Likewise Caliban is, as it were, introduced to Stephano and Trinculo and left to follow the course that Prospero at least foresees, elaborating the conspiracy that Prospero remembers in the strange moment of passion that brings the celebratory masque to such a sudden and confused end. Prospero *remembers*: so the conspiracy is no surprise to him and, even if he has been monitoring its progress off-stage (suggested by IV.i.171) [170], the fact that he has not bothered to immobilize the conspirators indicates that he desires the conspiracy to run its course. Clearly it is an essential element in his play—and 'the minute of their plot / Is almost come' (IV.i.141–2) draws neatly from the registers of both conspiracy and the theatre—yet it is an element that, paradoxically, he almost manages to forget.

Giving full weight to the notion of Prospero's play within the play would also allow the recuperation of at least some earlier *Tempest* criticism, which makes perfect sense if read as referring to Prospero's play alone, rather than to *The Tempest* as a whole. The dramatic structure of *The Tempest* has always looked too straight-forward to merit much detailed analysis, yet the five-act division, if accepted as original, appears a somewhat arbitrary arrangement of the play's materials.

A better starting point would be the observation that the structure of the play must be dual, with Prospero's play within the play considerably more formal and highly-wrought than *The Tempest* itself. Generically, in fact, Prospero's play is closest to a court masque of the elaborate Jacobean kind, a fitting form for Prospero to celebrate his reaccession to his rightful dukedom, with its contrast, proper to such ornamental state occasions, between order and disorder, between a stable society subject to a God-like monarch and an anarchic world of brutality and folly. The emphasis of the masque is on device and display, culminating in a spectacular sequence of events: the anti-masque of the disappearing banquet, the magnificent betrothal celebrations, the 'theophany' of Prospero's delayed appearance before his enemies, and the final moment of revelation which discovers Ferdinand and Miranda playing chess. Such a form, in the words of Enid Welsford, 'expresses, not uncertainty, ended by final success or failure, but expectancy crowned by sudden revelation'.[2] Of course only Prospero, the masque presenter and inductor, and Ariel, the assistant producer, are in a position to appreciate the full significance of this spectacle of state since the various 'actors' and 'spectators' on stage are unaware of their participation within Prospero's play. All in all the masque is distinctly Pirandellian. The dramatic analogy could be pressed further to suggest that the point of Prospero's elaborate deceit is to confuse Alonso as to the genre of his experiences on the island. He must—if Prospero's plans are to succeed—believe himself to be living a 'tragedy' which in the climactic *anagnorisis* turns into a 'comedy', its true status as masque being prudently reserved by Prospero for later revelation (V.i.303–5) [302–6]. *The Tempest contains* Prospero's masque but it is in no sense identical to or coterminous with it, as the dramatic structure reveals. The discovery of Ferdinand and Miranda is a fine and complex moment: we witness the amazement of the court party as they recognize Ferdinand, and we see Prospero's satisfaction at the triumphant climax of his masque as he also witnesses their amazement. But the revelation of Ferdinand and Miranda is no peripeteia for us since we have been privy to all the preparations.

The simplest way of stating the difference between Prospero's play and *The Tempest* would then be to say that *The Tempest* stages Prospero's staging of his play: only during the first scene are we unaware that everything happening on stage is in some sense under Prospero's control. So as well as watching the enactment of the masque, we also hear his reasons for staging it, see his preparation of the theatrical machines that will produce it, witness him watching that production from the wings, and observe the constantly changing audience on stage. This audience is probably the key to the distinction, yet it is a distinction that nearly disappears from view if we choose—as many critics have done—to view simply the performance on stage, rather than *that performance as attended by its audience.* Support for this surmise comes when, at the height of

2. Enid Welsford, *The Court Masque: A Study in the Relationship between Poetry and the Revels*, New York, 1962, p. 340. She recognizes Prospero as masque inductor, but does not distinguish between the masque and the play as a whole.

the betrothal celebrations (the most spectacular moment of both plays and when we are therefore most likely to be oblivious to the distinction between them) the machinery of the masque grinds to a halt. The Nymphs and Reapers, a moment ago in the middle of a graceful dance, heavily vanish to a strange, hollow, and confused noise, and we are forcefully reminded of the spectators on stage (at this juncture Ferdinand and Miranda) by hearing them comment on the breakdown in transmission: a moment of 'recognition'—that there is a play within the play—likely to constitute a true peripeteia for *The Tempest*'s audience. It is Ferdinand who speaks for the audience: 'This is strange: your father's in some passion / That works him strongly' (IV.i.143–4), to which Prospero's immediate response is a clever *tu quoque*: 'You do look, my son, in a mov'd sort, / As if you were dismay'd' (IV.i.146–7), thereby allowing him the 'revels' speech to regain his composure and to assume the guise of military officer ordering his troops ('*Pros.*: We must prepare to meet with Caliban / *Ari.*: Ay, my commander' (IV.i.166–7)). The text strikes a delicate balance here: our surprise at Prospero's disturbance is recent enough for our perspective still to be sufficiently askew from Prospero's to note the ludicrousness of elaborate preparations to deal with a woefully inadequate force who could be immobilized on the spot. On the other hand, our disturbance has been soothed, not to say anaesthetized, along with Ferdinand's, by the most beautiful poetry in the play, as Prospero tries to explain away his disturbance by insisting that the revels are properly concluded, just as everything comes to an end, even life itself—in the context of Prospero's play a brilliant piece of improvisation to cover a necessary change of scene and hustle Ferdinand and Miranda out of the way.

The improvisation is only necessary because of Prospero's sudden remembering of Caliban's conspiracy, the one moment in the play when his plans run less than smoothly. His perturbation has proved understandably perplexing. After all, politically, the conspiracy has no role to play whatsoever: strictly speaking, Alonso and Ferdinand are the objects towards whom Prospero's skill is directed—his ends can still be reached irrespective of Antonio's response, which is of course just as well. The conspirators are supplementary, a sub-plot in Prospero's play, and therefore 'understandably' forgettable in the celebration of his own power which is to precede the final dénouement—'some vanity of mine Art' (IV.i.41) may be self-deprecatory, but it is none the less true: the celebratory masque is in one sense a vain demonstration of power, purely the 'corollary' that Prospero himself calls it. He is guilty of celebrating before the story is over, and suffers for his presumption. But why is the 'supplementary' conspiracy there in the first place? And why, above all, is 'the strangeness of the disturbance . . .

strangely insisted on',[3] Prospero being in such a passion that Miranda can say: 'Never till this day / Saw I him touch'd with anger, so distemper'd' (IV.i.144–5)?

Prospero's play is in fact a subtle instrument of revenge and Caliban occupies a crucial role in it, though this is a fact kept hidden from Caliban for as long as possible: he, like the other 'actors', is not aware that he is in a play at all, let alone aware of the nature of his part. What might seem initially odd, though, is that whilst Caliban is the pivot around which the discursive axes of the play turn, and whilst his conspiracy clearly troubles Prospero, *dramatically* its importance appears undermotivated: Caliban is after all a mere slave of Prospero's, powerless against his magic, and incapable of mounting a serious coup. So, if the seemingly trifling sub-plot of Prospero's play causes such distress when its moment comes, it has to be because it is not trifling at all but, on the contrary, the very nub of the matter, representable at all by Prospero only in the differently-centred production staged by his desire.

\* \* \*

In its own terms Prospero's play is undoubtedly a success: it achieves what he wants it to achieve. Yet in always showing us more than this elaborate masquerade *The Tempest* leaves room for other questions to emerge. The most crucial of these questions concerns the relationship between Prospero's sub-plot and the main plot of his masque. The function of the masque is clear and its procedure, though complicated by the court party's dual role as actors and spectators, easily comprehensible given Prospero's initial premisses. From the perspective of Prospero's main plot the conspiracy is of minor importance. It merely echoes in a lower and more comic key the confusions of the noble Italians, but the two plots are not in any way dramatically interwoven: the courtiers have no glimpse of Caliban until less than a hundred lines before the end of the play, when Prospero ostentatiously completes *his* play by revealing how he has foiled the plot against his life. Of the principals only Prospero, then, is in the position of the ideal spectator able to view the progress of the respective plots. The masque *as a whole* is for his eyes only.

His dramatic construction makes it clear that the conspiracy is to take the subsidiary part in the production: in accordance with neoclassical criteria its action begins later and ends earlier than the main plot. This undoubtedly suits Prospero's purposes and corresponds to his perception of the conventions of the masque, where disorder is well and truly routed. But this is not necessarily our view of the conspiracy.

3. J. Middleton Murray, 'Shakespeare's dream' (from his *Shakespeare*, 1936), reprinted in *The Tempest: A Casebook*, ed. D. J. Palmer, London, 1968, p. 120.

We are in a position, for example, to see how Prospero's drama is in essence a series of repetitions. The courtiers must repeat Prospero's primary suffering: the distress at sea, the absence of food, and the powerlessness in a hostile environment. Prospero takes pleasure in their suffering and then, when the moment is right, brings the suffering to an end in order to obtain his final purpose. The last move in Prospero's psychological manoeuvring of Alonso is especially acute or, to put it another way, little short of psychopathic, showing Prospero's obsessive observance of the patterns of repetition. Alonso's genuine distress at the supposed loss of his son—the key element in Prospero's plan—has to be matched by Prospero's cruelly factitious grief for 'the like loss . . . for I have lost my daughter . . . in this last tempest' (V.i.143 [144], 147–8, 153), a shrewd blow which associates the two children in Alonso's mind and has him wishing them King and Queen of Naples, just as Prospero desires—thereby, of course, unwittingly plumbing Prospero's cleverly figurative meaning of 'losing' his daughter.

But the repetition does not stop there: it must be completed in the sub-plot by a controlled repetition of the primary trauma. Prospero stages a fantasized version of the original conspiracy with the difference that, this time, he will defeat it. Caliban must re-enact Antonio's usurpation, enabling Prospero to take a part in his own play. But, whereas the other 'actors' have to remain ignorant of the play's fictiveness, Prospero can indeed act—in both senses—in stark contrast to his earlier state of passive unpreparedness. Twelve years ago, 'rapt in secret studies', Prospero had been helpless before Antonio's determination to close the gap between—the words are Prospero's—'this part he play'd', as acting Duke, and the reality behind the role, 'Absolute Milan' (I.ii.107–9). This time it is Prospero who can 'play the part' of ruler under threat from disloyal subject, this time discover the plot before it comes to fruition, and this time triumph over it. The repetition cancels out the original, the twelve years are as nothing, and Prospero has created for himself a second chance. The pleasures of total revenge can be so easily forsworn because revenge presupposes an original insult and it is Prospero's intent to wipe the very record of that insult from his consciousness: 'Let us not burthen our remembrance with / A heaviness that's gone' (V.i.199–200).

The sub-plot, far from being the mere echo of his main plot that Prospero's dramatic ordering would have us believe, is therefore the enactment of a repression which takes from Prospero's consciousness the memory of his usurpation by Antonio, so that Prospero can resume his position—at least his fantasized position—as much-loved Duke of Milan, untroubled by a record of negligence.

Alongside the public performance of the masque runs this private psychodrama, this 'other scene' whose importance Prospero keeps to himself. The terms of the settlement make it clear, however, that the victory thereby achieved is indeed primarily psychic rather than in any meaningful sense political: the price Prospero pays for his restoration is the eventual envelopment of the Duchy of Milan into Ferdinand's Neapolitan empire. Prospero mortgages his inheritance for a chance to repress a history of failure. Thus ends the Mediterranean story.

On this reading Caliban, unbeknown to him, plays the part of Antonio who, this time, will fail. But Caliban is also, as it were, playing himself, except that 'himself' means the self that Prospero has cast for him—the treacherous slave. This is a complication that needs some unpacking. For Prospero, Caliban is playing the part of Antonio in the remake of his psychodrama, the new version with the happy ending. For Prospero, Caliban is an appropriate actor for this part because he is a 'natural' usurper, this nature only held in check by Prospero's power. This power is relaxed during the course of the play so that Caliban can impersonate Antonio—proving to Prospero's satisfaction that his assessment of Caliban's character is correct. If *The Tempest*'s critics have conceded that much turns on how you define Caliban, Prospero has no doubts: he offers Caliban the part of the treacherous slave with the silent entailment that acceptance—of what Caliban of course sees as a 'real' opportunity—will be taken as definition of being. For Prospero this is merely confirmation of what he knows already: Caliban, like Antonio and Sebastian, only has to act according to character. What is more, Prospero can in the end only see Caliban as acting according to character because Caliban does indeed seize upon the part offered to him and plays it with a gusto only diminished by the fatuity of his fellow-conspirators. It would be difficult, incidentally, to deny that *The Tempest* here has its finger on what is most essential in the dialectic between colonizer and colonized, offering a parable of that relationship probably never equalled for its compelling logic. So Caliban is, in other words, doubly inscribed in Prospero's play as both himself and a surrogate for Antonio, thereby putting into motion his double burden from the play's cast of characters, savage and slave, Atlantic and Mediterranean.

Yet Caliban's part in *The Tempest* is not coextensive with his part in Prospero's play, since he has appeared in that delayed prologue at the beginning of the second scene which includes some preparatory shaping up of Prospero's team, ensuring—via threat and bribe—that Ariel will obey orders, and—via invective and abuse—that Caliban will be in a suitably resentful frame of mind. Pros-

pero's moves are effective, but at the price of allowing us to hear
what Ariel and, more to the point, Caliban have to say for themselves. This scene repays close attention.

The confidence of the opening *coup de théâtre* has been immediately undermined by the evidently urgent need to hark back to
other earlier beginnings. For Prospero, the real beginning of the
story is his usurpation twelve years previously by Antonio, the opening scene of a drama which Prospero intends to play out during *The
Tempest* as a comedy of restoration. Prospero's exposition might
seem to take its place unproblematically as the indispensable prologue to an understanding of the present moment of Act I, no more
than a device for conveying essential information. But to see it simply as a neutral account of the play's prehistory would be to ignore
the contestation, which follows insistently throughout the rest of
that scene, of Prospero's version of true beginnings. In this narration the crucial early days of the relationship between the Europeans and the island's inhabitants are covered by Prospero's laconic
'Here in this island we arriv'd' (I.ii.171). And this is all we would
have, were it not for Ariel and Caliban. First Prospero is goaded by
Ariel's demands for freedom into recounting at some length how
his servitude began, when, at their first contact, Prospero freed him
from the cloven pine in which he had earlier been confined by
Sycorax. Caliban then offers his compelling and defiant counter to
Prospero's single sentence when, in a powerful speech, he recalls
the initial mutual trust between them 'When thou cam'st first', with
benefits bestowed by each on the other, Prospero making much of
Caliban, Caliban showing Prospero 'all the qualities o' th' isle'
(I.ii.334–40) [332–37]; a trust broken by Prospero's assumption of
the political control made possible by the power of his magic. Caliban, 'Which first was mine own King', now protests that 'here you
sty me / In this hard rock, whiles you do keep from me / The rest o'
th' island' (I.ii.344–6) [342–44].

It is remarkable that these contestations of 'true beginnings' have
been so commonly occluded by that uncritical willingness to identify Prospero's voice as direct and reliable authorial statement, and
therefore to ignore the lengths to which the play goes to dramatize
its problems with the proper beginning of its own story. Such identification hears, as it were, only Prospero's play, follows only his
stage directions. But although different beginnings are offered by
different voices in the play, Prospero has the effective power to im-
pose his construction of events on the others. While Ariel gets a
threatening but nevertheless expansive answer, Caliban provokes
an entirely different reaction. Prospero's words refuse engagement
with Caliban's claim to original sovereignty ('This island's mine, by
Sycorax my mother, / Which thou tak' st from me' (I.ii.333–4)

[332–33]); yet Prospero is clearly disconcerted. His sole—somewhat hysterical—response consists of an indirect denial ('Thou most lying slave' (I.ii.346) [1.2.344]) and a counter accusation of attempted rape ('thou didst seek to violate / The honour of my child' (I.ii.349–50) [1.2.347–48]), which together foreclose the exchange and are all that Prospero ever has to say about his early relationship with Caliban.

Nevertheless, this second scene opens up an important space which the play proceeds to explore. Prospero tells Miranda (and the audience) a story in which the island is merely an interlude, a neutral ground between extirpation and resumption of power. Ariel and Caliban immediately act as reminders that Prospero's is not the only perspective, that the island is not neutral ground for them. So right from the beginning Prospero's narrative is distinguished from the play's: we are made aware that Caliban has his own story and that it does not begin where Prospero's begins. A space is opened, as it were, behind Prospero's narrative, a gap that allows us to see that Prospero's narrative is not simply history, not simply the way things were, but a particular *version*. In that gap Caliban is at least allowed to begin his story. Not only—as has often been pointed out—can Prospero and Caliban be seen as archetypes of the colonizer and the colonized, but Prospero is also colonial historian, and such a convincing and ample historian that other histories have to fight their way into the crevices of his official monument.

Of course Prospero's arrival on the island occupied by Caliban and Ariel remains an event as inaccessible to us as the arrival of the first Europeans on the Caribbean islands. In one case we have only Columbus's opaque text. In the other we have three stories: Prospero's two accounts—the brief 'Here in this island we arriv'd' (I.ii.171), and the fuller version he gives to remind Ariel of his place; and Caliban's alternative version, which Prospero denies only with the vague 'Thou most lying slave' (I.ii.346) [1.2.344]. Speculation about what 'really' happened would be even more futile here in this fictional story than in the earlier chapter, but it is surely significant that Caliban's account of the beginning of the relationship is allowed to stand unchallenged, while Prospero responds by charging him with the attempted violation of Miranda. Shakespearean criticism has recently grown more sceptical towards Prospero's behaviour and achievements, especially with respect to Caliban.[4] There are various ways of looking at this. Even as master to slave, Prospero speaks and behaves with an excessive vehemence, threatening pun-

4. The earliest, most trenchant, example is probably Clifford Leech, who called Prospero's behaviour 'pathological' (*Shakespeare's Tragedies and Other Studies in Seventeenth Century Drama*, London, 1950, pp. 137–58). Philip Mason notes the unquestioning admiration for Prospero during the era of British colonialism (*Prospero and Caliban: Some Thoughts on Class and Race*, London, 1962, pp. 92–3).

ishments out of all keeping with the supposed crimes. This has
tended to become more of an issue as it has become less easy to see
Caliban as some sort of semi-human figure.

It is perhaps less of a strain than it was a hundred years ago to
see as genuinely human a figure described in animal terms by Europeans. Much also turns on the attempt at violation. Once upon a
time that would have been enough to justify any punishment in-
flicted on Caliban. Today it is possible for at least one critic—and a
religious one at that—to defend Caliban on the grounds that he
was simply refusing to accept the European code of ethics.[5] Perhaps more to the point is that Prospero's way of phrasing the insult
(he 'lodg'd thee / In mine own cell, till thou didst seek to violate /
The honour of my child' (I.ii.348–50) [346–48]) makes it clear that
Caliban's crime is ingratitude towards him, Prospero: violation of
Miranda would be a trespass on his property. Prospero's extraordinary possessiveness—at first mention Miranda, Ariel and Caliban
are respectively, 'my dear one' (I.ii.17), 'my Ariel' (I.ii.188), and 'my
slave' (I.ii.310) [308]—is open to both political and psychoanalytical readings, the two by no means incompatible. Miranda's virginity
is an important political card for Prospero, in some ways his only
one, and he takes great care—as all commentators note—to make
sure that it is not accidentally trumped by Ferdinand's premature
ardour. Like many Shakespearean fathers, Prospero needs such political incentives to loosen his grip on his daughter and, even so, he
goes through a ludicrous charade in order to gain what David Sundelson calls 'a symbolic victory over [Ferdinand's] confident sexuality'.[6] That is probably as far as the warrant of the play's words
themselves permits. Recent psychoanalytical criticism has gone further. Coppélia Kahn reads Prospero's actions as an intricate yet un-
successful attempt to work through his Oedipal past.[7] Mark Taylor
questions whether 'violation' may not be Prospero's interpretation
of 'a perfectly honourable action', on the grounds that 'Caliban's
pursuance of the normal forms of courtship, with or without
Miranda's responding positively to them, would be seen by him,
Prospero, as an effort to violate her'. So, 'rather than indict the
daughter for disloyalty in choosing a man other than himself, the
father castigates the suitor's dishonourable methods—a classic displacement, which allows the father to retain belief in his daughter's
loyalty'.[8] These can only be speculations—'reasonable inferences'

5. Sister Corona Sharp, 'Caliban: The Primitive Man's Evolution', *Shakespeare Studies*,
   XIV, 1981, p. 276.
6. David Sundelson, 'So Rare a Wondered Father: Prospero's *Tempest*', in Schwartz and
   Kahn, eds., *Representing Shakespeare: New Psychoanalytic Essays*, p. 46.
7. Kahn, pp. 236–40.
8. Mark Taylor, *Shakespeare's Darker Purpose: A Question of Incest*, New York, 1982,
   p. 143.

Taylor optimistically calls them[9]—but they find their justification in the seemingly consistent way in which the play undercuts Prospero's attempted explanations of the past, the best example being the self-induced tangle he gets into over his wife:

Pros.    Thy father was the Duke of Milan, and
         A prince of power.
Mir    .                    Sir, are not you my father?
Pros.    Thy mother was a piece of virtue, and
         She said thou wast my daughter; and thy father
                    Was Duke of Milan. (I.ii.55–8)

In a word, as Freudian readings force us to pay attention to suggestions that there is more to Prospero's accounts of past events than immediately meets the eye, we are likely in consequence to look carefully at what alternative versions of events we do have. It is not that Caliban somehow speaks the truth that undermines Prospero's false or misleading history: there is no way in which the status of their respective words could be thus accented. But Caliban is allowed to articulate a history, it is a history markedly distinct from Prospero's, and we see Prospero attacking Caliban for daring to speak it, without himself ever offering an alternative version of those early days on the island. Interestingly enough, his inadequate denial of Caliban's charge—'Thou most lying slave' (I.ii.346) [344]—is repeated three times by Ariel in the scene where he taunts Caliban (III.ii.40–150), as if to emphasize that there is no narrative counter to Caliban's arguments. Ariel himself is also accused by Prospero in identical terms during *their* disagreement over historical matters: 'Thou liest, malignant thing!' (I.ii.257).

For Caliban the issue is simple: 'I am subject to a tyrant, a sorcerer, that by his cunning hath cheated me of the island' (III.ii.40–2): Prospero's power, his magic, has usurped Caliban of his rights. But the text inflects this usurpation in a particular direction: Prospero has taken control of Caliban, made him his slave, and yet 'We cannot miss him' (I.ii.313) [311]—Caliban is indispensable to Prospero, the usurper depends upon the usurped. Why should this be if Prospero is so powerful a magician? Why should he have to depend upon a lowly slave like Caliban? We need to comprehend more clearly the precise nature of Prospero's magic.

This does not imply further investigation of Prospero as Renaissance magus on the way to enlightenment, or subtle distinctions between black and white magic. A simpler question needs answering: just how extensive is Prospero's power? In some ways this overlaps with the discussion of Prospero as playwright: he has the sort of

9. Taylor, p. xi.

power that can erect an invisible barrier, that can inflict physical punishment, and that can take human and animal form; but he does not have direct power over human thoughts, words and actions. But one can go beyond this, still on the basis of the play's own evidence: his magic is only effective within certain distances since he has depended on 'accident most strange' (I.ii.178) to bring the court party within his sphere of influence; it was not effective in Milan or else he could have defended himself against Antonio; or on the open seas since he and Miranda needed 'Providence divine' (I.ii.159) to come ashore: but it *was* effective either immediately upon, or soon after, reaching the island since he freed Ariel from the cloven pine. If Prospero's extraordinary speech of abjuration is to be believed (V.i.33–57), his powers extend to plucking trees out of the ground, and even to wakening the dead. But on the other hand he cannot, or will not, chop wood, make dams to catch fish or do the washing up, all tasks for which Caliban's services are required.

If such a listing seems open to the charge of excessive literalism, that is precisely the point. The text is not concerned with the exact configuration of Prospero's magical powers, but rather with two broad distinctions: Prospero's magic is at his disposal on the island but not off it; it can do anything at all except what is most necessary to survive. In other words there is a precise match with the situation of Europeans in America during the seventeenth century, whose technology (especially of firearms) suddenly *became* magical when introduced into a less technologically developed society, but who were incapable (for a variety of reasons) of feeding themselves. This is a topos that appears with remarkable frequency in the early English colonial narratives, as it had in the Spanish: a group of Europeans who were dependent, in some cases for many years, on food supplied by their native hosts, often willingly, sometimes under duress. One final Caribbean story, therefore, will be set alongside *The Tempest*.

In April 1605, the *Olive Branch* with some seventy passengers sailed from England to join Leigh's recently established colony in Guiana. According to the account of John Nicholl, one of the adventurers on board, the master seems to have missed his course and, after seventeen weeks at sea, with shortages of food and drink making 'our men's minds very much distracted, which bred amongst us many fearful and dangerous mutinies',[1] they fetched up

---

1. John Nicholl, 'An Houre Glasse of Indian News' (1607), ed. Rev. C. Jesse, *Caribbean Quarterly*, XII, no. I, 1966, p. 49. Nicholl speaks of dissension between the 'sea-men' and the 'land-men', 'which rested not only in the common sort, but rather and most chiefly in our captains' (p. 48).

on the shore of St Lucia, an island still without European settlements:

> And so having been seventeen weeks at sea, instead of our hopeful expectations of attaining to a pleasant, rich and golden Country, and the comfortable company of our friends and Country-men, there as we supposed then resident, we were brought to an Island in the West India somewhat distant from the main, called Santa Lucia, having about twelve degrees of North latitude, inhabited only with a company of most cruel Cannibals, and man-eaters, where we had no sooner anchored, but the Carebyes came in their Periagoes or Boats aboard us with great store of Tobacco, Plantains, Potatoes, Pines, Sugar Canes, and divers other fruits, with Hens, Chickens, Turtles, & Iguanas: for all which we contented and pleased them well. These Carrebyes at their first coming in our sight, did seem most strange and ugly, by reason they are all naked, with long black hair hanging down their shoulders, their bodies all painted with red, and from their ears to their eyes, they do make three strokes with red, which makes them look like devils or Anticke faces, wherein they take a great pride.[2]

The disjunction between the discursive and the experiential could hardly be clearer. 'Cannibal', it should be noted, is no longer the ethnic name it had been, for which 'Carebye' has become established; but the association between the two is so immediate that the text has no problem in speaking, before the moment of actual contact, of 'most cruel Cannibals, and man-eaters'. Even if this description were retrospective, bestowed in the light of Nicholl's perception of their subsequent behaviour, it would still sit uneasily with the welcome supply of food with which the Caribs chose to begin the intercourse with their visitors. The story that follows is in many ways predictable. The English were given a whole village in which to stay, in return for a single hatchet. The master wanted to leave the sick to fend for themselves but the captain disagreed, so the company split, half staying on St Lucia and half leaving on the *Olive Branch*. Those remaining were left a cannon from the ship but the two parties quarrelled and the gun was actually fired *at* the ship, with both sailors and settlers giving different stories to the Caribs, who must have been thoroughly bemused by these strange happenings.

After the departure of the *Olive Branch* relations were good between the Caribs and their guests: large amounts of vegetables, fruit and game were supplied by the Amerindians, and the Europeans made some effort to catch turtles, although they seem to

2. Nicholl, pp. 49–50.

have spent most of their time cutting down trees and building a stockade to defend themselves 'lest the Carrebyes should at any time assault us'.[3] Three events seem to have triggered the deterioration in the relationship. It was discovered that, contrary to instructions, one of the company had sold a sword to a Carib chief: the English captain reclaimed it without compensation. Then, inevitably, the English started asking about gold and got different answers from different Caribs: 'these contrary tales made us suspect some villany.'[4] And finally the Caribs stopped bringing food, so the English started stealing it from their gardens. Eventually the ambush came: the nineteen who survived it barricaded themselves in their stockade and prepared to die of hunger—but the Caribs brought them food:

> Thus for the space of 6 or 7 days, every day fighting for the space of three or four hours, and then our victual began to fail again, which caused us to hold out a Flag of truce: which the Indians perceiving, came in peaceable manner unto us.[5]

This way of fighting clearly had little to do with European ideas of warfare. In the end the English offered to leave behind all their hatchets, knives and beads in return for a canoe and some food. The offer was accepted and the survivors, not without further hardship, reached Venezuela and (some of them) thence Spain and England.

Behind Nicholl's narrative of heroism in the face of cruel cannibals it is possible to reconstruct a story of initial hospitality, increasing suspicion in the face of boorish behaviour, and eventual loss of patience with a hostile drain on the economy that showed little inclination to shift for itself. It seems probable that fear of guns dictated the early diplomacy but it cannot explain the continuing supply of food when there were less than twenty survivors. If the Caribs' main objective had been to kill the English rather than to get them to leave, they would only have had to deny them food. The magic of technology has its limits.

At issue is not the influence of Nicholl's account on *The Tempest* but rather the congruence between, on the one hand, his and numerous other New World narratives, and on the other, the words and actions of the play. Even the most cursory of structural analyses would reveal common features in almost all the early reports: initial native hospitality—especially supply of food; growing misunderstandings; and then violent conflict, perceived by the Europeans

---

3. Nicholl, p. 52.
4. Nicholl, p. 53.
5. Nicholl, p. 59.

as 'treachery'. There seems little doubt that as far as the Amerindians were concerned the turning point was always the realization
that their 'guests' had come to stay. The Europeans were blinded to
this by their failure to comprehend that what confronted them was
an agriculturally based society with claims over the land. Unable to
understand the effects of their own behaviour the only narrative
that they could construct to make sense of both the hospitality and
the violence was a narrative of treachery in which the initial kindness was a ruse to establish trust before the natives' 'natural'
violence emerged from behind the mask.

This can serve as the larger context within which to view the limits of Prospero's power and the essential offices that Caliban performs. For such a supposedly 'spiritual' play *The Tempest* has much
to say about food. One would perhaps expect such material concerns in the sub-plot where Caliban quickly appreciates—presumably having learned from his earlier visitors—that the way to
Stephano's heart is through his stomach: 'I'll show thee the best
springs; I'll pluck thee berries; / I'll fish for thee, and get thee wood
enough' (II.ii.160–1) [156–57]. But they appear no less insistently
elsewhere, particularly in the two masques where, first, Ariel shows
his devouring grace that Prospero finds so amusing and, later, the
betrothal is somewhat inappropriately presided over by Ceres rather
than the banished Venus, as if visions of golden harvests were more
suited to the present straitened circumstances than idylls of married bliss. Caliban makes it plain ('I must eat my dinner' (I.ii.332)
[330]) that Prospero's most powerful weapon over him is the with-
holding of food—the food that Caliban is himself responsible for
collecting and preparing. Here the master/slave relationship begins
to take on, if not exactly a Hegelian reciprocity, then at least a more
delicate balance than might at first be apparent. Prospero is dependent upon Caliban's labour for his food supply and general material requirements; Caliban is forced by Prospero's magic to labour
in order to be able to eat even a small portion of the food he prepares. We are now, finally, in a position to see that Caliban's second
inscription within Prospero's play is exactly parallel to the first in
its project of effacement, thereby continuing the dizzy sequence
of parallelisms. Just as the first inscription, as an Antonio figure,
effaces Prospero's original usurpation by his brother, so this inscription, as revolting slave, effaces both the *original* relationship
between Caliban and Prospero, a relationship of host to guest,
of Prospero's dependence—which has continued—on Caliban's
labour; and the moment of violence, the moment when Prospero
used his power to change host/guest into slave/master. Prospero's
usurpation of Caliban is effaced by the engineered drama of Cal-

iban's conspiracy against Prospero. The gap in Prospero's narrative is thereby filled: Caliban's 'treacherous' nature is 'proved' beyond dispute, and his continued subjection 'justified'.

Each of Caliban's two inscriptions is, just to complicate matters, disguised as the other. The repetition is not simply a fantasy—because Caliban really is conspiring to murder Prospero; but the conspiracy as enacted cannot genuinely be Caliban's attempt to regain what is rightfully his—because it is so clearly yet another plot against the rightful Duke. For Caliban his double inscription is a double bind. Either he is a slave who can only allege his usurpation, or he is a conspirator whose failure confirms his treachery; leaving Caliban little option but to 'seek for grace' in an attempt to minimize his suffering, whatever the justice of his claims may have been.

This brings the Atlantic story to a very satisfactory end as far as Prospero is concerned. Bewildering Alonso by means of that ultimate *anagnorisis* into agreeing to Ferdinand and Miranda's marriage was not a significant strain on Prospero's ingenuity: to give his daughter to his enemy's son is apparently a small price to pay for Alonso's recognition of Milan's temporary independence. The recognition afforded him by Caliban is altogether sweeter, since it franks that repression of the island's early history which we have watched the play enact. Caliban repudiates his claims *of his own volition*. The violence of slavery is abolished at a stroke and Caliban becomes just another feudal retainer whom Prospero can 'acknowledge mine' (V.i.276). This is the wish-fulfilment of the European colonist: his natural superiority voluntarily recognized.

We should now, finally, be in a position to understand the interrupted masque. Formally, the moment of Caliban's conspiracy is merely the working through of the sub-plot to its appointed conclusion. But that moment also triggers the screen behind which Prospero's usurpation of Caliban can be concealed, his proven treachery providing a watertight alibi against any claims of prior sovereignty that might be lodged. To remember Caliban is essential if that alibi is to be constructed, but to remember him is to remember why the alibi is needed in the first place. Prospero's sub-plot is a finely wrought piece, but the displeasure of that memory outweighs, for a moment, the need to put it into action. Hence the sudden perturbation.

This hiccough in the running order of the masque, this seemingly trivial moment over which commentators have fretted, is quite simply the major turning point in the larger play because, as Prospero's anger briefly but dramatically holds the two plays apart, we are able to glimpse the deeper import of that conspiratorial sub-plot, able to realize that, though it is kept to a minor place within

Prospero's play, that very staging is the major plot of *The Tempest* itself. The Atlantic material, seemingly at the periphery, proves to be at the centre.

The conclusion to Act IV is the culmination of the dramatic action, a powerful and deeply ambivalent scene in which the conspirators are hunted by dogs and hounds, one of them called Tyrant, another Fury. It is cast, as Prospero's entire sub-plot has been, in the comic mode, further evidence of his commitment to the dramatic adequacy of the Mediterranean tradition, and it has of course proved possible to read the scene in its entirety through that mode.[6] The one question that remains is whether *The Tempest*—allowing us to see Prospero's brilliant deployment of the paraphernalia of comedy—permits any ambiguities to attenuate that scene of farce. There are perhaps two.

The final chastisement of the conspirators is out of all proportion to their powerlessness: they may have plotted murder but their chance of success has been nil from the start. Admittedly the connotations of being hunted by hounds are open to discussion: some, like G. Wilson Knight, will see them as 'impregnated with a sense of healthy, non-brutal, and . . . man-serving virility';[7] others will feel uneasy, if not nauseous, at the sight of dogs hunting men—Las Casas's denunciation of the hunting of Amerindians with dogs had already been translated into English as part of the construction of the 'Black Legend' of Spanish cruelty.[8] They are not of course 'real' hounds; it is, after all, only a joke. But what is considered to be a joke is often as revealing as an action in earnest.

And, finally, Caliban is allowed to make desperate efforts to avoid the comic mode: almost all his words in this scene are warnings to his companions not to be diverted from their purpose, and he alone refuses the tempting finery on the lime-tree, thereby possibly foiling the very last piece in Prospero's jigsaw since he will not *dress* as Antonio—in Milanese clothes—for the culminating moment of the repeated coup. Admittedly the scene is classically ironic since the audience sees, as Caliban cannot, the all-powerful hand of his enemy behind even this opportunity for revenge, but the poignancy of his position should surely sour any possible laughter. Caliban, though defeated, is allowed to retain his dignity in spite of Prospero's best efforts to degrade him.

6. See Bernard Knox, 'The Tempest and the ancient comic tradition', in *English Stage Comedy*, ed. W. K. Wimsatt, New York, 1955, pp. 52–73.
7. G. Wilson Knight, 'The Shakespearian Superman' (from *The Crown of Life*, 1947), reprinted in *The Tempest: A Casebook*, ed. D. J. Palmer, London, 1968, p. 147.
8. Bartolomé de Las Casas, *The Spanish Colonie, or Brief Chronicle of the Acts and gestes of the Spaniardes in the West Indies, called the newe World, for the space of xl. yeeres*, trans. M.M.S., London, 1583, p. 3.

# ANDREW GURR

## *The Tempest*'s Tempest at Blackfriars†

At one fairly inconspicuous moment in Heywood's play *The Fair Maid of the West*, the Chorus to Act 5, the Chorus says, of a shipwreck scene,

> Our stage so lamely can express a sea
> That we are forc'd by Chorus to discourse
> What should have been in action.     (4.5.1–3)[1]

*The Fair Maid* was moderately well known even before Heywood wrote a sequel for the Cockpit company who played it at Court in the early 1630s, when the two plays were first published.[2] It was probably originally written in 1609–10, because *The Roaring Girl* refers to it, and that play can be dated precisely in 1611.[3] The dating, very close to the time *The Tempest* was written, raises the question whether Shakespeare heard Heywood's lament before he wrote the shipwreck scene to open his play, or alternatively whether Heywood's Chorus was commenting on the failure of *The Tempest*'s shipwreck scene. Either Shakespeare was showing Heywood what a different playhouse could do on its not-so-lame stage, or Heywood was disowning Shakespeare's failure.

† From *Shakespeare Survey* 41 (1989): 91–102. Reprinted by permission of Cambridge University Press. Line numbers to this Norton Critical Edition of the play appear in brackets following the author's original citation.

1. Thomas Heywood, *The Fair Maid of the West, Part I*, ed. Robert K. Turner, Jr, Regent's Renaissance Drama Series (London, 1968), 1–90.
2. Heywood published both plays together in 1631, when they were in the Cockpit's repertoire. The second play belongs stylistically to the 1630s, but the first has the characteristics of the 'citizen' playhouse repertoire of the first decade of the century, when Heywood was a 'fellow' of the Red Bull players. See G. E. Bentley, *The Jacobean and Caroline Stage*, 7 vols. (Oxford, 1941–68), vol. 4 (1956), pp. 568–9.
3. A. M. Clark, *Thomas Heywood: Playwright and Miscellanist* (Oxford, 1931), p. 110, dates the first play called *The Fair Maid* after 1609, because it seems to have taken the name 'Muly-sheck' from a pamphlet published in that year. This dating is supported by Brownell Salomon in his edition of the play (Salzburg, 1975, pp. 3–13). Clark also dates the play before 1611 because of an apparent allusion to its subtitle, 'A Girl Worth Gold', in *The Roaring Girl*, which was on stage early in 1611, according to Cyrus Hoy, *Introductions, Notes, and Commentaries to Texts in 'The Dramatic Works of Thomas Dekker edited by Fredson Bowers'*, 4 vols. (Cambridge, 1980), vol. 3, p. 9. P. A. Mulholland, 'The Date of *The Roaring Girl*', *Review of English Studies*, NS 28 (1977), 18–31, affirms 1611 as the date for at least the main composition of the play. *The Roaring Girl*, performed at the Fortune, does have two other references in the same scene, 4.2, to early plays in the Henslowe repertoire which were being run either at the Fortune or Red Bull. After the references to 'brave girles: worth Gold' at line 166, there is an allusion to *Friar Bacon and Friar Bungay* at lines 171–2 and to *A Knack to Know an Honest Man* at line 264. The two unmistakable allusions make the third, to Heywood's play, much more likely. The phrase 'a girl worth gold' was not proverbial, at least in the strict sense, and some such allusion to a play fits the context in *The Roaring Girl*. That in itself does not of course prove that it was a new play in 1611.

Another play of Heywood's, written rather earlier, *The Four Prentices of London*, has a broadly similar display of modesty, this time
prescribing exactly what he would have liked his stage to show. The
'presenter' in the second scene of Act I, like the Chorus in *Henry V*,
asks the audience to use its imaginary forces to conceive a shipwreck:

> Imagine now yee see the aire made thicke
> With stormy tempests, that disturbe the sea:
> And the foure windes at warre among themselves:
> And the weake Barkes wherein the brothers saile,
> Split on strange rockes, and they enforc't to swim.
>
> (sig. Ci<sup>r</sup> lines 7–19)[4]

I have always been inclined to resist the idea that Shakespeare very
often sat in on the plays of his rival playhouses. For one thing, he
should have been busy performing his job as a player at his own
playhouse when the rival companies were performing. He and Heywood were almost unique among the playwrights of their time in
having an urgent contractual reason not to attend the plays of other
writers. That is one minor cause for thinking that it was difficult for
either of them to have observed the other's plays. But by 1610 Heywood may have been making his living from his 220 plays alone,
and Shakespeare is widely assumed to have been retiring, at the
grand old age of forty-six, to his home in Stratford, so for both of
them acting may have ceased to be a daily necessity. Heywood does
appear to have seen *Pericles* and *The Winter's Tale* before he wrote
his first *Ages* plays.[5] Whether Shakespeare ever heard Heywood's
plays at the Red Bull is a more doubtful question.

And yet there is another consideration which in the end might
suggest that Heywood wrote innocently and first, and that it was
Shakespeare who took note of Heywood's disclaimer rather than
Heywood who mocked Shakespeare. *The Tempest* was the first play
Shakespeare unquestionably wrote for the Blackfriars rather than
the Globe. Much, probably too much, has been made about the
possible effects on Shakespeare's writing when, after a thirteen-

---

4. Thomas Heywood, *The Four Prentices of London* (London, 1615; *BEPD* 333a). *The Four
   Prentices* in its original form predates 1607, when it achieved a satirical mention at the
   Blackfriars in *The Knight of the Burning Pestle* (Francis Beaumont, *The Knight of the
   Burning Pestle*, in *The Dramatic Works in the Beaumont and Fletcher Canon*, gen. ed.
   Fredson Bowers, vol. 1 (Cambridge, 1966), p. 12. It was not printed, like *The Fair Maid
   of the West*, until 1632, and may have been revised by Heywood before its publication. In
   1632 he claimed he had written it fifteen or sixteen years earlier, which must mean either a revision or plain misrepresentation.
5. According to Ernest Schanzer, Heywood seems to have borrowed from, or at least have
   been familiar with, both *The Winter's Tale* and *The Tempest* in his *Golden Age* and *Silver
   Age*. See: 'Heywood's *Four Ages* and Shakespeare', *Review of English Studies*, 11 (1960),
   18–28.

year delay, the Blackfriars playhouse finally came into the possession of Shakespeare's company in 1608 and they began to play at
the hall venue throughout the long London winters. *Pericles* and
*Cymbeline*, as well as the post-1609 *Winter's Tale* and *Tempest*,
have been claimed as distinctive in the canon partly because of the
new playhouse and its more affluent customers. This is unaccep-
table if only because *Pericles*, for one, was on the Globe's stage
more than a year before the company could have had any inkling
that it was about to acquire the Blackfriars. Even *The Winter's Tale*
has nothing that could not have been staged as easily at the Globe
as at the Blackfriars. On the other hand, *The Tempest* is uniquely a
musical play among Shakespeare's writings, and the consort of musicians at Blackfriars was justly famous. Under the boy company
management before 1609 they offered concerts lasting an hour before the play began.[6] Of course the consort of Blackfriars musicians
might easily have played through the summer, when the Blackfriars
was closed, at the Globe in its newly installed music room on the
stage balcony. If they were not to play there, the creation of a balcony music room at the Globe to match the Blackfriars music room
would seem a redundancy.[7] The music, though, is not final evidence that Shakespeare wrote the play specifically for the Blackfriars. Much more significant is the fact that *The Tempest* is the first
of his plays to show unequivocal evidence that it was conceived
with act breaks in mind.

Plays on the amphitheatre stages ran non-stop, without pauses
for an interval or between the acts. On the hall stages, however, either as an acknowledgement of the formal five-act structure or for
the more practical purpose of getting time to trim the candles that
lit the stage and auditorium, brief pauses between the acts were
standard. In *The Knight of the Burning Pestle*, performed at Blackfriars by the boy company in 1607, there is an 'interact' between
each act of the play, during which music plays and a boy dances.
One of them features a burlesque 'Maylord' speech of a little over
thirty lines. The audience on stools on the stage, some of them
players disguised as audience, chat with one another during the
pauses and comment on features such as the stage hangings. Some
such pause, at least for music, must have been designed to inter-

---

6. Frederick Gerschow, visiting London in the train of the Duke of Stettin-Pomerania in
1602, wrote about the hour-long concert that preceded a play at Blackfriars. In later
years the fame of the Blackfriars consort of musicians was attested by Bulstrode White-
locke among others. See Bentley. *The Jacobean and Caroline Stage*, vol. 6 (1968), p. 32.
7. In the Induction to the 1604 version of *The Malcontent*, written for the Globe, the players speak of 'the not-received custom of music in our theatre': John Marston, *The Malcontent*, ed. George K. Hunter, The Revels Plays (London, 1975), Induction, line 84.
After about 1608 the plays begin to require a music room on the upper level. See
Richard Hosley, 'Was there a Music-Room in Shakespeare's Globe?', *Shakespeare Survey*
13 (1960), 113–23.

vene between Acts 4 and 5 of *The Tempest*.[8] Prospero and Ariel leave the stage together at the end of Act 4 and enter together again to open Act 5. Shakespeare evidently expected there would be a break between the acts. He has the same characters leaving and re-entering like this in none of his other plays. For that reason if no other it is clear that he had the Blackfriars in mind, not the Globe, when he wrote *The Tempest*.

Conceivably he knew his play would be first available for performing in the winter, between September and May when the company used the Blackfriars and the Globe was empty. But its unique exploitation of instrumental music as well as song, the plethora of magic and stage effects dependent on the music, makes the scoring for the hall playhouse a consequence of something more positive than the accidents of the seasonal timetable. It was not a fortuitous exercise, this scoring for the Blackfriars, and it certainly cannot be ascribed to Shakespeare's increasing distance from the stage, which is sometimes used as another way of explaining why the last plays are so distinct. It is, of course, rather too readily assumed that Shakespeare retired from the stage to Stratford in 1609, a year before he wrote *The Tempest*, and that he therefore withdrew from any direct engagement with the company's playhouses. His mother, who seems to have managed some of his business interests at home, died in September 1608 and left a number of matters which held his attention there.[9] It was nearly four years before he clearly reaffirmed his London interests by buying the Blackfriars gatehouse, in March 1613. That, as Schoenbaum suggests,[1] may have been no more than an investment, of the kind Richard Burbage was making in the same precinct at the same time, but its locality is nonetheless suggestive. I think there is a little evidence in *The Tempest*, besides the act-break, which indicates that he was definitely not remote from the new playhouse and its company when he composed the play for it. *The Tempest* was written with an exact knowledge of what the play's staging required, even to some precise line-counting to measure the time needed for different changes of costume.

8. If *The Knight of the Burning Pestle* is anything to go by, the length of the pause for an act-break amounted to not more than twenty-five or thirty lines of dialogue on the average, sometimes a little more. This amounts to less than two minutes and matches the thirty-three lines which Ariel might have needed between Acts 3 and 4. For the uniqueness of this act-break in Shakespeare, see C. M. Haines, 'The "Law of Re-entry" in Shakespeare', *Review of English Studies*, 1 (1925), 449–51. W. T. Jewkes showed that between 1583 and 1616 out of 67 indoor plays 59 mark act breaks, whereas out of 134 amphitheatre plays only 30 mark them: Wilfred T. Jewkes, *Act Division in Elizabethan and Jacobean Plays, 1563–1616* (Hamden, Conn., 1958). Even on these figures some of the allocations to types of playhouses are questionable. I cannot find any amphitheatre play which clearly calls for a pause between the acts.

9. Ernst Honigmann's paper, 'Shakespeare and Commerce', given at the World Shakespeare Congress in Berlin, April 1986, makes this point.

1. Samuel Schoenbaum, *William Shakespeare: A Compact Documentary Life* (Oxford, 1977), p. 273.

Ariel's airy speed on stage is marked not only by his frequent boasts about how fast he can girdle the earth but by his rapid changes of costume. He goes offstage, for instance, for only sixteen lines in 1.2, when Prospero tells him 'Go make thyselfe like to a nymph o' th'Sea' (TLN 433–Exit 437²) [301–4], before he returns in the new dress ('*Enter Ariel like a water-Nymph*' (TLN 453) [316SD]). We can assume he retains this dress and the invisibility which is said to go with it through the scene with tabor and pipe, 3.2, which ends with him invisibly leading the comic conspirators offstage (TLN 1512) [147SD]. He then has seventy-one lines to dress himself with the Harpy costume and wings before entering to the courtiers and their banquet at TLN 1583 [54SD], in 3.3. According to the stage direction '*He vanishes in thunder*' (TLN 1616) [84SD], he then has another seventy-one lines before he returns without the Harpy costume and wings at TLN 1687 [33SD], in 4.1. There is a difficulty here, since Prospero appears to address him at TLN 1619–20 [85–86] after the stage direction says he has vanished—'Bravely the figure of this *Harpie* hast thou / Perform'd, (my *Ariel*)'—and if he does remain on stage to hear this aside, as he hears all Prospero's other asides to him, he would not leave the stage until it is cleared at TLN 1649 [111]. This would allow him only thirty-eight lines to remove the wings and Harpy attire. But here too there is an act break. Either Ariel was allocated 71 lines to put on and 71 lines to take off the winged costume, or 71 lines to put it on and 38 plus an act-break to take it off. Since act-breaks seem to have lasted the equivalent of about thirty lines of dialogue, Ariel would then have about seventy lines to change out of the Harpy costume, matching the seventy-one he was given to put it on. This apparent symmetry of time allowed for dressing or undressing in a particular costume is repeated, and I suspect confirmed as a carefully calculated feature of the staging, by Ariel's third change of costume.

In the masque in 4.1 Ariel takes the part of Ceres. This piece of doubling became a routine tradition in nineteenth-century productions, sound practical sense given the need of a good singing voice for the two parts. It was first proposed as an editorial interpretation by John Dover Wilson,³ on the basis of Ariel's subsequent statement to Prospero that he 'presented Ceres' (TLN 1840) [166], and is generally accepted by modern editors as the explanation for this phrase. As before, to change into the costume for Ceres, Ariel is al-

---

2. Through Line Numbers (TLN) provide a rough guide to the elapsed time in a performance at the Globe, and, with pauses added for the act-breaks, also at the Blackfriars. The TLN used here is that of the Norton Facsimile of the First Folio.
3. *The Tempest*, eds. A. Quiller-Couch and John Dover Wilson, The New Shakespeare (Cambridge, 1921), p. 81.

lotted a strictly measured length of time. He gets 27 lines between his exit as Ariel at TLN 1706 [49] and his entry as Ceres at TLN 1733 [74], then has 29 lines, or 25 lines of dialogue plus some business, between his departure as Ceres at the end of the masque at TLN 1808 [137] and his re-entry at TLN 1837 [163] in 'Thy shape invisible', as Prospero calls it at TLN 1859 [184]. Altogether Ariel has four different costumes. The first, not an 'invisible' gear since Miranda has to be put to sleep before he enters, is only worn in 1.2 between his entry at TLN 299 [188] and his exit at TLN 437 [304]. The second is the 'water-Nymph' costume which marks him out as invisible, and which he wears through the rest of the play, as we know from Prospero's order in 4.1 (TLN 1859) [184] to remain invisible, and the reminder in 5.1 (TLN 2054) [97]. 'Invisible as thou art'. This takes sixteen lines to put on. The two changes from the water nymph costume are into the 'Harpey' (3.3), with the wings he can clap over the banquet table, and into Ceres for the masque in 4.1. It is, I think, no coincidence that a similar number of lines should have been allowed for the changes into and out of these non-routine costumes, and it is hardly surprising that the Harpy's wings should have required nearly three times as long as the Ceres costume, and more than four times the original change into the invisible water nymph. All in all *The Tempest* lays down more exacting demands for its staging than any play in the canon, even without the special functions the music undertakes. Ariel's costume changes suggest that Shakespeare was calculating quite precisely what his company could be asked to do.

Even without Heywood's modesty to set against it, the shipwreck scene which opens the play is a remarkably bravura piece of staging. It could have been done more easily on an amphitheatre stage than in a hall, and was a feature more familiar at such venues than in the halls, though even there it was done more often by Chorus than in action, as in Heywood and *Henry V*. Storms like *King Lear's* were not infrequent at the Globe, enough to make the opening of *The Tempest* quite disturbing to audiences accustomed to the quieter indoor conditions of the hall playhouses. And of course Shakespeare's play went further. There are no real precedents anywhere in earlier plays for mounting a storm complete with a shipwreck on stage. Indeed the musical effects, which do not appear until the second scene, might be considered the second and reassuring movement in a deliberate challenge to audience expectations. At the Blackfriars a wild and stormy scene like the middle act in *King Lear*, with drums rumbling and bullets crackling to make thunder offstage, might deliver an initial shock to the routine musical expectations of the Blackfriars audience, expectations which would be only slowly eased by the announcement of Prospero's magical

control of the storm and the music which follows. And yet even on
the amphitheatre stage of the Globe Heywood's modesty indicates
the size of the challenge. The technical aids available for creating a
storm amounted to little more than the offstage noises. Thunder
from a 'roul'd bullet' (a metal ball trundled down a metal trough)
and 'tempestuous drumme'[4] were standard accessories on both
types of stage. Fireworks or rosin for lightning flashes were available at the amphitheatres but unpopular at the halls because of the
stink. The stage directions in *The Tempest* 1.1 call only for thunder
and crashing noises offstage, not for flashes of lightning (the opening stage direction specifies a '*noise of thunder and lightning*' only).
The Blackfriars stage and auditorium might have been dimmed a
little by closing the hall windows, but there is nothing to suggest
that the lights were dowsed, and nothing about the windows either.
In fact it would have been uncharacteristic and cumbersome to
pause while the windows were reopened after the storm and I
doubt if that kind of atmospheric aid was attempted. The scene is
the plainest possible confrontation, in the most unlikely setting, to
the challenge implied in Heywood's disclaimer.

It is a bravura piece of staging not only in the way it deploys an
outdoor effect at an indoor playhouse, but because that effect sets
up the ruling conceit for the whole play. A thoroughly realistic
storm, with mariners in soaking work clothes being hampered in
their work by courtiers dressed for a wedding,[5] concludes in shipwreck for all. And immediately this realism is proclaimed to be only
stage magic, the art of illusion. The courtiers, supposedly as soaked
as the mariners, return with their clothes as fresh as ever. By the
end of the play even the mariners are dry again, the joke about the
realism of wet clothes being taken over by Stephano, Trinculo, and
Caliban in Act 4. The whole play depends on the initial realism of
the shipwreck scene. It is the verification of Prospero's magic and
the declaration that it is all only a stage play. If we accept that its
realism succeeds, it is also a supremely adroit and discreet upstag-
ing of Heywood and the Red Bull's modesty.

Shakespeare, of course, had himself previously used a Chorus to
'waft you o'er the seas', as Jonson derisively described it.[6] The Chorus in *Henry V* which opens Act 3 names several of the features
which appear in *The Tempest*. The later play did not actually show
'Upon the hempen tackle ship-boys climbing', but it does have
mariners hauling on ropes, or orders for them to do so. You can cer-

4. Jonson's terms, in the 1616 Prologue to *Every Man in his Humour: The Revised Version
   from the Folio of 1616, Ben Jonson*, eds. C. H. Herford and Percy Simpson, vol. 3 (Oxford, 1927), Pro. 18–19.
5. Gonzalo in 2.1 (TLN 743–5) [67–69] says their clothes are 'now as fresh as when we put
   them on first in Affricke, at the marriage of the Kings faire daughter *Claribel*'.
6. Jonson, Prologue, *Every Man in his Humour*.

tainly hear the Master's 'shrill whistle, which doth order give / To sounds confused'. The *Henry V* Chorus, as in Heywood, urges the audience to assume that the scene flies 'with imagined wing' and asks them to 'Suppose, that you have seen' and to 'Play with your fancies'.[7] Even without Heywood, it was an exceptional audacity in Shakespeare to launch a new play in a new playhouse on such a piece of realism, at the very beginning of the play, to a cold audience.

The Blackfriars, we know, had two entry doors and a central 'discovery space' in the tiring-house wall, a balcony above, flanked by the curtained music room, and a stage platform half the size of the Globe's with boxes along its flanks and up to fifteen gallants sitting on stools on the stage alongside the boxes. Apart from the cramping of platform space it was not dissimilar to the Globe's stage area and, in fact, the opening scene could have been done equally well on either. Minimally, all the scene itself needed for the original performance was two doors. More use might have been made of the fringe areas, especially the balcony room, but reconstructions of early staging are wise to stick with definitions of the minimal requirements and leave extensions to speculation. At 1.1.6 [2] the Master's shout for the Boatswain and the Boatswain's reply 'Heere Master' indicate that each of them comes on stage by a separate door. The Master then exits, presumably through the same door as he entered by, and the Mariners enter, presumably by the door the Boatswain appeared through, in order that they should not collide with the Master as he exits. The Master subsequently remains offstage, heard only by means of the whistle he must have round his neck. The only alternative way to do this, by no means impractical since this is the Master's only appearance in the scene, would have been for him to appear on the balcony and call to the Boatswain who stands below him at stage level. The Master's whistle could then be heard from the music room which we know was a curtained room on the upper level at Blackfriars. That would leave both doors free for the entrance of the mariners and courtiers, although the use of two doors would limit the effect of bustle and confusion which results from everyone fighting past one another for the same door.

There are some major uncertainties over the movements in the scene, chiefly because most of the exits are inadequately marked. Even multiple exits are scored in the singular and some are not marked at all. The worst uncertainty this creates is about the ropes. The question is whether realism went so literal-minded as to have real ropes dangling from the balcony for the mariners to haul on

---

7. *Henry V*, 3.0.1–10. Heywood must have written *The Four Prentices*, I suspect, with the *Henry V* choruses echoing in his mind.

when the Boatswain orders them to 'Take in the toppe-sale' (1.1.12) [6] and 'Downe with-the top-Mast' (1.1.43) [34]. There is some emphasis on rope-hauling, since the Boatswain says sarcastically to the courtiers at 1.1.31 [22–23], while the mariners are still on stage, 'wee will not hand a rope more'. Gonzalo's allusion at 1.1.39 [30] to the 'rope' of the Boatswain's 'destiny' would also gain more pungency if a visible piece of apparatus was dangling like a noose from above. Ropes hanging from the music room would give the mariners something to do and also allow the courtiers to get visibly in their way. Unfortunately the deficient notation of exits leaves two distinctly alternative possibilities, one with ropes and one without.

The Boatswain's instruction 'Downe with the top-Mast' might be directed either at mariners onstage tailing onto real ropes or to off-stage mariners on imaginary ropes. Striking the topmast in heavy weather was fairly new technology in Shakespeare's day, a practical piece of seamanship but one not easily realized on stage or recognized by a London audience, except through words. Paying out a rope to the music room might have given a visual indicator of the action of lowering the topmast to back up the words. If so, we have to assume two groups of mariners, one which exits with the Boatswain at 1.1.35 [27], the other remaining to haul on the ropes at lines 43–4 [34–35] when the Boatswain gives the order, and again at 1.1.57–8 [49–50] when he shouts 'lay her a hold, a hold, set her two courses off to sea againe, lay her off.' The other group would be the one to return 'wet' at 1.1.59 [50SD]. If, on the other hand, the ropes are imaginary and offstage, the whole body of the mariners would exit with the Boatswain at 1.1.35 [27], justifying his order to the courtiers, 'out of our way, I say', on behalf of the whole crew as they all exit. The Boatswain would then re-enter *solus* at 1.1.42 [33SD] as the courtiers leave, to shout his instructions about the offstage ropes at 1.1.43–4 [34–35] and 1.1.57–8 [49–50] before all the mariners re-enter 'wet' at 1.1.59 [50SD]. The absence of any *exeunt* for the mariners, or even some of them, leaves the staging of the rope-hauling unclear. Two considerations make the latter option more plausible. First, the relatively small number of supernumeraries likely to be available as crew would make their division into two groups less desirable. The smallish Blackfriars stage, already encumbered with fifteen stool-sitting gallants wearing ostrich-plumed hats and smoking long pipes, would not have taken large crowd scenes easily. The more the mariners were offstage and the fewer of them coming on stage the better. Secondly, the practical problem of how to make the ropes disappear after the topmast had been lowered—an action which required the ropes to be fastened to something after the hauling—would create too much risk of unhandy and possibly visibly ridiculous rearrangement. The ropes would have to disappear before Prospero and Miranda enter at the end of the scene, since they are supposed to be watching the shipwreck from the island, which would not be encumbered with dangling ropes. The ropes could not be hauled up silently into the music room without someone first releasing them and making such a public and all-too-visible readjustment look silly. All the hauling, therefore, must have happened offstage.

The main action dramatized in the scene is the contrast between the bustling Boatswain and the rabble of unhelpful courtiers, at least seven of whom enter at 1.1.14 [8]. The offstage noises include not only the thunder and tempest but the Master's whistle, which *Henry V* tells us gives order to sounds confus'd. This offstage shrilling makes the Boatswain tell the mariners at 1.1.12 [6]. 'Tend to th' Master's whistle' and makes King Alonso's question 'where's the Master?' when he enters at 1.1.14 [9] emphatically redundant. It does of course indicate Alonso's ignorance of ships as well as the level of mastery that he, as king, prefers to converse with. When the Boatswain ignores him and Antonio angrily renews the question the Boatswain makes it clear the offstage whistle is still sounding— 'Do you not heare him?' The courtiers are in his way. His concern is with the crew, telling them 'cheerely, good hearts'. His only word for the courtiers is 'Out of our way, I say' as all the crew-members rush off through the crowd of courtiers at 1.1.35 [27].

The incomplete marking of the mariners' exits is matched by that of the courtiers' exits, though in the latter case it is easier to deduce the sequence of their movements. They all go off at 1.1.41 [32], leaving the Boatswain briefly alone on stage to shout his orders. Theirs is the '*cry within*' at 1.1.45 [36] before three of them re-enter to hamper the Boatswain for a second time—'yet againe?'—at 1.1.47 [38]. On their re-entry the king is no longer with them. The three who speak are probably the only ones who return to the stage and they all help to identify themselves by speaking in the way the later development of their characters (in 2.1) would indicate. Sebastian and Antonio, the courtiers most likely to do so, angrily shout back at the Boatswain for his insolence. Gonzalo, who never speaks unselfconsciously in the king's presence—another reason for thinking that the king does not return—is more cheerful in adversity.

The second entry of the mariners at 1.1.59 [50], their spectacular condition '*wet*' making a perfect contrast to the splendours of the courtiers' apparel, is the beginning of the end. The ship's business, from the Master's whistling to the attempt to set more sail and steer offshore, all happens offstage, if my conclusion about the ropes is correct. So the return of the dampened mariners is a token that disaster is looming for the well-dressed passengers. The

Boatswain's second set of orders about rope-hauling is evidently too late to be of any help, and his directive 'off to Sea againe, lay her off', followed by the re-entry of the wet mariners, covers the ship's last moments before it is disabled. That appears to be signalled by the *'confused noyse within'* at 1.1.79 [60].

John Jowett[8] has proposed that several of the stage directions in *The Tempest* bear the signs of Ralph Crane rather than Shakespeare. Crane, a regular scribe for the King's Men in the 1620s, does seem on occasions to have used his memory of performances to supplement the stage directions of the texts he was transcribing. Descriptive stage directions, such as the *'queint device'* at 3.3.74 [52] with which the banquet vanishes, are in the terminology of a spectator, innocent of stage mechanisms and incapable of being prescriptive as authors and playhouse book-keepers commonly were. The adjective used for the offstage noise of the apparent shipwreck at 1.1.70 [60] has a similar air. 'Confused' might be the term a spectator not precisely sure what the crashing and banging is supposed to represent might give it. Possibly Crane, the scribe and spectator, was doctoring his text for the reader here.

There is also another possibility, which seems to me more likely, and which is also consistent with Jowett's reading of this passage. The Folio text appears to give the lines following the *'confused noyse'* to Gonzalo, who has spoken the preceding lines, and seems to go on to speak the odd gabble which follows. The Folio arranges the text as follows:

> *Gonz.* Hee'l be hang'd yet,
>     Though every drop of water sweare against it,
>     And gape at widst to glut him. *A confused noyse within.*
>     Mercy on vs.
>     We split, we split, Farewell my wife, and children,
>     Farewell brother: we split, we split, we split.
> *Anth.* Let's all sinke with' King
> *Seb.* Let's take leaue of him.                               *Exit.*
> (TLN 68–75) [1.1.58–64]

Editors since Theobald have given the lines from 'Mercy on vs' to the last 'we split' to voices *'off'*. Partly this is on the ground that Gonzalo has no brother on the ship to say farewell to, as the lines require, while both Sebastian and the offstage Alonso have. But Gonzalo, like the rest of the courtiers, has no wife and children on board either, so the cry is evidently not addressed to relatives present in the flesh. Children and brothers become important later in the play, of course, in Ferdinand and Miranda, and Antonio and Se-

---

8. John Jowett, 'New Created Creatures: Ralph Crane and the Stage Directions in *The Tempest*', *Shakespeare Survey* 36 (1983), 107–20.

bastian. I am inclined (like Jowett) to think that the three lines following from 'Mercy on vs' are the sounds made in the *'confused
noyse'*, and that they are offstage.[9] The positioning of the stage direction is similar to the conventional *'within'* which usually marks
offstage voices. The scribe merely failed to detach them from Gonzalo's onstage lines. The question this leaves unclear is whether the
*'confused noyse'* was only voices, or (as it might be if Crane was transcribing what he remembered of the performance) whether there
was some more material sound of the ship striking and splitting.

For reasons that in part depend on a more general view of what
this scene is meant to do, I think that voices alone make the noise
here. This is a dangerous kind of assumption, because it quickly
leads into circular arguments. It also assumes a deficient text.
However, a full transcription of these moments at the end of the
scene clearly is lacking, since no exit is marked for Boatswain and
mariners, and therefore some interpretation of the evidence has to
be made. Some offstage voices must have joined with Gonzalo's
even if they did not replace him, since the main events are happening offstage, where the splitting would be most pointedly observed.
The confusion would be the appropriate moment for the Boatswain
and mariners to leave the stage, probably accompanied by Antonio
and Sebastian as they say their exit lines. A mixture of mariners and
courtiers leaving together at this point would exemplify the general
disaster. Gonzalo would then be left to speak the last four lines *solus*. The lines are not addressed to anyone and nobody answers
him. Moreover his solo exit after the others by one door leaves the
opposite door free for the entry of robed Prospero and the agitated
Miranda for the start of 1.2.

That, in broad terms and with some necessary conjectures, is a
reconstruction of the minimal staging that Shakespeare seems to
have intended for the original performances. The supply of evidence is defective chiefly in the incomplete marking of exits. It is
consistent with what we know about the material design of the
stage at the Blackfriars. A. M. Nagler, who has given an account of
how he thinks the whole play was originally staged, would accept
this minimal rendering, only adding the possibility that more use
was made of the balcony, chiefly for the Master.[1] The main features
of this staging—bustle and agitation, the physical confusion in the

9. John Jowett sets out the text in precisely these terms in the Oxford *Complete Works* (Oxford, 1986).
1. A. M. Nagler, *Shakespeare's Stage*, enlarged edition (New Haven, 1981), has a chapter
entitled 'The First Night of *The Tempest*'. Apart from the fact that the first performance
would have been in an afternoon, not at night, Nagler's deductions about the original
staging of the opening scene are consistent with the version offered here. He assumes
that the Master would definitely have been on the balcony and makes no mention of
ropes.

clash of the busy mariners with the bothered courtiers, the noises off, the focus of everyone's attention on events happening just off-stage signalled by the noises and the wet mariners—are utterly realistic, however slight were the devices used to create the realistic effects. The wetting of the mariners is a wonderfully literal-minded and yet strikingly minimal realization of the storm effects. Such realism is vital as a precursor to the revelation in the lines next following, when Prospero tells Miranda that the tempest and shipwreck are only an illusion of his art, that the passengers and crew will be found safe, the ship trimly rigged, the wet clothes clean as if newly pressed.

There are a few points more which can be made about the necessary minimalism of this staging as it was designed for the Blackfriars. A criterion for it, and also perhaps an indication that Shakespeare was commenting on Heywood rather than the reverse, is Fletcher's imitation of Shakespeare's staging in the opening scene of *The Sea Voyage*.[2] Fletcher's play, written in about 1622, was also designed for the Blackfriars, since like *The Tempest* it has an act-break between Acts 4 and 5, where Crocale, Clarinda, and Julietta exit and then re-enter to start the final act. Fletcher's play generally overdoes Shakespeare's model. His play has two islands and two ships, though its stage effects are fairly similar, including 'Horid Musick' before the reunions which bring about the happy ending, and a banquet. The banquet, however, which is watched over by an Amazon in Prospero-like fashion, is not transformed by any magic, and is amazing only in having potatoes included in the food and drink. The play has none of Prospero's magic, and no Caliban.

The tempest and the threat of shipwreck in its opening scene is a benign version of Shakespeare's subtle literal-mindedness. Its use of sea-terms suggests that Fletcher knew the idioms of the sea less well, but was deliberately trying to remind his audience of the earlier Blackfriars play before setting his off on a different course. The initial stage direction is 'A Tempest, Thunder and Lightning. Enter Master and two Sailors'. The Master immediately delivers his echo.

> *Master.*
> Lay her aloof, the Sea grows dangerous,
> How it spits against the clouds, how it capers.
> And how the fiery Element frights it back.
> There be Devils dancing in the air I think
> I saw a *Dolphin* hang i'th' horns o' th' moon
> Shot from a wave, hey day, hey day.

---

2. I use the text first published in Francis Beaumont and John Fletcher, *Comedies and Tragedies* (London, 1647).

How she kicks and yerks!
Down with the Main Mast, lay her at hull,
Farle up all her Linnens, and let her ride it out.

The Master goes on to talk about the risk of the ship splitting, and
calls for the Boatswain, who suggests casting the lading overboard.
This is eventually done, much to the dismay of the courtiers, whose
valuables are thus lost. Altogether this scene does a good deal more
to establish the plot-line than Shakespeare's does. At 180 lines it is
well over double Shakespeare's 79 lines, much of it concerned with
the passengers. All the sea-talk is covered in the opening 60 lines,
including mention of leaks, the ribs being open, the rudder almost
spent, and a proposal to hoist out the boat. The scene then moves
on to the courtiers. The woman on board is the only one alarmed
for her life. She is told 'We ha storms enough already; no more
howling', and the Master threatens to clap her under the hatches.
The focus settles on throwing everyone's treasure overboard at the
demands of 'so rude a tempest', and there is talk of swimming. At
the end of the scene the Master demands that everyone help—'My
life now for the Land. / 'Tis high, and rocky, and full of perils'. They
all exit. Two men marooned on the island then enter, discussing the
storm and the ship, and make it clear that the ship has safely made
harbour.

Fletcher's scene is designed to be an immediately recognizable
echo and development of Shakespeare's and therefore cannot be
compared too closely with it. It alludes to its model and then moves
smartly on along its own plot-line. Some use is made in a subsequent scene, for instance, of the wet clothes device, but probably
not in the same literal fashion. At the beginning of 1.3 a courtier
says, 'Wet come ashore my mates, we are safe arrived yet', and a little later, 'I'll dance till I'm dry.' I would doubt whether the players
would want to afford the wetting of courtier clothes, as distinct
from the working dress of the mariners, and there is not the need
here of the striking appearance wet that Shakespeare's scene demands. Fletcher's play, being ostensibly realistic throughout, does
not need the emphatic though momentary illusion of reality which
Shakespeare's scene requires from the wet clothes.

Comparison with Fletcher's scene and its intertextual links clari-
fies two main features of Shakespeare's. The first is *The Tempest*'s
refusal to indicate any plot-line. All we see is the shipwreck, with
no indication of where the ship is going or who is on it, or why.
Shakespeare's courtiers are only sketched in. Alonso is in authority,
but helplessly lost. Sebastian and Antonio are sycophantic—as Antonio's angry renewal of the king's pointless question and later his
'Let's all sink wi' th' King' (1.1.74) [63] show—and bad-tempered.

Gonzalo is cheerful if verbose in adversity. Ferdinand is on stage for twenty-five lines and has no word to say. There are faint hints of what is to come in the king's helplessness when the Boatswain tells him 'Use your authoritie. If you cannot, give thankes you have liv'd so long and make your selfe readie in your Cabine for the mischance of the houre' (1.1.28–9) [23–25]. Even more obliquely, perhaps, the farewells to brother, wife, and children in the *confused noyse* hint at an element in the play to be developed later. These are all so fleeting and enigmatic that the effect is entirely given over to the tempest. After the wreck anything could happen.

For all the focus on the storm, very little action takes place on the stage itself. The offstage sounds, from the opening stage direction about the *tempestuous noise* and the Master's whistling to the confused hubbub of voices at the end, direct us to things happening tantalizingly out of vision. First one man, the Master, appears. He is joined by the Boatswain and a number of mariners, all in working clothes. Then at least seven gorgeously dressed courtiers enter, mixing amongst the men in working clothes and provoking four requests to go below from the Boatswain, increasingly curt: 'I pray now keepe below . . . Keepe your Cabines . . . to cabine, silence . . . make your selfe readie in your Cabine for the mischance of the houre.' The working men rush off leaving Gonzalo to try cheering the king up before all the courtiers leave and the Boatswain re-enters. He has hardly issued two orders when he is interrupted by an offstage cry from the courtiers and three of them re-enter. The Boatswain shouts at them and two shout back before the working clothes return, now wet, to announce the end. It is a scramble of anonymous functionaries and courtiers falling over one another in a limited space, calling to, or rather against, one another, their hubbub punctuated by entrances and exits and offstage thunder, whistling and cries of panic. It displays human helplessness in the face of natural violence.

The Blackfriars playhouse was the antithesis of disorder and natural storms. It was a candlelit hall, with seats for everyone, exclusively an enclave for the leisured class of courtiers, gallants, gentry, and their ladies. None of its seats cost less than sixpence, the price of a box at the Globe, and even the sixpenny seats were banished to the furthest remove in the galleries. The priorities in its auditorium were the reverse of the Globe's. At the ampitheatre, in a tradition going back to travelling companies performing in market places, the first priority was standing room around the stage, the minimal pennyworth. If you paid more you removed yourself to a bench in the galleries behind the 'understanders o' th' yard'. You might do so for comfort—twopence for a gallery seat, threepence for one with a cushion—or for a roof to protect you from rain. Whatever extra you paid, you saw the play from behind the crowd standing in the yard and the rain. At the Blackfriars the opposite priorities prevailed. The more you paid the closer to the stage you sat, in a box along the flank of the stage for half a crown—ten times the price of a cushioned seat at the Globe—or on a stool on the stage itself. The Blackfriars was indeed playgoing for the privileged.[3]

If *The Tempest* truly was the first play Shakespeare planned for the Blackfriars, his opening scene was a model of how to *épater les gallants*. The shock of the opening's realism is transformed into magic the moment Miranda enters. Her first two lines are reassuring—

> If by your Art (my deerest father) you have
> Put the wild waters in this Rore, alay them.

She knows what Prospero is capable of, and her appeal tells the audience what his magician's robe and staff ought already to signify. It is not after all going to be a rough-and-tumble amphitheatre play of the kind Heywood was writing for the Red Bull. But its course still does not run smooth. It is a play which consistently arouses, challenges, and disappoints courtier expectations. Eventually Shakespeare does offer some satisfaction to the taste of the masque-hungry courtier, but even that belated spectacle is broken off in disharmonies by the cold reality of the conspiracy. The audience, quite specifically a Blackfriars audience of gallants and courtiers, is being kept in suspense. Like the courtiers in the shipwreck, the audience is not to know what it is in for.


# BARBARA FUCHS

## Conquering Islands: Contextualizing *The Tempest*†

It is an axiom of contemporary criticism that *The Tempest* is a play about the European colonial experience in America. While this perspective has generated enormously enriched readings of the play, it runs the risk of obscuring the complicated nuances of colonial discourses in the early seventeenth century. When is America not

---

3. The contrasting conditions of the two auditoriums and audiences are described in the author's *Playgoing in Shakespeare's London* (Cambridge, 1987).

† From *Shakespeare Quarterly* 48 (1997): 45–62. Reprinted by permission of The Johns Hopkins University Press. Line numbers to this Norton Critical Edition of the play have been added in brackets when they differ from the author's original citation.

America? When it is Ireland, or North Africa, or Europe itself, or the no-man's-land (really every man's *desired* land) of the Mediterranean in-between. Just as the formal literary elements of a text—metaphors, puns, patterns—may signify in multiple ways, context, too, may be polysemous. By exploring other contexts for the insistent colonial concerns of Shakespeare's island play, I hope to show how a multiple historical interpretation can unpack the condensed layers of colonialist ideology. This type of reading depends not only on recent *Tempest* criticism—what one might call the American readings—but on studies of England's colonial role in Ireland. My aim is, first, to provide descriptions of the contemporary colonial contexts in both Ireland and the Mediterranean, which I believe shed light on the play, and, second, to suggest the advantages for political criticism of considering all relevant colonial contexts simultaneously. If, as I will argue, the superimposition of those contexts on the play reflects the way colonialist ideology is "quoted" from one contact zone to another in the sixteenth and early seventeenth centuries, criticism that attempts to trace that ideology will gain from identifying precisely such layering of referents.[1]

My purpose in this essay is not to refute American readings of *The Tempest*; I agree with Peter Hulme that placing New World colonialism at the center of the play has made it a fundamentally more interesting and, at least for twentieth-century readers, a more relevant text.[2] Instead, by highlighting the historical and political dimensions of the contemporary Mediterranean world and England's colonial experience in Ireland, I hope to continue to historicize the colonialist discourse that American readings first brought to the fore. Even in highly suggestive and politically sophisticated readings of *The Tempest*, the Mediterranean often equals the literary, the *Aeneid*, the essentially European, functioning largely as a

---

1. I take the term "contact zone" from Mary Louise Pratt's *Imperial Eyes: Travel Writing and Transculturation* (London and New York: Routledge, 1992). Pratt uses this term to replace "colonial frontier," a term "grounded within a European expansionist perspective" (6–7).

   In her suggestive "Rogues, Shepherds, and the Counterfeit Distressed: Texts and Infracontexts of *The Winter's Tale* 4.3," (*Shakespeare Studies* 22 [1994]: 58–76), Barbara A. Mowat explores the "infracontexts" of *The Winter's Tale*. In my analysis of *The Tempest*, I will show how such superimposition of contexts serves colonialist ideologies. In discussing what I shall call "colonial quotation," I adhere to a wide definition of intertextuality as a relation between not only literary but also cultural texts. This notion of intertextuality recognizes that, as Roland Barthes argues, "The logic that governs the Text is not comprehensive (seeking to define 'what the work means') but metonymic; and the activity of associations, contiguities, and cross-references coincides with a liberation of symbolic energy" ("From Work to Text" in *Textual Strategies: Perspectives in Post-Structuralist Criticism*, Josué V. Harari, ed. [Ithaca, NY: Cornell UP, 1979], 73–81, esp. 76). Unlike Barthes, I perceive such symbolic energy as driving a particular ideological project.
2. See Peter Hulme, *Colonial Encounters: Europe and the Native Caribbean, 1492–1797* (London and New York: Methuen, 1986), 106.

background to American *newes*[3]—what Hulme calls the first layer of a textual palimpsest.[4] The new transatlantic colonial discourse works itself out against this background of the *Aeneid* and classical Mediterranean travels. Yet this critical privileging of America as the primary context of colonialism for the play obscures the very real presence of the Ottoman threat in the Mediterranean in the early seventeenth century and elides the violent English colonial adventures in Ireland, which paved the way for plantation in Virginia.

Although twentieth-century historians can speak of the Ottoman Empire in the early seventeenth century as having "passed its peak,"[5] such a perspective was hardly available, as Samuel Chew points out, to contemporary observers of Islam's might.[6] As I hope to show, the sense of an Eastern empire encroaching on Europe pervades Shakespeare's play, making the European "center" of the text simultaneously the origin of colonial adventure and the target of another empire's expansionism. The general absence of Ireland from discussions of colonialism in the play is troubling, particularly since the devastation of a native population and its culture was more deliberate and vicious in England's first plantation than in its later ventures in Virginia. As Paul Brown has suggested, there are strong analogies between Prospero's island and Elizabethan Ireland, which locate them both "between American and European discourse."[7]

The Irish are the niggers of Europe, lads.
*The Commitments*

What are we to make of Roddy Doyle's equation—his rather tongue-in-cheek justification for an Irish band's focus on soul music? Doyle has found a parallel between the situation of African Americans within the U.S. and that of the Irish vis-à-vis postimperialist Europe. While his use of the ugly term *niggers* indicates the conflictive nature of such a comparison (in that the register of working-class/colonized solidarity fails to transcend racial prejudice, and in that the comparison problematically erases the presence in Europe of large black immigrant populations), Doyle's

3. William C. Spengemann, in *A New World of Words: Redefining Early American Literature* (New Haven, CT, and London: Yale UP, 1994), points out that America "was in fact the source of the genre called 'newes' " (97).
4. See Hulme, 108–9.
5. Bernard Lewis, *Islam and the West* (New York: Oxford UP, 1993), 16.
6. See Samuel C. Chew, *The Crescent and the Rose: Islam and England during the Renaissance* (New York: Oxford UP, 1937), 100.
7. Paul Brown, " 'This thing of darkness I acknowledge mine': *The Tempest* and the discourse of colonialism" in *Political Shakespeare: Essays in Cultural Materialism*, Jonathan Dollimore and Alan Sinfield, eds., 2d ed. (Ithaca, NY, and London: Cornell UP, 1994), 48–71, esp. 57.

comparison also parodies the discursive strategies of quotation which contribute to colonization. By comparing them to another oppressed population, Doyle establishes the right of the Irish to soul; ironically, the colonization of Ireland itself depended largely on strategies of comparison which represented its conquest as a repetition of earlier imperialist ventures to Africa and the Americas. As Nicholas P. Canny has pointed out, the colonization of Ireland functioned as an apprenticeship for England's plantation in the Americas.[8] I propose to focus here on the discursive dimension of this education—what I term colonial quotation.

By *quotation* I mean the references by colonial writers to the works of earlier explorers and planters as well as the larger rhetorical maneuver of assimilating the unknown by equating it with the already-known. Such quotation does not overlap perfectly with the notion of *translatio imperii*—the westward translation of Rome's imperial tradition to the nascent European empires. However, the quoted discourse may use *translatio imperii* as its particular justification.[9] The quotation of colonialist discourse from one instance to the next naturalizes expansion by bringing newly "discovered" lands and people under the conceptual domain of the already-known, the already-digested. Thus this particular kind of intertextuality advances a colonialist ideology.[1]

The equation between prior and ongoing colonial encounters may be achieved by literal textual quotation of authorities, by referring to the colonist's own previous experiences in another territory, or by reading a newly discovered culture as another manifestation of one already othered. Such a strategy underlies the remarkable encounter between Trinculo and Caliban in 2.2 of *The Tempest*, where the European does not know what the man/ fish is but certainly knows what to *make of it*: a for-profit display like the multiple "dead Indians" in London fairs: "Were I in England now, as once I was, and had but this fish painted, not a holiday-fool there but would give a piece of silver. There would this monster make a man—any strange beast there makes a man" (ll. 27–30).[2]

8. See Nicholas P. Canny, "The Ideology of English Colonization: From Ireland to America," *William and Mary Quarterly* 30 (1973): 575–98.
9. For one approach to the role of translation in colonization, see Eric Cheyfitz, *The Poetics of Imperialism: Translation and Colonization from* The Tempest *to* Tarzan (New York and Oxford: Oxford UP, 1991).
1. In his "Broken English and Broken Irish: Nation, Language, and the Optic of Power in Shakespeare's Histories" (*Shakespeare Quarterly* 45 [1994]: 1–32) Michael Neill suggests how a different form of quotation might serve to *counter* colonialism. If, as he argues, Irish nationalism was produced by the same English nationalism that violently redefined and colonized Ireland, then perhaps the strategy of quotation need not work entirely to the conquerors' advantage.
2. Quotations of *The Tempest* in this essay follow the Oxford text (ed. Stephen Orgel [Oxford: Clarendon Press, 1987]).

The context of exhibition that Trinculo quotes serves to frame the new and bring it under his dominion. The irony, of course, lies in the fact that the man "made" by such exhibition would be not Caliban attaining human status but Trinculo made rich.[3] Although Trinculo claims to "let loose" his earlier opinion when he realizes that Caliban is alive, even calling him an "islander," the framework of exhibition is immediately reinstated by Stephano, who says he would take the monster home to present to a ruler or sell for profit (ll. 67–68, 74–75). Alive or dead, Caliban fulfills the role of spectacular other and, throughout the comic process of recognition by which Stephano and Trinculo discover him, occupies an abject position. His monstrosity corresponds quite neatly to the Europeans' expectations. For Caliban himself, of course, the situation is framed by Prospero's abusive treatment, which has scripted him as victim.

Caliban's cloak plays a central part in this complicated series of misrecognitions and discoveries, especially as a signal of the play's Irish context. The presence of the cloak does not prove such a context, but it suggests how English domination of Ireland might *take cover* in the text under precisely such details. The cloak, I would argue, is the only native artifact allowed Caliban. He first shrouds under it in order to escape detection by Trinculo, who he fears is a spirit in Prospero's service. Trinculo does discover him and immediately joins him under his "gaberdine" to seek protection from the storm.[4] There Stephano finds the two of them—a curious hybrid creature with four legs and two mouths, recalling Iago's characterization of Othello and Desdemona's marriage as a miscegenistic "beast with two backs." Such unhallowed combinations are precisely the issue here, as Trinculo unwittingly becomes monstrous in Stephano's eyes. Given England's anxiety over distinguishing savage from civilized, islander from colonizer in Ireland, it is possible to read this episode in Shakespeare's text as one of the indices of this colonial adventure.

The English conquest of Ireland was a messy affair. The twelfth-century Anglo-Norman conquest had provided England with a foothold in Dublin and the eastern counties—an area known as the Pale—while large portions of Ireland remained, literally and figura-

---

3. I find Brown's identification of Trinculo with the "footloose Irish" (56) as a masterless barbarian unconvincing, given that Trinculo so clearly occupies the position of colonizer in this episode. This is not to suggest, however, that the text is not staging an anxiety about the *English* masterless classes.

4. In his introduction, Cheyfitz suggests that this reference to gaberdines links Caliban to the Jews (xii), although the main evidence in the *Oxford English Dictionary* for such a connection derives from Shakespeare's own usage in *The Merchant of Venice* (*Oxford English Dictionary*, prepared by J. A. Simpson and E.S.C. Weiner, 2d ed., 20 vols. [Oxford: Clarendon Press, 1989], 6:302). I would argue that the highly charged discourse about Irish coverings in the period provides a more immediate referent.

tively, beyond the Pale of English authority.[5] Cruel attempts to control the island during Elizabeth's rule were both enabled and impeded by this earlier conquest. Over the intervening four centuries the Old English settlers had become in cultural terms all but indistinguishable from the Irish, which hugely complicated English attempts to fight the colonial war on cultural turf by proscribing Irish custom, dress, and social institutions. One of the earliest English statutes in Ireland, enacted in 1297, had required the English to "relinquish the Irish dress," while the Statutes of Kilkenny in 1366 had expressly linked English adoption of the "manners, fashion, and language of the Irish enemies" to the decay of "the said land and its liege people, the English language, the allegiance due to our lord the king, and the English laws."[6] By the sixteenth century, despite such separatist legislation, Old English settlers had adopted many Irish ways. The imperfect allegiance of the Anglo-Irish nobility to Elizabeth and to her metropolitan power was reflected in their rather less ambivalent embrace of Irish culture.

The Irish mantle became a particularly loaded signifier of such cultural struggles.[7] In Spenser's *A View of the Present State of Ireland* (1596) the two interlocutors, Eudoxus and Irenius, propose several competing genealogies for such mantles. Irenius states that the Irish have such a custom "from the Scythians," to which Eudoxus responds with a long history tracing the mantle from Jews to "Caldees" and Egyptians, through Greeks and Romans. But Irenius—who is given an extensive last word on the matter—cuts that history short:

> I cannot deny but anciently it was common to most, and yet Sithence disused and laid away. But in this latter age of the world since the decay of the Roman Empire, it was renewed and brought in again by those northern nations, when breaking out of their cold caves and frozen habitation into the sweet soil of Europe, they brought with them their usual weeds, fit to shield the cold and that continual frost to which they had at home been enured; the which yet they left not off, by reason that they were in perpetual wars with the nations where they

5. For a good summary of this history, see David Beers Quinn, *The Elizabethans and the Irish* (Ithaca, NY: Cornell UP, 1966), or Canny, *The Elizabethan Conquest of Ireland: A Pattern Established 1565–76* (New York: Barnes and Noble, 1976).

6. The preamble to the Statutes of Kilkenny, excerpts reprinted in A. J. Otway-Ruthven, *A History of Medieval Ireland* (London: Ernest Benn; New York: Barnes and Noble, 1968), 291.

7. For a suggestive account of the role of the Irish mantle in terms of gender dynamics, see Ann Rosalind Jones and Peter Stallybrass, "Dismantling Irena: The Sexualizing of Ireland in Early Modern England" in *Nationalisms & Sexualities*, Andrew Parker, Mary Russo, Doris Sommer, and Patricia Yaeger, eds. (New York and London: Routledge, 1992), 157–71. Neill also discusses the mantle as a site for English anxieties about the "inscrutable" Irish other (26).

had invaded, but still removing from place to place carried always with them that weed as their house, their bed and their garment, and coming lastly into Ireland they found there more special use thereof, by reason of the raw cold climate, from whom it is now grown into that general use in which that people now have it; afterward the Africans succeeding, yet finding the like necessity of that garment, continued the like use thereof.[8]

The mantle—house, bed, and garment—becomes inextricably linked to Irish transhumance, the seasonal movement of people and their livestock in search of pastures, one of the practices that most disturbed the English and which they associated closely with barbarity and "enormities unto that commonwealth."[9] Yet this history looks forward, too, by projecting the mantle from the Irish to the Africans, despite the logic of climatic determinism. Irenius does not deny the mantle a genealogy but simply replaces the history of civil peoples with one of savagery, setting the stage for the kind of colonialist quotation that I shall analyze below.

The discussion of the mantle continues at some length, with Irenius paradoxically providing more examples of the usefulness of such garments the more he seeks to criticize them. The perspective from under the cloak differs greatly from that outside it—as Irenius says, "the commodity doth not countervail the discommodity. . . . for it is a fit house for an outlaw, a meet bed for a rebel, and an apt cloak for a thief."[1] One's appreciation of the mantle, then, will vary radically according to whether one is the persecuted or the persecutor. In Spenser's description the mantle becomes the reified signifier of Irish resistance, which cannot be fully penetrated by English authority, even with English ethnography leading the way. As Jones and Stallybrass argue, "The mantle represents Irishness as the refusal to adopt English order, English social categories, English style."[2] Moreover, as one of the prime signifiers of Irishness, the mantle served to assess the extent to which earlier settlers had "gone native": the adoption of the mantle was presumably the culminating move in such acculturation.[3] It is significant, then, that this problem is carefully avoided in Irenius and Eudoxus's discus-

8. Edmund Spenser, *A View of the Present State of Ireland*, ed. W. L. Renwick (Oxford: Clarendon Press, 1970), 51.
9. Spenser, 49.
1. Spenser, 51.
2. Jones and Stallybrass in Parker et al., eds., 166.
3. In discussing the contradictory English attitudes toward the mantle, Jones and Stallybrass note that "a miscegenation of clothes returns to haunt the colonizer" when a military supplier in Ireland suggests to Elizabeth that she provide her English troops there with an Irish mantle ( Jones and Stallybrass in Parker et al., eds., 168). Although the authors read the episode as a sign of fragile English cultural identity, to adopt the mantle might also be to incorporate the enemy's tricks.

sion, as the latter moves quickly from the mantle to a warning about English use of the "glib," or long bangs over the eyes:

> Sure I think Diogenes' dish did never serve his master more turns, notwithstanding that he made his dish his cup, his measure, his waterpot, then a mantle doth an Irishman, but I see they be all to bad intents, and therefore I will join with you in abolishing it. But what blame lay you to then glib? Take heed, I pray you, that you be not too busy therewith, for fear of your own blame, seeing our Englishmen take it up in such a general fashion, to wear their hair so unmeasurably long that some of them exceed the longest Irish glibs.[4]

The Irish glibs, Irenius answers, are "fit masks as a mantle is for a thief." The subject of English mimicry of Irish fashions, however, has once again been carefully avoided. If, as Sir John Davies wrote, the Old English imitating Irish ways are "like those who had drunke of Circes Cuppe, and were turned into very Beasts," the real threat lay not in the power of the witch but in the fact that her colonist victims "tooke such pleasure in their beastly manner of life, as they would not returne to their shape of men againe."[5] The metaphor takes on an interesting resonance if read back into Spenserian allegory in Book II of *The Faerie Queene*. In the Bower of Bliss, Acrasia/Circe's cup threatens not so much the disarmed knight (who can, after all, be disenchanted) as it does Grill, who stubbornly insists on going—and staying—native, famously refusing to be saved back into civilization.

The cultural warfare so well exemplified by Spenser's diatribe was just one front of attack in the English conquest of Ireland. As the violence escalated from the 1560s to the early part of the seventeenth century, anti-Irish rhetoric became ever more virulent, precisely to justify the widening attacks against Irish civilian populations. Ireland did eventually provide large estates for English gentlemen, but only after a bloody and extended struggle such as the English had not expected. Throughout this conflict, Ireland and America were both considered attractive options for expansionist ambitions; when particularly frustrated in their Irish campaigns, colonizers like Humphrey Gilbert and Walter Ralegh turned to America instead. Similarly, when the earliest English settlements at Roanoke proved impossible to sustain, such veterans of the American voyages as Thomas Hariot and John White tried planting in Ireland as an alternative.[6]

The connection between these desirable colonies as expansionist

4. Spenser, 53.
5. Sir John Davies, *A Discovery of the Reasons Why Ireland Was Never Entirely Subdued* (1612), 182; quoted here from Jones and Stallybrass in Parker et al., eds., 163.
6. See Quinn, 109ff.

sites was established rhetorically at a number of levels. The description of dress—to return to our discussion of Caliban's cloak—is one of the clearest instances of the quoting of a previous colonial experience in a new plantation. The English often perceived the Americas through an Irish filter. Thus Gabriel Archer described the natives' leggings in New England as "like to *Irish* Dimmie Trouses," and Martin Pring saw natives with "a Beares skinne like an *Irish* Mantle over one shoulder."[7] Even Powhatan's dress was described by one of John Smith's companions as "a faire Robe of skins as large as an Irish mantle."[8] As the comparisons expand beyond costume to other cultural practices, such as "wild" mourning, devil worship, and transhumance—all of which the English believed they had found on both sides of the Atlantic—it becomes easier to see how such comparisons contribute to the "othering" of a culture by assimilating it conceptually to one already subdued, if not conquered.[9] The resulting quotations function as the colonist's mirror image of miscegenation: instead of the confusion of racial boundaries that might actually threaten his dominion, he creates a purely rhetorical union of various colonial subjects. The others are insistently other but similar among themselves. I should stress, of course, that both the similarities and differences quoted belong to a constructed "text" of culture.[1]

Quoting from one colonial context to the other serves to domesticate the new—the American experience—and equate it with the already-advanced plantation of Ireland. Yet the considerable chronological overlap of European colonial experience in Ireland and America makes the temporal sequence more difficult to untangle. Although Ireland's subjection is the primary colonial context for England in the 1590s and early 1600s, that conquest is in turn justified by comparing the English role in Ireland to that of the Spaniards in America.[2] References to previous Spanish conquests introduce a kind of reciprocity in colonialist quoting, with Ireland as the middle term: the English quote the Spanish experience in America in order to justify England's role in Ireland, and then transfer that Irish experience to Virginia. Yet the process of quotation must reach increasingly farther back in history for additional

---

7. Samuel Purchas, *Purchas His Pilgrimes*, 4 vols. (London, 1625), 4:1647 and 1655.
8. John Smith, *Works. 1608–1631*, ed. Edward Arber (Birmingham: Privately Printed, 1884), 102; see also page 405.
9. Although I cannot address it here, such colonial quoting was also used to characterize African peoples newly encountered in the period, comparing them to the Irish.
1. Colonialism mediates English encounters with its several others, so that observation is never neutral or transparent. As Neill has shown, not only is ocular control essential to English domination in Ireland, but the construction of the Irish as different already brands them with a kind of guilt (26–27 and 6).
2. For a discussion of such triangulation, see Canny, "The Ideology of English Colonization."

terms to substantiate the comparison. Thus the similarity between the English situation in Ireland and the Spanish *Conquista*—a problematic one considering Elizabethan propaganda against Spain—is reinforced by allusions to the *Reconquista*, or expulsion of the Moors from Spain, to further buttress colonialist apologias. Davies justifies the forcible transplantation of the Irish in Ulster by referring to "the Spaniards [who] lately removed all the Moors out of Grenada into Barbary, without providing them any new seats there."[3] The end of the comparison gives away Davies's conscience: Spain was far more concerned with preventing the return of the Moors expelled from North Africa than with their resettlement. In Ireland what to do with a starving peasant population forcibly removed from its land was a question not easily addressed.

Nicholas Canny finds the main source for the English/Spanish connection in Richard Eden's translation of Peter Martyr's *De Orbe Novo* (1555), which was probably familiar to English notables in Ireland in the 1560s.[4] The Spanish conquest of the Americas became a model for the domination of savage peoples, so that the English comparison of their own role in Ireland to the Spanish conquests became closely imbricated with the construction of the Irish as barbarous. In this colonialist logic, once the Irish were thus characterized, they became appropriate subjects for the same treatment Native Americans had received at the hands of the Spanish. That the English reviled Spanish behavior, disseminating the infamous Black Legend of Spanish atrocities in the Indies, seems not to have impeded use of this model when the Irish situation made it expedient.[5] English characterizations of Irish savagery, based on the natives' supposed paganism and transhumance, proceeded apace: by 1560 Archbishop Matthew Parker could take such descriptions as a given, advocating the establishment of resident clergy in the north of England to prevent the inhabitants from becoming "too much Irish and savage."[6]

In constructing the Irish as savages, the English placed them within a temporal framework in which Ireland existed at a stage of social development long since surpassed by England. Ireland re-

---

3. Davies to Salisbury, 8 November 1610, quoted here from Davies, *Historical Tracts* (Dublin, 1787), 273–86, esp. 283–84.
4. See Canny, "The Ideology of English Colonization," 593–94.
5. The first translation of Bartolomé de las Casas's *Breve historia de la destrucción de las Indias* appeared in England under the title *The Spanish Colonie* (London. 1583). The English emulation of Spanish behavior is thus exactly contemporaneous with its condemnation. For an account of how this ambiguity played itself out in Ralegh's voyage to Guiana, see Louis Montrose, "The Work of Gender in the Discourse of Discovery" in *New World Encounters*, Stephen Greenblatt, ed. (Berkeley: U of California P, 1993), 177–217.
6. Matthew Parker, *Correspondence* (1833), quoted here from Quinn, 26.

quired civilizing by England in much the same way that England
had required colonizing by Rome.[7] Sir Thomas Smith engaged in
this rather partial relativism when he explained:

> This I write unto you as I do understand by histories of thyngs
> by past, how this contrey of England, ones as uncivil as Ireland
> now is, was by colonies of the Romaynes brought to under-
> stand the lawes and orders of thanncient orders whereof there
> hath no nacon more streightly and truly kept the mouldes even
> to this day then we, yea more than thitalians and Romaynes
> themselves.[8]

The recognition of one's own past in another by no means implies
an acceptance of that other; it instead establishes a temporal dynamic in which that other must be made the same—forcibly
brought up to date, so to speak. Here, England has already been
civilized, having accepted the imposition of the Roman mold. This
shapely civility then authorizes the imposition of a similar rule on
Ireland, as *translatio imperii* becomes a kind of *translatio morum*.

English emphasis on the need to civilize the savage Irish partly
replaces an earlier model of colonialist justification in which the
Old English had argued that the Irish needed to be liberated from
the tyranny of their own ruling class but were essentially fit subjects for English law and, indeed, desirable tenants or laborers.[9]
It is possible to read these shifting constructions of the colonial
subject in the two depictions of islanders in Shakespeare's text.
Although Ariel need not be read as the co-opted native, as some
modern rewritings of *The Tempest* insist, it *is* possible to view him
as the colonizer's fantasy of a pliant, essentially accommodating,
and useful subject. Of course, the play's ironic presentation of
Prospero's fantasy shows the tensions inherent in this model. Ariel's
gratitude is never as complete or as certain as Prospero would wish.
Perhaps, the text suggests, a liberated native tends to interpret liberation in terms rather different from those of his or her enlightened liberator. In the lively prehistory of the play, Prospero freed
Ariel from Sycorax's tyranny—wonderfully literalized in the pine
trunk that bound him; but it is unclear whether subjugation to the
new magician on the scene really means more liberty for the sprite.

Caliban, meanwhile, recalls the second model developed by the
English to justify colonization: the Irish subject in need of civiliz-

---

7. This strategy for disarming criticism of colonialism has had a long life. Compare Joseph
Conrad's evocation of a "primitive" London in *Heart of Darkness* (New York: Signet,
1978): after eulogizing the Thames as the artery of commerce and empire, Marlow says,
"And this also has been one of the dark places of the earth" and proceeds to evoke the
Roman arrival in Britain (67).
8. Sir Thomas Smith to Fitzwilliam, 8 November 1572; quoted here from Canny, *Elizabethan Conquest*, 588–89.
9. See Canny, *Elizabethan Conquest*, 580 and 589.

ing. Miranda's speech presents the colonizer's story of attempts to civilize the native and locates the supposed intractability of Caliban in his lack of language (1.2.350–61). Consider her description of his inability to express himself:

> I pitied thee,
> Took pains to make thee speak, taught thee each hour
> One thing or other. When thou didst not, savage,
> Know thine own meaning, but wouldst gabble like
> A thing most brutish, I endowed thy purposes
> With words that made them known.
>
> (ll. 352–57)

Emphasis on the impenetrability of Caliban's language—even he, according to Miranda, cannot understand it—evokes the English colonizers' frustration with Gaelic as a barrier to their penetration of the territory.[1] But Caliban cannot be "liberated" simply by being taught English. The end of Miranda's speech betrays the unspoken half of the colonialist argument: if the native's "vile race" makes him inherently unsuited to civilization, then violence is justified:

> But thy vile race—
> Though thou didst learn—had that in't which good natures
> Could not abide to be with; therefore wast thou
> Deservedly confined into this rock,
> Who hadst deserved more than a prison.
>
> (ll. 357–61)

Here the duplicitous logic of colonialist ideology is exposed: if one explanation for Caliban's subjection doesn't work, a more essentialist one will be found. Language is more useful than Caliban knows.

My point is not that the elements of colonialist discourse in the text do not apply to the Americas. It would be ridiculous to deny that the English experienced a similar or even greater disorientation when confronted with American languages and cultures than with Gaelic. Instead, I am attempting to display the layering of such contexts in the play, from the basic discourse of savagery developed by the English in Ireland to their eventual experiences in the Americas. To read only America in *The Tempest* is to ignore the connections that colonial quotation establishes between England's two main Western plantations, connections perhaps expressed most graphically in the instability of their geographic referents. In the first part

---

1. The English address the threatening incomprehensibility of the natives' language itself through the mechanisms of colonial quotation. The term *hubbub*, originally used to describe an Irish war cry or outery, migrates to Virginia, where Henry Spelman hears the Indians making a "whoopubb" (Smith, cv). The *OED* itself incorporates the strategies of colonial quotation, defining *hubbub* as "a confused noise of a multitude shouting or yelling; esp. the confused shouting of a battle-cry or 'hue and cry' by *wild or savage races*" (7:459, my emphasis).

of the seventeenth century, Ireland could be, as it was to Bacon, "the second island of the ocean Atlantic," or it could migrate to a completely different conceptual context, as in Fynes Moryson's description of "This famous Island in the Virginian Sea."[2]

—§—

This Tunis, sir, was Carthage.
(2.1.82) [81]

Even within these pages it has not been possible to separate Irish and Mediterranean colonial contexts without postponing the insistent presence of the latter, as the English in Ireland compare themselves to the Spaniards expelling the Moors and the Irish mantle is sighted not only in America but in Africa. Our inability to describe simultaneously the bewildering number of ways in which early modern Europe experienced other civilizations prevents us from uncovering all the connections among those experiences, but a focus on one area of contact should not preclude consideration of others. Ann Rosalind Jones has tried to bring together multiple cultural encounters by exploring the often-made comparison of Vittoria Colombina's Moorish maid Zanche to the Irish in Webster's *The White Devil*.[3] The attribution to Zanche of both Irish and Moorish savagery is particularly evocative if we consider that two terms of the comparison represent, respectively, a newly established Western colony *of* England and an Eastern empire that was a threat *to* England. Such a conflation of attributes in the figure of the Moorish maid may suggest how the English import a gendered discourse into their cultural negotiations with the Moors in order to disable the Islamic threat.

Textual signs of English anxiety about Islamic power in the Mediterranean abound in the play, though critics generally relegate those signs to a literary register. When discussing the marriage of Alonso's daughter Claribel to the king of Tunis, Gonzalo points out that Tunis *is*, in a fundamental way, Carthage: "This Tunis, sir, was Carthage." Critics hastily explain *Carthage*, with its baggage of Virgilian associations, as though the mention of Tunis were self-explanatory.[4] While

---

2. Francis Bacon, *The Letters and the Life of Francis Bacon*, 4th ed. (1868), and Fynes Moryson, *An Itinerary* (1617); both quoted here from Quinn, 121–22.

3. See Ann Rosalind Jones, "Italians and Others: Venice and the Irish in *Coryat's Crudities* and *The White Devil*," *Renaissance Drama* 18 (1987): 101–19.

4. See, for example, Robert Wiltenburg, "The *Aeneid* in *The Tempest*," *Shakespeare Survey* 39 (1987): 159–68; and John Pitcher, "A Theater of the Future: *The Aeneid* and *The Tempest*," *Essays in Criticism* 34 (1984): 193–215. Orgel does mention Spain's repeated attempts to invade Tunis in the sixteenth century (40).

It must be noted that the imperial name of Carthage itself travels far beyond the classical world. By the seventeenth century Cartagena was the name of both a city in Spain and a Spanish settlement in what is now Colombia. Orgel cites Richard Eden's mention of this West Indies harbor as "Carthago" in *The Decades of the New World* (London, 1555), a translation of Peter Martyr's *De Orbe Novo*.

some recent criticism has explored the early seventeenth-century construction of Islam in the English theater,[5] there are specific textual traces of the imperial Ottoman threat in *The Tempest*. Even though by the 1580s trade was established between England and the Turkish world, the perceived menace of Islam was still great. Writing his *Generall Historie of the Turkes* in 1603, Richard Knolles calls them "the greatest terrour of the world" and advocates the reading of his text because the Ottoman Empire "in our time so flourisheth, and at this present so mightily swelleth as if it would ouerflow all, were it not by the mercie of God."[6] The threat of Islam existed on two fronts: southeastern Europe (which will not concern us here) and the Mediterranean. Knolles shows great respect for Ottoman power on both land and sea: "With the great Ocean [the Ottoman monarch] much medleth not, more than a little in the gulfes of Persia and Arabia: most of his territories lying upon the Mediterranean and Euxine seas. . . . Now for these seas, no prince in the world hath greater or better means to set forth his fleets than hath he."[7]

During the sixteenth century the Barbary Coast that figures so prominently in Shakespeare's play had come gradually under Turkish power.[8] In fact, Algiers, Sycorax's home before her banishment, had been captured by the Turks in the 1530s. Charles V led an expedition against it in 1541 but without success. Tunis itself had very recently been the site of a European struggle against the Ottoman Empire: captured by the Spanish in 1572, it was reconquered by the Turks in 1574.[9]

Morocco had never been part of the empire, and a substantial diplomatic relationship developed between its rulers and Elizabeth, allied together against both the Spanish and the Turks.[1] After James's peace with Spain, England abandoned its rather fanciful plans for invading Spain with Morocco's help and instead considered invading Morocco. Writing to King James, Henry Roberts suggested that the campaign be carried out with "Irish solduars and they of the Out Isles," as "the countrey wilbee the better to bee ridd of them, for they bee but idle and will never fall to worke but steale

---

5. See especially Lynda E. Boose, " 'The Getting of a Lawful Race': Racial discourse in early modern England and the unrepresentable black woman"; Jean E. Howard, "An English Lass Amid the Moors: Gender, race, sexuality, and national identity in Heywood's *The Fair Maid of the West*"; and Patricia Parker, "Fantasies of 'Race' and 'Gender': Africa, *Othello*, and bringing to light," all in *Women, "Race," and Writing in the Early Modern Period*, Margo Hendricks and Patricia Parker, eds. (London and New York: Routledge, 1994), 35–54, 101–17, and 84–100.

6. Richard Knolles, *The Generall Historie of the Turkes*, 2d ed. (London, 1610), A4$^v$ and A6$^v$.

7. Knolles, Aaaaaa6$^r$.

8. See, for example, Prospero's account of Sycorax (1.2.261–70) and the discussion of Claribel's marriage to the king of Tunis (2.1.68–84 and 244–58).

9. For a concise summary of these events, see Chew, 551–55.

1. For a detailed account of the history of Anglo-Moroccan relations, see Jack D'Amico, *The Moor in English Renaissance Drama* (Tampa: U of South Florida P, 1991), 7–40.

as longe as they remaine in Ireland."[2] Once again the colonized—here proposed as mercenaries—return to English rhetoric as new conquests are envisioned.

The possibility of conquering Morocco, however remote, might account for the representation of non-Turkish Moors, in plays such as Heywood's *Fair Maid of the West*, as embodying a "dangerous but effeminate otherness that finally renders them safely inferior to their European visitors," as Jean Howard puts it.[3] But Howard makes race the main cause of such a representation, minimizing the difference between Turks and Moroccan Moors in terms of an expansionist imperative. I think that the difference in terms of an imperial threat is fundamental: isolated Morocco could be an ally or, treacherously, could be turned into a colony; under the Ottoman Empire the rest of North Africa remained a much greater threat. Thus England's willingness to consider Moroccan Islam a lesser threat than Spanish Catholicism: Morocco was not an expansionist power, or at least not in the direction of Europe.

The perceived threat from the Ottoman Empire itself, however, did not abate, even after the decisive victory at Lepanto. This 1571 naval battle was hailed as the triumph of Christendom over the Turks, but it was soon clear that the intra-European alliances necessary to mount a credible challenge to Ottoman power would not last. One textual record of the unusual place that Lepanto occupied in the history of the European struggle against Islam is King James's epic poem on the subject, written after the battle and republished when he acceded to the English throne.[4] The poem caught Richard Knolles's attention, and he dedicates his history to James, "for that your Majestie hath not disdained in your *Lepanto* or *Heroicall Song*, with your learned Muse to adorne and set forth the greatest and most glorious victory that euer was by any the Christian confederat princes obtained against these the *Othoman* Kings or Emperors."[5] Perhaps the most interesting signs of the European tensions that made the Lepanto victory unrepeatable appear in James's preface to the reader, where he provides an extensive set of justifications for a Protestant monarch's praise of the Catholic alliance: "And . . . I knowe, the special thing misliked in it, is, that I should seeme, far contrary to my degree and Religion, like a Mercenary Poët, to penne a worke, *ex professo*, in praise of a forraine

2. Henry De Castries, *Les Sources Inédités de L'Histoire du Maroc* (1918): quoted here from D'Amico, 38.
3. Howard in Hendricks and Parker, eds., 113.
4. For the poem's publication history and an account of the battle as the background for *Othello*, see Emrys Jones, " 'Othello', 'Lepanto' and the Cyprus Wars," *SS* 21 (1968): 47–52.
5. Knolles, A3ʳ.

Papist bastard. . . ." Although the extraordinary circumstances of the battle justify his praise of Don Juan of Austria "as of a particular man," James suggests, the reader should not extrapolate from that praise any sympathy for the Catholic League: "Next follows my invocation to the true God only, and not to all the He and She Saints, for whose vain honors, DON- IOAN fought in all his wars."[6] In James's ambivalent unwriting of the poem's epic praise, we see reflected the fragility of the European unity that had led to the great naval triumph.

In the years after Lepanto, as English trade with the Turks was gradually established, England developed a complex relationship to the Ottoman threat. While a healthy respect for the Turks' imperial might prevailed, Islam (especially in the Moroccan version) also became a term in an elaborate set of rhetorical constructions which played it off against Catholicism as a lesser, or merely equivalent, evil. An observer like Knolles, however, thought that Spain, given its American riches, was the most appropriate power to deal with the Turkish emperor:

> There remaineth only the king of Spaine, of all other the great princes either Christians or Mahometanes (bordering vpon him) the best able to deale with him; his yearely reuenewes so farre exceeding those of the Turkes. . . .[7]

Knolles suggests that the Spanish have the best chance of defeating the Turks but regrets that their resources are spread too thin over their many possessions "for the necessarie defence and keeping of his so large and dispersed territories."[8]

For England the situation vis-à-vis the Turks was further complicated by piracy in the Mediterranean. As the sixteenth century drew to a close, petty piracy gradually replaced large naval encounters.[9] English merchants were prey to Barbary pirates from Algiers or Tunis, but English piracy also flourished, glorified during Elizabeth's reign as privateering against the Spanish and alternately condemned and condoned once peace with Spain had been reached. When English pirates fell out of favor at home, they "turned Turk." Purchas locates the scandalous confusion of Moors and English renegades in Algiers, which he calls "the Whirlepoole of these Seas, the Throne of Pyracie, the Sinke of Trade and the Stinke of Slavery; the Cage of uncleane Birds of Prey, the Habitation of Sea-Devils, the Receptacle of Renegadoes of God, and Traytors to their

6. "Lepanto" in *The Poems of James VI of Scotland*, ed. James Craigie, 2 vols. (Edinburgh: William Blackwood and Sons, 1955), 1:198.
7. Knolles, Bbbbbb[r].
8. Knolles, Bbbbbb[r].
9. See Fernand Braudel's encyclopedic *The Mediterranean and the Mediterranean World in the Age of Philip II*, trans. Siân Reynolds, 2 vols. (London: Collins, 1973), 2:1186–95.

Country."[1] But the figure of the English renegade seemed threatening, I conjecture, mainly because it shattered the carefully constructed mirroring of Barbary Coast pirates in English privateering. As long as this mirror image was maintained, the English could imagine a role for themselves in controlling the Mediterranean. Once English pirates became, effectively, outlaws and went over to the other side, England was at a disadvantage, having no official expansionist presence in such contested territory. This complicated background of piracy on the sea and traditional Islamic expansionism on land lies behind the Algiers described as Sycorax's birthplace in *The Tempest*, 1.2. Yet even that origin is made more complicated by the location of the main action of the play on an island somewhere between Tunis and Italy.

In some ways the Mediterranean islands themselves were the most volatile territories in the region. Malta had withstood the Turkish assault in 1565, but the Knights of St. John had moved there only when it proved impossible to defend Rhodes. Cyprus, too, was in Turkish hands, as even the victory at Lepanto had proved insufficient to reconquer it. All the islands were especially vulnerable, of course, to pirate raids. Any island imagined in the Mediterranean at the time of the play, then, would be understood to exist in a hotly contested space, permanently threatened by the Ottoman Empire if not directly under its control.

If one focuses on Tunis and the threat it posed to the Christian areas of the Mediterranean, the indecorous marriage that sets the royal party in *The Tempest* on their journey becomes ever more outrageous. If the marriage of Desdemona to Othello is controversial, it could at least be partly redeemed by the fact that Othello the Moor fights against the Turks on the side of Venice. To marry a daughter to the king of Tunis, while perhaps expedient in political terms, is a far more radical move than to pair her off in some convenient European alliance. To Lynda Boose's argument that "the black male–white female union is, throughout this period and earlier, most frequently depicted as the ultimate romantic-transgressive model of erotic love,"[2] I would add that the chastening tragic end of *Othello* cannot be discounted as one vision of such unions. The threat of violence to Christian women from irascible foreign husbands is well chronicled in Knolles, who tells the story of Manto, a Greek lady taken prisoner by the Turks, who marries Ionuses Bassa, an official in Suleiman's army. After an initial interlude of married bliss, Bassa, "after the manner of sensual men still fearing least that which so much pleased himselfe, gaue no lesse contentment to others also," becomes madly jealous.[3] Manto

---

1. Purchas, quoted here from Chew, 344.
2. Boose in Hendricks and Parker, eds., 41.
3. Knolles, 357.

tries to leave him and return to her country but is betrayed by a
eunuch, whereupon her husband kills her. This story could have
served as a source for *Othello*; whether or not it did so, it highlights the dangers that Europe imagined for a woman married into the
empire of Islam. Such a union would probably be more acceptable
in European eyes when (as with Othello fighting for Venice or the
Prince of Morocco coming to Belmont to woo Portia unsuccessfully
in *The Merchant of Venice*) it involved the domestication of the foreign male rather than the removal of a European woman to North
Africa or Asia Minor. As Sebastian points out, rubbing salt in Alonso's
wounds:

> Sir, you may thank yourself for this great loss,
> That would not bless our Europe with your daughter,
> But rather lose her to an African,
> Where she, at least, is banished from your eye,
> Who hath cause to wet the grief on't.
>                    (2.1.121–25) [120–24]

The description of Claribel's forced marriage recalls grim accounts
of Christians captured by Barbary Coast pirates rather than stories
of transgressive romance. Sebastian continues to insist upon the
near-sacrificial nature of the union:

> You were kneeled to and importuned otherwise
> By all of us, and the fair soul herself
> Weighed between loathness and obedience at
> Which end o'th' beam should bow. . . .
>                    (ll. 126–29) [125–28]

What does this marriage tell us, then, about the sexual politics of the
play as a sublimated arena for imperial struggles? Knolles suggests
the reason for the Claribel-Tunis union when he describes Naples as
the European border of the Ottoman Empire. Alonso is thoroughly
chastised for his decision to marry off his daughter (presumably to
contain Islamic attacks on Naples), but the reproaches come from
one who wishes him ill and would usurp his crown. The thoroughly
negative characterization of the island conspirators somewhat relegit-
imizes the marriage, since it is mainly Sebastian who condemns it.
Yet the most telling reaction to the supposed alliance with Tunis
comes when Sebastian and Antonio discuss murdering Alonso for his
crown. At this point Claribel entirely replaces her Moorish consort,
as her femaleness is used to fix Islam firmly in Africa. When Antonio
asks Sebastian who, after Ferdinand, is next in line to the crown of
Naples, Sebastian answers "Claribel." Antonio then places Claribel at
a further and further remove from the crown by insisting on the impossible distances that separate her from Europe:

ANTONIO    She that is Queen of Tunis; she that dwells
　　　　　　Ten leagues beyond man's life; she that from Naples
　　　　　　Can have no note unless the sun were post—
　　　　　　The man i' th' moon's too slow—till newborn chins
　　　　　　Be rough and razorable; she that from whom
　　　　　　We all were sea-swallowed, though some cast again—
　　　　　　And by that destiny, to perform an act
　　　　　　Whereof what's past is prologue, what to come
　　　　　　In yours and my discharge.
SEBASTIAN　　　　　　　　　　　　What stuff is this? How say you?
　　　　　　'Tis true my brother's daughter's Queen of Tunis,
　　　　　　So is she heir of Naples, 'twixt which regions
　　　　　　There is some space.
ANTONIO　　　　　　　　　　　　A space whose every cubit
　　　　　　Seems to cry out, 'How shall that Claribel
　　　　　　Measure us back to Naples? Keep in Tunis,
　　　　　　And let Sebastian wake.'
　　　　　　　　　　　　　　　　(2.1.244–58) [243–57]

Sebastian's commonsense rejoinder about "some space" is perfectly reasonable, considering that the distance from Tunis to Naples, as Stephen Orgel points out, is three hundred miles.[4] But what interests me here is the incredible amplification of space that Antonio imagines, as he expands the Mediterranean into an immense ocean. His hyperbole not only makes the crossing impossible but also neatly obscures its possible agents. Although Antonio measures the length of the voyage by a man's lifespan, by the man in the moon's speed, and by the time it takes for a baby boy to reach manhood, the actual man Claribel has married is nowhere to be found in the passage. Presumably, however, the king of Tunis would support his royal consort's claims to a European throne; perhaps his interest in conquering that throne justified the marriage in the first place. Antonio's exclusive focus on the possibility of Claribel's return should thus be read as a strategy for containing the role of Islam in the play. In a perverse metonymy, the European woman, instead of her threatening husband, becomes "Tunis." Unlike "Norway," "Denmark," "Morocco," "Aragon," and other heroic national appellations, the name of "Tunis" signifies only an infinitely distant Claribel. Much as the Turks in *Othello* are conveniently drowned in a single line of dialogue—"News, friends: our wars are done; the Turks are drown'd" (2.1.202)—in order to allow the domestic action to proceed, Antonio's relocation of Claribel to faraway Tunis and his erasure of her husband define the power struggles within the play as essentially European, regardless of the place where they are occurring. Of course Alonso's party is itself an exception to the

4. Orgel, ed., 2.1.245n.

supposed impossibility of getting to Tunis. Antonio admits this but points to their being "sea-swallowed" on their return. And yet the very urgency of the conspiracies on the island would indicate that the Italians have little doubt they will eventually return home. The play's containment of "Tunis"—a pressing, contemporary imperial threat—by focusing on Claribel's distance rehearses the earlier containment of a historical empire, Carthage, through the jocund references to "Widow Dido" in 2.1.

In *The Tempest* gender does the work of imperialism rather than of discovery.[5] The containment of the Islamic threat to European sovereignty or Mediterranean expansion plays itself out once again in the peculiar story of Sycorax's banishment from Algiers. This expulsion functions as a screen for European fears of Islamic control of the Mediterranean islands. Sycorax—cast as too awful even for the rough society of Algiers—is banished, as Prospero (whose source for this knowledge is somewhat unclear) tells Ariel, "For mischiefs manifold and sorceries terrible / To enter human hearing" (1.2.264–65). Yet her banishment was a commuted sentence; her life was spared "for one thing she did"—that is, her pregnancy. This ascription of mercy to the Algerians, reflecting European law, effectively replaces the Barbary pirates or Ottoman galleys—whose power so impressed Knolles—with the flimsy bark of sailors on a charitable mission who deposited the pregnant Sycorax on the island. Again, the metonymic reduction of Islam to the figure of the witch is perverse, for what is at stake in the Mediterranean is not the "Satanic" side of Islam—which Sycorax might represent—but its military might. The rewriting of Islamic expansionism into an errand of mercy operates once again through a female figure—a type of containment far more subtle than the effeminization Howard points to in Heywood's play, or even than the commonplace associations of the East with luxury and sensuousness. Here the female figures take the place of the threatening Moors, so that the latter are disarmed at a remove. By indirectly neutralizing the threat of Islam, the text of *The Tempest* prevents any direct engagement with its forces, addressing instead a female version, which is more easily conquered, at least in rhetoric. As the action of the play proves, Sycorax represents a temporary presence rather than an effective Islamic conquest of the island; her son Caliban loses it immediately to the Europeans. Moreover, this second instance of containment through figuration is presented by Prospero, who, whatever his colonialist failings, clearly represents a center of moral authority in the text. Thus it is not only conspirators who turn to the feminine as a strategy for ensuring European power; Prospero's story emas-

---

5. I allude to Montrose's discussion of Ralegh in Guiana ("The Work of Gender" in Greenblatt, ed.).

culates Algerian naval power just as Antonio and Sebastian's fantasies erase the king of Tunis.

The gendered dynamics of Mediterranean containment in the play recall the more common gendered colonialist trope of ravishing a newly discovered land. Clearly this particular island no longer has her maidenhead; she is thoroughly known by Caliban, who was familiar with her secrets even before Prospero arrived, and who showed Prospero "all the qualities o'th' isle" (l. 337). Instead of rhapsodizing the European rape of the island, then, the text provides as counter-metaphor another rape—Caliban's attempt on Miranda— as colonialist justification (ll. 347–48).[6] Caliban's attack on Prospero's daughter once more genders the colonizing impulse; here it is the defense of the European woman that justifies repression of the non-European.

The triad of female figures which I have considered (two of them absent, two largely submissive daughters) thus participates in the text's containment of Islamic expansionism and its more complex espousal of European colonialism. The rhetorical representation of the women, through hyperbole, metonymy, and the anti-metaphor of Miranda's near-rape, performs European imperial goals at the discursive level, and it is only by interrupting that performance through, for example, a consideration of the play's multiple contexts that the illusionism can be examined.

Thus the discursive work of gender functions as yet another set of colonialist strategies. Much like the use of quotation which I identified when discussing the connections between English experiences in Ireland and America, these rhetorical strategies in *The Tempest* make sense only when viewed from the perspective of multiple contexts. Europe's experience of being another empire's goal was closely bound up, temporally, materially, and rhetorically, with its burgeoning experience of empire-building; it is no wonder, then, that the multiple dimensions come together in a text as complex and polysemous as *The Tempest*. By purposely conflating and collapsing these contexts, I have attempted to give a political reading of the play which insists on what Richard Knolles would call "the four parts of the world," in order to prevent Shakespeare's island play from itself becoming isolated somewhere in the Americas.

---

6. In another variation on this theme, the natives' alleged sexual violence toward the Europeans' intended land was sometimes offered as a colonialist justification, as in Purchas's description of the vulnerable Virginia: ". . . howsoeuer like a modest Virgin she is now vailed with wild Couerts and shadie Woods, expecting rather rauishment then Mariage from her Natiue Sauages . . ." (4:1818).

# LEAH MARCUS

## The Blue-Eyed Witch†

In Act I, scene 2 of *The Tempest*, Prospero describes Caliban's mother Sycorax as a "damn'd Witch" condemned to death in "*Argier*" on account of her "mischiefes manifold" and "sorceries terrible." I quote here from the First Folio, the only early text of the play, although most modern edited versions introduce only minor changes to the lines in question. Because of "one thing" Sycorax "did / They wold not take her life" but banished her instead: "This blew ey'd hag, was hither brought with child"—her child being Caliban, born somewhat later on the island where he, Prospero, Miranda, and the others presently reside (TLN 391–96) [1.2.266–69].[1]

Our discussion will focus on the witch's blue eyes, but we may wish to pause briefly over her crime. What was it that Sycorax did to avoid execution? Until the second half of the nineteenth century, readers and editors were in a quandary over this matter. Charles Lamb found the passage puzzling "beyond measure." It aroused "infinite hopeless curiosity" in him until he read of the infamous career of an actual Algerian witch (unnamed in his source) who had earned a reprieve from death by delivering Algiers from the siege of Emperor Charles V.[2] Staid Victorian editions tended to avoid what now appears the obvious explanation, while displaying unease over the passage's sexual innuendo. The matter remained in debate until the early twentieth century; since then, editors have regularly noted that the "one thing" Sycorax did to avoid execution was become pregnant, as actual female convicts sometimes did in early modern England to postpone execution.

This is an example of a genuinely helpful editorial intervention, but it leaves open the question of Caliban's parentage. Was Sycorax pregnant by the devil, as Prospero repeatedly asserts, or by some other father? At some point in her history, Sycorax "with Age and Envy / Was growne into a hoope" (TLN 384–5) [1.2.258–59], and she died sometime before Prospero's and Miranda's arrival on the island. But that deformity was the effect of age and malice: what was

---

† From *Unediting the Renaissance: Shakespeare, Marlowe, Milton* (London: Routledge, 1996), pp. 5–17. Reprinted by permission of the author. Line numbers to this Norton Critical Edition of the play appear in brackets following the author's original citation.
1. TLN is the Through Line Number, quoted from Charlton Hinman's Norton facsimile version of the First Folio (London and New York: Paul Hamlyn, 1968).
2. "Nugae Criticae," *London Magazine*, November, 1823; as cited in *Charles Lamb on Shakespeare*, ed. Joan Coldwell (London: Colin Smythe; New York: Barnes & Noble, 1978), pp. 62–64.

she like before that? In this passage and throughout the play, Sycorax is a shadowy figure, and even here, the seemingly specific information we are offered is Prospero's recounting of a story Ariel had apparently told him previously, a narration of events even Ariel had in all likelihood not witnessed himself. Nearly everything we know about Sycorax we know only through Prospero's secondhand information, which may or may not be accurate but is certainly not without prejudice: he has supplanted her son on the island and his magic has rivalled and exceeded hers. To what degree might he, or even Ariel, have "edited" her story? To what extent, if we were editing *The Tempest*, would we want to align ourselves with his perceptions?

Let us return to Sycorax's blue eyes—"blew" in the First Folio, but regularly modernized to "blue" in recent editions. Why has so little been made of their color in recent critical studies of the play? The mention of eye color in Shakespeare is rare, and blue eyes are particularly rare. Why are the witch's eyes blue? Much of the interpretive energy surrounding *The Tempest* in the late twentieth century has gone toward the deconstruction of the play's apparent opposition between the properly European (Prospero, Miranda, Ferdinand) and the colonial or otherwise alien stranger (Caliban, Sycorax). We might have supposed that Sycorax's eye color would be a prominent piece of evidence in such critical revisionism, since blue eyes, in our culture at least, are associated with the Anglo-American imperialist and with the "self," rather than with the colonized peoples and with the "other." As a blue-eyed Algerian, Sycorax would fail to fit our racial stereotypes in a number of interesting ways. We tend not to think of Africans as blue eyed, even though North Africans of "Argier" and elsewhere sometimes are. But the witch's blue eyes scarcely surface in the critical discussions I have read: the critics have dutifully read the explanatory notes to the play in the editions they have used, and modern editions overwhelmingly reject the possibility that "blue-eyed" in this instance can possibly mean blue eyed.

In nearly all modern editions, "blew ey'd," "blue-ey'd," or "blue-eyed" is glossed in a way that cancels out its potential for disrupting the self/other binary that has characterized most readings of the play. Among popular teaching editions of the complete works of Shakespeare, the Riverside glosses "blue-ey'd" as "with dark circles around the eyes"; the Bevington fourth edition suggests, "with dark circles under the eyes or with blue eyelids, implying pregnancy", the Signet edition offers, "referring to the livid color of the eyelid, a sign of pregnancy."[3]

3. Cited respectively from *The Riverside Shakespeare*, ed. G. Blakemore Evans (Boston: Houghton Mifflin, 1974), p. 1615; *The Complete Works of Shakespeare*, ed. David Bevington, 4th edition (New York: Harper Collins, 1992), p. 1534; and *The Complete Signet Classic Shakespeare*, ed. Sylvan Barnet (New York and Chicago: Harcourt Brace Jovanovich, 1972), p. 1547.

Standard single-play editions are only slightly more informative.
Frank Kermode's Arden edition glosses "blue-ey'd" as "Alluding to the
eyelid; blueness there was regarded as a sign of pregnancy."
G. L. Kittredge suggests, somewhat more creatively, "with blueish
settled streaks (often called *circles*) under and partly surrounding her
eyes—a sign of exhaustion or debility" and follows the suggested
reading with a long list of analogues from other Renaissance texts.
John Dover Wilson's notes to the New Shakespeare offer paleograph-
ical evidence for a possible emendation of "blew-ey'd" to "blear-ey'd":
in the passage of *Sir Thomas More* which had been suggested only a
few years before Dover's edition as a sample of Shakespeare's hand-
writing, final *r* and final *w* are almost indistinguishable. Wilson
suggests that Shakespeare may have written "bler-ey'd" and been
misread by the compositor.[4] In the hand of the *Sir Thomas More* passage, the two letters are indeed easily confused, but we have no conclusive evidence that the hand in *Sir Thomas More* is Shakespeare's.
As Paul Werstine has pointed out, a recent volume of essays on the
subject succeeds in demonstrating only that none of the contributors
is willing to rule out Shakespeare as possible author of the *More* passage.[5] In most Renaissance hands, final *r* and final *w* are quite easy
to distinguish. Wilson's argument is cogent only if we have already
accepted his assumption that Sycorax could not possibly be blue
eyed. Only a few twentieth-century single-volume editors of *The
Tempest* have left the line unannotated: most notably, Northrop Frye
and Alfred Harbage in the Pelican Shakespeare. Most editions that
do not annotate the line supply the requisite information in a glossary: "blue-eyed" in Shakespeare means with "a dark circle round the
eye" or "with blueness about the eyes."[6]

Why are twentieth-century editors so relatively uniform in their
interpretation of the line, which would seem, on the face of it, to
be receptive to a wide range of explications? In this, as in many
other editorial matters, they have followed the lead of William Aldis
Wright's prestigious Clarendon edition of *The Tempest* (1874),
which contended that " 'blue-eyed' does not describe the colour of

---

4. See Frank Kermode, ed., *The Tempest*, The Arden Shakespeare, 6th edition (London:
Methuen, 1958), p. 27 n.; George Lyman Kittredge, ed., *The Tempest* (Boston: Ginn,
1939), pp. 96–97; and Sir Arthur Quiller-Couch and John Dover Wilson, eds, *The Tempest* (Cambridge: Cambridge University Press; New York: Macmillan, 1921), p. 93. Most
other twentieth-century single-play editions follow the standard formula, with Alfred
Harbage and Northrop Frye's Pelican editions of *The Tempest* (Baltimore: Penguin,
1959; reprinted 1970) representing a prominent exception: the Pelican editors leave the
line unglossed.
5. Paul Werstine, review of T. H. Howard-Hill, ed., *Shakespeare and* Sir Thomas More: *Essays on the Play and its Shakespearian Interest* (Cambridge: Cambridge University Press,
1989), in *Essays in Theatre* 9 (1990): 91–94.
6. Cited from the glossaries to *The Comedies of Shakespeare*, ed. W. J. Craig and Edward
Dowden (London: Oxford University Press, 1932); and *The Temple Shakespeare: The
Tempest*, ed. Israel Gollancz (London: J. M. Dent, 1910). Interestingly, Peter Alexander's
editions, which do not have notes but do include a glossary, do not gloss the phrase.

the pupil of the eye, but the livid colour of the eyelid, and a blue eye in this sense was a sign of pregnancy. See Webster, *Duchess of Malfi*, ii, I, 'The fins of her eyelids look most teeming blue.' "[7] But nineteenth-century editors were by no means so formulaic as their successors have been in their interpretation of the witch's startling blue eyes. In fact, the idea that Sycorax could not possibly be blue eyed in our usual sense of the term seems to have been hatched around mid-century along with the dissemination of Charles Darwin's theory of evolution.

Surprisingly enough, the phrase "blue-eyed hag" went unannotated in editions of Shakespeare from the early folios (which were, of course, not annotated), through all of the eighteenth- and early nineteenth-century annotated editions, until the late 1850s. Even Thomas Bowdler's *Family Shakespeare* (1818) left the description of the pregnant, blue-eyed Sycorax intact, despite his resolve to remove words and expressions "which cannot with propriety be read aloud in a family."[8] The first edition of *The Tempest* to take issue with Sycorax's eye color was the Gilbert Shakespeare (1858–60), edited by Howard Staunton. Staunton suggested emendation of "blew-ey'd" to "blear-ey'd" as a more appropriate epithet for the "damn'd witch." His edition also happened to anticipate Darwin's *Descent of Man* by depicting Caliban as a "missing link" between primate and human. In one of Sir John Gilbert's illustrations, a simian Caliban is attended by his close cousin, the monkey. The page on which Sycorax is described is adorned with a portrait of her in standard witch-like garb. She is apparently on the point of imprisoning Ariel, who recoils from the hunched forms of the witch and her half-human son.[9] A decade and a half later, Daniel Wilson's *Caliban: The Missing Link* (1873) accepted the emendation as settled, referring several times to the "blear-eyed" Sycorax as part of his discussion of Caliban's borderline status between the animal and the human. Wilson contended:

> Sycorax is spoken of with every term of loathing: as a "foul witch," a "hag," a "damned witch," &c. There seems no propriety in coupling with these the term *blue-eyed*—one of the tokens, according to Rosalind, in "As You Like It," whereby to know a man in love.

7. William Aldis Wright, ed., *The Tempest*, The Clarendon Shakespeare (Oxford: Clarendon Press, 1874), pp. 91–92; see also Alexander Schmidt's supporting definition in his authoritative *Shakespeare-Lexicon: A Complete Dictionary of All the English Words, Phrases and Constructions in the Works of the Poet*, 2 vols (Berlin: Georg Reimer; London: Williams & Norgate, 1874–75), 1: 123.
8. Thomas Bowdler, ed., *The Family Shakespeare, in Ten Volumes* (London: Longman, 1818), title page.
9. See the survey of visual depictions of Caliban in Alden T. Vaughan and Virginia Mason Vaughan, *Shakespeare's Caliban: A Cultural History* (Cambridge: Cambridge University Press, 1991), pp. 215–51; and Howard Staunton, ed., *The Plays of Shakespeare*, vol. 3 (London and New York: Routledge, Warne & Routledge, 1860), pp. 12 and 23.

Some Victorian stage Calibans followed Gilbert and Wilson, modelling their portrayals of the savage on the behavior patterns of great apes.[1]

Although Staunton's and Wilson's textual emendation was not followed by later editors, who at most admitted it into their notes as conjectural, the rationale behind the suggested emendation was generally accepted. In nineteenth-century literature and culture, blue eyes were commonly associated with beauty, innocence, and transcendence, as in Keats' "beauteous woman's large blue eyes" or Shelley's eyes "like the deep, blue, boundless heaven" or Arnold's "eyes, so blue, so kind."[2] Blue eyes were also associated, at a time of expanding colonization and racial consciousness, with British culture and national heritage, with the "white man's burden," and with the superior moral elevation attained by English-speaking peoples. To imagine Sycorax as "blue-eyed" in any positive sense of the term was to violate deeply engrained cultural assumptions.

Some nineteenth-century editors searched for ways of associating "blue" with malevolence: Sycorax's eyes might be a blue like that "cold, startling blue which suggests malignity so strongly," or like the "pale-blue, fish-like, malignant eye, which is often seen in hag-like women."[3] As Charles and Mary Cowden Clarke explained in their popular edition designed to elevate Shakespeare for families and purge his texts of phrases "coarse and unfit for modern utterance," the "epithet [blue-eyed], as applied by Shakespeare; is far from being commendatory, as at present. He uses it here to describe the dull, bleared, neutral colour seen in the eyes of old crones."[4] Charles Cowden Clarke was a noted lecturer on literary subjects; he had been intimate with several of the Romantics and had tutored John Keats. He, as much as any other single person, helped to popularize the strict separation in late nineteenth-century editions of *The Tempest* between the heavenly blue eyes of the English cultural ideal and the malignant eyes of the she-demon Sycorax.

1. Daniel Wilson, *Caliban: The Missing Link* (London: Macmillan & Co., 1873), p. 227. For a history of nineteenth-century stage Calibans, see Stephen Orgel, ed., *The Tempest*, The Oxford Shakespeare (Oxford and New York: Oxford University Press, 1987; paperback reprint, 1991), pp. 71–75.
2. Cited respectively from "To J. H. Reynolds, Esq.," line 53, in *The Poetical Works of John Keats*, ed. H. W. Garrod, 2nd edition (Oxford: Clarendon Press, 1958), p. 485; *Prometheus Unbound* 2.1.114, in *Shelley's* Prometheus Unbound, A Variorum Edition, ed. Lawrence John Zillman (Seattle: University of Washington Press, 1959), p. 187; and "A Memory Picture," line 41, in *The Poems of Matthew Arnold*, ed. Kenneth Allott, 2nd edition, ed. Miriam Allott (London and New York: Longman, 1979), p. 115.
3. See J. Surtees Phillpotts, ed., *The Tempest*, The Rugby edition (London: Rivington's, 1876), as cited in Horace Howard Furness, ed., *A New Variorum Edition of Shakespeare*, vol. 9 *The Tempest* (Philadelphia and London: J. B. Lippincott, 1892), p. 61 n.; and Richard Grant White, *Studies in Shakespeare* (Boston and New York: Houghton Mifflin; Cambridge, Massachusetts: The Riverside Press, 1885), p. 324.
4. Charles and Mary Cowden Clarke, eds, *The Plays of William Shakespeare* (London, Paris, and New York: Cassell, Petter & Galpin, [1864–68]), vol. 3, *The Tragedies*, Preface, p. vii, and vol. 1, *The Comedies*, p. 10 n.

The main piece of cultural business performed by annotations of "This blue-eyed hag" in nineteenth-century editions was the policing of boundaries between the acceptably civilized and the loathsomely, dangerously alien. But the range of suggested interpretations during that period was free and wide-ranging by comparison with that of twentieth-century editions, which have frozen earlier editorial speculation into dogma. The only annotated edition since the Pelican to depart from reigning orthodoxy on the subject of the "blue-eyed" witch (at least among the editions that I have encountered) is Stephen Orgel's recent Oxford edition (1987), which repeats the usual explanations but offers them more as hypothesis than as self-evident truth.

Having indicated some of the cultural pressures underlying the typical annotation of "blue-eyed hag," however, we have by no means completed our task. Editors have not only registered discomfort with the idea of a witch who is blue eyed, they have also done exhaustive historical research into the meaning of "blue-eyed" in the Renaissance to support their annotation of the line. They have, in fact, uncovered considerable evidence that the phrase in English Renaissance culture could be used in senses very different from our own. If twentieth-century editions may be said to be impoverished in terms of their interpretation of the line, they are often copious in providing historical evidence to support the reigning dogma. And indeed, if they are correct in concluding, as they have, that "blue-eyed" could not possibly refer simply to eye color in Shakespeare's culture, then perhaps their intervention is helpful rather than obfuscating.

We in the twentieth century have inherited the nineteenth century's marked cultural emphasis on blue eyes, particularly insofar as they are found in young women and accompanied by the requisite blond hair and an aura of combined innocence and sexual availability, as in Marilyn Monroe, blond-haired Barbie dolls, and so on. If Shakespeare's "blew-ey'd" did not resonate for his culture in the ways that "blue-eyed" tends to resonate in ours, then perhaps the editorial intervention is justified. We will note, however, that twentieth-century explications of the line, like their forebears from the previous century, serve to smooth out an apparent incongruity. The witch cannot have blue eyes, because the cultural image of blue eyes is overwhelmingly positive and Sycorax has to be understood as negative.

Part of the purpose of a good edition has traditionally been to bridge historical distance—to make a text and its cultural milieu accessible to people with different practices and assumptions. But that process always involves the risk of over-normalization, of making the past over to accommodate one's own, and one's readers', sense of what constitutes acceptable meaning. Particularly in our own poststructural critical climate, an edition allowing for cultural dissonance and distance might well be more desirable than one that consistently irons out interpretive difficulties. At what point does editorial assistance become unwanted intrusion? We plunge to the heart of the matter when we investigate the range of signification carried by blue eyes in the Renaissance. No doubt many of the unfortunates hanged as witches in early seventeenth-century England had eyes of a color that we would now describe as blue, but the naming of eye colors, then as now, was as much cultural construction as perception. What perceptions matched the phrase "blue-eyed" in England of the early modern era?

According to Wright and most subsequent editors, "blue-eyed" refers not to the iris of the eye, but to the area around the eye. And there are indeed many instances of such usage in the Renaissance. Kittredge cites Shakespeare's *Lucrece* (1587): "And round about her tear-distained eye / Blue circles stream'd" and Davenant's *The Cruel Brother*: "His eyes . . . Encircled with the weakly colour blue" (Kittredge p. 96). But much more commonly cited is the example from *The Duchess of Malfi*, already quoted above from Wright's edition, which brings in the association with pregnancy: "The fins of her eyelids look most teeming blue." Although each of these examples refers explicity to the area around the eye while the Shakespearean passage does not, there are other contemporary instances in which the phrase "blue eyes" seems clearly to mean what we would call "black and blue eyes" or "eyes with dark circles around them." Kittredge cites Dekker's *Honest Whore*, Part II, "Out, you blue-eyed Rogue" and, following Wright, Davenant's *The Playhouse to be Let*: "Her eyes look blue; pray heav'n she be not breeding!" (pp. 96–97). The examples do not all support the same precise reading of the origin of Sycorax's "blue-eyed" demeanor: some imply pregnancy, while others suggest grief or physical bruising. But all of them together demonstrate fairly conclusively that in late sixteenth- and early seventeenth-century England, "blue-eyed" did not necessarily mean what we mean by blue eyed.

The case against the standard emendation is not yet lost, however. To pursue it further, we need to probe into the cultural construction of eye color. For if editors are to be allowed to annotate the line with the interpretive assurance conveyed by most twentieth-century editions, they need to demonstrate not only that "blue-eyed" *could* mean "blue circled" as a result of pregnancy or some other debility; they should be willing to demonstrate an overwhelming likelihood that it meant "blue circled" as opposed to "blue." As we have noted, by no means did all nineteenth-century editors agree about the eyes of Sycorax—some of them opted for eyes of a baleful or malignant blue. Horace Howard Furness queried in his *New Variorum Edition* of *The Tempest* (1892):

Is it not possible to accept the blueness as referring not only to the dark eyelids and circles round the eyes, but also to the pupil itself, where the *arcus senilis*, as the ophthalmologists call it, is wont to give the baleful expression which we associate with witches?

Following an earlier hint by Edmund Malone, Furness made the interesting suggestion that some of the positive connotations associated with blue eyes in recent Anglo-American culture were in Shakespeare attached to gray eyes:

> Instances are as plenty as blackberries where what we now call blue eyes were by Shakespeare called grey eyes. There are two in *Rom. & Jul.*, where the Friar speaks of "The grey-ey'd morn," and Mercutio of "Thisbe, a grey eye or so." Since, then, our "blue eyes" and Shakespeare's "blue eyes" are not the same, I think we are at liberty to include, in the present phrase, whatsoever tends to add abhorrence to the repulsive witch.[5]

If we combine all of these suggestions about historical differences in meaning, a Shakespearean taxonomy of eye-color would run something like this: his blue eyes = our dark circled eyes, his gray eyes = our blue eyes. And in fact, in pre-Shakespearean literature the eyes of the desired woman are often gray rather than blue. In Chaucer, for example, the desirable woman typically has "eyen greye as glas" or at least "greye." John Skelton gives her "eyen grey and steep."[6] "The phrase "grey as glasse" occurs in *Two Gentlemen of Verona* 4.4.196 (F TLN 2010), Olivia has grey eyes in *Twelfth Night* 1.5.256 (F TLN 538), and there are similar references in *Romeo and Juliet* 2.4.45 and 3.5.19. The OED confirms that "blue eye" gradually migrated in signification from what we would term a "black eye" in the sense of black-and-blue to "blue eye" in our sense of blue, but the precise chronology of the change is left unclear. Unlike most eye colors, "blue eye" receives its own entry in the OED. The first cited usage of "blue eyes" in the nineteenth- and twentieth-century sense appears to be to 1735 (Alexander Pope's *Moral Essay* 2.284.[7]) The OED glosses our specific crux—Shakespeare's description of Sycorax—to mean black or blue around the eyes rather than blue-eyed in the more recent sense of the term.

At this point, as Smedley Force would be happy to inform us, our

5. Furness, ed. (see above), 9: 62 n.
6. See *The Works of Geoffrey Chaucer*, ed. F. N. Robinson, 2nd edition (Boston: Houghton Mifflin, 1961), p. 18 (*General Prologue*, 152), p. 56 (*Reeve's Tale*, 3974); and John Skelton, *Philip Sparrow*, line 1014, in *The Complete Poems of John Skelton, Laureate*, ed. Philip Henderson 1931, revised edition (London and Toronto: J. M. Dent and Sons, 1948), p. 89.
7. Alexander Pope, *Epistles to Several Persons*, ed. F. W. Bateson, The Twickenham Edition of the Poems of Alexander Pope (London: Methuen; New Haven: Yale University Press, 1951: 2nd edition, 1961), vol. 3 part ii, p. 73.

potential case against the standard annotation of "blue-eyed hag" appears lost. If the OED and standard editions confirm each other, we are confronted with a powerful array of authority. We need to remind ourselves, however, that the OED, however invaluable, is not without its biases: it is a product of the same late nineteenth-century codifying impulse that has given us our standard editions of Shakespeare and many other writers. Some of the same minds who prepared the Shakespearean editions also participated in the monumental cultural enterprise of the OED, and a similar cultural agenda is to be expected in both. Indeed, a major purpose of the OED entry on "blue eyes" may have been to help solidify the post-Wrightian interpretation of the Shakespearean line, rather than vice versa. We need to go beyond the OED itself if we are to determine whether Sycorax's eyes could have been blue.

In English Renaissance literature, there are hordes of golden-tressed women—particularly in blazons à la Petrarch of an idealized beloved—but there are precious few blue eyes. As we have already seen, the traditional eye color for the beautiful woman in earlier literature appears to have been gray. This does not necessarily mean, of course, that people in early modern England favored gray eyes over blue eyes; they may simply have perceived the blue-gray that we call blue as gray. In literature of the late sixteenth and seventeenth centuries, however, black eyes come strongly into favor: Philoclea in the Old Arcadia is black-eyed, and so, famously, is Sidney's Stella in Astrophil and Stella. Shakespeare's dark lady is also described in Sonnet 127 as having eyes of "raven black," and there are numerous other examples from the period.[8] Part of this preference may relate to the eye color of actual women celebrated in the verse, as in the case of Shakespeare's dark lady and Sidney's Stella: other poets also celebrated Penelope Devereux Rich's "black sparckling eyes."[9]

On stage or in verse celebrating a generic mistress, such specificity might have been a drawback, limiting the range of actors who could play a given part, or the range of women who could be wooed with the aid of a given poem. English Petrarchan poetry is strongly fixated on the beautiful woman's eyes, but more for their power than for their color. Most frequently, the woman's eyes are likened to stars, suns, or some other emitter of celestial light, without their color being specified. Often they are crystal, which may or may not connote a color like our blue: it tends to be associated in verse of the period with the heavens and with "crystal streams" (both of

8. See Stephen Booth, ed., Shakespeare's Sonnets (New Haven and London: Yale University Press, 1977), p. 111; and for other examples from among many, James Shirley's "To Odelia" and Sir John Suckling's Sonnet II as printed in Ben Jonson and the Cavalier Poets, ed. Hugh Maclean (New York: W. W. Norton, 1974), pp. 188 and 258.
9. See, for example, The Poems of Henry Constable, ed. Joan Grundy (Liverpool: Liverpool University Press, 1960), Sonnet Seven, p. 158.

which we might be more inclined to think of as blue) but sometimes it seems to suggest a translucent paleness. Often the eyes
are diamonds, or other precious stones. Following Petrarch, whose
Laura was clearly what we would call blond-haired and blue-eyed,
English poets sometimes described their mistress's eyes as "sapphire," as in Spenser's *Amoretti* and the famous blazon from the
*Epithalamion*: "Her goodly eyes lyke Saphyres shining bright."[1]

In Spenser, as in the case of Sidney's Stella, we may be dealing
with the perceived eye color of an actual woman, except that
Spenser's beloved, unlike Sidney's, happens to conform to the Petrarchan ideal. But only rarely in the English Renaissance verse that
has survived are the beautiful woman's "sapphire" eyes explicitly associated with the word "blue." One popular and widely anthologized
exception is Sidney's *contreblason* of Mopsa the Shepherdess from
the *Arcadia*; it mocks the Petrarchan ideal by interchanging the conventionalized colors of Mopsa's physical attributes. She is as fair as
Saturn and as chaste as Venus. "Her forhead jacinth like, her
cheekes of opall hue, / Her twinkling eies bedeckt with pearle, her
lips of Saphir blew:"[2] The pearls that in the usual Petrarchan blazon
would represent teeth here suggest a dropping rheum about the
eyes; the sapphire blue that should shine from the eyes is instead
the color of her lips. The joke depends on a conventionalized expectation that eyes will be blue and teeth pearly white, rather than vice
versa. Obviously, at least some members of a cultural elite in the sixteenth century were able to imagine eyes that were "blue" in our
sense rather than in the commoner Renaissance meaning.

The evidence I have collected suggests that the Shakespearean
taxonomy of eye color accepted by earlier editors may be too
simple. In Renaissance culture, "blue eyes" sometimes suggested
black-and-blue eyes, or eyes rimmed with black as a result of pregnancy or fatigue, but, *pace* the *OED*, "blue eyes" sometimes meant
what we mean by blue eyes today. The phrase "blue eye" seems to
have carried then some of the ambiguity that "black eye" carries in
our own culture, where the phrase can be used for an eye with a
dark brown or black iris, or for an eye that is black and blue. We
can speculate that "blue eyes" in the twentieth-century sense may

1. *The Poetical Works of Edmund Spenser*, ed. J. C. Smith and E. de Selincourt (London
and New York: Oxford University Press, 1929), pp. 565 (Sonnet XV) and 581 (*Epithalamion*, line 171). For another example, see the poem attributed to Thomas Lodge in *The
Phoenix Nest 1593*, ed. Hyder Edward Rollins (Cambridge: Harvard University Press,
1931), p. 58. On the Petrarchan construction of beauty more generally, see Elizabeth
Cropper, "The Beauty of Woman: Problems in the Rhetoric of Renaissance Portraiture,"
in *Rewriting the Renaissance: The Discourses of Sexual Difference in Early Modern Europe*, ed. Margaret W. Ferguson, Maureen Quilligan, and Nancy J. Vickers (Chicago and
London: University of Chicago Press, 1986), pp. 175–90.
2. Cited from *The Poems of Sir Phillip Sidney*, ed. William A. Ringler, Jr (Oxford: Clarendon Press, 1962), p. 12.

have been a recent import in early modern England, associated with foreign models and with elite culture rather than with the native English tradition of gray-eyed beauty. Within Shakespeare's own corpus, the color blue is at least once associated with the heavens, but the reference appears in one of his last plays: in a famous textual crux, *Cymbeline* describes Imogen's closed eyes and/or eyelids as "White and Azure lac'd / With Blew of Heauens owne tinct" (F TLN 929–30). A little after Shakespeare, blue eyes become more common in poetry, but may still have been regarded as exotic. Charles Cotton wrote a blazon of his sister's beauty in which he praised her black eyes above "English grey, or French blue eyes," seeming to suggest an equivalence between the two colors: what the French (and Italians?) conventionally termed blue or sapphire eyes the English traditionally called gray.[3]

And indeed, if we move outside the realm of lyric poetry, we find a similar equivalence. In the standard modern translations of Homer, Athena's most customary epithet is "gray-eyed." In Chapman's Homer, however, composed about the same time as Shakespeare's *Tempest*, Athena is regularly described as either "blue-eyed" or "gray-eyed." In translating Athena's Homeric epithet γλαυκῶπις, Chapman uses "blue" and "gray" indifferently: there is no clear contextual reason for the choice of one color over the other; Athena in her irenic, as opposed to her martial, demeanor, is repeatedly called "blue eyed," and her eyes are also associated with things we think of as blue, such as the sky. By the time Dryden translated Homer, Virgil, and Ovid toward the end of the century, Athena was regularly described as "blue-eyed" in our sense of the term.[4] We can safely assume that for neither Chapman nor Dryden did calling the virgin goddess "blue-eyed" connote that she had bleary eyes "ringed in blue, as in pregnancy."

We have turned up a number of alternative possibilities for reading Shakespeare's description of Sycorax. Her eyes may have been "blue" in the popular sense of rimmed with blue or black, but there is at least the possibility that Prospero's brief and fragmentary description of the witch can be read in terms of the Petrarchanists' mock blazon: at the time that she was exiled to the island, she had the blue eyes of

---

3. See *Poems of Charles Cotton 1630–1687*, ed. John Beresford (New York: Boni & Liveright, n.d.), p. 124.
4. See George Chapman, trans., *The Iliads of Homer Prince of Poets* (London: for Nathaniell Butter [1612]), p. 20, line 24; p. 64, line 4; p. 66, line 18; p. 71, line 44; p. 96, line 17; p. 106, line 1, etc.; and Chapman, trans., *Homers Odysses* (London: for Nathaniell Butter [1614]), p. 4, line 31; p. 7, line 28; p. 83, line 48; p. 209, line 7, etc. Since Dryden never translated a Homeric epic in full, the examples are more scattered, and sometimes from Latin rather than Greek. But see his "Last Parting of Hector and Andromache," (*Examen Poeticum*, 1693), line 19 "blue-ey'd progeny of Jove"; *The Second Book of the Aeneis*, line 243 "blue-ey'd maid"; and *The Twelfth Book of Ovid His Metamorphoses*, line 208 "blue-ey'd maid"; all cited from *The Poetical Works of Dryden*, ed. George R. Noyes, new revised and enlarged edition (Cambridge, Massachusetts: The Riverside Press, 1950).

a Petrarchan heroine but was (monstrously) pregnant. Can we imagine that at the time of her exile, as opposed to the time of her death, she may have been physically attractive rather than repulsive, that she may have radiated an aura of eroticism? Interestingly enough, eighteenth and nineteenth-century adaptations of the play regularly retain the description of Sycorax as "blue-eyed," even though by those periods the phrase had lost the ambiguity of its earlier meaning. In Restoration adaptations of *The Tempest*, one of which survived on stage until the early nineteenth century, Sycorax is regularly brought to life as a character on stage—Caliban's sister, daughter of his blue-eyed mother. The Restoration stage Sycorax is comically loathsome but sexually available—perhaps like her mother?[5] The witch's sexuality seems to have been a more acceptable subject for Restoration and eighteenth-century audiences than for their Victorian descendants. At least one adaptation makes Sycorax the subject of a mock blazon like Sidney's on Mopsa.[6] In such an eroticized conceptualization of the witch, "blue-eyed" might well mean "blue-eyed."

Or, alternatively, the "blue-eyed" Sycorax could be associated through her exotic eye color with the blue-eyed Athena as popularized by Chapman, much in the way that the play appropriates for Prospero's own magic spells some of the incantatory language of the Ovidian witch Medea. As Orgel's edition has recently emphasized, Prospero's magic has not always been envisioned as benign before our own century: on the eighteenth-century stage, in particular, it carried sinister overtones of black magic, and Prospero's spirits were sometimes referred to as "devils."[7] For both Prospero and Sycorax, the play's surface moral valuation of an enchanter is complicated by resonances that contradict the superficial impression. The eyes of Sycorax, like the charms of Prospero, eerily reverberate with their supposed moral opposites, and the play's many Virgilian echoes facilitate a contextualization of "blue eyes" in terms of classical epic tradition rather than in terms of the native English tradition. To associate Sycorax's mysterious eye color with the uncanny power and attributes of a goddess rather than with the debility of pregnancy is to achieve rather a different perspective on her nature and activities, and on those of her inheritor, Caliban. It is also to adopt a reading of the "hag" that is far from the one pro-mulgated by Prospero.

5. See in particular John Dryden, *The Tempest or The Enchanted Island. A Comedy* (London: for Henry Herringman, 1670), available in George Robert Guffey's collection of facsimile editions, *After* The Tempest (Los Angeles: William Andrews Clark Memorial Library, 1969).

6. See T[homas] Duffett, *The Mock-Tempest or The Enchanted Castle* (London: for William Cademan, 1675), p. 52. This play is also available in the Guffey facsimile edition.

7. Orgel, ed., *The Tempest*, The Oxford Shakespeare, pp. 72, 189–90. On the play's classical echoes, see also Donna B. Hamilton, *Virgil and* The Tempest: *The Politics of Imitation* (Columbus: Ohio State University Press, 1990).

All of Shakespeare's linkings of "blue" with eyes are difficult cruxes, and we will never know certainly what he "meant." Nor, if we wish to operate within a traditional intentionalist scheme of explanation, can we expect that Shakespeare was utterly consistent in his conceptualization of "blue eyes." But even if we were able (by some miracle) to establish that chimerical entity, the meaning of the passage as the author intended it, we would still be left with the strong likelihood that in Shakespeare's culture, the phrase "blue-eyed" was highly ambiguous and likely to be understood differently by different segments of his audience, depending on their social class, education, and life experience. *The Tempest* is a play that dramatizes a series of encounters between Europeans and denizens of a strange island that appears alien to the Europeans. It was written at a time when similar Europeans were embarked on actual voyages of discovery, and beginning to confront racial and cultural difference in an unprecedentedly radical form through their encounters with natives of the New World. What greater likelihood than that the play itself should record a sense of dissonance, even shock, over the difficulty of using physical characteristics to separate the cultural "self" from the "other"?

How, then, should the "blue-eyed hag" be explicated in our modern editions? Our investigation has been inconclusive in that it has not allowed us to settle on any single eye color or condition as properly glossing the phrase, but it has been highly conclusive about the suspect origins of the standard emendation. If the edition's format allows only very brief indications of meaning, I would suggest that the phrase is best left unglossed, rather than glossed in a way that replicates nineteenth-century cultural assumptions and removes too much of its Renaissance range of signification. In an edition permitting more copious annotation, however, the phrase should be annotated with due respect to the broad perspective of meanings "blue-eyed" could have carried in early modern culture; the highly restrictive interpretation of "with dark circles about the eyes as a result of pregnancy" should be offered to readers only as one possibility among others. In thinking about Shakespeare's "blue-eyed hag," we need to remember that the whole rickety twentieth-century superstructure of historical investigation of "blue eyes" was reared on a base of nineteenth-century assumptions about what was acceptably English as opposed to unacceptably alien and threatening. To unedit the phrase "blue-eyed hag" is to cast off a set of strict cultural delimitations by which the witch has been kept under control in modern editions of *The Tempest*. It is to declare a preference for variability over fixity of meaning. It is to open the play once more to an unsettling, polysemous menace that Prospero and modern editors have worked very hard to contain.

# REWRITINGS AND
# APPROPRIATIONS

# Drama and Film

## JOHN FLETCHER AND PHILIP MASSINGER

[John Fletcher (1579–1625) was one of the most prolific writers for the Renaissance stage and is best known for his collaborations with Francis Beaumont, Philip Massinger, and William Shakespeare himself. Fletcher consistently explored the tragicomic and romantic possibilities suggested by *The Tempest*, and many of his plays featured travel and trade in exotic settings. In the opening scenes from *The Sea Voyage* (written in 1622 and published in 1647), Fletcher and Massinger offer their own version of a dramatic tempest off the coast of a "desert island."]

## The Sea Voyage†

The scene: first at sea, then in the desert islands

*A tempest, thunder and lightning. Enter Master and two sailors.*

MASTER
    Lay her aloof, the sea grows dangerous:
    How it spits against the clouds, how it capers,
    And how the fiery element frights it back!
    There be devils dancing in the air, I think.
    I saw a dolphin hang i' th' horns of the moon,
    Shot from a wave: hey day, hey day!
    How she kicks and yerks?
    Down with'e main mast, lay her at hull,
    Fardel up all her linens, and let her ride it out.
1 SAILOR
    She'll never brook it, Master.
    She's so deep laden that she'll bulge.
MASTER                              Hang her.
    Can she not buffet with the storm a little?
    How it tosses her! She reels like a drunkard.

† From *The Sea Voyage* [1622], first printed in Francis Beaumont and John Fletcher, *Comedies and Tragedies* (London: Humphrey Robinson and Humphrey Mosely, 1647). From Act 1, scene 1, and Act 1, scene 4.

301

2 SAILOR
>  We have discovered the land, sir.
>  Pray let's make in, she's so drunk; else,
>  She may chance to cast up all her lading.

1 SAILOR
>  Stand in, stand in, we are all lost else,
>  Lost and perished.

MASTER                    Steer her a-starboard there.

2 SAILOR
>  Bear in with all the sail we can. See Master,
>  See, what a clap of thunder there is,
>  What a face of heaven, how dreadfully it looks?

MASTER
>  Thou rascal, thou fearful rogue, thou hast been praying;
>  I see't in thy face, thou hast been mumbling,
>  When we are split, you slave. Is this a time,
>  To discourage our friends with your cold orisons?
>  Call up the Boatswain. How it storms! Holla!
>      [*Enter* BOATSWAIN.]

BOATSWAIN
>  What shall we do, Master?
>  Cast over all her lading? she will not swim
>  An hour else.

MASTER          The storm is loud,
>  We cannot hear one another. What's the coast?

BOATSWAIN
>  We know not yet; shall we make in?

>      *Enter* ALBERT, FRANVILE, LA-MURE, TIBALT DU-PONT, MORILLAT.

ALBERT
>  What comfort, sailors?
>  I never saw, since I have known the sea
>  (Which has been this twenty years) so rude a tempest.
>  In what state are we?

MASTER                Dangerous enough, Captain.
>  We have sprung five leaks, and no little ones;
>  Still rage; besides her ribs are open;
>  Her rudder almost spent; prepare yourselves;
>  And have good courages, death comes but once,
>  And let him come in all his frights.

ALBERT                          Is't not possible
>  To make in to th' land? 'Tis here before us.

MORILLAT
>  Here, hard by, sir.

MASTER          Death is nearer, gentlemen.
>  Yet do not cry, let's die like men.

TIBALT

Shall's hoist the boat out
And go all at one cast? The more the merrier.

MASTER

You are too hasty, Monsieur.
Do ye long to be i' th' fish-market before your time?
Hold her up there.

\* \* \*

*Enter* SEBASTIAN *and* NICUSA.

AMINTA

But ha! What things are these?
Are they human creatures?

TIBALT                                    I have heard of sea-calves.

ALBERT

They are no shadows, sure: they have legs and arms.

TIBALT

They hang but lightly on, though.

AMINTA

How they look! Are they men's faces?

TIBALT

They have horse-tails growing to 'em, goodly long manes.

AMINTA

Alas, what sunk eyes they have!
How they crept in, as if they had been frightened!
Sure they are wretched men.

TIBALT                                    Where are their wardrobes?

Look ye, Franvile, here are a couple of courtiers.

AMINTA

They kneel, alas, poor souls.

ALBERT

What are ye? Speak: are ye alive,
Or wand'ring shadows, that find no place on earth
Till ye reveal some hidden secret?

SEBASTIAN

We are men as you are;
Only our miseries make us seem monsters.
If ever pity dwelt in noble hearts—

ALBERT

We understand 'em, too: pray mark 'em, gentlemen.

SEBASTIAN

Or that heaven is pleased with human charity;
If ever ye have heard the name of friendship;
Or suffered in yourselves the least afflictions;
Have gentle fathers that have bred ye tenderly,
And mothers that have wept for your misfortunes,

Have mercy on our miseries.

ALBERT                                                Stand up, wretches;
Speak boldly, and have release.

NICUSA                                                If ye be Christians,
And by that blessed name, bound to relieve us,
Convey us from this island.

ALBERT                                                Speak: what are ye?

SEBASTIAN
As you are, gentle born. To tell ye more
Were but to number up our own calamities,
And turn your eyes wild with perpetual weepings.
These many years in this most wretched island
We two have lived, the scorn and game of fortune.
Bless yourselves from it, noble gentlemen;
The greatest plagues that human nature suffers
Are seated here, wildness, and wants innumerable.

ALBERT
How came ye hither?

NICUSA
In a ship, as you do, and as you might have been
Had not heaven preserved ye for some more noble use;
Wracked desperately; our men and all consumed
But we two, that still live and spin out
The thin and ragged threads of our misfortunes.

ALBERT
Is there no meat above?

SEBASTIAN                                Nor meat nor quiet;
No summer here, to promise anything;
Nor autumn, to make full the reapers hands;
The earth obdurate to the tears of heaven,
Let's nothing shoot but poisoned weeds.
No rivers, nor no pleasant groves, no beasts;
All that were made for man's use fly this desert;
No airy fowl dares make his flight over it,
It is so ominous.
Serpents and ugly things, the shames of nature,
Roots of malignant tastes, foul standing waters;
Sometimes we find a fulsome sea-root,
And that's a delicate; a rat sometimes,
And that we hunt like princes in their pleasure;
And when we take a toad, we make a banquet.

# THOMAS HEYWOOD

[Thomas Heywood (1573?–1641) captured the vital energies of English writing in an age that saw both the revival of classical learning and the expansion of geographical horizons. *The English Traveller* (first performed c. 1624 and first printed in 1633) takes a skeptical look at the period's vogue for travel and draws heavily on the themes and vocabularies of *The Tempest*, as in this scene comparing the gallants' drunken revelry to the experience of a shipwreck.]

## The English Traveller†

*Enter* YOUNG LIONEL, RIOTER, BLANDA, SCAPHA, *two* GALLANTS *and two* WENCHES, *as newly waked from sleep.*

YOUNG LIONEL.   We had a stormy night on't.
BLANDA.                                               The wine still works,
  And with the little rest they have took tonight
  They are scarce come to themselves.
YOUNG LIONEL.                              Now 'tis a calm,
  Thanks to those gentle sea-gods that have brought us
  To this safe harbour. Can you tell their names?
SCAPHA.   He with the painted staff I heard you call
  Neptune.
YOUNG LIONEL.   The dreadful god of seas,
  Upon whose back ne'er stuck March fleas.
FIRST GALLANT.   One with the bill keeps Neptune's porpoises,
  So Ovid says in's *Metamorphoses*.
SECOND GALLANT.   A third the learned poets write on,
  And as they say, his name is Triton.
YOUNG LIONEL.   These are the marine gods to whom my father
  In his long voyage prays, too. Cannot they,
  That brought us to our haven, bury him
  In their abyss? For if he safe arrive,
  I, with these sailors, sirens and what not,
  Am sure here to be shipwracked!
FIRST WENCH.   [*To* RIOTER]         Stand up stiff.
RIOTER.   But that the ship so totters; I shall fall.
FIRST WENCH.   If thou fall, I'll fall with thee.
RIOTER.                                               Now I sink,
  And, as I dive and drown, thus by degrees
  I'll pluck thee to the bottom.         *They fall.*

† From *The English Traveller* [c. 1624] (London: Robert Raworth, 1633). From Act 2, scene 2.

*Enter* REIGNALD

YOUNG LIONEL.    Amain for England! See, see,
  The Spaniard now strikes sail.
REIGNALD.                               So must you all.
FIRST GALLANT.    Whence is your ship? From the Bermoothes?
REIGNALD.    Worse, I think: from Hell.
  We are all lost, split, shipwracked and undone;
  This place is a mere quicksands.
SECOND GALLANT.                        So we feared.
REIGNALD.    Where's my young master?
YOUNG LIONEL.                        Here man. Speak. The news?
REIGNALD.    The news is, I, and you—
YOUNG LIONEL.    What?
REIGNALD.    She, and all these—
BLANDA.    I?
REIGNALD.    We, and all ours, are in one turbulent sea
  Of fear, despair, disaster and mischance
  Swallowed. Your father, sir—
YOUNG LIONEL.                        Why, what of him?
REIGNALD.    He is—
  O, I want breath—
YOUNG LIONEL.        Where?
REIGNALD.                        Landed, and at hand.
YOUNG LIONEL.    Upon what coast? Who saw him?
REIGNALD.                                    I, these eyes.
YOUNG LIONEL.    O Heaven, what shall I do, then?
REIGNALD.                                    Ask ye me
  What shall become of you that have not yet
  Had time of study to dispose myself?
  I say again, I was upon the quay,
  I saw him land and this way bend his course.
  What drunkard's this, that can outsleep a storm
  Which threatens all our ruins? Wake him.
BLANDA.    Ho, Rioter, awake!
RIOTER.                        Yes, I am wake.
  How dry hath this salt water made me. Boy,
  Give me th'other glass.
YOUNG LIONEL.            Arise, I say.
  My father's come from sea.
RIOTER.                        If he be come,
  Bid him be gone again.
REIGNALD.                Can you trifle
  At such a time, when your inventions, brains,
  Wits, plots, devices, stratagems and all

Should be at one in action? Each of you
That love your safeties, lend your helping hands,
Women and all, to take this drunkard hence
And to bestow him elsewhere.

BLANDA.                                    Lift, for heaven's sake! *They carry
him in.*

REIGNALD.    But what am I the nearer? Were all these
Conveyed to sundry places, and unseen,
The stain of our disorders still remain,
Of which the house will witness, and the old man
Must find when he enters; and for these
I am left here to answer.

    *Enter again* [YOUNG LIONEL *and the others*].

                      What, is he gone?

YOUNG LIONEL.    But whither? But into the self-same house
That harbours him, my father's, where we all
Attend from him surprisal.

REIGNALD.                          I will make
That prison of your fears your sanctuary.
Go, get you in together.

YOUNG LIONEL.                    To this house?

REIGNALD.    Your father's, with your sweetheart, these and all.
Nay, no more words, but do't.

BLANDA.                                That were
To betray us to his fury.

REIGNALD.                      I have't here
To bail you hence at pleasure. And in th'interim
I'll make this supposed gaol to you as safe
From th'injured old man's just incensèd spleen
As were you now together i'the Low Countries,
Virginia, or i'th'Indies.

BLANDA.                          Present fear
Bids us to yield unto the faint belief
Of the least hopèd safety.

REIGNALD.                        Will you in?

ALL.    By thee we will be counselled.

    [*All except* YOUNG LIONEL *and* REIGNALD *go in.*]

# JOHN DRYDEN AND WILLIAM DAVENANT

[Many of Shakespeare's plays were revived for the Restoration stage, and the author and critic John Dryden (1631–1700) and the playwright and theater manager William Davenant (1606–1668) were responsible for several of the most successful adaptations. As a play (first staged in 1667) and an opera (first produced in 1674, with additions by Thomas Shadwell and music by some of the period's greatest composers), this version of *The Tempest* all but displaced Shakespeare's from the stage for nearly two centuries. Dryden and Davenant simplified Shakespeare's language, updated the political nuances, and put new emphasis on dramatic spectacle; and they added several new characters, giving Miranda a sister (Dorinda) and a counterpart in Hippolito—a young man, also raised by Prospero, who has never seen a woman.]

## The Enchanted Island†

*Enter* PROSPERO *alone*

PROSPERO:   'Tis not yet fit to let my Daughters know I kept
  The infant Duke of *Mantua* so near them in this Isle,
  Whose Father dying bequeath'd him to my care,
  Till my false Brother (when he design'd t'usurp
  My Dukedom from me) expos'd him to that fate
  He meant for me. By calculation of his birth
  I saw death threat'ning him, if, till some time were
  Past, he should behold the face of any Woman:
  And now the danger's nigh.—*Hippolito!*

*Enter* HIPPOLITO

HIPPOLITO:   Sir, I attend your pleasure.
PROSPERO:   How I have lov'd thee from thy infancy,
  Heav'n knows, and thou thy self canst bear me witness,
  Therefore accuse not me for thy restraint.
HIPPOLITO:   Since I knew life, you've kept me in a Rock,
  And you this day have hurry'd me from thence,
  Only to change my Prison, not to free me.
  I murmur not, but I may wonder at it.
PROSPERO:   O gentle Youth, Fate waits for thee abroad,
  A black Star threatens thee, and death unseen
  Stands ready to devour thee.
HIPPOLITO:   You taught me not to fear him in any of his shapes:

† From *The Tempest; or, The Enchanted Island* (1667), in *Dryden: The Dramatic Works*, ed. Montague Summers (London: The Nonesuch Press, 1932), 2:177–81.

Let me meet death rather than be a Prisoner.

PROSPERO:     'Tis pity he should seize thy tender youth.

HIPPOLITO:     Sir, I have often heard you say, no creature liv'd
Within this Isle, but those which Man was Lord of;
Why then should I fear?

PROSPERO:     But there are creatures which I nam'd not to thee,
Who share man's soveraignty by Nature's Laws,
And oft depose him from it.

HIPPOLITO:     What are those Creatures, Sir?

PROSPERO:     Those dangerous enemies of men call'd women.

HIPPOLITO:     Women! I never heard of them before.
But have I Enemies within this Isle, and do you
Keep me from them? do you think that I want
Courage to encounter 'em?

PROSPERO:     No courage can resist 'em.

HIPPOLITO:     How then have you, Sir,
Liv'd so long unharm'd among them?

PROSPERO:     O they despise old age, and spare it for that reason:
It is below their conquest, their fury falls
Alone upon the young.

HIPPOLITO:     Why then the fury of the young should fall on them
again.
Pray turn me loose upon 'em: but, good Sir,
What are women like?

PROSPERO:     Imagine something between young men and Angels:
Fatally beauteous, and have killing Eyes;
Their voices charm beyond the Nightingales;
They are all enchantment; those who once behold 'em,
Are made their slaves for ever.

HIPPOLITO:     Then I will wink and fight with 'em.

PROSPERO:     'Tis but in vain, for when your eyes are shut,
They through the lids will shine, and pierce your soul;
Absent, they will be present to you.
They'l haunt you in your very sleep.

HIPPOLITO:     Then I'le revenge it on 'em when I wake.

PROSPERO:     You are without all possibility of revenge;
They are so beautiful that you can ne're attempt,
Nor wish to hurt them.

HIPPOLITO:     Are they so beautiful?

PROSPERO:     Calm sleep is not so soft, nor Winter Suns,
Nor Summer Shades so pleasant.

HIPPOLITO:     Can they be fairer than the Plumes of Swans?
Or more delightful than the Peacocks Feathers?
Or than the gloss upon the necks of Doves?
Or have more various beauty than the Rain-bow?

These I have seen, and without danger wondred at.

PROSPERO:   All these are far below 'em: Nature made
Nothing but Woman dangerous and fair:
There if you should chance to see 'em,
Avoid 'em streight, I charge you.

HIPPOLITO:   Well, since you say they are so dangerous,
I'le so far shun 'em as I may with safety of the
Unblemish'd honour which you taught me.
But let 'em not provoke me, for I'm sure I shall
Not then forbear them.

PROSPERO:   Go in and read the Book I gave you last.
To-morrow I may bring you better news.

HIPPOLITO:   I shall obey you, Sir.          [*Exit* HIPPOLITO]

PROSPERO:   So, so; I hope this lesson has secur'd him,
For I have been constrain'd to change his Lodging
From yonder Rock where first I bred him up.
And here have brought him home to my own Cell,
Because the Shipwrack happen'd near his Mansion.
I hope he will not stir beyond his limits,
For hitherto he hath been all obedience:
The Planets seem to smile on my designs,
And yet there is one sullen cloud behind;
I would it were disperst.

> *Enter* MIRANDA *and* DORINDA

How, my daughters! I thought I had instructed
Them enough—Children! retire;
Why do you walk this way?

MIRANDA:   It is within our bounds, Sir.

PROSPERO:   But both take heed, that path is very dangerous.
Remember what I told you.

DORINDA:   Is the man that way, Sir?

PROSPERO:   All that you can imagine ill is there,
The curled Lyon, and the rugged Bear
Are not so dreadful as that man.

MIRANDA:   Oh me, why stay we here then?

DORINDA:   I'le keep far enough from his Den, I warrant him.

MIRANDA:   But you have told me, Sir, you are a man;
And yet you are not dreadful.

PROSPERO:   I child! but I am a tame man; old men are tame
By Nature, but all the danger lies in a wild
Young man.

DORINDA:   Do they run wild about the Woods?

PROSPERO:   No, they are wild within Doors, in Chambers,
And in Closets.

DORINDA:   But Father, I would stroak 'em and make 'em gentle,
Then sure they would not hurt me.

PROSPERO:   You must not trust them, Child: no woman can come
Neer 'em but she feels a pain full nine Months:
Well I must in; for new affairs require my
Presence: be you, *Miranda*, your Sister's Guardian.

[*Exit* PROSPERO]

DORINDA:   Come, Sister, shall we walk the other way?
The man will catch us else, we have but two legs,
And he perhaps has four.

MIRANDA:   Well, Sister, though he have; yet look about you
And we shall spy him e're he comes too near us.

DORINDA:   Come back, that way is towards his Den.

MIRANDA:   Let me alone; I'le venture first, for sure he can
Devour but one of us at once.

DORINDA:   How dare you venture?

MIRANDA:   We'll find him sitting like a Hare in's Form,
And he shall not see us.

DORINDA:   I, but you know my Father charg'd us both.

MIRANDA:   But who shall tell him on't? we'll keep each
Others Counsel.

DORINDA:   I dare not for the world.

MIRANDA:   But how shall we hereafter shun him, if we do not
Know him first?

DORINDA:   Nay I confess I would fain see him too. I find it in my
Nature, because my Father has forbidden me.

MIRANDA:   I, there's it, Sister; if he had said nothing I had been
quiet. Go softly, and if you see him first, be quick and becken me
away.

DORINDA:   Well, if he does catch me, I'le humble my self to him,
And ask him pardon, as I do my Father,
When I have done a fault.

MIRANDA:   And if I can but scape with life, I had rather be in pain
nine Months, as my Father threatn'd, than lose my longing.

[*Exeunt*]

*The Scene changes, and discovers* HIPPOLITO *in a Cave walk-
ing, his face from the Audience*

HIPPOLITO:   *Prospero* has often said that Nature makes
Nothing in vain: why then are women made?
Are they to suck the poyson of the Earth,
As gaudy colour'd Serpents are? I'le ask that
Question, when next I see him here.

*Enter* MIRANDA *and* DORINDA *peeping*

DORINDA:     O Sister, there it is, it walks about like one of us.
MIRANDA:     I, just so, and has legs as we have too.
HIPPOLITO:    It strangely puzzles me: yet 'tis most likely
Women are somewhat between men and spirits.
DORINDA:     Heark! it talks, sure this is not it my Father meant,
For this is just like one of us: methinks I am not half
So much afraid on't as I was; see, now it turns this way.
MIRANDA:     Heaven! what a goodly thing it is!
DORINDA:     I'le go nearer it.
MIRANDA:     O no, 'tis dangerous, Sister! I'le go to it.

# THOMAS DUFFETT

[The Dryden/Davenant *Tempest* was a box-office hit for Davenant's Duke's Company, and, in 1675, the rival theater company (Thomas Killigrew's King's Company) commissioned a parody by Thomas Duffett (fl. 1672–1684). Duffett's irreverent *Mock-Tempest* not only mocked the style of Restoration adaptations but anticipated the Shakespearean burlesques of the eighteenth and nineteenth centuries, shifting the play to the London underworld and turning Prospero into the Keeper of Bridewell (the chief prison for prostitutes).]

## The Mock-Tempest†

### Act 1, Scene 2

*The Scene changed to Bridewell.*

*Enter* PROSPERO *and* MIRANDA.

PROSPERO    Miranda, where's your sister?
MIRANDA     I left her on the dust-cart-top, gaping after the huge noise that went by.—
PROSPERO    It was a dreadful show.
MIRANDA     O woe, and alas, ho, ho, ho! I'm glad I did not see it though.
PROSPERO    Hold in thy breath, and tell thy virtuous body there's no harm done, they're all reserved for thine and thy sister Dorinda's private use.
MIRANDA     And shall we have 'em all, a-ha! That will be fine i'fads; but if you don't keep 'em close, pray father, we shall never have 'em long to ourselves, pray; for now ev'ry gentlewoman runs

† From *The Mock-Tempest: or, The Enchanted Castle. Acted at the Theatre Royal* (London: for William Cademan, 1675), pp. 9–12.

huckst'ring to market, the youth are bought up so fast that poor publicans are almost starved, so they are so.

PROSPERO   Leave that to my fatherly care.

MIRANDA   And shall we have 'em all, ha, ha, he! O good dear how, how the citizens' wives will curse us.—

PROSPERO   Miranda, you must now leave this tom-rigging and learn to behave yourself with a grandeur and state befitting your illustrious birth and quality.—Thy father, Miranda, was 50 years ago a man of great power, Duke of my Lord Mayor's dog-kennel.—

MIRANDA   O lo, why father, father, are not I Miranda Whiff, sooth, and aren't you Prospero Whiff, sooth, Keeper of Bridewell, my father?

PROSPERO   Thy mother was all mettle.—As true as stell, as right's my leg, and she said thou wert my daughter. Canst thou remember when thou wert born? Sure thou canst not, for then thou wert but three days old.

MIRANDA   I'fads, I do remember it father, as well as 'twere but yesterday.

PROSPERO   Then scratch thy tenacious poll, and tell me what thou findest backward in the misty black and bottomless pit of time.

MIRANDA   Pray father, had I not four or five women waiting upon top of me, at my mother's groaning, pray?

PROSPERO   Thou hadst, and more, Miranda, for then I had a tub of humming stuff would make a cat speak.

MIRANDA   O Gemine! Father, how came we hither?

PROSPERO   While I despising mean and worldly bus'ness, as misbecoming my grave place and quality, did for the bett'ring of my mind apply myself to the secret and laudable study of nine-pins, shuffleboard, and pigeon-holes—dost thou give ear, infant?

MIRANDA   I do, most prudent sir.

PROSPERO   My brother, to whom I left the manage of my weighty state, having learned the mysterious craft of coupling dogs and of untying them, and by strict observation of their jilting carriage, found the time when Venus, Countess, Lady, Beauty, and the rest of my she-subjects were to be obliged, by full allowance of their sports, soon grew too popular, stole the hearts of my currish vassals, and so became the ivy-leaf which covered my princely issue and sucked out all my juice. Dost observe me, child?

MIRANDA   Yes, forsooth father, this story would cure kibed-heels.

PROSPERO   This miscreant, so dry he was for sway, betrayed me to Alonso, Duke of Newgate; and in a stormy and dreadful night opened my kennel gates, and forced me thence with thy young sister and thy howling self.

MIRANDA    Father! did they kill us then, pray, father?

PROSPERO    Near the kennel they dared not for the love my dogged subjects bore me.—In short to Newgate we were carried,—And thence all in a cart, without a cov'ring or a pad of straw, to Hyde Park Corner, we were hurried there on the stubbed carcass of a leafless tree, they hoisted us aloft to pipe to winds, whose mur-m'ring pity whistling back again did seem to show us cursed kindness.

MIRANDA    O poor father!—But whereof, how did we 'scape, father?

PROSPERO    Some friends we had, and some money, which gained the assistance of a great man called Gregoria Dunn, appointed master of that black design. Now luck begins to turn.—But ask no more; I see thou grow'st pink-eyed, go in and let the nurse lay thee to sleep.

MIRANDA    And shall she give me some bread and butter father?

PROSPERO    Ay, my child,—go in.—                    *Exit* MIRANDA.
So, she's fast.—Ariel, what ho my Ariel?

   *Enter* ARIEL *flying down.*

ARIEL    Hail most potent master, I come to serve thy pleasure, be it to lie, swear, steal, pick pockets, or creep in at windows—

PROSPERO    How didst thou perform the last task I set thee?

ARIEL    I gathered the rabble together, showed them the bawdy house, told 'em they used to kill prentices, and make mutton pies of 'em—I led them to the windows, doors, backward, forward, now to the cellar, now to the house top—Then I ran and called the constable, who came just as the rabble broke in, and the de-fendants were leaping from the balcony, like sailors from a sink-ing ship. The Duke and his train I clapped into a coach.

PROSPERO    Are they all taken and safe?

ARIEL    All safe in several parts of this thy enchanted castle of Bridewell; and not a hair of 'em lost.

PROSPERO    'Twas bravely done, my Ariel! What's o-clock?

ARIEL    Great Tom already has struck ten:
   Now blessed are women that have men,
   To tell find tale, and warm cold feet,
   While lonely lass lies gnawing sheet.

PROSPERO    We have much to do ere morning come: follow me, I'll instruct thee within.
   Before the gorgeous sun upon house top doth sneer,
   The Laud knows what is to be done, the Laud knows where.
                                        *Exeunt.*

# ROBERT AND WILLIAM BROUGH

[The Brough brothers were part of a lively reaction against the high literary culture of Victorian England: Robert (1826–1860) and William (fl. 1848) sent up not just *The Tempest* but a wide range of European plays, operas, and novels. Their *Enchanted Isle*, first performed in November 1848, engaged in a light-hearted way with the serious political upheavals of that year: both Prospero and Alonso are deposed monarchs; Caliban moves from down-trodden slave to revolutionary; and Ariel leads a group of constables called in to suppress protests and rebellions.]

## [Raising the Wind]†

SCENE IV. *Before* PROSPERO's *Cell, a combination of a Cave and a modern Dwelling, being a rock,* L., *with a street door and a window let into it. On the door a plate, with 'Sig. Prospero'. A board,* R., *on which is pasted a poster, with 'Blaze of Triumph!! Positively the last week of Sig. Prospero, the celebrated Wizard of the Isle!! who is about to Break his Staff and Drown his Book!!!'*
    *A Landscape and Sea View in the back.*

*Enter* MIRANDA *from door,* L.

MIRANDA.    Now he may come as soon as e'er he pleases.
    I think this style—as fast men say—'the cheese' is.
                                        [*Looking at her dress.*]
    I wonder who he is, and what he's like,
    And if his fancy I may chance to strike.
    But where's that Caliban! He's never near
    When wanted. Caliban, where are you?
CALIBAN.    [*Within.*]                    Here!
MIRANDA.    Come here, slave!

*Enter* CALIBAN, *with a Wellington boot on one arm and a brush in his hand.*

CALIBAN.    Slave! Come, drop that sort of bother;
    Just let me ax, 'Ain't I a man and a brother?'
MIRANDA.    The airs that servants give themselves just now,

† From *The Enchanted Isle, or 'Raising the Wind' on the Most Approved Principles. A drama without the smallest claim to legitimacy, consistency, probability, or anything else but absurdity; in which will be found much that is unaccountably coincident with Shakespeare's 'Tempest'* (London: National Acting Drama Office, 1848), pp. 14–19. First performed at the Royal Amphitheatre, Liverpool, August 7, 1848, and at the Adelphi Theatre, London, November 20, 1848.

They are the 'Greatest Plague in Life', I vow.
Don't answer me, but work, you gaping swine;
Polish those boots, or else there'll be a shine.
Then come to me.                                        [*Exit.*

CALIBAN.                There, now; her dander's riz—
It's jolly hard upon a cove, it is.
List to my story; when it meets your ears
I'm sure the *Boxes* will be all in *tears*,
And in the *gentle pit* each *gent'll pity* me.
I'm plain, straightforward, honest, every *bit* o' me;
And though in polished articles I deal,
'A round unvarnished tale' I will reveal.

　　　TUNE—'*Georgy Barnwell, good and pious*'.

Sons of freedom, hear my story,
　　Pity and protect the slave;
Of my wrongs the inventory
　　I'll just tip you in a stave.
　　　　　　　　Tiddle ol, &c.
　　　　　　[*Brushes the boot to the chorus.*
From morn till night I work like winkin',
　　Yet I'm kicked and cuffed about,
With scarce half time for grub or drinkin',
　　And they never lets me have a Sunday out.
　　　　　　　　Tiddle ol, &c.

And if jaw to the gov'nor I gives vent to,
　　He calls up his spirits in a trice,
Who grip, squeeze, bite, sting, and torment—oh!
　　Such friends at a *pinch* are by no means nice.
　　　　　　　　Tiddle ol, &c.

But I'll not stand it longer, that I'll not,
I'll strike at once, now that my *mettle's* hot.
Ha, here he comes! Now soon I'll make things better;
'Hereditary Bondsmen', hem! Et cetera.
　　　　　　[*Folds his arms and looks dignified.*

　　　*Enter* PROSPERO.

PROSPERO.    Well, sir, why don't you work?
CALIBAN.    [*Giving the boot a single rub.*] Ay, there's the rub.
PROSPERO.    What, mutinous! Out, vile, rebellious cub!
CALIBAN.    [*With sudden vigour.*] Oh, who's afraid? Blow you and
　　your boots together!                          [*Throws boot down.*
　　My soul's above your paltry upper leather.
PROSPERO.    [*Aside.*] That's democratic, and by no means morall

[*To* CALIBAN.] Pick up that boot, unless you'd pick a quarrel.
You'd best not raise a breeze.

CALIBAN.                               Oh, blow your breezes!
   The love of liberty upon me seizes;
   My bosom's filled with freedom's pure emotions,
   And on the 'Rights of Labour' I've strong notions.

PROSPERO.    You want work, then?

CALIBAN.                               No—up for my rights I'll stick;
   I've long enough been driven—now I'll kick.

    TUNE—'*When the Heart of a Man*'.

When the back of a donkey's oppress'd with wares,
Which weigh rather more than his strength well bears,
   Instead of submitting he stoutly—stoutly
Plucks up a spirit and shows some airs.
   Stripes are administer'd—kicks also,
   But his stout ribs no emotion show.
            Press him,
            Caress him,
            Try kicking
            Or licking,
The more he is wallop'd the more he won't go.

PROSPERO.    This sort of thing at once I'd better crush;
   I'll stand no more—pick up that boot, then brush.
                  [*Pointing off with staff.*

CALIBAN.    Never—I swear.

PROSPERO.                    Oh, very good; we'll see, sir.

    *Taps his wand on the stage.* FAIRY SPECIALS *appear from all
    parts, and commence laying on to* CALIBAN *with their staves,
    chasing him round the stage.*

CALIBAN.    [*Picks up the boot.*] Oh no, sir—don't sir—please, sir—
    twasn't me, sir!                    [*Runs off, followed by* FAIRIES.

PROSPERO.    Thus disaffection should be timely checked.
   Now for the prince, whom shortly I expect;
   He little thinks, in his perambulations,
   How soon he'll drop upon some blood relations,
   Nor that he stands on matrimony's edge;
   For at his *uncle's* he must leave a *pledge*—
   His heart; Miranda from his breast must pick it,
   And on it lend her own—ay, that's the ticket.
   I have a plan their passion to ensure—
   All sorts of trouble I'll make him endure;
   And on their intercourse I'll lay restriction,
   So that they'll fall in love from contradiction.

MIRANDA.   *[From door.]* Pa!

PROSPERO.            Yes, dear!

MIRANDA.               Come, and put some tidy things on.

PROSPERO.   Well, look me out a collar, one with strings on.  *[Exit.*

> *Railway music; a bell and steam whistle. A* FAIRY SPECIAL *rises through trap,* C. *with a flag, and holds it out as Railway policemen do. A noise of an approaching Train is heard. Shortly after enter a fairy Locomotive,* R. *with* ARIEL *and a* SPECIAL *as engineer and stoker, attached to a car, in which sits* FERDINAND, *attended by* FAIRY SPECIALS. *Train stops at* C. ARIEL *and* FERDINAND *get out.*

ARIEL.   Now then, sir, for the Wizard Cavern Station;
   Your ticket, please—this is your destination.
                               *[Jumps into train.*

FERDINAND.   *[Looking round amazed.]* Nay, pray explain—just say
   why here you bring me.          *[Train drives off,* L.
   Gone, like the baseless fabric of a thing' me!
   The train has vanished into sheer vacuity;
   That engine shows the greatest ingenuity.
   The very line's gone. Oh, it's clear as day
   That line was but a 'Pencilling by the way';
   And something's rubbed it out; or 'tis perhaps
   One of those airy atmospheric chaps.       *[Sees the door.*
   But ho! What's here? 'A local habitation?'
   Ay, 'and a name'. Now for some explanation.
                                 *[Reads the bill.*
   'Um! 'Blaze of triumph!' That's a flaming placard;
   I'll knock, and boldly; yes, egad, I'll whack hard   *[He knocks.*

> PROSPERO *comes out suddenly followed by* MIRANDA.

PROSPERO.   *[Fiercely.]* 'Who am dat a knocking at de door?'

FERDINAND.                            It's me!

PROSPERO.   And pray, sir what may your intentions be?

FERDINAND.   Pity the sorrows of a poor young man,
   Whom fairy sprites have brought unto your door,
   Who wishes you to give him—if you can,
   A simple explanation—nothing more.

MIRANDA.   *[Aside.]* 'Tis he, I know; with Cupid's darts I'm struck.

FERDINAND.   *[Seeing* MIRANDA.*]* Good Heavens! What a captivating
   duck!

PROSPERO.   *[Aside.]* They're smitten. *[Aloud and sternly.]* For the
   questions you have put,
   I've but one answer, which is simply 'Cut!'  *[Motioning his wand.*

FERDINAND.    [*Astonished.*] Cut?
MIRANDA.                               Cut?
PROSPERO.                             Yes, cut!
MIRANDA.                                    Well really, Pa, I call
    That cut the most unkindest cut of all.
PROSPERO.    Silence, bold minx! Now, once for all, sir—hook it!
    This is no inn—was it for such you took it?
FERDINAND.    An inn your house by me was never *thought* to be,
    Tho' I confess I really think it *ought* to be.
    It might accommodation find at least
    For man, since it accommodates a beast.
MIRANDA.    Pa, I'm ashamed of you. [*To* FERDINAND.] Sir, don't sup-
    pose
    That rudeness such as that my father shows
    Runs in the family. I've none of it;
    I don't take after him.
FERDINAND.              You don't, a bit.
    All I can say is—if from him you came,
    'Deny thy father and refuse thy name',
    And in return please to accept of me.          [*Opens his arms.*
MIRANDA.    I like the barter, most amazingly.
                                    [*About to rush into his arms.*
PROSPERO.    [*Stopping her.*] Back, forward puss! Egad, 'twas time to
    stop her;
    Advances such as these are most improper.
FERDINAND.    Our passion's sudden, but the style's not new,
    We're 'Romeo and Juliet' number two.
    Maiden, I swear—
PROSPERO.             Pooh, pooh! Your vows are *hollow* as
    Drums. And besides, we don't allow no *follow*ers,
    Save men whose minds are honorably bent—
    Not such as you—a trickster and a gent.
FERDINAND.    [*Drawing his sword à la De Mauprat in 'Richelieu'.*]
    Gent! Zounds—Sir Conjuror!
PROSPERO.                    Ho, my angry child!
    You've drawn your sword—you'd best have drawn it mild.

        [*Waves his wand.* FERDINAND *is transfixed and unable to move.*

FERDINAND.    Holloa! What's this? Quite powerless I'm grown;
    From a real *brick* I'm changed into a *stone*.
    I don't half like it—it quite spoils one's pleasure;
    This is a most unfair Coercive Measure.
    Come, please to set me free, old fellow, will you?
    And 'pon my word, I'll promise not to kill you.
PROSPERO.    You plead in vain; no, there take up your dwelling,

A fatal column of my magic spelling.

MIRANDA.   You can't be such a brute, Pa, surely no;
I'll be his bail, if you will let him go.

FERDINAND.   Thou art my *bale* of precious goods the rarest,
Within my heart locked up, and safely ware'us'd.
How I'd embrace thee, were I only free!

MIRANDA.   'More free than welcome' you could never be.

PROSPERO.   [*Aside.*] All right! I've changed my mind another way;
I'll punish you; therefore be free, I say.

[FERDINAND *goes through pantomime expressive of being free.*

FERDINAND.   As the first sign of liberty I seize
The freedom of the *press*, or rather squeeze. [*Embraces* MIRANDA.

PROSPERO.   Phew! Here's an open armed and public meeting.
Egad! It's time that the *rappel* was beating.

Knocks his wand on the stage as policemen do. The sound is
answered, and FAIRY SPECIALS flock in from all parts and group
around.

[*To* FERDINAND *and* MIRANDA.] Now then, disperse.

FERDINAND.                              Divide us if you can.
I s'pose you call yourself a loyal man.
And here you're getting up an agitation,
Our union to repeal by separation.

MIRANDA.   Though as in Parliament, on every side
They stun our ears and cry 'Divide, divide',
Yet we'll not part.

PROSPERO.          You won't?

FERDINAND.                        No!

PROSPERO.                                    Then, of course.
The law's authority I must enforce.
Tear them asunder! [*The* SPECIALS *pull them apart.*] Now, my
    loving pair,
I'll teach you both my mighty power to dare.
[*To* MIRANDA.] You, miss, I sentence, ere the moon is full,
To work six ottomans in Berlin wool.
[*Turning to* FERDINAND.] And as for him, who'd 'steal what isn't
    his'n,'                                    [*Indicating* MIRANDA.
Now that he's 'cotched', of course 'he goes to pris'n'.
Off with him—let him have some bread—nought richer;
His bed some straw; his only friend a pitcher.

SONG—PROSPERO *and* CHORUS.
TUNE—'Nix my Dolly'.

In a box of the stone-jug all forlorn,
Whose walls your efforts will treat with scorn,
             To break away,

All covered with irons, you'll have to lay,
Which will put a stop to your capers gay.
      Fixed, my jolly pal, there you'll stay,
      Fixed, my jolly pal, there you'll stay.
[*Exit into house.* FAIRIES *march to music of the chorus, one detach-
      ment taking* MIRANDA *off by the door,* L., *the others taking*
                                        FERDINAND *off,* R.

# AIMÉ CÉSAIRE

[Born in Martinique in 1913, Aimé Césaire is both poet and playwright. *A Tempest* was written in 1969 and first performed in Tunisia.
Subtitled "Adaptation for a Black Theatre," it highlights matters of
race, specifying a black Caliban and a mulatto Ariel, although the
opening stage direction has actors choosing masks in "the ambiance of
a psychodrama." Despite the play's being more overtly about colonial
and racial issues than its original, the exchanges between Caliban and
Prospero are written with lyricism and humor.]

## A Tempest†

CALIBAN:
  You must understand, Prospero:
  for years I bowed my head,
  for years I stomached it,
  stomached all of it:
  your insults, your ingratitude,
  and worst of all, more degrading than all the rest,
  your condescension.
  But now it's over!
  Over, do you hear!
  Of course, for the moment you're still
  the stronger.
  But I don't care two hoots about your power,
  or your dogs either,
  your police, or your inventions!

† From *A Tempest* (1969), translated from the French by Philip Crispin (London: Oberon
  Books, 2000), pp. 26–28, 44–47, 59–61. Reproduced from 1840021438 by permission
  of Oberon Books.

And do you know why I don't care?
Do you want to know?
It's because I know I'll have you!
You'll be impaled! And on a stake
you'll have sharpened yourself!
You'll have impaled yourself!
Prospero you're a great illusionist:
you know all about lies.
And you lied to me so much,
lied about the world, lied about yourself,
that you ended up by imposing on me
an image of myself:
underdeveloped, in your words,
incompetent,
that's how you forced me to see myself,
and I hate that image! And it is false!
But now I know you, you old cancer,
and I also know myself!

And I know that one day
my bare fist, my bare fist alone
will be enough to crush your world!
The old world is falling apart!

Isn't it true? Just look!
It even bores you to death!
And by the way, you have a chance to finish it off:
You can get the hell out.
You can go back to Europe.
But there's no hope of that!
I'm sure you won't leave!
That makes me laugh—your 'mission',
your 'vocation'!
Your vocation is to get on my wick!
And that's why you'll stay,
like those men who established the colonies
and can no longer live elsewhere.
An old addict, that's what you are.

PROSPERO:   Poor Caliban! You're well aware that you're heading
toward your own perdition. That you're rushing toward suicide! That I will be the stronger, and stronger each time! I pity
you!

CALIBAN:   And I hate you!

PROSPERO:   Beware! My generosity has limits.

CALIBAN:    (*Chanting.*)
Shango marches with strength
across the sky, his covered way!
Shango is a fire-bearer,
each step he treads shakes the heavens
shakes the earth
Shango, Shango oh!

PROSPERO:
I have uprooted the oak, roused the sea,
shaken the mountain, and baring
my breast against adversity,
I have exchanged thunder with Jupiter, bolt for bolt.
Better still! From the brute monster I made man!
But oh!
To have failed to find the path
to the man's heart, if that really is where man
is to be found.

*To* CALIBAN.

Well, I hate you as well!
For you are the one who
made me doubt myself
for the first time.

    *Addressing the Lords.*

. . . My friends, come closer. I take my leave of you. I am going
no longer. My fate is here: I shall not flee it.

ANTONIO:    What, Your Grace!

PROSPERO:
Understand me well.
I am not, in the ordinary sense
the master, as this savage thinks,
but rather the conductor of a vast score:
this isle.
Teasing out voices, myself alone,
and coupling them at my pleasure,
arranging out of the confusion
the sole intelligible line.
Without me, who would be able
to derive music from all this?
Without me, this island is dumb.
Here then, my duty.
I will remain.

GONZALO:    Oh miraculous day to the end!

PROSPERO:    Do not be distressed. Antonio, remain lieutenant of my estates and use them as regent until Ferdinand and Miranda may take effective possession of them, joining them with the Kingdom of Naples. Nothing that has been ordained for them must be postponed: let their marriage be celebrated in Naples with due royal splendour. Honest Gonzalo, I place my trust in your good faith. At this ceremony, you shall stand as father to our Princess.

GONZALO:    You may rely on me, Your Grace.

PROSPERO:    Gentlemen, farewell.

   *They exit.*

And now, Caliban, there's only us!
What I have to tell you will be brief:
Ten times, a hundred times, I've tried to save you,
above all from yourself.
But you have always answered me with rage
and venom, like
the opossum that hoists itself up by its own tail
the better to bite the hand
that pulls it from the darkness.
Well, boy, I shall spurn my indulgent nature
and, from now on, I will answer your violence
with violence!

   *Time passes by, symbolised by the curtain's being lowered halfway and then being taken up again. In semi-darkness,* PROSPERO *appears, aged and weary. His gestures are stiff and automatic, his speech weak and listless.*

Funny, for some time now, we've been invaded by opossums. They're everywhere . . . Peccaries, wild boar, all those unclean beasts! But, above all, opossums. Oh, those eyes! And that hideous leer! You'd swear the jungle wanted to invade the cave . . . But I'll defend myself . . . I will not let my work perish . . . (*Roaring.*) I will defend civilisation! (*He fires in all directions.*) They've got what was coming to them . . . Now, this way, I'll have some peace for a blessed while . . . But it's cold . . . Funny, the climate's changed . . . Cold on this island . . . Have to think about making a fire . . . Ah well, my old Caliban, we're the only two left on this island, just you and me. You and me! You-me! Me-you! But what the hell's he up to? (*Roaring.*) Caliban!

*In the distance, above the sound of the surf and the mewing of birds, snatches of* CALIBAN'*s song can be heard.*

LIBERTY, OH-AY! LIBERTY!

# PETER GREENAWAY

[Peter Greenaway (b. 1942) is one of Britain's leading experimental filmmakers, known for highly structured and visually excessive films drawing as much on dance, opera, and the visual arts as on classic cinematography. His 1991 film of *The Tempest*, *Prospero's Books*, takes as its central concern—and structuring device—the twenty-four books that Prospero might have taken with him to the island.]

## Prospero's Books†

These are the twenty-four books that Gonzalo hastily threw into Prospero's boat as he was pushed out into the sea to begin his exile. These books enabled Prospero to find his way across the oceans, to combat the malignancies of Sycorax, to colonise the island, to free Ariel, to educate and entertain Miranda and to summon tempests and bring his enemies to heel.

**1**  *The Book of Water.* This is a waterproof-covered book which has lost its colour by much contact with water. It is full of investigative drawings and exploratory text written on many different thicknesses of paper. There are drawings of every conceivable watery association—seas, tempests, rain, snow, clouds, lakes, waterfalls, streams, canals, water-mills, shipwrecks, floods and tears. As the pages are turned, the watery elements are often animated. There are rippling waves and slanting storms. Rivers and cataracts flow and bubble. Plans of hydraulic machinery and maps of weather-forecasting flicker with arrows, symbols and agitated diagrams. The drawings are all made by one hand. Perhaps this is a lost collection of drawings by da Vinci bound into a book by the King of France at Amboise and bought by the Milanese Dukes to give to Prospero as a wedding present.

**2**  *A Book of Mirrors.* Bound in a gold cloth and very heavy, this book has some eighty shining mirrored pages; some opaque, some

† From *Prospero's Books: A Film of Shakespeare's "The Tempest"* (London: Chatto & Windus, 1991), pp. 17, 20–25. Reprinted by permission of The Random House Group Ltd.

translucent, some manufactured with silvered papers, some coated in paint, some covered in a film of mercury that will roll off the page unless treated cautiously. Some mirrors simply reflect the reader, some reflect the reader as he was three minutes previously, some reflect the reader as he will be in a year's time, as he would be if he were a child, a woman, a monster, an idea, a text or an angel. One mirror constantly lies, one mirror sees the world backwards, another upside down. One mirror holds on to its reflections as frozen moments infinitely recalled. One mirror simply reflects another mirror across a page. There are ten mirrors whose purpose Prospero has yet to define.

3   *A Book of Mythologies*. This is a large book—Prospero on some occasions has described it as being as much as four metres wide and three metres high. It is bound in a shining yellow cloth that, when polished, gleams like brass. It is a compendium, in text and illustration, of mythologies with all their variants and alternative tellings; cycle after cycle of interconnecting tales of gods and men from all the known world, from the icy North to the deserts of Africa, with explanatory readings and symbolic interpretations. Its authority and information is richest in the Eastern Mediterranean, in Greece and Rome, in Israel, in Athens and Rome, Bethlehem and Jerusalem, where it supplements its information with genealogies, natural and unnatural. To a modern eye, it is a combination of Ovid's *Metamorphoses*, Frazer's *The Golden Bough* and Foxe's *Book of Martyrs*. Every tale and anecdote has an illustration. With this book as a concordance, Prospero can collect together, if he so wishes, all those gods and men who have achieved fame or infamy through water, or through fire, through deceit, in association with horses or trees or pigs or swans or mirrors, pride, envy or stick-insects.

4   *A Primer of the Small Stars*. This is a small, black, leather-covered navigational aid. It is full of folded maps of the night skies that tumble out, belying the modest size of the book. It is a depiction of the sky reflected in the seas of the world when they are still, for it is complete with blanks where the land masses of the globe have interrupted the oceanic mirror. This, to Prospero, was its greatest usage, for in steering his leaky vessel to such a small blank space in a sea of stars, he found his island. When opened, the primer's pages twinkle with travelling planets, flashing meteors and spinning comets. The black skies pulsate with red numbers. New constellations are repeatedly joined together by fast-moving, dotted lines.

**5** *An Atlas Belonging to Orpheus.* Bound in a battered and burnt, enamelled-green tin cover, this atlas is divided into two sections. Section One is full of large maps of the travel and usage of music in the classical world. Section Two is full of maps of Hell. It was used when Orpheus journeyed into the Underworld to find Eurydice, and the maps, as a consequence, are scorched and charred by Hellfire and marked with the teeth-bites of Cerberus. When the atlas is opened, the maps bubble with pitch. Avalanches of hot, loose gravel and molten sand fall out of the book to scorch the library floor.

**6** *A Harsh Book of Geometry.* This is a thick, brown, leather-covered book, stippled with gold numbers. When opened, complex three-dimensional geometrical diagrams rise up out of the pages like models in a pop-up book. The pages flicker with logarithmic numbers and figures. Angles are measured by needle-thin metal pendulums that swing freely, activated by magnets concealed in the thick paper.

**7** *The Book of Colours.* This is a large book bound in crimson watered silk. It is broader than it is high, and when opened the double-page spread makes a square. The three hundred pages cover the colour spectrum in finely differentiated shades moving from black back to black again. When opened at a double spread, the colour so strongly evokes a place, an object, a location or a situation that the associated sensory sensation is directly experienced. Thus a bright yellow-orange is an entry into a volcano and a dark blue-green is a reminder of deep sea where eels and fish swim and splash your face.

**8** *The Vesalius Anatomy of Birth.* Vesalius produced the first authoritative anatomy book; it is astonishing in its detail, macabre in its single-mindedness. This *Anatomy of Birth*, a second volume now lost, is even more disturbing and heretical. It concentrates on the mysteries of birth. It is full of descriptive drawings of the workings of the human body which, when the pages open, move and throb and bleed. It is a banned book that queries the unnecessary processes of ageing, bemoans the wastages associated with progeneration, condemns the pains and anxieties of childbirth and generally questions the efficiency of God.

**9** *An Alphabetical Inventory of the Dead.* This is a funereal volume, long and slim and bound in silver bark. It contains all the names of the dead who have lived on earth. The first name is Adam and the last is Susannah, Prospero's wife. The names are written in many inks and many calligraphies and are arranged in long columns that sometimes reflect the alphabet, sometimes a chronology of history, but often use taxonomies that are complicated to unravel, such that you may search many years to find a name, but be sure it will be there. The pages of the book are very old and are watermarked with a collection of designs for tombs and columbariums, elaborate headstones, graves, sarcophagi and other architectural follies for the dead, suggesting the book had other purposes, even before the death of Adam.

**10** *A Book of Travellers' Tales.* This is a book that is much damaged, as though used a great deal by children who have treasured it. The scratched and rubbed crimson leather covers, once inlaid with a figurative gold design, are now so worn that the pattern is ambiguous and a fit subject for much speculation. It contains those marvels that travellers talk of and are not believed. 'Men whose heads stood in their breasts', 'bearded women, a rain of frogs, cities of purple ice, singing camels, Siamese twins', 'mountaineers dewlapped like bulls'. It is full of illustrations and has little text.

**11** *The Book of the Earth.* A thick book covered in khaki-coloured webbing, its pages are impregnated with the minerals, acids, alkalis, elements, gums, poisons, balms and aphrodisiacs of the earth. Strike a thick scarlet page with your thumbnail to summon fire. Lick a grey paste from another page to bring poisonous death. Soak a further page in water to cure anthrax. Dip another in milk to make soap. Rub two illustrated pages together to make acid. Lay your head on another page to change the colour of your hair. With this book Prospero savoured the geology of the island. With its help, he mined for salt and coal, water and mercury; and also for gold, not for his purse, but for his arthritis.

**12** *A Book of Architecture and Other Music.* When the pages are opened in this book, plans and diagrams spring up fully-formed. There are definitive models of buildings constantly shaded by moving cloud-shadow. Noontime piazzas fill and empty with noisy crowds, lights flicker in noctural urban landscapes and music is played in the halls and towers. With this book, Prospero rebuilt the island into a palace of libraries that recapitulate all the architectural ideas of the Renaissance.

**13** *The Ninety-Two Conceits of the Minotaur.* This book reflects on the experience of the Minotaur, the most celebrated progeny of bestiality. It has an impeccable classical mythology to explain provenances and pedigrees that include Leda, Europa, Daedalus, Theseus and Ariadne. Since Caliban-like centaurs, mermaids, harpies, the sphinx, vampires and werewolves—is the offspring of bestiality, he would find this book of great interest. Mocking Ovid's *Metamorphoses*, it tells the story of ninety-two hybrids. It should have told a hundred, but the puritanical Theseus had heard enough and slew the Minotaur before he could finish. When opened, the book exudes yellow steam and it coats the fingers with a black oil.

**14** *The Book of Languages.* This is a large, thick book with a blue-green cover that rainbow-hazes in the light. More a box than a book, it opens in unorthodox fashion, with a door in its front cover. Inside is a collection of eight smaller books arranged like bottles in a medicine case. Behind these eight books are another eight books, and so on. To open the smaller books is to let loose many languages. Words and sentences, paragraphs and chapters gather like tadpoles in a pond in April or starlings in a November evening sky.

**15** *End-plants.* Looking like a log of ancient, seasoned wood, this is a herbal to end all herbals, concerning itself with the most venerable plants that govern life and death. It is a thick block of a book with varnished wooden covers that have been at one time, and probably still are, inhabited by minute tunnelling insects. The pages are stuffed with pressed plants and flowers, corals and seaweeds, and around the book hover exotic butterflies, dragonflies, fluttering moths, bright beetles and a cloud of golden pollen-dust. It is simultaneously a honeycomb, a hive, a garden and an ark for insects. It is an encyclopedia of pollen, scent and pheromone.

**16** *A Book of Love.* This is a small, slim, scented volume bound in red and gold, with knotted crimson ribbons for page-markers. There is certainly an image in the book of a naked man and a naked woman, and also an image of a pair of clasped hands. These things were once spotted, briefly, in a mirror, and that mirror was in another book. Everything else is conjecture.

**17** *A Bestiary of Past, Present and Future Animals.* This is a large book, a thesaurus of animals, real, imaginary and apocryphal. With this book Prospero can recognise cougars and marmosets and fruit-bats and manticores and dromersels, the cameleopard, the chimera and the cattamorrain.

**18** *The Book of Utopias.* This is a book of ideal societies. With the front cover bound in gold leather and the back bound in black slate, it has five hundred pages, six hundred and sixty-six indexed

entries and a preface by Sir Thomas More. The first entry is a consensus description of Heaven and the last is one of Hell. There will
always be someone on earth whose utopian ideal will be Hell. In
the remaining pages of the book, every known and every imagined
political and social community is described and evaluated, and
twenty-five pages are devoted to tables where the characteristics of
all societies can be isolated, permitting a reader to sort and match
his own utopian ideal.

**19**  *The Book of Universal Cosmography.* Full of printed diagrams
of great complexity, this book attempts to place all universal phenomena in one system. The diagrams are etched into the pages—
disciplined geometrical figures, concentric rings that circle and
countercircle, tables and lists organised in spirals, catalogues
arranged on a simplified body of man, who, moving, sets the lists in
new orders, moving diagrams of the solar system. The book deals in
a mixture of the metaphorical and the scientific and is dominated
by a great diagram showing the Union of Man and Woman—Adam
and Eve—in a structured universe where all things have their allot-
ted place and an obligation to be fruitful.

**20**  *Love of Ruins.* An antiquarian's handbook, a checklist of the
ancient world for the Renaissance humanist interested in antiquity.
Full of maps and plans of the archaeological sites of the world, tem-
ples, towns and ports, graveyards and ancient roads, measurements
of one hundred thousand statues of Hermes, Venus and Hercules,
descriptions of every discovered obelisk and pedestal of the
Mediterranean, street plans of Thebes, Ostia and Atlantis, a direc-
tory of the possessions of Sejanus, the tablets of Heraclitus, the sig-
natures of Pythagoras; an essential volume for the melancholic
historian who knows that nothing endures. The book's proportions
are like a block of stone, forty by thirty by twenty centimetres, the
colour of blue-veined marble, chalky to the touch, with crisp, stiff
pages printed in classical fonts with no W or J.

**21**  *The Autobiographies of Pasiphae and Semiramis* is a pornogra-
phy. It is a blackened and thumbed volume whose illustrations leave
small ambiguity as to the book's content. The book is bound in black
calfskin with damaged lead covers. The pages are grey-green and
scattered with a sludge-green powder, curled black hairs and stains
of blood and other substances. The slightest taint of steam or smoke
rises from the pages when the book is opened, and it is always
warm—like the little heat apparent in drying plaster or in flat stones
after the sun has set. The pages leave acidic stains on the fingers
and it is advisable to wear gloves when reading the volume.

**22** *A Book of Motion.* This is a book that at the most simple level describes how birds fly and waves roll, how clouds form and apples fall from trees. It describes how the eye changes its shape when looking at great distances, how hairs grow in a beard, why the heart flutters and the lungs inflate involuntarily and how laughter changes the face. At its most complex level, it explains how ideas chase one another in the memory and where thought goes when it is finished with. It is covered in tough blue leather and, because it is always bursting open of its own volition, it is bound around with two leather straps buckled tightly at the spine. At night, it drums against the bookcase shelf and has to be held down with a brass weight. One of its sections is called 'The Dance of Nature' and here, codified and explained in animated drawings, are all the possibilities for dance in the human body.

**23** *The Book of Games.* This is a book of board games of infinite supply. Chess is but one game in a thousand in this volume, merely occupying two pages, pages 112 and 113. The book contains board games to be played with counters and dice, with cards and flags and miniature pyramids, small figures of the Olympic gods, the winds in coloured glass, Old Testament prophets in bone, Roman busts, the oceans of the world, exotic animals, pieces of coral, gold putti, silver coins and pieces of liver. The board games represented in the book cover as many situations as there are experiences. There are games of death, resurrection, love, peace, famine, sexual cruelty, astronomy, the cabbala, statesmancraft, the stars, destruction, the future, phenomenology, magic, retribution, semantics, evolution. There are boards of red and black triangles, grey and blue diamonds, pages of text, diagrams of the brain, Arabic carpets, boards in the shape of the constellations, animals, maps, journeys to Hell and journeys to Heaven.

**24** *Thirty-Six Plays.* This is a thick, printed volume of plays dated 1623. All thirty-six plays are there save one—the first. Nineteen pages are left blank for its inclusion. It is called *The Tempest.* The folio collection is modestly bound in dull green linen with cardboard covers and the author's initials are embossed in gold on the cover—W.S.

# Poems

## PERCY BYSSHE SHELLEY

[*The Tempest* was the favorite play of English Romantic poet Percy Bysshe Shelley (1792–1822), and "Ariel" was his choice of name for the ill-fated sailboat upon which he drowned in July 1822. In "With a Guitar. To Jane" Shelley casts himself in the role of Ariel, to the Miranda and Ferdinand of Jane and Edward Ellerker Williams. In the summer of 1822, the Shelleys shared with the Williamses the Casa Magni, near the bay of San Terenzo, in Italy; and Edward drowned along with Shelley. The guitar that accompanied Shelley's poem can now be found at the Bodleian Library, Oxford.]

## With a Guitar. To Jane.†

*Ariel* to *Miranda*;—Take
This slave of music for the sake
Of him who is the slave of thee;
And teach it all the harmony,
In which thou can'st, and only thou.
Make the delighted spirit glow,
'Till joy denies itself again
And too intense is turned to pain;
For by permission and command
Of thine own *prince Ferdinand*
Poor Ariel sends this silent token
Of more than ever can be spoken;
Your guardian spirit Ariel, who
From life to life must still pursue
Your happiness, for thus alone
Can Ariel ever find his own;
From Prospero's enchanted cell,
As the mighty verses tell,

† From *Shelley's Poetry and Prose*, A Norton Critical Edition, Second Edition (New York: W. W. Norton), 2002. Copyright © 2002 by Donald H. Reiman, Neil Fraistat, and Rebecca Thompson. Copyright © 1977 by Donald H. Reiman and Sharon B. Powers. Reprinted by permission of W. W. Norton & Company.

To the throne of Naples he
Lit you o'er the trackless sea,
Flitting on, your prow before,
Like a living meteor.
When you die, the silent Moon
In her interlunar swoon
Is not sadder in her cell
Than deserted Ariel;
When you live again on Earth
Like an unseen Star of birth
Ariel guides you o'er the sea
Of life from your nativity;
Many changes have been run
Since Ferdinand and you begun
Your course of love, and Ariel still
Has tracked your steps and served your will.
Now, in humbler, happier lot
This is all remembered not;
And now, alas! the poor sprite is
Imprisoned for some fault of his
In a body like a grave.—
From you, he only dares to crave
For his service and his sorrow
A smile today, a song tomorrow.

The artist who this idol wrought
To echo all harmonious thought
Felled a tree, while on the steep
The woods were in their winter sleep
Rocked in that repose divine
On the wind-swept Apennine;
And dreaming, some of autumn past
And some of spring approaching fast,
And some of April buds and showers
And some of songs in July bowers
And all of love,—and so this tree—
O that such our death may be—
Died in sleep, and felt no pain
To live in happier form again,
From which, beneath Heaven's fairest star,
The artist wrought this loved guitar,
And taught it justly to reply
To all who question skilfully
In language gentle as thine own;
Whispering in enamoured tone

Sweet oracles of woods and dells
And summer winds in sylvan cells
For it had learnt all harmonies
Of the plains and of the skies,
Of the forests and the mountains,
And the many-voiced fountains,
The clearest echoes of the hills,
The softest notes of falling rills,
The melodies of birds and bees,
The murmuring of summer seas,
And pattering rain and breathing dew
And airs of evening;—and it knew
That seldom heard mysterious sound,
Which, driven on its diurnal round
As it floats through boundless day
Our world enkindles on its way—
All this it knows, but will not tell
To those who cannot question well
The spirit that inhabits it:
It talks according to the wit
Of its companions, and no more
Is heard than has been felt before
By those who tempt it to betray
These secrets of an elder day.—
But, sweetly as its answers will
Flatter hands of perfect skill,
It keeps its highest holiest tone
For our beloved Jane alone.—

# ROBERT BROWNING

[Robert Browning (1812–1889) was one of Victorian England's most influential poets. First published in his *Dramatis Personae* of 1864, Browning's dramatic monologue "Caliban Upon Setebos" was primarily intended as a satire of Victorian theologians, but it also offers a strikingly original meditation on Caliban's peculiar language and his vexed relationship to creation and power.]

## Caliban upon Setebos; or, Natural Theology in the Island†

'Thou thoughtest that I was altogether such a one as thyself.'

['Will sprawl, now that the heat of day is best,
Flat on his belly in the pit's much mire,
With elbows wide, fists clenched to prop his chin.
And, while he kicks both feet in the cool slush,
And feels about his spine small eft-things course,
Run in and out each arm, and make him laugh:
And while above his head a pompion-plant,
Coating the cave-top as a brow its eye,
Creeps down to touch and tickle hair and beard,
And now a flower drops with a bee inside,
And now a fruit to snap at, catch and crunch,—
He looks out o'er yon sea which sunbeams cross
And recross till they weave a spider-web
(Meshes of fire, some great fish breaks at times)
And talks to his own self, howe'er he please,
Touching that other, whom his dam called God.
Because to talk about Him, vexes—ha,
Could He but know! and time to vex is now,
When talk is safer than in winter-time.
Moreover Prosper and Miranda sleep
In confidence he drudges at their task,
And it is good to cheat the pair, and gibe,
Letting the rank tongue blossom into speech.]

Setebos, Setebos, and Setebos!
'Thinketh, He dwelleth i' the cold o' the moon.

'Thinketh He made it, with the sun to match,
But not the stars; the stars came otherwise;

---

† From "Caliban upon Setebos; or, Natural Theology in the Island," in *The Poetical Works of Robert Browning* (London: Smith, Elder, & Company, 1889), 7:149–50, 161.

Only made clouds, winds, meteors, such as that:
Also this isle, what lives and grows thereon,
And snaky sea which rounds and ends the same.

'Thinketh, it came of being ill at ease:
He hated that He cannot change His cold,
Nor cure its ache. 'Hath spied an icy fish
That longed to 'scape the rock-stream where she lived,
And thaw herself within the lukewarm brine
O' the lazy sea her stream thrusts far amid,
A crystal spike 'twixt two warm walls of wave;
Only, she ever sickened, found repulse
At the other kind of water, not her life,
(Green-dense and dim-delicious, bred o' the sun)
Flounced back from bliss she was not born to breathe,
And in her old bounds buried her despair,
Hating and loving warmth alike: so He.
                    *    *    *
[What, what? A curtain o'er the world at once!
Crickets stop hissing; not a bird—or, yes,
There scuds His raven that has told Him all!
It was fool's play, this prattling! Ha! The wind
Shoulders the pillared dust, death's house o' the move,
And fast invading fires begin! White blaze—
A tree's head snaps—and there, there, there, there, there,
His thunder follows! Fool to gibe at Him!
Lo! 'Lieth flat and loveth Setebos!
'Maketh his teeth meet through his upper lip,
Will let those quails fly, will not eat this month
One little mess of whelks, so he may 'scape!]

# JOAQUIM MARIA MACHADO DE ASSIS

[The Brazilian Machado de Assis (1839–1908) is best known as one of Latin America's finest novelists, but he was also a distinguished poet. "No alto" ("At the Top") is, perhaps significantly, the final poem in his collection *Ocidentais*, "western" poems first published in his *Poesias completas* (1901). The hand of "the other one" (Caliban) held out to the poet prefigures the twentieth-century interest in Caliban throughout America.]

## At the Top†

A poet had reached the mountain peak;
wending his way down the western slope,
he saw a strange thing,
a fell figure.

He turns his eyes to the subtle, sky-born,
delightful Ariel, his companion from the start,
and fearfully asks
who or what is that?

Like a merry sweet sound lost in the air
or as it were
a vain thought

Ariel dissolved without further word.
To help him down the hill
the other one held out his hand.

---

† Translated from the Portuguese by Lúcia Sá and Gordon Brotherston.

# RAINER MARIA RILKE

[Rainer Maria Rilke (1875–1926) is regarded as the finest German modernist poet, one of the creators of new forms of lyricism and sensuality. Rilke's work culminated in the *Duino Elegies* and the *Sonnets to Orpheus*, both published in 1923. "The Spirit Ariel," perhaps another meditation on the role of the artist, belongs to this late period.]

## The Spirit Ariel†

### (After reading Shakespeare's *Tempest*)

Sometime, somewhere, you had set him free
with the jerk with which you flung yourself in youth
full upon greatness, far from all respect.
Then he grew willing: and since then a servant,
after each service waiting for his freedom.
Half-domineering, half almost ashamed,
you make excuses, that for this and this
you still require him, and insist, alas!
how you have helped him. Though you feel yourself
how everything that you detain in him
is missing from the air. Sweet and seductive,
to let him go, and then, abjuring magic,
entering into destiny like others,
to know that henceforth his most gentle friendship,
without all tension, nowhere bound by duty,
a something added to the space we breathe,
is busied thoughtless in the element.
Dependent now, having no more the gift
to form the dull mouth to that conjuration
that brought him headlong. Powerless, ageing, poor,
yet breathing *him* like infinitely wide
divided perfume making the Invisible
at last complete. Smiling, to think how once
your nod could bind him, now with such great acquaintance
grown so familiar. Perhaps weeping, too,
when you remember how he loved you and
    desired to leave you, always both at once.

    (And there I left it? Now he terrifies me,
    this man who's once more duke.—The way he draws

† From *Later Poems* (London: Hogarth Press, 1938), trans. J. B. Leishman, pp. 57–58. Reprinted by permission of The Random House Group.

the wire into his head, and hangs himself
beside the other puppets, and henceforth
asks mercy of the play! . . . What epilogue
of achieved mastery! Putting off, standing there
with only one's own strength: "which is most faint.")

# H.D.

[The American expatriate Hilda Doolittle (1886–1961), known as
H.D., was one of the founders of the Imagist school of poetry. Her al-
lusive and musical writing intertwined female identity, literary history,
and personal psychology. H.D.'s poem on *The Tempest* (part of her
1949 tribute to Shakespeare, *By Avon River*) emerged from visits to
Stratford-upon-Avon in the wake of a personal breakdown and the col-
lective trauma of World War II; it is one of the few creative responses
to *The Tempest* to focus on the figure of Claribel.]

## By Avon River†

### I

Come as you will, but I came home
Driven by *The Tempest*; you may come,

With banner or the beat of the drum;
You may come with laughing friends,

Or tired, alone; you may come
In triumph, many kings have come

And queens and ladies with their lords,
To lay their lilies in this place,

Where others, known for wit and song,
Have left their laurel; you may come,

Remembering how your young love wept
With Montague long ago and Capulet.

---

† From *By Avon River* (New York: Macmillan, 1949), pp. 5–7, 9.

II

I came home driven by *The Tempest*;
That was after the wedding-feast;
*'Twas a sweet marriage*, we are told;
And she *a paragon . . . who is now queen*,
*And the rarest that e'er came there*;

We know little of *the king's fair daughter*
*Claribel*; her father was Alonso,
King of Naples, her brother, Ferdinand,
And we read later, *in one voyage*
*Did Claribel her husband find at Tunis*:

Claribel was outside all of this,
*The Tempest* came after they left her;
Read for yourself, *Dramatis Personae*.

III

Read for yourself, *Dramatis Personae*,
Alonso, Sebastian, Prospero,
Antonio, Ferdinand, Gonzalo,
Adrian, Francisco, Caliban
(Whom some call Pan),
Trinculo, Stephano, Miranda,
Ariel, Iris, Ceres, Juno;

These are the players, chiefly,
Caliban, a savage and deformed slave,
Ariel, an airy Spirit, Miranda,
The magician's lovely daughter,
The magician—ah indeed, I had forgot
Boatswain, Mariners, Nymphs and Reapers,

And among these, are other
Spirits attending on Prospero.

IV

Read through again, *Dramatis Personae*;
She is not there at all, but Claribel,
Claribel, the birds shrill, Claribel,
Claribel echoes from this rainbow-shell,
I stooped just now to gather from the sand;

Where? From an island somewhere . . .
Some say the *Sea-Adventure* set out,
(In May, 1609, to be exact)

For the new colony, Virginia;
Some say the *Sea-Adventure* ran aground
On the Bermudas; but all on board
Were saved, built new ships
And sailed on, a year later;

It is all written in an old pamphlet,
Did he read of her there, Claribel?

\* \* \*

VIII

Awkwardly, tenderly,
We stand with our flowers,
Separate, self-consciously,
Shyly or in child-like
Delicate simplicity;

Each one waits patiently,
Now we are near the door;
Till sudden, wondrously,
All shyness drops away,
Awkwardness, complacency;

Ring, ring and ring again,
'Twas a sweet marriage,
So they say, *my beloved is mine*
*And I am his*; Claribel
The chimes peel;

Claribel, the chimes say,
The king's fair daughter
Marries Tunis; O spikenard,
Myrrh and myrtle-spray,
'Twas a sweet marriage;

Tenderly, tenderly,
We stand with our flowers,
Our belovèd is ours,
Our belovèd is ours,
To-day? Yesterday?

# SUNITI NAMJOSHI

[Suniti Namjoshi (b. 1941) is a Canadian-born writer of Indian descent, living and teaching in England. Her poetry and prose "fables"
draw on both her Hindu background and her position as a lesbian and
feminist. In the sequence "Snapshots of Caliban," Namjoshi shifts
freely between voices and identities, exploring alternative and re-
pressed gender dynamics among Miranda, Caliban, and Prospero.]

## Snapshots of Caliban†

### VI

There's something wrong with Caliban.
    Is it her shape? Is it her size?
If I could say that Caliban is stupid,
then that might help, but she can read and write
    and sometimes her speech is so lucid.
She does not feel? But I've heard her howling:
she howls like a dog or some tiresome animal.
    and she sobs at night.
Yet she is Caliban. I've seen her gaping
    at the blue heavens, or at me,
and I fear her dream. For there is something
I dislike so thoroughly about Caliban:
if she had her way, she would rule the island,
    and I will not have it.

### VII *From Caliban's Notebook*

They dreamed it. There was no storm,
no shipwreck, nobody came. Prince Ferdinand
was a rock or a tree. M dreamed it.
She said to the tree, "Bow gracefully,"
and the tree bowed with Ariel in it.
As for revenge—the old man's dream—
even in his dream he could not change them,
not utterly; they still plotted, still schemed—
as though in a play—until Ariel once again
was sent to intervene.
         And they never got away,
for here we all are, M and myself
and doddering P, still islanded,

† From *Because of India* (London: Onlywomen Press, 1989), pp. 91, 92, 94. Reprinted by
  permission of the author.

still ailing, looking seaward
                    for company.

## IX *Prospero's Meditations*

Two monsters are crawling out of my eyes
and onto the sand, scrabbling and scuttling,
climbing and sliding on top of one another,
tipping over stones, doing themselves,
and one another too, some damage perhaps.
Of the two crabs which is more dainty?
Which one of the two least crab-like?
Most graceful? Is there a lovelier sheen
on one curved carapace, a subtler shine?
Their function escapes me.
                    They have broken their claws.
Oh my pretty playthings,
                    my shining instruments!

# LEMUEL JOHNSON

[Lemuel Johnson (1942–2002) was brought up in Freetown, Sierra
Leone, and later lived in France, Austria, and the United States, where
he taught English. His collection of poems, *Highlife for Caliban*, addresses the colonial history of West Africa very much in the spirit of
George Lamming (see above). Johnson also wrote the important critical
work *Shakespeare in Africa (and Other Venues)* (1998).]

## Calypso for Caliban†

ackee rice salt fish is nice

*as when I set down to substance
and to sum, but, seduced, think
to be elf with printless foot
is admiration and nice*

this is the place
my inheritance
a chain of leached bones
my inheritance
mother this

---

† From *Highlife for Caliban* (New Jersey: Africa World Press, Inc., 1995), pp. 39–42.
Reprinted with the kind permission of Mrs. Marian A. Johnson.

chain of leached stones
airless quays
dust that rises
to coast on water

but they walk on water
for you
they walk on water
papa prospero
atibo legba
the whores
with water will
walk on water

papa prospero
jig me mama
an' jig she mama
papa prospero jig
jig me mama
to born the beast

prospero
atibo legba
is him goin to make
all so, and thee,
prosperous so;

to make the beast
is him goin to kiss
in his own true-true name
the whores
until the red part white
more so than black can
white in she certain parts.

Mary-Miranda and mother
and holy virgin,
so come to us
so pray for us
in all your own
true-true name—that the will
be done too for dem mamas with
the derelict vaginas,
though defunct; that they be
holy maid and ready
now to make the beast
with two backs

with atibo prospero
even till the kingdom.

come, keep too the air
out of Sycorax hole:

let this, that I am
set to be, choke unborn
where she think to born
me black; lacking
in air that is light,

for is so things happen,
prospero,
if a whore put
to black lips, sir,
on her private vagina, sir.

but, you, virgin
daughter of god's
own true self,
admired so in
your body's own self,
keep open the carnival,
this feast of ashes,
and Lent (this dance
of flex knee
and tight thigh)
for when the black
beast to come
prowls so about
the derelict pasture
that is man's
braincase sometimes;

when I will prowl
these quays,
dissatisfied, with my face
prospero
against the face
prospero
of your daughter
prospero
prowling the fringes
of the tempest.

god's own daughter,
*ora pro nobis,*
and again be admired

when I turn the corners
of these my eyes
for a vision of hulks
and black flesh
drugged in vomit and fart,
　　*ora pro nobis*

when I set down to substance
and to sum and think to be
elf with printless foot
is admiration and nice;

when, the wind breaks
　　in derelict places,
and I grow to be at last
　　not ariel-spirit
　　not daughter-flesh,
but prey for us,

be present at the table,
and in your own
true-true admiration;
when I am myself again
only in this or that corner
of a dissatisfied face;

　　　　be present
while and still I am ready,
if the revel end,
to wake and cry to dream again.

# HEINER MÜLLER

[The East German playwright Heiner Müller (1929–1995) was best known in the English-speaking world for his radical adaptation of *Hamlet*, *Hamletmachine* (1978). His rewritings of Shakespeare are dislocated and provocative, drawing on Marx's political philosophies and Brecht's theatrical strategies in an attempt to unsettle our relationship to Shakespearean authority.]

## [Go Ariel]†

Go Ariel silence the tempest and
throw the dazed ones on the beach
               I need them
living so I can kill them
For me              Father
        Why

† From *PAJ* 65 (2000), trans. Carl Weber. Reprinted by permission of Carl Weber.

# EDWIN MORGAN

[The Scottish poet Edwin Morgan (b. 1920) is the first Poet Laureate
of Glasgow, where he has spent his entire life. His playful, learned, and
moving work ranges from sonnets and libretti to concrete poetry and
translations of continental classics (often into Scots rather than English). For Morgan, poetry is a space for linguistic invention and imaginative travel—through the literary and historical figures of the past and
our everyday experiences and aspirations.]

## Ariel Freed†

I lifted my wings at midnight.
Moonlit pines, empty paths,
broochlike lagoons dwindled below me.
Oh I was electric: my wingtips
winked like stars through the real stars.
Cold, brisk, tingling that journey,
voyage more than journey, the night
had waves, pressures I had to breast,
thrust aside, I had a figurehead or
perhaps I was a figurehead with
dolphins of the darkness as companions.
Only to have no shore, no landfall,
no runway, no eyrie, no goal and no fall!

† From *Virtual and Other Realities* (Manchester: Carcanet Press Ltd., 1997), 101.
Reprinted by permission of the publisher.

# TED HUGHES

[One of twentieth-century Britain's most celebrated writers, Ted Hughes (1930–1998) engaged with Shakespeare as both a critic and a poet. His final collection of poems, *Birthday Letters* (1998), offered an unexpectedly intimate poetic account of his marriage to the American poet Sylvia Plath (who committed suicide in 1963, and who herself borrowed names and themes from *The Tempest* for her major collection, *Ariel*). In "Setebos," Hughes maps the characters of *The Tempest* onto the drama of his life with Plath.]

## Setebos†

Who could play Miranda?
Only you. Ferdinand—only me.
And it was like that, yes, it was like that.
I never questioned. Your mother
Played Prospero, flying her magic in
To stage the Masque, and bless the marriage,
Eavesdropping on the undervoices
Of the honeymooners in Paris
And smiling on the stair at her reflection
In the dark wall. My wreckage
Was all of a sudden a new wardrobe, unworn,
Even gold in my teeth. Ariel
Entertained us night and day.
The voices and sounds and sweet airs
Were our aura. Ariel was our aura.
Both of us alternated
Caliban our secret, who showed us
The sweetest, the freshest, the wildest
And loved us as we loved. Sycorax,
The rind of our garden's emptied quince,
Bobbed in the hazy surf at the horizon
Offshore, in the wings
Of the heavens, like a director
Studying the scenes to come.

Then the script overtook us. Caliban
Reverted to type. I heard
The bellow in your voice
That made my nape-hair prickle when you sang
How you were freed from the Elm. I lay

† From *Birthday Letters* (London: Faber & Faber Ltd., 1998), 132–133. Reprinted by permission of Faber & Faber Ltd. and Farrar, Straus & Giroux.

In the labyrinth of a cowslip
Without a clue. I heard the Minotaur
Coming down its tunnel-groove
Of old faults deep and bitter. King Minos,
Alias Otto—his bellow
Winding into murderous music. Which play
Were we in? Too late to find you
And get to my ship. The moon, off her moorings,
Tossed in tempest. Your bellowing song
Was a scream inside a bronze
Bull being roasted. The laughter
Of Sycorax was thunder and lightning
And black downpour. She hurled
Prospero's head at me.
A bounding thunderbolt, a jumping cracker.
The moon's horns
Plunged and tossed. I heard your cries
Bugling through the hot bronze:
'Who has dismembered us?' I crawled
Under a gabardine, hugging tight
All I could of me, hearing the cry
Now of hounds.

# Selected Bibliography

Sound introductions to Shakespeare and to Shakespearean studies can be found in *The Cambridge Companion to Shakespeare*, ed. Margreta de Grazia and Stanley Wells (Cambridge: Cambridge University Press, 2001); *The Oxford Companion to Shakespeare*, ed. Michael Dobson and Stanley Wells (Oxford: Oxford University Press, 2001); and *The Bedford Companion to Shakespeare: An Introduction with Documents*, ed. Russ McDonald (Boston: Bedford Books, 1996).

## Essay Collections

Hulme, Peter, and William H. Sherman, eds. *"The Tempest" and Its Travels*. London: Reaktion Books, 2000.
Murphy, Patrick M., ed. *The Tempest: Critical Essays*. New York: Routledge, 2001.
Palmer, D. J., ed. *Shakespeare: The Tempest*. Basingstoke: Macmillan, 1991.
Phelan, James, and Gerald Graff, eds. *The Tempest: A Case Study in Critical Controversy*. New York: Bedford/St. Martin's Press, 2000.
Vaughan, Virginia Mason, and Alden T. Vaughan, eds. *Critical Essays on Shakespeare's "The Tempest."* New York: G. K. Hall & Co., 1997.
White, R. S., ed. *The Tempest: Contemporary Critical Essays*. London: Macmillan, 1999.
Wood, Nigel, ed. *The Tempest*. Buckingham: Open University Press, 1995.

## Other Works

• indicates works included or excerpted in this Norton Critical Edition.

Baker, David J. "Where Is Ireland in *The Tempest?*" In Mark Thornton Burnett and Ramona Wray, ed., *Shakespeare and Ireland*. Basingstoke: Macmillan, 1997. 68–88.
Baldo, Jonathan. "Exporting Oblivion in *The Tempest*." *Modern Language Quarterly* 56 (1995): 111–44.
Barker, Francis, and Peter Hulme. " 'Nymphs and Reapers Heavily Vanish': The Discursive Con-texts of *The Tempest*." In John Drakakis, ed., *Alternative Shakespeares*. London: Methuen, 1985. 191–205.
Barton, Anne. "Introduction" to William Shakespeare, *The Tempest, The New Penguin Shakespeare*. London: Penguin, 1968. 7–51.
Bate, Jonathan. *Shakespeare and Ovid*. Oxford: Clarendon Press, 1993.
Bender, John. "The Day of *The Tempest*." *ELH* 47 (1980): 235–58.
Berger, Harry, Jr. "Miraculous Harp: A Reading of Shakespeare's *Tempest*." *Shakespeare Studies* 5 (1969): 253–83.
Berger, Karol. "Prospero's Art." *Shakespeare Studies* 10 (1977): 211–39.
Black, James. "The Latter End of Prospero's Commonwealth." *Shakespeare Survey* 43 (1991): 29–41.
Breight, Curt. " 'Treason Doth Never Prosper': *The Tempest* and the Discourse of Treason." *Shakespeare Quarterly* 41 (1990): 1–28.
Brockbank, Philip. "*The Tempest*: Conventions of Art and Empire". In J. R. Brown and B. Harris, ed., *Later Shakespeare*. London: Edward Arnold, 1966. 183–201.
Brotton, Jerry. " 'This Tunis, Sir, Was Carthage': Contesting Colonialism." In Ania Loomba and Martin Orkin, ed., *Post-Colonial Shakespeares*, London: Routledge, 1998. 23–42.

Brown, Paul. " 'This Thing of Darkness I Acknowledge Mine': *The Tempest* and the Discourse of Colonialism." In Jonathan Dollimore and Alan Sinfield, ed., *Political Shakespeare: New Essays in Cultural Materialism.* Manchester: Manchester UP, 1985. 48–71.

Bruster, Douglas. "Local *Tempest*: Shakespeare and the Work of the Early Modern Playhouse." *Journal of Medieval and Renaissance Studies* 25:1 (1995): 33–53.

Brydon, Diana. "Re-writing *The Tempest.*" *World Literature Written in English* 23:1 (1984): 75–88.

———. "Sister Letters: Miranda's *Tempest* in Canada." In Marianne Novy, ed., *Cross-Cultural Performances: Differences in Women's Re-Visions of Shakespeare.* Urbana: U of Illinois P, 1993. 165–84.

Bullough, Geoffrey, ed. *Narrative and Dramatic Sources of Shakespeare.* London: Routledge & Kegan Paul, 1975. 8:275–339.

Burnett, Mark Thornton. " 'Strange and Woonderfull Syghts': *The Tempest* and the Discourses of Monstrosity." *Shakespeare Survey* 50 (1997): 187–99.

Busia, Abena P.A. "Silencing Sycorax: On African Colonial Discourse and the Unvoiced Female." *Cultural Critique* 14 (1989–90): 81–104.

Cartelli, Thomas. *Repositioning Shakespeare: National Formations, Postcolonial Appropriations.* London: Routledge, 1999.

Chedgzoy, Kate. *Shakespeare's Queer Children: Sexual Politics and Contemporary Culture.* Manchester: Manchester UP, 1995.

Chickering, Howell. "Hearing Ariel's Songs." *Journal of Medieval and Renaissance Studies* 14:1 (1994): 132–72.

Cholij, Irena. " 'A Thousand Twangling Instruments': Music and *The Tempest* on the Eighteenth-Century London Stage." *Shakespeare Survey* 51 (1998): 79–94.

• Coleridge, Samuel Taylor. "Notes on *The Tempest.*" In *The Literary Remains of Samuel Taylor Coleridge,* coll. and ed. Henry Nelson Coleridge. London: W. Pickering, 1836. 2: 92–102.

Dobson, Michael. " 'Remember / First to Possess His Books': The Appropriation of *The Tempest.*" *Shakespeare Survey* 43 (1991): 99–107.

———. *The Making of the National Poet: Shakespeare, Adaptation, and Authorship, 1660–1769.* Oxford: Clarendon Press, 1992.

Dolan, Frances E. "The Subordinate('s) Plot: Petty Treason and the Forms of Domestic Rebellion." *Shakespeare Quarterly* 43 (1992): 317–40.

• Dryden, John. "[The Character of Caliban]." From the Preface to *Troilus and Cressida, or, Truth found too late* (1679), in *Dryden: The Dramatic Works,* ed. Montague Summers. London: Nonesuch Press, 1932. 5:21–22.

Dymkowski, Christine, ed. *The Tempest.* Shakespeare in Production, Cambridge: Cambridge UP, 2000.

Esolen, Anthony M. " 'The Isles Shall Wait for His Law': Isaiah and *The Tempest.*" *Studies in Philology* 94:2 (1997): 221–47.

Evans, Malcolm. "Some Subtleties of the Isle." In his *Signifying Nothing: Truth's True Contents in Shakespeare's Text.* Brighton: Harvester Press, 1996. 17–38.

Fernández Retamar, Roberto. *Caliban and Other Essays,* trans. Edward Baker et al. Minneapolis: U of Minnesota P, 1989.

Fiedler, Leslie. *The Stranger in Shakespeare.* New York: Stein and Day, 1972.

Frey, Charles. "*The Tempest* and the New World." *Shakespeare Quarterly* 30 (1979): 29–41.

• Fuchs, Barbara. "Conquering Islands: Contextualizing *The Tempest.*" *Shakespeare Quarterly* 48 (1997): 45–62.

Gibbons, Brian. "*The Tempest* and Interruptions." *Cahiers Elisabethains* 45 (1994): 47–58.

Gilbert, A. H. "*The Tempest*: Parallelism in Characters and Situation." *Journal of English and German Philology* 14 (1915): 63–74.

• Gillies, John. "Shakespeare's Virginian Masque." *ELH* 53 (1986): 673–707.

———. *Shakespeare and the Geography of Difference.* Cambridge: Cambridge UP, 1994.

Greenblatt, Stephen. "Learning to Curse: Aspects of Linguistic Colonialism in the Sixteenth Century." In Fredi Chiappelli, ed., *First Images of America: The Impact of the New World on the Old.* 2 vols. Berkeley: U of California P, 1976. 561–80.

———. "Martial Law in the Land of Cockaigne." In his *Shakespearean Negotiations: The Circulation of Social Energy in Renaissance England.* Oxford; Clarendon Press, 1988. 142–63.

———. *Marvellous Possessions: The Wonder of the New World.* Oxford: Oxford UP, 1992.

Griffiths, Trevor R. " 'This Island's Mine': Caliban and Colonialism." *Yearbook of English Studies* 13 (1983): 159–80.

Guffey, George Robert, ed. *After "The Tempest."* Los Angeles: U of California, 1969.

• Gurr, Andrew. "*The Tempest's* Tempest at Blackfriars." *Shakespeare Survey* 41 (1989): 91–102.

Hadfield, Andrew. *Literature, Travel, and Colonial Writing in the English Renaissance, 1545–1625*. Oxford: Oxford UP, 1998.

Hall, Kim F. *Things of Darkness: Economies of Race and Gender in Early Modern England*. Ithaca: Cornell UP, 1995.

Halpern, Richard. " 'The Picture of Nobody': White Cannibalism in *The Tempest*." In David Lee Miller et al., eds., *The Production of English Renaissance Culture*. Ithaca: Cornell UP, 1994. 262–92.

Hamilton, Donna B. *Virgil and "The Tempest": The Politics of Imitation*. Columbus: Ohio State UP, 1990.

Hamlin, William M. "Men of Inde: Renaissance Ethnography and *The Tempest*." *Shakespeare Studies* 22 (1994): 15–44.

Hawkes, Terry. "*The Tempest*: Speaking Your Language." In his *Shakespeare's Talking Animals*. London: Edward Arnold, 1973. 194–214.

———. "Swisser-Swatter: Making a Man of English Letters." In John Drakakis, ed., *Alternative Shakespeares*. London: Methuen, 1986. 26–46.

Hendricks, Margo, and Patricia Parker, eds. *Women "Race," and Writing in the Early Modern Period*. London: Routledge, 1994.

Holderness, Graham. "*The Tempest*: Spectacles of Disenchantment." In Graham Holderness, Nick Potter, and John Turner, *Shakespeare: Out of Court*. London: Macmillan, 1990. 136–94.

Holland, Norman. "Caliban's Dream." *Psychoanalytical Quarterly* 37 (1968): 114–25.

Holland, Peter. "The Shapeliness of *The Tempest*." *Essays in Criticism* 45:3 (1995): 208–29.

———. "Modernizing Shakespeare: Nicholas Rowe and *The Tempest*." *Shakespeare Quarterly* 51 (2000): 24–32.

———. "Introduction" to William Shakespeare, *The Tempest*, The Pelican Shakespeare. New York: Penguin Books, 1999. xxvii–xli.

• Hulme, Peter. "Prospero and Caliban." In his *Colonial Encounters: Europe and the Native Caribbean, 1492–1797*. London: Methuen, 1986. 89–134.

• James, Henry. "Introduction" to *The Tempest*. In Sidney Lee, ed., *The Complete Works of William Shakespeare*. New York: George D. Sproul, 1907. 16: ix–xxxii.

Jameson, Anna. "Miranda." In her *Shakespeare's Heroines* [1832]. London: George Newnes, 1897. 148–55.

Johnson, Lemuel A. *Shakespeare in Africa (and Other Venues): Import & the Appropriation of Culture*. Trenton, N.J.: Africa World Press, 1998.

Johnson, Nora. "Body and Spirit, Stage and Sexuality in *The Tempest*." *ELH* 64 (1997): 683–700.

Joseph, May. "The Scream of Sycorax." In her *Nomadic Identities: The Performance of Citizenship*. Minneapolis: U of Minnesota P, 1999. 127–39.

Kahn, Coppélia. "The Providential Tempest and the Shakespearean Family." In Murray M. Schwartz and Coppélia Kahn, ed., *Representing Shakespeare: New Psychoanalytic Essays*. Baltimore: Johns Hopkins UP, 1980. 217–43.

Kastan, David Scott. " 'The Duke of Milan / And His Brave Son': Dynastic Politics in *The Tempest*." In Virginia Mason Vaughan and Alden T. Vaughan, eds., *Critical Essays on Shakespeare's "The Tempest"*. New York, G. K. Hall & Co, 1997. 91–103.

• Kemble, Frances Anne. "Some Notes on *The Tempest* (Parts I, II and III)." In her *Notes upon Some of Shakespeare's Plays* [1882]. Reprinted in Ann Thompson and Sasha Roberts, eds., *Women Reading Shakespeare, 1660–1900: An Anthology of Criticism*. Manchester: Manchester UP, 1997. 121–25.

• Kermode, Frank. "Introduction" to William Shakespeare, *The Tempest*, The Arden Shakespeare. London: Methuen & Co., 1954. xi–xciii.

Kingsley-Smith, Jane. "*The Tempest's* Forgotten Exile." *Shakespeare Survey* 54 (2001): 223–33.

Knapp, Jeffrey. *An Empire Nowhere: England, America, and Literature from "Utopia" to "The Tempest,"* Berkeley: U of California P, 1992.

• Knight, G. Wilson. *The Shakespearean Tempest, with a Chart of Shakespeare's Dramatic Universe*. Oxford: Oxford UP, 1932.

• ———. "The Shakespearian Superman: A Study of *The Tempest*." In his *The Crown of Life: Essays in Interpretation of Shakespeare's Final Plays* [1947]. London: Methuen & Co., 1964. 203–55.

Kott, Jan. *The Bottom Translation: Marlowe and Shakespeare and the Carnival Tradition*, trans. Daniela Miedzyrzecka and Lillian Vallee. Evanston: Northwestern UP, 1987.

• Lamming, George. "A Monster, a Child, a Slave." In his *The Pleasures of Exile* [1960]. London: Allison & Busby, 1984. 95–117.

Lanier, Douglas. "Drowning the Book: Prospero's Books and the Textual Shakespeare." In James C. Bulman, ed., *Shakespeare, Theory, and Performance*. London: Routledge, 1996. 187–209.

Lie, Nadia, and Theo D'haen. ed. *Constellation Caliban: Figurations of a Character*. Amsterdam/Atlanta, Ga: Rodopi, 1997.

• Lindley, David. "Music, Masque, and Meaning in *The Tempest*." In David Lindley, ed., *The Court Masque*. Manchester: Manchester UP, 1984. 47–59.

———. "Introduction" to William Shakespeare, *The Tempest*, The New Cambridge Shakespeare. Cambridge: Cambridge UP, 2002. 1–86.

Linton, Joan Pong. *The Romance of the New World: Gender and the Literary Formations of English Colonialism*. Cambridge: Cambridge UP, 1998.

Loomba, Ania. "Seizing the Book." In her *Gender, Race, and Renaissance Drama*. Manchester: Manchester University Press, 1989. 142–58.

———. "Shakespeare and Cultural Difference." In Terence Hawkes, ed., *Alternative Shakespeares Volume 2*. London: Routledge, 1996. 164–91.

Lupton, Julia Reinhard. "Creature Caliban." *Shakespeare Quarterly* 51 (2000): 1–23.

McDonald, Russ. "Reading *The Tempest*." *Shakespeare Survey* 43 (1991): 15–28.

Mackenthun, Gesa. "A Monstrous Race for Possession: Discourses of Monstrosity in *The Tempest* and Early British America." In Tim Youngs, ed., *Writing and Race*. London: Longman, 1997. 52–79.

Magnusson, A. Lynne. "Interruption in *The Tempest*." *Shakespeare Quarterly* 37 (1986): 52–65.

Maquerlot, Jean-Pierre, and Michèle Willems, eds. *Travel and Drama in Shakespeare's Time*. Cambridge: Cambridge UP, 1996.

• Marcus, Leah. "The Blue-Eyed Witch." In her *Unediting the Renaissance: Shakespeare, Marlowe, Milton*. London: Routledge, 1996. 1–37.

Marienstras, Richard. "Prospero ou le machiavélisme du bien." *Bulletin de la Faculté des Lettres de Strasbourg* 43 (1965): 899–917.

———. "Elizabethan Travel Writing and Shakespeare's *The Tempest*." In his *New Perspectives on the Shakespearean World* [1981], trans. Janet Lloyd. Cambridge: Cambridge UP, 1985. 160–85.

Marx, Leo. "Shakespeare's American Fable." In his *The Machine in the Garden: Technology and the Pastoral Ideal in America*. New York: Oxford UP, 1964. 37–72.

Miko, Stephen J. "Tempest." *ELH* 49 (1982): 1–17.

• Mowat, Barbara A. "Prospero, Agrippa, and Hocus Pocus." *English Literary Renaissance* 11 (1981): 281–303.

———. "Prospero's Book." *Shakespeare Quarterly* 52 (2001): 1–33.

———. "*The Tempest*: A Modern Perspective." In Barbara A. Mowat and Paul Werstine, eds., *The Tempest*, The New Folger Library Shakespeare. New York: Washington Square P, 1994. 185–99.

Muñoz Simonds, Peggy. " 'Sweet Power of Music': The Political Magic of 'the Miraculous Harp' in Shakespeare's *The Tempest*." *Comparative Drama* 29 (1995): 61–90.

Nilan, Mary N. " 'The Tempest' at the Turn of the Century: Cross-currents in Production." *Shakespeare Survey* 25 (1972): 113–23.

Nixon, Rob. "Caribbean and African Appropriations of *The Tempest*." *Critical Inquiry* 13 (1987): 557–78.

Norbrook, David. " 'What Cares These Roarers for the Name of King?': Language and Utopia in *The Tempest*." In Gordon McMullan and Jonathan Hope, eds., *The Politics of Tragicomedy*. London: Routledge, 1992. 21–54.

• Orgel, Stephen. "Prospero's Wife." *Representations* 8 (1985): 1–13.

———. "Introduction" to William Shakespeare, *The Tempest*. Oxford: Oxford UP, 1987. 1–87.

Pasternak Slater, Ann. "Variations within a Source: From Isaiah XXIX to *The Tempest*." *Shakespeare Survey* 25 (1972): 125–35.

Patterson, Annabel. " 'Thought Is Free': *The Tempest*." In her *Shakespeare and the Popular Voice*. Oxford: Basil Blackwell, 1989. 154–62.

Potter, Lois. "A Brave New *Tempest*." *Shakespeare Quarterly* 43 (1992): 450–55.

Powell, Jocelyn. "*The Tempest, or The Enchanted Island*." In his *Restoration Theatre Production*. London: RKP, 1984. 62–83.

Purkiss, Diane. "The Witch on the Margins of 'Race': Sycorax and Others." In her *The Witch in History: Early Modern and Twentieth-Century Representations*. London: Routledge, 1996. 251–75.

Raley, Marjorie. "Claribel's Husband." In Joyce Green MacDonald, ed., *Race, Ethnicity, and Power in the Renaissance*. Cranbury: Associated University Presses, 1997. 95–119.

• Rowe, Nicholas. "[The Magic of *The Tempest*]." In *The Works of Mr. William Shakespear*. London: for Jacob Tonson, 1709. 1:xxiii–xxvi.

Sachdev, Rachana. "Sycorax in Algiers: Cultural Politics and Gynecology in Early Modern England." In Dympna Callaghan, ed., *A Feminist Companion to Shakespeare*. Oxford: Blackwell, 2000. 208–25.

Schmidgall, Gary. "*The Tempest* and *Primaleon*: A New Source." *Shakespeare Quarterly* 37 (1986): 423–39.

Skura, Meredith Anne. "Discourse and the Individual: The Case of Colonialism in *The Tempest*." *Shakespeare Quarterly* 40 (1989): 42–69.

Smith, James. "The Tempest." In his *Shakespearian and Other Essays*. Cambridge: Cambridge UP, 1974. 159–261.

Sokol, B. J. "*The Tempest*: 'All Torment Trouble, Wonder and Amazement': A Kleinian Reading." In B. J. Sokol, ed., *The Undiscover'd Country: New Essays on Psychoanalysis and Shakespeare*. London: Free Association Books, 1993. 179–216.

———, and Mary Sokol. "*The Tempest* and Legal Justification of Plantation in Virginia." In Holger Klein and Peter Davidhazi, eds., *Shakespeare Yearbook* IV (1997): 353–80.

Solomon, Julie Robin. "Going Places: Absolutism and Movement in Shakespeare's *The Tempest*." *Renaissance Drama*, n.s., 22 (1991): 3–45.

• Strachey, Lytton. "Shakespeare's Final Period." In his *Books and Characters*. London: Chatto & Windus, 1922. 60–64.

Sturgess, Keith. " 'A Quaint Device': *The Tempest* at the Blackfriars." In his *Jacobean Private Theatre*. London: RKP, 1987. 73–96.

Summers, Joseph H. "The Anger of Prospero." *Modern Quarterly Review* 12 (1973): 116–35.

Sundelson, David. "So Rare a Wondered Father: Prospero's *Tempest*." In Murray M. Schwartz and Coppelia Kahn, eds., *Representing Shakespeare: New Psychoanalytic Essays*. Baltimore: The Johns Hopkins University Press, 1980. 33–53.

Taylor, Mark. "Prospero's Books and Stephano's Bottle: Colonial Experience in *The Tempest*." *Clio* 22:2 (1993): 101–13.

Thompson, Ann. " 'Miranda, Where's Your Sister?': Reading Shakespeare's *Tempest*." In Susan Sellers, ed., *Feminist Criticism: Theory and Practice*. London: Harvester Wheatsheaf, 1991. 45–56.

• Tieck, Ludwig. "Shakespeare's Treatment of the Marvellous" [1793], trans. Louise Adey. In Jonathan Bate, ed., *The Romantics on Shakespeare*. Harmondsworth: Penguin, 1992. 60–66.

Tudeau-Clayton, Margaret. "Shaking Neptune's 'Dread Trident': *The Tempest* and Figures of Virgil." In her *Jonson, Shakespeare and Early Modern Virgil*. Cambridge: Cambridge UP, 1998. 194–244.

Vaughan, Alden T., and Virginia Mason Vaughan. *Caliban: A Cultural History*. New York: Cambridge UP, 1992.

Vaughan, Virginia Mason, and Alden T. Vaughan. "Introduction" to *The Tempest*, The Arden Shakespeare. London: Thomas Nelson and Sons, 1999. 1–138.

Warren, Roger. "Rough Magic and Heavenly Music: *The Tempest*." In his *Staging Shakespeare's Late Plays*. Oxford: Clarendon P, 1990. 158–207.

Wickham, Glynne. "Masque and Anti-Masque in *The Tempest*." *Essays and Studies*, n.s., 28 (1975): 1–14.

Wikander, Matthew H. " 'The Duke My Father's Wrack': The Innocence of the Restoration *Tempest*." *Shakespeare Survey* 43 (1991): 91–98.

Wilson, Richard. "Voyage to Tunis: New History and the Old World of *The Tempest*." *ELH* 64 (1997): 333–57.

Yates, Frances A. "Prospero: The Shakespearean Magus." In her *The Occult Philosophy in the Elizabethan Age*. London: Routledge, 1979. 159–63.

Zabus, Chantal. *Tempests After Shakespeare*. New York: Palgrave, 2002.